JUST LAWYERS: SEVEN PORTRAITS

PATRONS OF THE SOCIETY

Aird & Berlis

Blake, Cassels & Graydon

Davies, Ward & Beck

Holden Day Wilson

McCarthy Tétrault

Osler, Hoskin & Harcourt

Reynolds, Mirth, Richards & Farmer

The Harweg Foundation

Tory Tory DesLauriers & Binnington

Weir & Foulds

The Society also thanks the Law Foundation of Ontario and the
Law Society of Upper Canada for their continuing support.

Just Lawyers

Seven Portraits

DAVID RICARDO WILLIAMS

The Osgoode Society for Canadian Legal History

© The Osgoode Society for Canadian Legal History 1995
Printed in Canada

ISBN 0-8020-0747-3

Printed on acid-free paper

Canadian Cataloguing in Publication Data
Williams, David Ricardo, 1923–
Just lawyers

Includes bibliographical references and index.
ISBN 0-8020-0747-3

1. Lawyers – Canada – Biography.   I. Osgoode Society
for Canadian Legal History.   II. Title.

KE415.W55 1995   349.71'092'2   C95-931517-9
KF345.Z9A1W5 1995

For Katharine and Charlotte

An advocate, by the sacred duty which he owes his client, knows in the discharge of that office but one person in the world, that client and none other. To save that client by all expedient means – to protect that client at all hazards and costs to all others and among others to himself – is the highest and most unquestioned of his duties; he must not regard the alarm, the suffering, the torment, the destruction which he may bring upon any other.

Henry Brougham, 1820

Contents

Illustrations follow page 154.

Foreword

THE OSGOODE SOCIETY FOR CANADIAN LEGAL HISTORY

The purpose of The Osgoode Society for Canadian Legal History is to encourage research and writing in the history of Canadian law. The Society, which was incorporated in 1979 and is registered as a charity, was founded at the initiative of the Honourable R. Roy McMurtry, former attorney general for Ontario, and officials of the Law Society of Upper Canada. Its efforts to stimulate the study of legal history in Canada include a research support program, a graduate student research assistance program, and work in the fields of oral history and legal archives. The Society publishes (at the rate of about one a year) volumes of interest to the Society's members that contribute to legal-historical scholarship in Canada, including studies of the courts, the judiciary, and the legal profession, biographies, collections of documents, studies in criminology and penology, accounts of significant trials, and work in the social and economic history of the law.

Current directors of The Osgoode Society for Canadian Legal History are Jane Banfield, Tom Bastedo, John Brown, Charles Harnick, Brian Bucknall, Archie Campbell, J. Douglas Ewart, Martin Friedland, John Honsberger, Kenneth Jarvis, E. Susan Elliott, Allen Linden, Virginia MacLean, Wendy Matheson, Colin McKinnon, Roy McMurtry, Brendan O'Brien, Peter Oliver, Paul Reinhardt, James Spence, and Richard Tinsley.

The annual report and information about membership may be obtained by writing The Osgoode Society for Canadian Legal History, Osgoode Hall, 130 Queen Street West, Toronto, Ontario, Canada

M5H 2N6. Members receive the annual volume published by the Society, of which the present book is one.

In this collection of lively biographical essays, David Ricardo Williams portrays the careers of seven eminent Canadian lawyers whose contributions to the legal fabric of the country have been immeasurable. Representing all Canadian regions, Williams's portraits transcend the biographical to deal with several of the themes which defined the nature of legal practice in Canada between 1910 and the 1980s. In so doing, they reveal the radical differences between the practice of these years and that prevailing today.

Based on extensive research in hard-to-locate sources, *Just Lawyers* demonstrates the importance, in the first half of this century, of appeals to the Privy Council. It emphasizes the dominant role played in the profession by the barrister as opposed to the solicitor, and it illustrates the value system and attitudes of a generation of lawyers who regarded the law as a profession rather than a business.

R. Roy McMurtry
President

Peter Oliver
Editor-in-Chief

Preface

This work has had a long gestation. It is five years since I first discussed the concept with Professor Peter Oliver, the general editor of The Osgoode Society, who, along with several other directors of The Society (Jane Banfield among them), had broached the idea of a series of biographical essays about lawyers. Early on, to give the work a theme, or at least a common thread, I decided that I should confine myself to those lawyers who had elected to remain in the profession, resisting the supposed blandishments of the judicial life, and, moreover, that the lawyers chosen should represent the various regions of the country in an effort to give the work a national scope. I concluded also that those pillars of the legal community who had active political careers, such as R.B. Bennett, J.L. Ralston, Louis St Laurent, and John Diefenbaker, should be excluded, and that my choices should be limited to lawyers who flourished in this century. Four of the candidates I selected, Isaac Pitblado, William Norman Tilley, Eugene Lafleur, and Aimé Geoffrion, started practice in the nineteenth century but their eminence lay in the twentieth.

In making a regional selection I have tried to make some allowance for population and the number of members of the bar in a given area but the process has been uneven and certainly unscientific. I hope the fact that I have chosen only one representative from British Columbia, from the prairie provinces, and from the Atlantic region will not rankle. In determining the selection I had also to try to balance the constraints of space – both The Osgoode Society and I wished the manuscript to be of manageable size – with the desire to afford reasonably full biographical treatment of each subject. We all wanted to avoid capsule portraits and this consideration in itself was obviously a limiting factor in the number of subjects chosen. Also, I could not, and did not intend to, write complete biographies of each subject and then reduce them to essay form. The approach I have taken instead is to emphasize those characteristics of each man that distinguished him in some way from the others. I have tended to take the eminence of each person as a given without spending a lot of time in proving it, but the basis for the assumptions naturally will be apparent to the reader.

In the end, I restricted my subjects to seven, a number that I believed would permit reasonably ample treatment without placing an undue financial burden on the publisher. Determining who the seven should be was very troublesome. How does one go about selecting lawyers thought to be distinguished above all others? I had my own ideas, of course. In particular, I did not think that there could be much argument about the selection of Senator J.W. de B. Farris as the representative for British Columbia – but still, there were other candidates in that province, E.P. Davis for one. A key factor in Farris's case was that many of his papers and much of his correspondence have been preserved and are available.

None the less, I sought advice from various people whose judgment I respected. Professor John McLaren of the faculty of law, University of Victoria (formerly dean of law at the University of Calgary), made suggestions about legal personages on the prairies, including Isaac Pitblado. Wilbur F. Bowker devoted much time and thought to nominees from the prairies and I am grateful to him. Professor D.G. Bell of the faculty of law of the University of New Brunswick was also helpful. Professor Philip Girard of Dalhousie Law School together with the then dean, Innis Christie, both suggested Frank Covert as the logical choice for the Atlantic region, and I have followed their advice. Aimé Geoffrion and Eugene Lafleur seemed obvious choices, at least to me, as representatives of Quebec. The choice of nominees for Ontario was far more difficult. Tilley was an evident candidate but I wanted to write about someone else of more recent prominence. Gordon Henderson, son of a distinguished lawyer, was the man I eventually selected. He was alive when I embarked on this work, but, sadly, he will not be present to comment on my treatment of him.

There was yet another difficulty in making a selection. In deciding on Tilley, Lafleur, and Geoffrion, I did so in spite of the fact that virtually all their personal papers, business correspondence, and office files have been destroyed – thrown away, I gather. To me, it seems incredible, scandalous in fact, that their successor law firms should not have preserved the papers of such adornments of the profession as those three.[1] In any event, I took the view that the overriding eminence of Tilley, Lafleur, and Geoffrion was such that they could not be ignored, even though few personal papers have survived. Such a gap obviously makes the task of a biographer more difficult; I hope the reader will agree with my decision. Fortunately, in the cases of Farris, Pitblado, Henderson, and Covert, there are rich sources of available material.

Some who read this collection of essays will maintain that so-and-so ought to have been included rather than those who have been. I am not unmindful of this potential criticism and can only reiterate that the confines of space have necessarily resulted in the exclusion of many worthies. As well, I must admit that the final choice is in part the result of my own, perhaps idiosyncratic, views. The reader will observe that most of my subjects have been essentially courtroom lawyers rather than solicitors, and that fact is a reflection of my own thirty-five years' experience as a trial lawyer. Yet any author must have a certain predilection or bias: there must be some aspect of a proposed subject that has a certain attraction for the biographer.

There may be other grounds of criticism of my selection. Six of my subjects were supporters of the Liberal Party. Only one – Farris – held elected political office, for a few years in British Columbia. The others never sought office although they remained committed to the party with varying degrees of enthusiasm. Of those six, Pitblado was the chief waverer. Until the formation of the Union government in 1917, he was a dedicated Liberal, but his admiration for Arthur Meighen led him to support the Conservatives in the 1920s. Thereafter, it is difficult to determine his political views – he was either a closet Liberal, or a closet Conservative. I assure the reader that the political affiliation of those about whom I have written is pure coincidence. In fact, it was not until I had concluded my research that I realized that my intentions might be misconstrued. Alone of my subjects, Gordon Henderson was, as he told me, always a-political.

All my subjects are male. There are, of course, outstanding female lawyers but many have become judges – one thinks of Mary Southin, Beverley McLachlin, Bertha Wilson, and others – and hence are beyond the terms of reference of this work. At this date, no female remaining at the bar has achieved the eminence of those of whom I have written; that will inevitably change, but it will have to be another author who records their careers.

All I can say is that, if some feel my subjects are less worthy than others, let them take up the pen. Whatever frailties there are in my selection, those portrayed were utterly devoted to the practice of law, having no interest in being judges. They believed that their highest calling was to remain at the bar and to instruct judges, and not be instructed by them. Not only were they passionately devoted to the practice of law – they were all passionate Canadians. Finally, I want to say that this book is written not just for the lawyer, practising or academic, but for the general reader and in particular for the general reader who has some perception that an orderly system of the administration of law is fundamental to the well-being of society.

In the preparation of this work, I have had much assistance from others not already mentioned. R.E. Parsons, a grandson of Eugene Lafleur, was extremely helpful in giving me recollections of his grandfather and making available to me such materials as have survived, including Lafleur's opinion books now held at McCarthy Tétrault in Montreal, Lafleur's successor firm. Guillaume Geoffrion of Montreal, the only surviving son of his father, was also of great assistance in locating and making available such papers and documents of his father that have survived, and in shepherding me around points of interest in Montreal relating to his father. Professor Ron Macdonald of the University of Toronto Law School cheerfully offered insights into the careers of Lafleur and Frank Covert, and the late John Humphrey of McGill also recalled Lafleur for me. Gordon Henderson not only assisted me in describing his own career but also passed on recollections of several others of my subjects. John Robinette ('Why have you not written about him?' I am often asked) was helpful in assessing Tilley, as were John Carson, Susan Binnie, Ian Kyer, and John Honsberger, all of Toronto. The Hon. Willard Estey told me pertinent anecdotes about several of my subjects. E. Peter Newcombe, Hyman Soloway, and Mr Justice James Chadwick helped me with aspects of Gordon Henderson's career, as did a group of colleagues at the University of Ottawa: Marcel Hamelin, rector and vice-chancellor, Father Roger Guindon, the former rector, and Antoine D'Iorio and Dean D.M. McRae of the faculty of law. Professor Trevor Anderson of the faculty of law at the University of Manitoba performed yeoman service in my preparation of Isaac Pitblado's profile, sending me much material and many useful leads. James Pitblado of Toronto, a grandson, was helpful with details of his family and in providing me with an excellent photograph of his grandfather. I am grateful to Debora Prokopchuk of the Department of Archives and Special Collections at the University of Manitoba for drawing to my attention the most interesting Thomas Glendinning Hamilton collection. Douglas Johnston, an expert on the law of the sea and a colleague of mine at the law school of the University of Victoria, was helpful in my writing about Tilley and the arbitration of the dispute over the North Atlantic coast fisheries; another colleague, Robert Howell, an expert on intellectual property, was of great assistance in my chapter on Gordon Henderson. The Rt Hon. John Turner, a former minister of justice, took an afternoon out of a very busy schedule to talk to me about the judiciary and to offer his recollections of some of my subjects. Brendan O'Brien of Toronto, a fellow author, provided me with revealing anecdotes of Tilley, and, in particular, described for me the feud between Tilley and R.R. Cromarty, publisher of the *Dominion Law Reports*; as well, he made helpful suggestions about the manuscript.

I cannot mention here those whom I interviewed; their names are collected in the bibliography, and I am grateful to all of them. One of the true pleasures of the biographer is interviewing, even if the person interviewed is unsympathetic to the biographee. Regardless of the project I am engaged in, I find that virtually everyone I ask for an interview is willing, indeed pleased, to respond. Special note, however, must be taken of the Covert family, specifically Frank Covert's widow, Mollie, and two of his children, Michael and Susan. As well, J.W.E. Mingo of Covert's old firm (now Stewart McKelvey Stirling Scales) was extremely helpful in various ways. The late John Farris and his widow, Dorothy, who is still very much alive, spoke freely about Senator Farris. Mrs Marion Tilley Greey, daughter of W.N. Tilley, offered insights into the character of her father which no one else could have done. I must record how helpful Freda Kardish, my secretary at the law school of the University of Victoria, has been in the preparation of my research notes and the manuscript, assisted from time to time by Sheila Talbot. And, finally, my thanks go to Peter Oliver, Marilyn MacFarlane, and the directors of The Osgoode Society for their continuing interest in, and support of, this project.

JUST LAWYERS: SEVEN PORTRAITS

Introduction

Each of the seven lawyers portrayed in this book attained, in his own particular way, the pinnacle of the legal profession not only in his own province and region but also in the entire country. Significantly, too, there was a substantial overlap in their careers. Four of them, Lafleur, Tilley, Geoffrion, and Pitblado, were called to the bar in the closing years of the last century. A fifth, Farris, qualified as a lawyer just after the turn of the century. Gordon Henderson came much later, starting practice in the late 1930s, but he knew all these men (except Lafleur) and they, in turn, knew each other, often as opponents in the courtroom though occasionally as colleagues. They were also linked by ties of friendship and common membership in professional bodies such as the Canadian Bar Association. Geoffrion and Lafleur in particular were the Castor and Pollux, 'the heavenly twins,' of the Quebec and Canadian bars, and like those mythological persons they occupy a prominent place in the firmament – the legal firmament. For the first three decades of this century, the careers of Lafleur, Tilley, and Geoffrion were so intertwined that one would be hard pressed to find an important case in which one or the other did not participate. Often, all three would be involved, sometimes on the same side of the fence, and after Lafleur's death Tilley and Geoffrion carried on a *pas de deux*, joined now and then by Farris to form a *pas de trois*. Covert, whose career started just before Lafleur's death and who barely knew Geoffrion, though the latter's reputation was well known to him, knew Pitblado, Farris, and Henderson reasonably well and had professional dealings with them. Remarkably – although one really should not be surprised because the Maritimes have always been an exporter of brains – three of the seven were born in the Atlantic region, Pitblado and Covert in Nova Scotia and Farris in New Brunswick. Pitblado and Farris received a significant part of their education in the provinces of their birth and Covert received all his in Nova Scotia.

These men approached the practice of law from the British tradition of the separation of barristers from solicitors. The separation was never formalized in Canada – as in the United Kingdom – but it existed none the less and barristers tended to view themselves as just a cut above their solicitor colleagues. For the most part, there would be little overt parading by a barrister of his belief in the superiority of a courtroom lawyer. Still, while Lafleur, Geoffrion, Pitblado, Covert, and Henderson were too polite to lord it over non-courtroom lawyers, there is no doubt that they looked on advocacy as the highest attainment of a lawyer. Tilley and Farris were not so tactful: they made no bones about their preference for the courtroom arena. Either would have viewed the prospect of drawing a will, or a land document, even if they knew how, with distaste.

In Canada, the distinction between barristers and solicitors has blurred somewhat. Both Covert and Henderson did substantial work as solicitors in the latter years of their practices (as did Pitblado in his latter years). As well, barristers in England traditionally did not become company directors but solicitors did. In Canada, however, pure barristers such as Tilley and Geoffrion did become corporate directors, and so did Pitblado, Covert, and Henderson. Even Farris for some years was a director of a publicly traded company. In the case of all these men, their directorships resulted from legal work done for the corporations. Today, the presence on the board of directors of a major publicly traded company of its principal legal adviser would be looked at askance because of the potential for a perceived conflict of interest, a subject of more concern than it formerly was.

Nor did English barristers run businesses, as did Covert and Henderson. Covert's business skills were employed on his clients' affairs, not his own, but Henderson successfully owned and operated a cable-television network. His entrepreneurial activities were an extension of his legal interests, which embraced the law relating to communications and regulation by government. (Of course, the very operation of a successful law firm is a form of entrepreneurship, with the engagement of accountants, para-legal staff, and office managers as the firms grow larger. However, lawyers do not regard their firms as businesses *per se* but as structures for the deployment of their professional skills.) Thus it is fair to say that all these highly successful lawyers looked on themselves as inheritors of an ancient and honourable professional tradition.

In England barristers were not members of law firms but independent practitioners. In Canada Lafleur spent his entire career as a member of a law firm consisting of no more than half a dozen lawyers, and the same was true of Tilley and Geoffrion. These men did not need a stable of lawyers to feed them business in-house, so to speak. Virtually all their business was referred by governments or other lawyers (they thus practised much in the manner of medical specialists today). Likewise, Pitblado was nurtured in a succession of small firms, the last of which did mature into a large metropolitan firm. Farris, who started practice in Vancouver in 1903 as a single practitioner, had, until the end of the Second World War, only a handful of partners and associates. Covert's experience was much the same, as was Henderson's. This circumstance illustrates the point made in the chapter on Farris, namely that until the end of the Second World War law firms revolved around the stellar reputations of leading counsel, other figures being relegated to a lesser position in the legal hierarchy.

The decade of the 1940s was as much a watershed for the legal profession as it was for every other aspect of Canadian society. Before 1939, the Depression had laid a heavy hand on commercial activity, such as it was, and Canada was still undergoing the transition from an essentially agrarian economy to an industrial one. The Second World War accelerated the process dramatically. Government regulation had been minimal until then – the Income War Tax Act of 1917 could be read and understood by an intelligent layman – but it proliferated during the war and then persisted into the post-war era, establishing a tradition of state control which has steadily become more entrenched. For lawyers, the change was profound. The growth in population and the increased complexity of the rules governing business and industrial activity dictated marked changes in how law firms in this country were organized and operated. Gone were the days when a man such as Lafleur could stand astride the legal world like the Colossus of Rhodes; gone were the days, too, when brilliant lawyers such as Tilley and Geoffrion could dominate the profession. Henceforth, law firms could survive only on knowledge of commercial and tax laws, areas in which barristers were often at sea – the age of the solicitor had arrived. Accordingly, law firms grouped themselves into specialized pens – the real estate section, the trust section, the securities group – with the result that barristers tended to be shunted to the wings, called on whenever necessary.

Concurrent with this development was the increase in size of law firms, which became in effect legal department stores – wills at that counter, trust deeds over there, separation agreements down on the main floor. Growth occurred not just in the steady expansion in size of a particular firm but, more dramatically, in the merger of already large firms with others to form, by Canadian standards, mega-firms. Thus Henderson's firm, which when he joined it had perhaps six lawyers, had grown by the time of his death to number hundreds and was one of the largest firms in Canada. And after Covert's death, his firm merged with leading firms in St John's, Charlottetown, and Saint John to form the largest law firm in the Atlantic region. Moreover, some mergers have been cross-country ventures, and so there are now national law firms. Lawyers, even those in the merged firms, worry about the trend, fearing that unwieldy and inefficient structures will result in increased costs to the client. (There is probably more concern on this score, in fact, among the nationally merged firms than among the regional ones.)

And where do the latter-day Lafleurs and Geoffrions, assuming there are any, stand in all this reorganization? All the men portrayed in this work were generalists, that is to say they would accept virtually any case offered to them within the constraints of their own time and availability and, of course, if accompanied with suitable fees. Nowadays, like the solicitors, barristers are being herded into their various pens: the criminal bar, the admiralty bar, the medical-malpractice group, the personal injury group, the family law bar, the labour bar, the commercial and taxation bar – and the list goes on. Besides the complexity of law and litigation, another factor is at work here – the fear of the lawyers themselves about being sued by disgruntled clients. As an act of self-defence, therefore, they have segregated themselves on the theory that one person cannot know everything, nor be expected to make the attempt. And so the type of lawyer epitomized in this book is disappearing. That is not necessarily a bad thing for the client, whose interests may be better served by the new scheme of things, but the job of legal biographers may be more difficult – and possibly less interesting.

This book has much to say about the roles of counsel and judges, and the relationship between them, as well as the process by which decisions are reached. The first thing to remember in this regard, and it particularly applies to younger or less experienced lawyers in the courts, is that the judge who happens to sit on the bench during the hearing does not possess all-encompassing knowledge. In most cases, or at least in many cases, lawyers appearing in court know or ought to know a great deal more about the case at hand than do the judge or judges presiding. This is not accidental. The lawyers have been, or should have been, working on the case for a long time and hope that the judge has sufficient intelligence – or interest – to understand the arguments being presented. The process of arriving at a decision in a certain case and, more important, in a case of significance which may shape the future development of the law, depends upon a sensible working relationship between a lawyer and a judge. Various elements come into play in this process: the temperament of the judge and the temperament of the lawyer, and the climate of the times, particularly in this day and age when the courts are increasingly faced with Charter of Rights cases in which social issues tend to outweigh legal ones (or 'legal' as that word has been used traditionally).

Until comparatively recent times, roughly the end of the Second World War, it was common for judges to be rude and overbearing. Any lawyer whose memory goes back fifty years or more can reel off the names of judges whose manners on the bench were often atrocious. By the custom of the day they were able to get away with it, though less often when confronted by experienced and thick-skinned lawyers. There is no question that as lawyers practise longer at the bar they become more used to the ways of judges and are easier and more comfortable and free of intimidation by them no matter how rude they may be. One recalls the celebrated exchange between F.E. Smith (later the Earl of Birkenhead, the lord chancellor of England) and a presiding judge which wound up with the judge telling F.E. Smith that he was offensive. Smith rejoined by confessing that indeed he was, but, whereas he was being deliberately offensive, with the judge rudeness came naturally. Although lawyers have as much right as judges to put their point of view as forcefully as they can, Smith certainly strayed over the boundary of appropriate behaviour. Such was his stature at the bar, however, that he could do so without fear of the consequences. This brings up the point that younger and less experienced lawyers, with some exceptions of course, do not have the same temerity when appearing in the courts to take on judges who have been on the bench for longer than the particular lawyer has been at the bar. Having said that, it is nevertheless true that the norm of judicial behaviour has markedly improved in the last thirty or forty years and seldom now does one encounter the type of judge whom Smith demolished. As for our subjects, as young barristers they often contended with the pressure of defending their clients' interests in the face of hostility from the presiding judge. Each, however, soon adopted a style of advocacy and a method of going about a case in a workmanlike fashion that never changed much over the ensuing years.

Lafleur, the classic advocate of the 1920s, was not much different from what he had been forty years earlier and the same could be said of the others. It is hard to imagine Tilley, for example, ever being intimidated by a judge. He was jealous of the rights of those at the bar and would not sanction them being trampled upon by rude judges.

A right relationship between the lawyer-counsel and the judge is critical because from association between professionals come decisions that shape the law and influence society. One is more likely to gain a defensible result from rational discussion between equals than from the squabbles of Kilkenny cats. And that word 'equals' is crucial to the discussion. Nothing, perhaps, illustrates better the relationship that ought to exist between bench and bar than an episode in the 1920s involving Lafleur. During the course of an argument he was putting to the Supreme Court of Canada, one of the judges curtly interrupted him to say that what he was arguing was utterly without merit. Lafleur was not a man who took a case to the Supreme Court of Canada unless he believed that there was a rational basis for advancing an argument, and indeed he often declined to take cases which he thought had no merit even though the client was well able to pay for it and eager to do so. (Without being cynical about it, however, for it is only human nature, a lawyer offered a large fee sometimes finds merit in a case which previously had gone unnoticed.) After the judge's outburst, Lafleur bowed to the court and, with a mixture of great charm and conviction, said that in view of the remark it would be inappropriate for him to continue his argument and that it would be best simply for him to withdraw. He folded his brief, bowed once more, and quietly left the courtroom. His exit threw the court and the judges into a quandary and the hearing was adjourned. A couple of hours later the chief justice came to visit Lafleur at his room in the Chateau Laurier and asked Lafleur to return to court the next morning to continue his argument, which Lafleur did as if nothing had happened. Lafleur firmly believed that he was at least equal to the judges of the highest court of the land and that both counsel and the bench should be devoted to discussing the issues of the case without casting aspersions on the other's views. That the chief justice of the Supreme Court of Canada should come to Lafleur's hotel room, as a suppliant, to persuade him to continue his argument remains one of the great triumphs of the Canadian bar.

Four of the subjects of this work were barristers, working in the courtroom exclusively, but the other three spent significant portions of their careers pleading causes for their clients. The task of an advocate – one may use the term interchangeably with 'barrister' or 'pleader' – is to persuade, and, as Chief Justice Sir Lyman Duff put it when paying tribute to Lafleur's qualities, the advocate must have the 'power to captivate, to fire, to hold the attention of the tribunal [and] the power to predispose the tribunal to a favourable view of the cause' of the client. To that end, Duff went on, the advocate must summon, 'all his powers and talents' and his 'supreme concern within the limits of honour' must be 'to secure a favourable decision.' In the performance of that task the lawyers look to precedents, prior rulings by courts equivalent or superior to the present forum made on the same or similar facts. Moreover, by the rule of *stare decisis*, to use the legal term, rulings are hierarchical – one made by a higher court will be binding on a lower. There is often a great deal of agility employed by lawyers – and also by judges – to circumvent the principle when for some reason – social change, public policy, or moral outrage – its inflexible application may result in injustice. Skilled advocates, such as those described in this work, have the knack of knowing when to rely on strict precedent and when to argue for flexibility. This process, to the layman, is mysterious, if not preposterous, but it is routine for barristers.

In both England and Canada, judges have led lives remote from the general public. This has begun to change in Canada during the last decade – our judges are now more visible, and vocal, outside the courtroom – but the old ways prevailed for the seven lawyers described here. By accepting a judgeship these men would effectively have cut themselves off from contact with the community at large, for by custom they would have been prohibited from participating in virtually all its organized activities. To Lafleur and the others, such a prospect was daunting. To forego independence of action – freedom – was too much. Moreover, although judges in Canada have been well paid, relative to income levels of their time, their salaries have been less than the fees charged by prosperous lawyers. Our seven lawyers earned far more money than they would have on the bench. When Lafleur was offered the chief justiceship of Canada, the highest judicial post in the country, the annual salary was $12,000. He was then earning at least five times that amount. (The disparity today is not so marked, with judges' salaries coming closer to, and sometimes exceeding, the average net income of busy lawyers.) Though other considerations deterred Lafleur from acceptance, the gap demonstrates a second formidable obstacle to people such as him who might have considered going on the bench – a massive drop in income. Besides, they believed that they were far more useful in the administration of justice, in the broad sense, by continuing to employ their legal talents as lawyers.

On learning of Lafleur's death, Viscount Dunedin of the Privy Council commented on the 'assistance' which he had rendered to the tribunal in all his cases. *There* was a true description of the role of counsel, one that Lafleur himself unquestionably would have endorsed: a lawyer should not be merely a contender for the interests of a client but a participant with the judge in the solution of a legal conundrum.

Lawyers often debate whether they make the law by advancing arguments or whether judges are entitled to the credit. It is generally a mutual process but there are occasions when one can unmistakably assign the accolade. In the well-known Alberta newspapers case of 1938, the Supreme Court of Canada considered the constitutional validity of a law passed by the William Aberhart government in Alberta restricting the power of the press to report government activities. The decision of the court, presided over by the chief justice, Sir Lyman Duff, held that press freedom was an inherent right stemming from the British parliamentary system which could not be abridged by a provincial legislature. The judgment was that of Duff, but the proposition was that of Geoffrion – a notable example of the influence of counsel on the outcome of an important case. Sometimes judges strike out on their own to make law in a particular matter that was not argued during the actual court hearing. As an example, the chief justice of British Columbia held in an Indian landclaims case of 1991 that, although aboriginal title did not exist in British Columbia (he was later overruled on this point), the crown provincial had a fiduciary duty to take into account the interests of Indians who might be affected by the alienation of hitherto unoccupied crown lands.[1]

Most of our seven lawyers practised at a time when the appointment of judges was blatantly political. If the Liberal Party was in power, only its adherents could expect to go to the bench and Conservatives would have to wait the turn of the political wheel. Once the Conservatives themselves were in power, they were no different from Liberals and only their supporters were appointed. Lawyers accepted this state of affairs as a fact of professional life though they would complain, if not of the system, of particular appointments. Because in this century the Liberal Party has formed the government in Ottawa more often than the Conservatives, the bench has been dominated by Liberal appointees, a circumstance that sometimes embarrassed even diehard Liberal partisans such as Farris. In 1943, writing to Ian Mackenzie, the ranking cabinet minister from British Columbia and the dispenser of patronage in that province, Farris discussed the imminent death of an incumbent on the Court of Appeal: 'In addition you will have to consider the fact that with MacQuarrie's passing all the remaining judges on that Bench are Liberals and all except Robertson on the Supreme Court Bench are Liberals ... Harold Robertson is the senior Judge on the Supreme Court; he is a Conservative ... I think his promotion would best meet your political problems and would, at the same time, be satisfactory to the profession.' He went on to recommend A.D. Macfarlane, a Liberal from Victoria, to replace Robertson, should the latter be promoted. Robertson was promoted (an excellent judge, incidentally) and Macfarlane took his place on the trial court. That's how the system worked – not just in British Columbia – and it did not begin to change until 1968 when Trudeau became prime minister, with John Turner as his minister of justice. Turner introduced measures to lessen partisanship in judicial appointments, a process that has continued so that today one seldom hears criticism of an appointee on political grounds. A complicating factor in the political appointment of judges was that, in British Columbia and some other provinces outside Quebec, an unwritten rule dictated that there must always be at least one Roman Catholic on the county or supreme courts and the courts of appeal, and so a proposed appointment had to satisfy the twin criteria of politics and religion. A good example was C.H. O'Halloran of the Court of Appeal in British Columbia, who, after a relatively undistinguished career as a lawyer, became a first-rate jurist.[2]

A notable feature of the careers of six of the subjects was their part in the setting of railway freight rates. Writers of legal history in Canada tend to forget, or do not acknowledge, the importance of freight-rate litigation, though 'litigation' may not be quite the appropriate word.[3] For the first forty years of this century, grain was the principal commodity hauled by the railroads, and grain haulage and the setting of rates for its transportation to the Great Lakes and to the Pacific coast gave rise to legal work which, after constitutional cases, was the most important in the country. Indeed, when one takes into account the shipment by rail of other commodities, and the fixing of rates for them, one can argue that litigation involving freight tariffs was central to the economic health of the country and therefore more significant than constitutional disputes about the legislative jurisdictions of the provinces and the federal government under the British North America Act. The Board of Railway Commissioners (latterly the Board of Transport Commissioners), a quasi-judicial body, exercised the statutory authority to fix rates, a jurisdiction later extended to telegraphs and express shipments. Its decisions were appealable to the governor-in-council – in practice a committee of the cabinet – but only in exceptional cases would the cabinet overrule a board decision. Also, appeals could be taken to the Supreme Court of Canada in cases where some legal principle was involved as distinct from a question of fact – for example, the cost of shipping five thousand widgets from Red Jacket to Moosonee. The commissioners enjoyed much the same status as judges of the Supreme Court of Canada and appointments to the board were prized very nearly as much as those to that court. Mr Justice A.C. Killam of the Supreme Court of Canada was persuaded to resign from that court to head up the board in 1905 and, many years later, a judge from New Brunswick, H.A. McKeown, also resigned to lead the regulatory body. Political hacks were seldom appointed: the work was too important to entrust to dunderheads. The number of lawyers involved in this lucrative business was small because the subject was both difficult and complex. So far as grain haulage was concerned, the issue was, depending upon one's point of view, bedevilled or blessed, by the Crow's Nest Pass Agreement, the 'Crow rate,' which came into existence as the result of a federal subsidy to the Canadian Pacific Railway to construct a line from Lethbridge into British Columbia through the Crow's Nest Pass.

Appearances before the Judicial Committee of the Privy Council, or the 'Privy Council' as lawyers commonly referred to it, were a significant part of the careers of Lafleur, Tilley, Geoffrion, and Farris. Pitblado made but one appearance there, Covert had been on the verge of one but the case was settled at the last moment, and Henderson never appeared. It is not too much to say that the reputations of the first three men were made in London, and Farris's appearances, though slightly less frequent, undoubtedly enhanced his domestic reputation. The Privy Council was the highest judicial tribunal in the British empire and commonwealth. Although strictly speaking a 'committee,' it was in fact a court whose members after hearing an appeal made a recommendation to the monarch, who by constitutional convention invariably accepted the advice tendered and so in effect rendered that opinion a binding judgment. At its inception the Privy Council was composed entirely of British judges, but in later years distinguished jurists from overseas came to London to sit on the 'Board,' as such a panel of judges is correctly known. In the latter years of the nineteenth century it became customary for the chief justice of the Supreme Court of Canada to be named to the Privy Council (and hence be styled the 'Right Honourable') though there was a departure from this pattern in the case of Lyman Duff, who in 1919 was named to the Privy Council while still a puisne judge. The board sat – and still does for those countries who continue appeals to it, Jamaica, Hong Kong, and Singapore among others – in a large, elegantly proportioned, finely panelled eighteenth-century room on Downing Street, close to the prime minister's official residence. Unlike their counterparts in other courts, the judges take their places before the lawyers enter and wear ordinary street clothes. The barristers, who are fully robed and bewigged, then troop in and the case begins. Even Canadian lawyers were required to wear wigs, though their use had been discontinued in Canada after the turn of the century.

Appeals took two forms, those from provincial courts of appeal which went directly to London provided there was compliance with provincial rules of court – the so-called *per saltum* ('leaping over') appeals – and those which went to the Supreme Court of Canada. A litigant wishing to appeal a provincial ruling had to weigh the alternatives, bearing in mind that success in Ottawa might result in an appeal to the Privy Council by the unsuccessful litigant. In each instance, compliance with certain conditions was required – for example, a stated sum of money needed to be involved – but there were other considerations. Obviously, an appeal to Ottawa followed by a further appeal to London entailed considerable expense. As well, if the case involved a constitutional issue only, the Privy Council tried to discourage *per saltum* appeals, preferring to have the views of the Supreme Court of Canada first. It became a fine art for lawyers to gauge whether in a particular case one would more likely gain a favourable ruling from Ottawa or from London.

Appeals to the Privy Council were costly. To start with, one hired an expensive lawyer to give an opinion on the advisability of an appeal. Since the right of appeal from the Supreme Court of Canada was not automatic but depended upon special leave being granted, it was necessary to make an appearance in an attempt to obtain it. In cases where that task appeared so easy that counsel's relative unfamiliarity with the facts would not be a major disadvantage, Canadian counsel would sometimes instruct English barristers to make the application on their behalf. More often, however, if a Canadian client could afford it the Canadian lawyer would travel to London for the purpose. If successful, the appeal process would go forward and eventually there would be a second journey to London for the hearing itself. Thus clients had to be prepared to pay the costs of two journeys as well as for preparation and conduct of the appeal. In an effort to cut expenses, lawyers would endeavour to arrange matters so that they would conduct several cases on the same journey, and Privy Council officials cooperated by assembling as far as possible

Canadian appeals or applications for appeal into one block. In deciding whether to grant leave to appeal, the Privy Council took much the same attitude as that taken today by the Supreme Court of Canada: was the case of sufficient importance in itself to warrant hearing it, or was there a difference of judicial opinion on a particular point which it was desirable to settle? In constitutional cases, the Privy Council was much more inclined to hear an appeal than in a routine civil case, but, with a handful of exceptions, it refused to hear appeals from Canada in criminal cases.

It was a marvellous life for lawyers lucky enough to be retained for an appeal; Lafleur, Geoffrion, and Tilley appeared more often, singly and collectively, than any other Canadian lawyers and seemed never to tire of it. It was hard to become jaded when one travelled saloon-class across the Atlantic in the most comfortable liners; when one stayed in posh hotels in London; when one spent agreeable weekends in the country homes of judges or English barrister friends; when one brushed friendly shoulders with the élite of the English legal establishment and dined at their clubs and Inns of Court, and, to top it all off, when one was handsomely paid to enjoy all this. There was, of course, some work to be done – arguing the appeal, a process marked by civility in the behaviour of both counsel and members of the board. There was a special camaraderie among the Canadian lawyers who gathered in London for the Canadian appeals, and sometimes it was also evident among them and the judges – when the hearings were concluded. On one occasion Farris enjoyed an even more special camaraderie. He was appearing on an appeal from a decision of the Supreme Court of Canada at a time when Mr Justice Lyman Duff was also in London to sit on the board, though Duff made it a rule never to sit on an appeal from his court even in cases in which he had not participated. He and Farris were good friends. Farris, after adjournment of his case for the weekend, by chance bumped into Duff. The latter, who guessed from Farris's disconsolate manner that his appeal was not going well, learned that such indeed was the situation and suggested to Farris that the two get together the next day, Saturday, at Duff's hotel to see what could be done. Over a bottle of gin, Duff offered various suggestions to his old friend for overturning a majority judgment of his own court which had been written by Chief Justice Anglin but in which Duff had concurred. As events proved, they were both unsuccessful: the Privy Council dismissed Farris's appeal. Such an episode could easily have occurred with Geoffrion – but certainly not with Tilley or Lafleur.[4]

Lest it be thought that in the accounts of these seven men too much emphasis has been placed on the role of some of them in the Privy Council, it must be recalled that until 1950 the ultimate judicial power of Canada lay with it. The reason partly was hierarchical – it was the final stage on the judicial step-ladder – but partly, perhaps mainly, it was due to the weakness of the Supreme Court of Canada, a weakness stemming from the presence on it of such judicial non-entities as Louis Davies and P.B. Mignault. Moreover, during the first three decades of this century many cases that went to the Supreme Court of Canada, leaving aside the constitutional and freight-rate cases, were trivial, placing no demands whatever on the intellects of judges. As a result, judges of mediocre talents appointed to repay political debts could do no real harm – there was, after all, the Privy Council to set matters right if need be.

Of the four giants of the courtroom, Lafleur, Tilley, Geoffrion, and Farris, the latter three enjoyed an equal success rate in the Supreme Court of Canada, each winning roughly 60 per cent of their cases. Lafleur, though he appeared in that court far more often than any of the others, did not achieve the same rate of success, winning just less than 50 per cent of his cases. Yet Duff, who for decades had observed at close range all four giants, ranked Tilley at the head of the list as one who knew more law on more subjects than anyone else in his time, but Lafleur and Geoffrion were not far behind. Farris, in Duff's eyes, was not quite in the same league. (On another occasion Duff referred to E.P. Davis of Vancouver, a contemporary of Lafleur, as the most 'powerful advocate' he had known, which is a somewhat different attribute than an all-encompassing knowledge of the law.) Lafleur appeared in the Supreme Court of Canada nearly 300 times in cases that reached the published reports, and on countless other unrecorded occasions, probably more often than any other lawyer before or since. It may be that affluent clients wanting to have one more kick at the can saw Lafleur as counsel of last resort, yet, as already noted, he was not the sort of man to argue a case in the Supreme Court of Canada unless he thought that it had some merit.

Tracking the records of these four men in the Privy Council is more difficult. Not until 1935 do the official records – the minutes – disclose the names of counsel. Unless, therefore, a case reached the published law reports, one cannot determine which lawyers acted on which cases. Yet not all cases reached the law reports, presumably because some were deemed by editors to be of insufficient significance to warrant publication. For example, at Tilley's death, it was stated that he had appeared before the Privy Council more than 100 times, but the official records and the reported decisions show him to have been there on only 70 occasions (a substantial number nevertheless). As for the other three men, the records show Lafleur there 30 times, Geoffrion 49, and Farris 27. In fact, however, they also would have been in London on many occasions to apply for leave. In brief, the total number of appearances for each of these men was undoubtedly greater than the number of identifiable occasions, but by how much one cannot say. On the basis of published decisions one *can* say, however, that Geoffrion's rate of success was higher than that of the others, a circumstance that tends to give the lie to any suggestion that his rate of success in the Supreme Court of Canada was due to his friendship with Duff. If arithmetic alone is the gauge of success, Geoffrion goes to the head of the class.

But is this a fair measurement of distinction? It may be for those who spend all their lives in the courtroom, but what about those who do not? It could well be argued that lawyers whose legal careers are more bound up with business and commercial activity than litigation are entitled to at least equal recognition. They help nourish the economic underpinnings of the country and in so doing make it possible for barristers such as Farris and the others to ply their craft. No doubt the latter helped shape the constitutional direction of the country but economic prosperity paid their fees. Which type of lawyer, therefore, is more important? It is a matter often debated when lawyers reflect on the careers of other lawyers – and their achievements. And what about political influence as a criterion? Here Farris is well ahead though Covert is not far behind. As attorney general for British Columbia for five years, Farris brought forward and sponsored much progressive legislation. Moreover, for all his long life he was a confidant of governments in Ottawa and Victoria, even on those relatively rare occasions when his political opponents, the Conservatives, were in power. If the respect of one's peers is the true measure of success, Lafleur is the winner. In preparing this work I was struck by how deeply Lafleur was admired by those who knew him, an admiration born not only of his accomplishments but also of his gentleness and thoughtfulness.

All seven men were *passionate* Canadians. The adjective is not an exaggeration. They were devoted to their individual provinces, certainly, but their devotion to country was paramount. It appears in the careers of all of them. Farris frequently spoke of Canadian nationhood in, and out of, the courtroom, most notably in the Senate debate on a bill to change July 1st from 'Dominion Day' to 'Canada Day.' In opposing any change, he spoke eloquently of Canada's history. Covert time and again in speeches and articles proclaimed his patriotism, deploring the creeping growth of separatism in Quebec, and he was an early and enthusiastic supporter of Trudeau's nationalism. Tilley's view of nationhood was shaped by his experience in the constitutional law of the country. Although his view of the distribution of powers under the British North America Act accorded with that of the Privy Council, which in his day tended to favour provincial rights when competing interests were involved, he was proud of his many appearances before that tribunal as a Canadian, not a provincial, lawyer. Henderson, a companion of the Order of Canada, though headquartered in Ottawa – the supposed centre of the Canadian universe – was the senior member of a national law firm. He was thoroughly familiar with all sections of the country and enjoyed travelling to them. Pitblado, at the geographical centre of the country, looked both east and west like Janus and saw the railways as the principal instrument of national unity. He travelled numberless times by rail to both coasts and, through his experiences with royal commissions on transportation and in railway freight-rate hearings, understood the interdependence of the different regions of Canada. And Geoffrion and Lafleur? If a person not knowing either man were to have met them in the lobby of the Empress Hotel in Victoria, the stranger would have taken them to be thoroughgoing 'anglos,' perhaps even, in Lafleur's case, an Englishman. Yet if the same person had met them in Rimouski, he would have considered them cultured francophones. With Geoffrion, French was the working language of choice but English was the language of his household. With Lafleur, English was the language of his household and his working language; even in instances where he rendered an opinion in French to a French-speaking client, a handwritten note made on it for his own purposes would be in English. Both men advised governments and individuals across the country. Each was as familiar with the English common law as with the Quebec civil code. Both were bilingual, bicultural, and bi-legal. But, above all, they were uni-Canadian.

There is a current tendency for members of the public to be cynical about the role of lawyers in society. This is not the place or occasion to examine the basis of that opinion, but it is belied by the careers of these seven men.

1

Eugene Lafleur

In December 1928 a merry group assembled at the University Club in Montreal, a reunion of the surviving members of that city's Shakespeare Club, which, founded in the 1870s, had faded out of existence in 1904. Among the luminaries present were Sir Andrew MacPhail, William deM. Marler, F.E. Meredith, the Venerable Archdeacon Frederick George Scott, and, presiding, Eugene Lafleur, who had been a member of the old club from 1883 until its demise. On the printed menu, the courses of the elaborate dinner – soup, salad, savory, entrées, desserts, wine, cigars, and coffee – were interspersed by appropriate quotations from the Bard. Two quotations from *Twelfth Night* began and ended the program: 'I'd warrant there's vinegar and pepper in it,' and 'Enough, no more.' At the cigar stage was found a line from *Cymbeline*, 'And let our crooked smokes climb to their nostrils,' which was followed by two other lines at the end of the menu, 'My will is even this – that presently you hie home to bed,' from *Two Gentlemen from Verona*, and 'I have yet room for six Scotches more,' from *Antony & Cleopatra*. (The latter is a clever play on words, for Scotch whisky was not known to Elizabethans. One meaning of the noun 'scotch' is 'cut' or 'incision.' In the drama, the bleeding warrior Scarus dismisses Antony's concern for his wounds by replying, 'I have yet room for six scotches more,' in other words, he could easily take a lot more punishment.) In the old days, Lafleur invariably regaled the amateur Shakespeare scholars with a song, *Le Brigadier*. It had nothing whatever to do with Shakespeare but it had a resounding chorus in which all joined, led by Lafleur with his fine singing voice. The account of the 1928 gathering does not mention whether Lafleur, then aged seventy-two, recalled the glory of his former vocal prowess, but one likes to think that the members present hazarded a chorus or two for old times sake.

At the University Club, founded in 1907, Lafleur was on familiar ground since he had been a member for many years and had been president in 1923. The founders were mostly McGill men, two of whom were Stephen Leacock and Dr John McCrae, later to be famous for *In Flanders Fields*; they were colleagues of Lafleur, who then held a professorship of international law at McGill. Lafleur's is the first French name on the club's roster of presidents (there have only been a handful since), but he could not really be described as a francophone. The club, on Mansfield Street, was within easy walking distance of Lafleur's sumptuous three-storey residence which he had built on Peel, just a couple of blocks off Sherbrooke, towards Mount Royal, but on that cold winter evening Lafleur probably got a ride home. His brick house still stands, now the clubhouse of the Newman Society of McGill. Though the mansion looks the worse for wear, a visitor today can glean some idea of its former grandeur. There were many rooms, richly but tastefully furnished and decorated. Carved plaster ceilings were found in all the main rooms – dining-room, sitting-rooms, and occasional rooms – and expensive rugs on the floors. The very large dining-room featured a handsome marble fireplace and other rooms also had fireplaces, but less imposing ones. Lafleur's spacious study, not surprisingly, was lined with books. Comfortable lounge chairs were ranged about and in the centre, facing the fireplace, stood Lafleur's commodious desk.

In the yard was a stable. It was Lafleur's habit before breakfast, when the weather permitted, to saddle up his horse, or have his groomsman do so, and ride up to the slopes of Mount Royal for a brisk canter. Although he had an expensive automobile – he fancied a Packard, which was the car of choice of the wealthy in his day, and at one time had an electric runabout – he preferred to go to his office by tram. It was his pleasant custom to take his beloved Scotty dog with him and, after getting off at the tram stop near his office, he consigned the animal to the good care of the conductor (all conductors on the tram route knew him very well), who dropped the dog off at the tram stop opposite Lafleur's house. Lafleur insisted on paying a human fare for the canine's return journey: the charming habits of a bygone age. As well as his groom, Lafleur employed a chauffeur and a gardener and live-in maids and nannies for his wife and children. The luxurious, but draughty, house required some eighty tons of coal annually to keep the occupants warm. But Lafleur was well able to pay for all this. He was not by nature profligate – indeed the opposite, for he was conservative in all his financial dealings – but there was no reason for him not to be comfortable. Records of his earnings prior to 1919 have not survived but in the early 1920s they averaged roughly $55,000 annually and for the last four years of his life $85,000. One would have to multiply those amounts by at least ten to arrive at today's equivalent while bearing in mind also that in the 1920s income tax was a mere pin prick. He also owned a substantial 240-hectare farm in Hudson, Quebec, which he sold a few years before his death. He and his family spent as much of each summer as possible at his large, comfortable seaside house at Kennebunkport, Maine, which remained in the family for twenty years after his death.

Lafleur's achievements, professional and financial, did not result from old Quebec family ties or indeed from any influential connections but simply from innate God-given ability. A Protestant of Swiss lineage, he was not born into the Quebec establishment but long before his death had certainly become part of it. At a time when the gap in Quebec between Roman Catholics and Protestants was far wider and of more social significance than it is now, and when the gap between the English-speaking commercial and professional classes and the Quebec intelligentsia was far wider, Lafleur – notwithstanding his Swiss lineage and Protestant religion – bridged these social divisions and was readily accepted on both sides. Most of the French-speaking people he dealt with, not knowing him, would have been surprised to learn that he was not of an ancient Quebec family. He was, in fact, an anomaly. His paternal name had originally been Di Coussi, a family from the Canton Vaud in Switzerland, a member of which had emigrated to Quebec. One of Lafleur's paternal forebears with a penchant for gardening had been familiarly known as 'Lafleur' and became 'Di Coussi Lafleur.' Eventually the 'Di Coussi' was dropped and 'Lafleur' stuck. Both Eugene's grandfather and father were born and lived at St Pie-de-Bagot on the south shore of the St Lawrence. The grandfather, a man of strong opinions, had a heated row with his parish priest, presumably over some doctrinal matter, and renounced Roman Catholicism to become a Baptist, in which faith he raised Lafleur's father. For his part, the parish priest was so incensed by this act of apostasy that he tore out from the baptismal register the page recording the births of the rebellious parishioner and of his son, Lafleur's father; he then rewrote the page, omitting the offending names and inserting it into the register. Since parish registers, in the days before central registries, constituted the official record of a person's existence, the parish priest had in effect made it appear as if the two Lafleurs had never been. Eugene Lafleur's father, Theodore, became a Baptist minister, conducting his ministry in various rural areas of the Eastern Townships. Lafleur, though raised as a Baptist, became an Anglican in adulthood.

Young Eugene, born in 1856 at Longueuil, also on the south shore, and raised in an English-speaking household, first went to school at a mission in the townships named LaGrande Ligne (later known as the Fellar Institute), but the family later moved to Montreal where Lafleur, at the age of fourteen, enrolled at the High School of Montreal in the classical program. At the end of his first term he was ranked either first or second in the many subjects he studied, including English, with two exceptions: oddly, considering his father's vocation, he did not do well in religious studies, and also oddly, given his later career, he did poorly at elocution. In French he did particularly well, standing at the head of his class and drawing the commendation 'superior examination' from the principal. Because he had been born with a malformation of the spine which gave him a slight stoop, he did not engage in 'gymnastics.' The principal noted that he was 'well spoken of by all the Masters.' Lafleur's highly creditable scholastic record continued into the succeeding year. He significantly improved his standing in religious studies and showed some slight improvement in elocution. But in French he was outstanding. His teacher noted in French (all other entries on his report were in English) that he was so far ahead of the rest of his class that there really was not much the teacher could impart to him.

Graduating at the top of his class in 1873, Lafleur enrolled at McGill to study classics and took his BA in 1877 at the age of twenty-one. He set his sights on a professorship in classics at the University of New Brunswick but his application was turned down. Disappointed, he decided to take up law and entered the law faculty at McGill; he graduated in civil law in 1880, winning the gold medal. By the regulations of the time he was required to serve articles with a lawyer contemporaneous with his university studies. John S. Archibald (later a judge) indentured him and testified to his satisfactory progress, with the result that on 11 January 1881 Lafleur was admitted to practice. He was immediately successful and, only five years after qualifying, he made his mark by representing a former Quebec minister of justice in a successful libel action against a Toronto newspaper; the suit recovered damages of $10,000, a large sum for the time. Seven years afterwards, he achieved his first notable victory in the Supreme Court of Canada in a highly publicized Quebec case involving the validity of a will. Professional attainments followed: he was conseiller (the Quebec equivalent of bencher) between 1894 and 1897 and, after being named Queen's counsel in 1899, he became treasurer of the Law Society for four years ending in 1905. That year he also became batonnier of the Montreal bar, and the year following he was made batonnier general for the province. He started practice on his own, but, though joined later by a few partners, his firm remained small – and cohesive. A bookkeeper who came to work for him in 1897 recalled the self-effacing manner and courtesy that marked Lafleur's relations with his staff and partners and also with lawyers in other firms.

But Lafleur, while achieving professional eminence and the honours that went with it, had not neglected his scholastic pursuits, for from the day of his call to the bar he continued his studies both in the common law and the civil code. He became interested in private international law, or conflict of laws, as the subject is more commonly known today. Lafleur himself preferred a more cumbersome title, 'The Extra-territorial Effect of Law,' but, always pragmatic, readily conceded that 'private international law' and 'conflicts of laws' were terms so entrenched in the literature that one could not displace them. Whatever it is called, this field of law focuses on private disputes between foreign nationals. When citizens of one country encounter legal entanglements in another, marriage or divorce for example, or engage in commercial activities outside their own country, it often becomes difficult to decide which country, that of the citizen's origin or the foreign, has jurisdiction over any ensuing disputes. A body of law has been built up to formulate rules for solving such disputes (that is, disputes between individuals as distinct from squabbles between nations, the latter type being categorized as 'public international law').

Lafleur was an undoubted Canadian pioneer in conflict of laws and his mastery of the subject led to an offer by McGill of a professorship in the law school in 1891, which he accepted, thus achieving, no doubt in an unexpected fashion, his ambition for an academic appointment. One cannot tell how it was that Lafleur became interested in this complex subject, but Professor Ron Macdonald of the University of Toronto speculates that his European antecedents may, subliminally, have prompted him, since much of the literature had been written by Europeans, such as Pothier. Regardless of the origins of his interest, Lafleur, in lecturing on the subject as early as 1891, was certainly ahead of his time. If confirmation were needed, one finds it in the publication of his text *The Conflict of Laws in the Province of Quebec*, the first text on the subject by a Canadian author. In the introduction to this work Lafleur points out the chaos that would result from the insistence by one nation that its laws must always override any legal rights which its nationals acquired elsewhere, adding: 'It is universally admitted among civilized nations that such a Procrustean method cannot be adopted for the solution of these conflicts but that, on the contrary, the tribunals of each country must give recognition to and enforce vested rights acquired under foreign jurisdictions.' Lafleur wrote elegant prose and the lucidity of his language illuminates the difficult, and, it must be admitted, rather dry topic. The author has not been able to locate anyone who took lectures from Lafleur – there cannot be many former students still alive – or to discover any written references to his lecturing style. Yet, if his book (which undoubtedly would have been part of the course material) is any indication, he must have been a delightful teacher.

Curiously, Lafleur seems to have had only two cases in the higher courts involving conflicts of laws, both of which, not surprisingly, he won; the first was in the Supreme Court of Canada and the other was in the Privy Council, with Geoffrion as his opponent. Still, in his day conflicts, to shorten the phrase, was a required subject at McGill Law School and elsewhere, and though the subject is no compulsory at law schools it is viewed as an important area of instruction none the less. Where it is taught Lafleur's text is not used, being of historical interest only. Indeed, one would be hard pressed to find any mention of it; even Walter Johnson of McGill, who delivered one of the eulogies at the unveiling of Lafleur's bust at McGill in 1934, and who himself later wrote a substantial text on the subject, does not refer anywhere to Lafleur's views or even cite his work. The subject itself may experience some revival, so Professor Macdonald suggests, as the result of the current fragmentation of European and other states. One may also observe that, if Quebec ever separates from the rest of Canada, a circumstance that Lafleur would have shuddered to contemplate, there will be a fertile field for the application of the principles of conflicts of law.

About 1909 Lafleur turned from private international law to public international law or, simply, international law, a subject that he taught at McGill for another dozen years. Altogether then, he held a chair at McGill for thirty years, and, although his appointment was for part-time lecturing only, his long association with the university was a remarkable achievement considering his extraordinarily busy professional life. Eugene Forsey studied under Lafleur, and also under his two brothers at McGill, Paul, the head of the department of English, and Henri, a medical doctor and heart specialist. In his memoirs, Forsey speaks of his 'good fortune' in being taught by this 'trio of brilliant French-Canadian Protestant brothers,' describing Eugene Lafleur as 'the leading constitutional lawyer of his day.'[1]

Lafleur's reputation in international law, both private and public, led to his nomination by the Canadian government in 1928 for membership on the International Court of Justice at The Hague, and in 1929 Canada named him as its arbitrator in the celebrated *I'm Alone* incident (see chapter 3). Sadly, Lafleur died before the hearings and Mr Justice Lyman Duff replaced him. Had Lafleur survived, he would have heard submissions prepared for the government of Canada by his familiar adversaries and sometime colleagues, W.N. Tilley and Aimé Geoffrion. The calibre of these three men is well illustrated in their selection by Canada, which, taking the incident very seriously, chose the best to represent it.

But Lafleur's reputation did lead to one solid piece of lucrative work and renown in 1911. That year a long-festering quarrel between the United States and Mexico over a disputed tract of land known as the Chamizal came to a head. The Chamizal, consisting of about 240 hectares, lay between the cities of El Paso in Texas and Juarez in Mexico. The dispute arose as a result of a shift in the course of the Rio Grande River, which forms much of the boundary between the two countries and flows between the two cities; dry land exposed by the retreat of the river was claimed by both nations. El Paso, in 1911, was a thriving city with a population of roughly 40,000 which had expanded into, or appropriated, depending on whether one took the American or Mexican point of view, the Chamizal. The Americans contended that the river's shift had been the result of a natural process and not man-made forces so that the ordinary rule of riparian accretion, which would confer title on them, applied. The Mexicans disagreed, holding that the shift had been induced by extraneous non-natural events caused by the Americans.

Whatever the cause, the river had changed its course by 1896 and since that time the two countries had been locked in a dispute, Mexican squatters claiming possession and El Paso asserting that the now developed Chamizal was part of the city and that to concede it to Mexico would necessitate laying out large sums to compensate American citizens who would be displaced after settling in the area in good faith. Suggestions for resolving the tricky question included arbitration by the presidents of Chile or Colombia, the president of the Swiss Federation, or by the king of Belgium. But in 1910 the two countries agreed to a tribunal formed by a representative of each and a Canadian jurist as chairman, who would have the casting vote in matters not agreed upon by the national representatives; a convention between the two nations signed that year stipulated that the decision of the commission, whether unanimous or by majority vote, would be 'final and conclusive upon both governments and without appeal.' These proved to be hollow words. Overtures were made to Canada to name a jurist and Lafleur was chosen precisely because of his reputation in international law. He spent six weeks in El Paso and Juarez hearing submissions and inspecting the disputed areas.

The Rio Grande, which flows into the Gulf of Mexico, had been designated a boundary by the Treaty of Guadalupe Hidalgo signed by the United States and Mexico in 1848 to end the war between the two countries. As is customary where rivers form international boundaries, the mid-channel was the point of reference. By a further treaty in 1884, the boundary was defined more precisely and it was the language of the later treaty that lay at the heart of the dispute, for it stated that the 'dividing line shall forever be that described in the aforesaid treaty [Guadalupe Hidalgo] following the normal channel' and should not be affected by any 'slow and gradual erosion.' Any other change in the channel, resulting from man-made cause or from rapid change, would have no effect on the boundary line, which should 'continue to follow the middle of the original channel bed.'

In earlier attempts to solve the dispute, the Mexicans had always relied on the argument that the shifting of the river was due not to 'slow and gradual' forces but rather to 'violent' forces. As originally presented to Lafleur and his colleagues, Colonel Anson Mills of the United States and Senor Puga of Mexico, the problem was to determine just what events had caused a shift that had laid bare some 240 hectares of valuable land. Like the river itself, however, the Mexicans changed their position not long before the hearings started, much to the consternation of the Americans. In brief, the Mexicans turned a purely factual inquiry into one focused on the legal interpretation of the 1848 and 1884 treaties, the effect of which, they contended, was to fix the 1848 boundary 'forever' (as the treaty itself specified) regardless of what alterations to the channel had since occurred and of the causes of such changes. The Americans countered that the usual principles of international law relating to mobile boundaries of rivers must apply and, moreover, the fact that the countries signed a second treaty in 1884 impliedly contradicted any notion that the 1848 treaty constituted a fixed boundary. Lafleur agreed, siding with Mills on this issue. However, he sided with the Mexicans in rejecting the American claim based on prescription. By international law, continuous undisputed possession by one nation of land of another will confer title, but Mexico could clearly establish various challenges it had made to American ownership. Even Mills sided with Lafleur, and Puga, on that issue. Those questions disposed of, the tribunal faced the problem initially presented, namely the causes of erosion, and, after hearing much argument on the question, Lafleur agreed that the evidence overwhelmingly favoured the Mexican contention that erosion had been 'violent' and rapid, induced by man-made improvements elsewhere on the river, rather than 'slow and gradual' as the treaty contemplated. The Mexican, Puga, fell in with Lafleur's views, with the result that the tribunal by a majority awarded the bulk of the Chamizal to Mexico.

Lafleur thought that he had settled this thorny international quarrel, but both the United States and Mexico at first refused to accept the award. In doing so, each country relied on a clause in the 1910 convention creating the arbitral tribunal which stated: 'The commission shall decide solely and exclusively as to whether the international title to the Chamizal tract is in the United States or Mexico.' The question was whether this wording required an award of the entire parcel to one country or the other so that an award of part only was a decision outside the mandate of the tribunal. The opposite view held that the clause merely stated the jurisdiction of the tribunal without limiting its function. Such is the stuff of lawsuits. Eventually Mexico accepted the award, realizing that it had got the best of the bargain, but the United States persisted in its refusal for more than fifty years, an action that put a continuing strain on relations between the two countries. Presidents Truman and Eisenhower grappled unsuccessfully with the conundrum but it was left to President Kennedy to settle the affair. Viewing the unfulfilled award as a blot on the good name of the United States, he wanted to improve relations with Mexico as well as with the Organization of American States. In 1963, at his insistence, the United States signed a new treaty by which the 1911 award was approved. Some 3,700 Americans living in the Chamizal were resettled and received $20 million in compensation for their lands and improvements. Lafleur's award was at last vindicated.

Under the arbitration arrangements, the United States was to pay his fee (and his out-of-pocket expenses). He sent a bill for $50,000. The United States, through its consul in Montreal, told Lafleur that his bill was excessive and sent him instead a cheque for $25,000. Lafleur's partner, Gordon MacDougall, believed it would be prudent to take the smaller amount and hope that the United States could be persuaded to pay the rest. Lafleur was furious, both with the United States and with his partner. He tore the cheque in half and sent the pieces to the consul, telling him that he was in a better position to value his services than government officials and refusing to accept one cent less than the $50,000. Six weeks later, the consul asked for an appointment with Lafleur and brought with him a cheque for the full amount. Lafleur, normally the mildest mannered of men, did not brook interference with his fees by his partner or anyone else. On another occasion, he had set a fee at $1,000. MacDougall thought that Lafleur had undervalued his services and ordered the office clerk to increase the fee to $10,000. Again, Lafleur was furious and warned Mac-Dougall that he would break up the partnership if there was a repetition of the action, which, in a way, was at the other end of the spectrum from the Chamizal matter. The bill went out at $1,000 and the partnership continued until Lafleur's death. (MacDougall was an extremely capable lawyer, more oriented to the corporate world than Lafleur was but with great talents in the courtroom as well.)[2]

By 1911 Lafleur had reached the pinnacle of his career and he was to remain there for the last twenty years of his life. From 1906 onward he made regular appearances at the Privy Council and argued cases in the Supreme Court of Canada from every province, although he became a member of only one other provincial law society, that of Alberta. The law society of that province required an intending out-of-province applicant to sit for an examination. The treasurer (presiding officer) of the society was embarrassed by the prospect of subjecting Canada's most eminent lawyer to such a procedure and, rather like the putting of a skill-testing question to a claimant for a lottery prize, asked Lafleur for one piece of information – his age. By this time, his legal skills, always a matter of remark and admiration by his contemporaries, were fully developed. As Sir Lyman Duff observed when extolling Lafleur at the unveiling of his bust at McGill in 1934, it is very difficult to 'decompose' the elements of great advocacy – one can recognize them in action but it is hard to define them. Lafleur's compendious knowledge of the law, his ability to master a new subject quickly and to discourse on it with apparent ease but with complete understanding, his mind well nourished by extensive reading of the great authors in both French and English, his extraordinary capacity for sustained concentration on the work at hand, his elegance of phrase whether uttered in French or English, his self-effacing manner – all these certainly were among the chief elements of his advocacy but by themselves do not explain his uniqueness. What set him apart was his absolute integrity. His philosophy was: Never try to flim-flam a court, never put an argument that does not have a rational basis, never take unfair advantage of an opponent, and always be willing to concede a point if it is well made.

Lafleur's courtesy and consideration for others was legendary. A.K. Hugesson, a lowly articled student to Lafleur, cited a typical instance. He had accompanied Lafleur to London in 1912 for a hearing of the Privy Council. Instead of a peremptory summons, Lafleur sent him a considerate note: 'A consultation has been arranged in the Outremont case at 5:30 tomorrow afternoon at Sir Robert Finlay's chambers, 4 Temple Gardens, and I should be glad to see you there if you have no other engagement. If you prefer it you might call for me here at 5 o'clock and we can go down together.' Sir Robert Finlay was an eminent English lawyer who often represented Canadian clients at the Privy Council and in this instance was associated with Lafleur on the same case, which was an appeal from the Supreme Court of Canada. The case seems trivial but must evidently have been thought of great importance. At issue was the monetary jurisdiction of the Supreme Court of Canada, to which appeals could be taken if more than $2,000 was involved. The town of Outremont, for whom Lafleur and Finlay acted, had sued unsuccessfully to recover an instalment of taxes amounting to $1,100, which was part of a much larger total bill. It appealed to the Supreme Court of Canada, which held that it had no jurisdiction because the amount at issue was less than $2,000, and it was from this decision that the appeal to the Privy Council was taken. Lafleur and Finlay were, however, unsuccessful.

But Lafleur could be sharp-tongued in private. He once attended an examination for discovery (a pre-trial procedure) conducted by a rude lawyer who behaved objectionably. Lafleur remarked to a companion afterward that the lawyer was 'a son-of-a-bitch from Texas which I believe is a particularly virulent kind.' (Perhaps Lafleur had met examples of his type when on the Chamizal arbitration.) On another occasion Lord Birkenhead, the former F.E. Smith and later the lord chancellor, before whom Lafleur sometimes appeared in the Privy Council, was a guest of the Canadian Bar Association at its annual meeting in Montreal; the president of the American Bar Association was also a guest. Birkenhead had a reputation for brilliant speeches, but he was a notoriously heavy drinker and on this night, in an after-dinner speech, evidently in his cups, he insulted and ridiculed the American visitor, to the shock and embarrassment of the gathering. Lafleur's terse comment was, 'That man has a black heart.'

Birkenhead's social gaffe appalled Lafleur, who in any case seldom made after-dinner speeches or any other variety for that matter. As a conversationalist, however, he was much treasured by his companions, for wide reading in a variety of topics informed his mind. He was always delighted to share his knowledge unobtrusively with like-minded friends: on scientific subjects, music, theatre (he loved the theatre), feats of engineering, even Sanskrit. But he listened to others as willingly as he imparted his own views. His eclectic reading tastes led him to become a member of PEN – the international literary organization of 'Poets, Essayists and Novelists.' It is still a very active organization, nowadays much devoted to freeing writers from oppression, such as Salman Rushdie. The members of the organization in Lafleur's time would not have been surprised by the presence in their midst of a cultured lawyer. His literary tastes were not, however, confined to serious literature, for on the hundreds, if not thousands, of journeys he made to Ottawa by train going to or from the Supreme Court of Canada he never read his legal briefs but 'whodunnits.' In any case, his preparatory notes of argument were, literally, brief. Every case in the Supreme Court of Canada necessitated the filing of formal documents and argument, a practice that of course Lafleur was bound to follow, but by the time Lafleur had worked up a case he required only the slightest of *aides-mémoires*. In presenting an argument, however elaborate, his well-ordered mind needed little jogging from printed or written material, and he generally addressed the court using only a handful of written notes.

In 1907 Lafleur rejected the first of two prime ministerial offers of judicial appointment. (The second, much more significant, was to take place in 1924.) A vacancy had opened on the Court of King's Bench, appeal side, and A.B. Aylesworth, the federal minister of justice, wrote Lafleur to enquire if he would take an appointment, adding that no one of his acquaintance was 'so well qualified' in 'natural qualities of mind, in legal attainment and in professional standing.' The next day Laurier himself wrote, telling Lafleur that he had a 'bundle of letters from the Bar of Montreal' pressing for his appointment and that 'I now write not so much to ask as – if you will permit me – to urge you to accept.' (Laurier, interestingly, wrote in English. Not even he regarded Lafleur as a francophone.) If Lafleur replied in writing, his letters have not survived and so one cannot tell if he was, at that stage of his career, interested in judicial office. Family tradition, however, has it that he was at least prepared to think about the offer, but Aylesworth was dissuaded from making the appointment by a delegation of Roman Catholic prelates who convinced him that it would not do to appoint a Protestant.

Family tradition also claims that the newly elected Borden government offered Lafleur in 1912 an appointment to the Supreme Court of Canada and was dissuaded for the same reason, namely that Lafleur was a Protestant. But the tradition is wrong for there was no vacancy until 1918. Still, there may be something in it. Sir Charles Fitzpatrick resigned as chief justice on 21 October 1918 and that very day Borden persuaded his cabinet to promote Mr Justice Davies to succeed him; this left a vacancy to be filled. Borden's diaries reveal that the cabinet debated at length whether to appoint Lafleur; one of the latter's proponents was Tilley. Borden even went so far as to suggest increasing the number of members of the court so that, if someone other than Lafleur were to be appointed, there would still be room for him anyway. In the upshot, it was decided not to increase the size of the court and to appoint P.B. Mignault, a Roman Catholic Conservative from Montreal, an inferior appointment by any standard. Nothing in the material indicates whether Lafleur, in 1907 or 1918, would have accepted the appointment if formally offered, but certainly intervention by Quebec Roman Catholics in 1907 with Aylesworth and in 1918 with C.J. Doherty, the minister of justice and a Roman Catholic from Quebec, were possible – if not probable – events. It was a similar form of intervention in 1924 that denied Duff the chief justiceship that year. On balance, however, it seems more likely that Lafleur, after reflection, decided that he was not interested in Laurier's offer in 1907. As regards his consideration by the Borden cabinet in 1918, the picture is less clear. Borden's own entries make no reference to an offer actually being made, yet Mackenzie King in his diary suggests, as will be seen, that one was. If so, however, there is no indication of Lafleur's reasons for turning it down.[3]

Lafleur experienced a personal tragedy in 1920, when his wife, Marie, thirteen years younger, died prematurely. They had married in Geneva in 1896 and, because they were first cousins, special dispensation had to be obtained from the État Civil de la Ville de Genève at a cost of 21 francs and 40 centimes. They had a son, Gilbert, and two daughters, Madeline and Violette. On her mother's death, Violette, who never married, succeeded her as chatelaine of the Peel St establishment, but there was not much entertaining. Small dinner parties for old friends were more convenient at the University Club.

Lafleur, meanwhile, still had his work. As noted in the preface, few of his personal papers have survived and virtually none of his personal correspondence. One important source, however, that has been fortunately preserved is the collection of his legal opinions to clients which span the period from 1883, two years after he started his practice, until ten days before his death in 1930. There is a remarkable uniformity of style in the approximately 2,000 opinions rendered by him in this period: reading the first, and comparing it to his last, one can detect no difference either in the approach taken to a problem presented or in the linguistic expression of the solution offered. In almost every instance, a calm judicious manner prevails. His dispassionate attitude towards the infinite variety of situations presented to him makes it extremely difficult for a researcher to detect Lafleur's personal views, as distinct from those that he offered to assist clients, even on matters of great public importance, such as the continuance of appeals to the Privy Council. In a letter to an American professor requesting information about the Canadian constitution, written before passage of the Statute of Westminster in 1931, Lafleur conveyed the impression that he saw the abolition of appeals to the Privy Council as inevitable, though he expressed no dismay at the prospect. He anticipated, correctly, the eventual ruling both by the Supreme Court of Canada and by the Privy Council itself that the parliament of Canada could abolish the *per saltum* appeals from the provinces. As well, he referred to the debate in the Senate in 1916 over the abolition issue and to the then current debate in the Ontario legislature on the subject but observed merely that many still thought it 'inexpedient to abolish this ancient right of appeal.' He made no reference to the irony that many in Quebec who opposed continuance of the British connection favoured retention of appeals to the Privy Council as a defence against an intrusive government in Ottawa.

More easy to discern is the principle that motivated Lafleur to accept or reject a brief: he had to be persuaded by his reasoning and convictions, and not by the prospect of handsome fees, that a case was sufficiently meritorious for him to argue it. In 1923 he was asked by the Lord's Day Alliance of Canada to act for it in an appeal to the Privy Council from a decision of the Manitoba Court of Appeal upholding an enactment of the province relaxing somewhat the strictures of the provincial Lord's Day Act. The alliance, which spawned much litigation in the zealous pursuit of its puritanical objects – some of it of considerable importance in the evolution of the Canadian constitution – insisted on an appeal to London. Lafleur declined, politely, to represent it, telling the head of the alliance: 'After mature reflection, I do not think it would be in your interests that I should argue this case on behalf of the Alliance, as I am strongly of the opinion that the legislation in question is within the powers of the Manitoba legislature [and did not therefore infringe the powers of the dominion government] and, entertaining this conviction, I would find it difficult to do justice to your side of the case.' The alliance went elsewhere, retaining Newton Wesley Rowell, a superb lawyer and a teetotaller, as its counsel. The government of Canada, represented by deputy minister of justice

E.L. Newcombe (later a judge of the Supreme Court of Canada), intervened to support the alliance in its appeal, and an English lawyer, Geoffrey Lawrence (later Lord Oaksey), acted for the province. Lafleur proved right: the Privy Council dismissed the appeal.

Seldom does any note of personal disapproval evidence itself in Lafleur's opinions, but religious matters could arouse him. In 1924 a distraught man consulted him about the burial of his brother. He told Lafleur that his brother, alone among his siblings, was a Protestant – a Presbyterian – who had purchased a grave plot in the cemetery of a Presbyterian church as his final resting place. The brother died intestate, leaving no instructions for his burial. The surviving brothers and sisters, except for the client, forbade burial in the Presbyterian cemetery. Although allowing a Presbyterian minister to offer prayers for the repose of the soul of the deceased in his residence prior to burial, his relatives then arranged burial, with the consent of the parish priest, in an unconsecrated section of a Roman Catholic graveyard. Even though he himself was a Roman Catholic, the man was so distressed by this violation of his brother's wishes that he asked Lafleur if his brother's body could be exhumed and reinterred in the Presbyterian cemetery. Lafleur said it was 'inconceivable that our courts should, in presence of such a clear manifestation of intentions, permit certain of his relatives to keep him buried in the unconsecrated territory of the cemetery of a church to which the deceased did not belong.' Unfortunately, one cannot tell what the outcome was, but one can certainly tell what Lafleur's feelings were.

Lafleur was not directly involved in the negotiations leading to formation of the United Church of Canada in 1924, nor in the litigation that followed, but he was consulted by the Presbyterian Church in Montreal about the pending legislation. He correctly anticipated the difficulties later experienced in dividing church assets between the new United Church, which would include at least some Presbyterian congregations, and those Presbyterian congregations that did not join union, the continuing congregations as they were known, and in devising a mechanism to allow those Presbyterian congregations who wished to do so to withdraw from union. Most Presbyterian congregations were believed to be opposed to union. Accordingly, Lafleur said, they should be excluded with the option to enter union rather than be lumped into union with the power to withdraw.

Lafleur was involved in two important pieces of religious litigation. The ramifications of one, the mixed-marriages case of 1911–12, lasted for over fifty years; the ramifications of the other, a 1924–5 school board case involving Jews and Protestants in Quebec, survive to this day. In 1908 the papal decree *Ne Temere*, which forbade marriages between Roman Catholics and Protestants unless celebrated by specially licensed Roman Catholic priests, became effective in Quebec and was reinforced by a provision in the civil code allowing priests to refuse marriage to couples who did not conform to church doctrine. Heated opposition to these measures by various Protestant denominations outside Quebec was a factor in the defeat of Wilfrid Laurier's Liberal government in 1911. After a Conservative backbencher in the newly elected parliament introduced, amidst great controversy, a private member's bill which, in effect, nullified the papal decree, Prime Minister Robert Borden referred the matter by a reference to the Supreme Court of Canada. A 'reference' was a device by which the cabinet could refer to the Supreme Court of Canada a question for its opinion on a matter of great public interest, usually on projected, or enacted, legislation regarding which there was doubt about constitutionality. Much of the constitutional history of the country has been settled in this fashion though there was a tendency by judges both in the Supreme Court and the Privy Council to deplore the method; the courts preferred to deal with a concrete rather than an hypothetical case. In the mixed-marriages case, the constitutional question was whether the proposed federal legislation was within the competence of Ottawa, which by the BNA Act had exclusive authority over 'marriage and divorce,' or of Quebec, which had by the same act exclusive jurisdiction over 'solemnization of marriage.'

Before the decree became effective, Lafleur believed that mixed marriages celebrated by a Protestant would be held valid, even though the Roman Catholic Church would likely call the marriage 'gravely illicit.' After the decree, he pencilled a notation on his opinion that 'now' – that is, in the light of the decree – such a marriage would be 'illegal in the eyes of the church.' Once more Lafleur's personal opinion surfaced: he deplored any restrictions on mixed marriages. Early in 1912 Lafleur told a client that he did not think the federal legislation would survive a constitutional challenge, and he indicated to an overseas friend that the bill invaded the exclusive jurisdiction of Quebec. Notwithstanding these views, he agreed to act for a group of Protestants in the ensuing reference to the Supreme Court of Canada; he thought there was an argument to be made that mere church ritual ought not to be allowed to affect validity of a marriage. The argument found no favour with the Supreme Court of Canada, where, incidentally, his principal opponent was Aimé Geoffrion acting for the province of Quebec. Lafleur's clients decided to appeal to the Privy Council but Lafleur did not represent them, no doubt having advised them that further proceedings would be futile. He was right: the Privy Council dismissed the appeal. Vestiges of *Ne Temere* lingered in Quebec until the 1960s.

On Armistice Day in 1924, Lafleur worked overtime to produce a very long opinion on the validity of Quebec legislation which, in effect, turned Jewish people into Protestants for the purpose of membership on the Protestant separate, but publicly funded, school boards. Section 93 of the BNA Act guaranteed (and still does guarantee) the status of separate schools at Confederation in 1867 according to religious class, Protestant or Roman Catholic. The Quebec government, in a remedial effort to confer upon Jewish people a voice in the school system (there were no Jewish separate schools in 1867), incorporated them into Protestant school boards. The Protestants objected and then consulted Lafleur. There was no doubt in his mind about the invalidity of the legislation, however well intentioned it was, because it deprived 'Protestants of their undivided control of the administration of their schools.' The so-called *Hirsch* case went to the Supreme Court of Canada but, curiously, Lafleur did not appear. The two principal legal adversaries were both Roman Catholics, Aimé Geoffrion, who represented the province in arguing for constitutionality of the legislation, and Louis St Laurent, who advanced the rights of the Protestants. The Supreme Court of Canada decided that the legislation was valid and at that stage the Protestant committee (a body distinct from the actual Protestant school board) was granted leave by the Privy Council to intervene and hired Lafleur to argue the case before it. (Geoffrion, however, successful at the Supreme Court of Canada, did not appear in London.) The Privy Council overturned the decision of the Supreme Court, holding, in effect, that Jewish people were Jewish, Protestants were Protestant, and, since the BNA Act gave no constitutional guarantee of separate school education to Jewish people, it could not be done through the back door, so to speak. And there the matter rests today.[4]

Almost exactly at the same time as Lafleur was considering the status of Protestants and Jews in the Quebec separate school system, he was up to his ears in mastering the intricacies of the effect of the Crow's Nest Pass Agreement of 1897 upon the rate structure of Canadian railways in the post–First World War era. If one were asked to name the most important single case of commercial litigation in Canada, the Crow's Nest Pass dispute in 1924 and 1925 would be on the short list if not at the top, and Lafleur was in the thick of it. (So were Tilley and Pitblado.) The 'Crow rate' had originated as part of the railway rate structure of the country because of an agreement reached between the Canadian Pacific Railway and the government of Canada by which the railway, in return for a subsidy to construct a rail line through the Crow's Nest Pass from Alberta to British Columbia, agreed to carry certain commodities, chiefly grain and other farm products, at a fixed rate between certain western and eastern shipping points and vice versa. The amount of the government subsidy, by today's standards, seems picayune, less than four million dollars, but the Crow rate, which never varied in spite of rising costs of railway transportation, became so enshrined in the prairie grain economy, with farmers relying on it as an inalienable right, that politicians dared not tamper with it. The Crow rate still exists, though in somewhat altered form; the government of Canada now compensates the railways for hauling grain at the lower rates, but farmers still enjoy the benefit. As this is written, however, the government has announced its intention to eliminate the subsidy, an action that would have the effect of requiring the producers to pay a higher rate. Strictly speaking, the Crow rate applied only to the CPR but as a practical matter the CNR was obliged to haul the same commodities at the Crow rate from competing shipping points in order to remain competitive. During the First World War, however, it was apparent that the railways, faced with rising costs, could not transport large quantities of grain and other supplies at rates fixed twenty years earlier. So the government of Canada, under the authority of the War Measures Act, granted them temporary relief by setting higher rates, which were later extended by legislation into the post-war era. But there were challenges to these higher rates by farm groups and the prairie provinces, both of whom contended that the Crow rate should be restored.

The legal position was complicated by the fact that the Board of Railway Commissioners, the regulatory body overseeing freight rates, was bound by the statutory provisions of the Railway Act to set freight tariffs in a non-discriminatory fashion. Thus the precise question presented to the board in 1924 was whether the freight rates sanctioned by wartime measures and extended in peacetime were valid notwithstanding the Crow's Nest Pass Agreement, which, the railways claimed, discriminated because it granted prairie grain farmers lower rates for the shipment of their product than those paid by shippers of grain for destinations outside the prairie region and by shippers of commodities not included within the lower Crow rate. The board held hearings at which Lafleur, Isaac Pitblado from Winnipeg, G.G. McGeer (from British Columbia), W.N. Tilley, and an array of other lawyers appeared. Lafleur often represented the railway companies in hearings before the board, sometimes acting for the CPR, sometimes for the Grand Trunk Railway, and sometimes for the Canadian Northern Railway Company. He was almost always associated with or opposed to the likes of Tilley, Geoffrion, and Pitblado. He was always opposed to Gerry McGeer, the redoubtable freight-rate warrior from British Columbia. (It was of McGeer that Sir Edward Beatty once remarked, apropos of the mountain differential rate, that McGeer could persuade the Board of Railway Commissioners that trains through the Rockies ran downhill in both directions.) In the epochal 1924 hearings before the board – and it is not too much to say that much of the economic life of the country hung on the outcome – Lafleur represented the Canadian Railway Association; acting for a different client but allied to the same cause was W.N. Tilley. Lafleur and his colleagues succeeded; the board held that it had power to allow tariffs higher than the Crow rate. The prairie provinces then appealed to the Supreme Court of Canada, which in a landmark decision reversed the board, holding that the Crow rate was in effect inviolable. However, Lafleur and the other lawyers representing the railways persuaded the court to limit the rate to those shipping points in existence as of the date of the agreement, 1897, and to no others, a major victory.

But victory was short-lived. There had been such a stir in the country, and the business community had been so unsettled by its inability to calculate costs for future shipments of goods because of uncertainty, that the government decided to act. Hardly four months after the decision of the Supreme Court, parliament directed the board to hold a full, public inquiry into the rate structure in the country as a whole, with hearings to commence on 5 January 1926. Moreover, parliament also legislated an end to the Crow rate on all eastward-bound commodities except grain. The board, seizing the moment, and without waiting for the General Rate Inquiry, as it came to be known, equalized rates on eastbound grain and flour from all prairie shipping points and two months later, in an even more momentous ruling, applied the Crow rate to grains and flour shipped to Pacific points for export, though westbound grain and flour for domestic use was unaffected. The combined effect of these rulings robbed Lafleur's railway clients of much of the fruit of their earlier victory, and, moreover, they would be put on the defensive at the General Rate Inquiry, which lasted for well over a year. Lafleur was not involved in it, undoubtedly because at his stage of life he decided that he simply could not devote a whole year to the tedium of cross-country hearings.[5]

For nearly fifty years Lafleur rendered opinions on a bewildering variety of topics to a bewildering variety of clients, the humble and meek and the mighty in their seats: private clubs such as the St James Club in Montreal that were coping with liquor regulations and dissident members; business corporations large and small; banks, trust companies, railways, and governments. Not all these matters wound up in court, of course; most consultations in fact were simply for guidance and advice on non-litigious matters. Thus, when the Bell Telephone Company proposed installing 'slot machines,' the name then used for what today we call 'pay-phones,' the licensing laws of Quebec had to be considered. He frequently advised what we would now refer to as multi-national corporations on patents and trademarks. When the Nobel Company proposed to manufacture dynamite at a plant in Hamilton, it wished to secure the trademark 'Nobel Gelignite.' Lafleur told Nobel there could be no protective trademark in a name, as the Singer Sewing Machine Company well knew. And a similar problem arose when both the Horlick and the Borden companies marketed 'malted milk.' Lafleur advised Horlicks that the words were merely descriptive and that either company was free to use the phrase without infringement. A more difficult problem arose when the R.J. Reynolds tobacco company began selling 'Camel' cigarettes ('I'd walk a mile for a Camel'). The package depicted a riderless camel against a desert backdrop. Imperial Tobacco had trademarked its design for 'Ali Baba' cigarettes in a package showing an Arab astride a camel while smoking, also against a desert backdrop. Lafleur told Imperial Tobacco that no court in the land would find an infringement of its trademark by the Reynolds Company, whose product had come onto the market after 'Ali Baba' cigarettes. Then there was Lady Marie Chapleau's lace. The widow of the eminent Quebec politician, Sir Joseph-Adolphe Chapleau, she lived in queenly splendor at the Ritz-Carlton Hotel in Montreal. At her death she bequeathed to a friend all her personal effects in her possession at the hotel, but earlier she had, for safekeeping, placed numerous pieces of valuable Belgian lace in a safety deposit box at a bank. The executors asked Lafleur whether these objects were part of her hotel possessions because the storage was only temporary. He gave a plain answer: they were not in the hotel room when she died and so they were not included within the gift.

But it was as an adviser to governments across the country that Lafleur gained his deserved national prominence. He acted as counsel, or gave advice, in important cases for British Columbia and the prairie provinces, frequently for Quebec, occasionally for a Maritime province, and he often acted as counsel for and adviser to the government of Canada, whatever its political stripe at the time. It was not unusual for him to appear for one government, provincial or federal, in opposition to another which he had but lately represented. It seemed to be a matter of which one hired him first. Lafleur's first retainer by the British Columbia government was to argue a case in the Supreme Court of Canada involving a dispute between the province and Ottawa over the proposed construction of a hydro-electric dam on a navigable river. (The case was much like later contests between Ottawa and Quebec in which, as will be seen, Lafleur was much involved.) W.J. Bowser, the attorney general, who met with Lafleur in Ottawa and sat in on the appeal, reported to his deputy, H.A. Maclean: 'I found Mr. Lafleur knew absolutely nothing about our constitutional questions, but after spending two days with him in the library he got up the Water case in splendid shape and made a good argument. He is certainly very clear headed and able.' The court ruled against the province, which then instructed Lafleur to appeal to the Privy Council; but he had no better luck there. Bowser's rather amusing appraisal of Lafleur rings true. A busy courtroom lawyer does not have everything at his fingertips but an able one can soon grasp the essential points. Neither Bowser nor Lafleur held high expectations of success, British Columbia joining in the litigation on the side of a power company as a matter of principle. Notwithstanding the result, Bowser was sufficiently impressed by Lafleur to engage him for two other important matters in 1910.

In that year the British Columbia government led by the Conservative Sir Richard McBride contemplated a reference to the courts for an opinion as to whether 'Indian,' or aboriginal, title existed in the province. In doing so, his government had been prodded by a group of activists in the Indian cause headed by the Reverend A.E. O'Meara, an Anglican cleric trained in the law, and by the Nishga Indians on the Nass River, in north-central British Columbia. O'Meara urged the government to submit to the courts the question of whether 'Indian title' existed in the province, and, if it did, to give a definition of it and to decide whether there had been full or partial extinguishment. He wanted a reference directly to the Privy Council, but everyone else including officials in London agreed that this was impossible for procedural reasons and any reference would have to be initiated in Canada. If there was to be a reference at all, McBride favoured one to the British Columbia Supreme Court, which would give him control over the matter and allow him to appeal to the Privy Council if faced with an adverse decision. Federal Minister of Justice A.B. Aylesworth would not countenance McBride's proposal, however, for under the BNA Act Ottawa had jurisdiction over Indians (even though the land affected was under provincial jurisdiction), and he insisted that any reference be made to the Supreme Court of Canada. Accordingly, discussions ensued between Maclean, the deputy attorney general for British Columbia, and E.L. Newcombe, the federal deputy minister of Justice, to settle the wording of the questions to be submitted to the court. At that point, when the drafting became tricky, British Columbia retained Lafleur not only to advise on the proposed aboriginal title question but also on the associated questions of Indian claims to fish and which government had the power to regulate coastal fisheries.

So far as the former issue was concerned, Lafleur, Maclean, and Newcombe met in Ottawa to thrash out the wording of three lengthy issues for reference to the Supreme Court. They drafted a series of complex questions revolving around the nature and extent of 'Indian title' and the effect upon such title of the establishment of British Columbia as a colony and the terms of union upon its entry into confederation. It is evident that one of the issues considered was whether the Indians of British Columbia had an interest in unalienated crown lands that represented less than full title and something more than mere rights to traditional use – for example, hunting – and whether they enjoyed a 'beneficial interest' of some kind in those lands. It was anticipated that the reference would be heard by the Supreme Court at its fall sitting in 1910, but McBride, who was never enthusiastic about a reference, decided for himself at the last minute that there was no such thing as Indian title, that there was therefore nothing to argue about, and that he would not agree to any reference on that large, or any smaller related, issue. There the matter rested until the land-claim litigation in British Columbia in the 1960s and 1970s, which culminated in the landmark case of *Delgamuukw v. The Queen* in 1991. In that case, as Lafleur and his colleagues had contemplated, Chief Justice Allan McEachern, although rejecting aboriginal title as a basis for claiming ownership, found that British Columbia Indians enjoyed a limited beneficial interest in unalienated lands. McEachern's decision was appealed to the British Columbia Court of Appeal, which held that aboriginal title did exist and had not been extinguished, and, as this is written, an appeal to the Supreme Court of Canada is pending. Lafleur, in effect, had become a pioneer of native land-claim litigation, working on the problem before the Oka case – dealt with in chapter 3 – began to wind its way through the courts. It is fascinating to speculate on what might have resulted from his appearing before the Supreme Court of Canada on behalf of British Columbia to argue against the concept of aboriginal title. The problem did not go away and festered for eighty years; the Nishga people to this very day are pressing their claims, as they did with McBride.

Lafleur was, however, instructed by British Columbia to continue with the fishery problem and that question did indeed come before the Supreme Court of Canada, on a reference in 1912 at which Lafleur represented the province. The contest was between British Columbia, supported by some other provinces including Quebec (for whom Geoffrion acted), and Ottawa over the extent of the exclusive right given to the dominion to legislate in regard to 'Sea Coast and Inland Fisheries,' the first in a line of disputes over aspects of fisheries between Ottawa and British Columbia. Lafleur had warned the provincial government that he was pessimistic about the outcome and his forebodings proved well founded. The Supreme Court decided that the province could not grant exclusive rights to fish within a marine league of the shore. An appeal to the Privy Council, at which both Lafleur and Geoffrion appeared, was equally unsuccessful.

Under no obligation to act for a particular province, Lafleur was ethically free to act on behalf of private clients against a province, as happened with British Columbia in 1918. Lafleur, representing the Esquimalt and Nanaimo Railway Company, on Vancouver Island, petitioned the federal cabinet to disallow provincial legislation granting settlers the right to take up homesteads within the railway belt which had been granted to the railway company as an inducement to construct the line, notwithstanding that the courts in British Columbia had declared illegal any occupation of these lands by settlers. Lafleur's successful argument was that the legislation constituted undue interference with vested rights. His position, in this case and others, was that the federal power to disallow provincial legislation should be used in cases of unfairness or injustice and particularly when vested rights were abrogated without compensation – in other words, in cases where constitutionality might not be an issue but where the facts cried out for relief from legislative oppression. By 1918 the power had begun to atrophy; by the time of Lafleur's death in 1930 it was seldom used and has not been used at all since 1943.

Six months after Lafleur successfully obtained disallowance of the British Columbia statute, J.W. de B. Farris, the province's attorney general, asked his advice on a troublesome matter affecting the validity of a guarantee given to British Columbia by a bonding company. Four months after that, Lafleur was consulted once again, this time by a mining company, to consider petitioning for disallowance of another British Columbia statute. Farris, now on the other side of the fence, told the minister of justice, to whom petitions for disallowance were referred, that the dispute should be settled in the courts and, in an effort to head off disallowance, agreed to submit the case to the courts for an opinion. Lafleur withdrew the petition and then learned that the British Columbia legislature, at Farris's instance, had passed a second piece of legislation which Lafleur interpreted as barring access to the court. Lafleur seldom grew heated in discussion of a legal problem but this piece of trickery, as he saw it, enraged him. Yet he appears to have over-reacted, for the legislation that he so hotly impugned was a sensible attempt to deal with a failed mining venture in a manner fair to the interests of the mine owners, their creditors, and the government itself. Even Homer nodded sometimes. Nevertheless, after Lafleur's diatribe (though it is not clear whether he expressed his feelings directly to Farris), he found himself acting once again for British Columbia, associated with Farris himself at the trial and arguing the appeal alone before the Supreme Court of Canada. The case involved duties levied by Ottawa on liquors imported into British Columbia, which viewed such taxes as an unjustified intrusion into provincial jurisdiction in the aftermath of the end of prohibition.[6]

Lafleur was a member of the Alberta bar, a fact that may have been responsible in part for his representing that province in a major constitutional case, the Board of Commerce case. The Combines and Fair Prices Act of 1919 prohibited unfair profits on the sale of the necessities of life, and the federal government argued for its constitutional validity on the ground that even if it intruded into provincial jurisdiction over 'property and civil rights' the circumstances of the immediate post-war era made it a legitimate exercise of the general power to legislate for 'peace, order and good government.' The Supreme Court was divided; Duff and two other judges declared the legislation invalid, holding that only in cases of 'unquestioned Canadian interest and importance,' an element lacking in this instance, could such legislation be upheld. Alberta, for whom Lafleur appeared in Ottawa, went to the Privy Council. Though Lafleur did not argue the appeal in London, his views found favour there; indeed, Lord Haldane took Duff's pronouncement a trifle farther by enunciating for the first time the so-called 'emergency test' of the extent of the general power, a decision of continuing ramifications. In another Alberta case, a most unusual one arising from confused federal legislation that had had the effect of naming two chief justices, Lafleur represented one of the contenders, Horace Harvey; the other, D.L. Scott, chose not to participate in the litigation which he obviously found distasteful but chose simply to abide by the decision of the Supreme Court of Canada to which the embarrassing dilemma had been referred; Harvey emerged the winner.

And in another highly unusual situation, in January 1928 J.F. Lymburn, the Alberta attorney general, asked Lafleur for his opinion on draft legislation providing for the sterilization of mental defectives; he wanted advice not about the desirability, medical or political, of such surgery but strictly about its constitutionality. In view of the debate brewing today over the sterilization of repeat or dangerous sexual offenders, even if the deviant requests the procedure, Lafleur's views are worth noting (although they might have to be tempered by the provisions of the Charter of Rights). He was of the view that such legislation came clearly within the 'property and civil rights' clause of the BNA Act and hence fell within provincial power. Yet a difficulty might occur, he pointed out, because a given province could exercise such power only within its own jurisdiction and therefore it was doubtful if an inmate in Alberta who was domiciled in another province could lawfully be sterilized; to be safe, he said, only discharged inmates domiciled in Alberta should be sterilized. Since the legislation also gave immunity to surgeons from prosecution for assault, Lafleur had to consider whether this was an invasion of exclusive federal authority over 'criminal law.' He thought not: 'The obedience of a surgeon to an enactment validly passed by the legislature of the province could not constitute a crime.' No doubt comforted by this opinion, Lymburn introduced the legislation, which came into force on 21 March 1928. One cannot tell what modifications to the draft, if any, resulted from Lafleur's opinion, but the effect of the legislation as enacted was limited to inmates who, on discharge, would be examined by a medical doctor; the latter's report was to be considered by a four-person board, which had the power to order sterilization if, in its view, the risk of procreation might result in transmission of the mental illness. But – and it was an important qualification – the patient, if *compos mentis*, had to give consent and, if non *compos mentis*, such consent must be given by family members or, failing them, by the minister of health. The act was amended over the years but the broad scheme remained law in Alberta until its repeal in 1972. (Over 2,800 persons were sterilized.)

Lafleur did less for the Saskatchewan and Manitoba governments. In his most significant work for the former his advice was disregarded. Late in 1924 Saskatchewan asked him whether the dominion government was obliged to account to the province for lands within the present provincial boundaries but alienated before 1905, when Saskatchewan entered confederation. At issue was the validity of the transfer to the dominion government by the Hudson's Bay Company of the lands and natural resources in what formerly had been Rupert's Land. Lafleur, in a very long opinion, said that any action by Saskatchewan to claim those resources would be 'doomed to failure.' The matter did not come to court until 1931, and by then Lafleur had died. The arguments addressed by the federal government both to the Supreme Court of Canada and later to the Privy Council were along the lines of the opinions advanced by Lafleur to Saskatchewan, whose claim was indeed turned down.

Of the provinces, Quebec was far and away the most frequent and important client. Lafleur rendered a vast number of opinions, often to Charles Lanctot, the assistant attorney general, with whom he worked in close association for many years. Lafleur's first appearance for the province in the Supreme Court of Canada was in 1906 in a successful appeal involving provincial authority over navigable rivers and riparian rights on their banks. That subject, the control of water either for purposes of navigation or for hydro-electric power generation, involved a conflict of jurisdictions between Ottawa, which had legislative authority over navigable waters and canals, and Quebec, with its control over property and civil rights. It gave rise to numbers of hotly contested legal battles between Ottawa and Quebec, some of which were of high commercial importance, and for nearly twenty-five years Lafleur, always acting for Quebec and never for Ottawa, was concerned with the issue both as counsel in litigation and as backroom adviser. At one point, the contentious matter became the subject of a reference to the Supreme Court of Canada concerning the line to be drawn between public works constructed by Ottawa in the legitimate protection of navigability of a river and those other projects that might, under the guise of protecting navigation, make it impossible for the province to utilize the flow of water for power generation. The reference was heard by the Supreme Court in 1929 following a joint opinion rendered by Lafleur and Geoffrion on behalf of Quebec and Tilley on behalf of Ontario to the premiers of the two provinces, which were united in common cause against the federal government. Some idea of the importance of the issue in the minds of Quebec and Ontario is found in their hiring, between them, the top three Canadian lawyers of the day. Reading the decision of the Supreme Court, one is reminded of the old man in Browning's poem who described the Battle of Blenheim to young Peterkin as a 'famous victory' without being able to say why it was so.

Just as the dominion government was barred from constructing works that interfered with the undoubted power of the provinces to appropriate water for provincial purposes, so the provinces could not use that water if by so doing it interfered with navigation. All the judges of the court voiced their opinions at length but those of Duff were the weightiest, and by and large he agreed with the views of Lafleur and his colleagues. At the end of his judgment Duff expressed some exasperation that the problem had appeared before the court in an abstract fashion, in the form of a reference, and that if a practical, real-life case were to be presented it was conceivable that the court might take views different from those currently expressed. The federal government took the hint and prepared a memorandum offering 'practical' policies for 'water power development in navigable waters.' In the last opinion he rendered to anybody, written only ten days before his death, Lafleur told Charles Lanctot that the federal proposals were objectionable. One of these stipulated: 'Should the Dominion Government at any time undertake or authorize the construction of any canal or other work for the improvement of navigation, it would be prepared to make available to an approved provincial agency the surplus water power developed beyond that needed for the operation of the locks and purposes of navigation on a basis equivalent to that which would govern if the provincial agency had itself undertaken the work as a power development scheme.' Lafleur, ever zealous for provincial rights, told Lanctot: 'The legal objection to this is that it assumes the right of the Dominion Government to develop water power in the course of construction of navigation works. In my opinion the water powers, being the exclusive property of the province, cannot be developed at all by the Dominion. Of course, in building navigation dams and canal locks the Dominion cannot help storing water and creating potential water power, but the development and utilization of this is exclusively within the power of the province.' The litigation illustrates the teething problems experienced by a mainly agrarian economy transforming itself into an industrial one. It also illustrates the central roles played by Lafleur and his two colleagues, Geoffrion and Tilley, in that march towards industrialization.

Lafleur and Geoffrion had teamed up on two other occasions on behalf of Quebec, the first in 1910 when they both went to the Privy Council in an unsuccessful attempt to overturn a decision of the Supreme Court of Canada on a dispute between Ontario and Quebec over distribution of income from school funds set aside by an 1870 award reached pursuant to section 142 of the BNA Act. If Quebec were to separate from Canada, there would be much squabbling over division of common funds and the decision of the Privy Council, which has languished in oblivion, would perhaps become of interest. And the two lawyers also joined forces, this time successfully, against the federal government in one of the many cases heard before 1920 on the conflicting powers of the provinces and Ottawa in the regulation of provincially or federally incorporated bodies. Again, these cases today are of interest only to scholars of constitutional law and students of political science, but in Lafleur's time they were very much part of the growing commercial activity in the country.

Lafleur does not seem to have given advice to the federal government in any significant matter prior to 1912. A federal act of 1910 had required insurance companies to take out a licence, to post security deposits, and to submit to inspection for solvency, but insurance companies operating exclusively within a province were exempted. Even so, both the Supreme Court of Canada and the Privy Council held the legislation invalid because it attempted to regulate a specific industry, control of which was reserved to the provinces by virtue of their jurisdiction over property and civil rights. The case was an example of the tug of war between Ottawa and the provinces over regulating increased commercial activity. Lafleur appeared for Canada in the Supreme Court in November 1912 but not in London. On another occasion, he represented Canada before the Privy Council in a case which resulted in a ruling that Alberta – or any other province for that matter – could not construct a railway that would interfere with the physical structure or operation of a railway under federal jurisdiction. This appeal was argued in wartime. Though sea travel early in the war was not so hazardous as it was to become in its later stages, Lafleur could not have relished his journey as much as he had similar trips in the halcyon days of peace. In still another case, the federal government – then the Union administration of Robert Borden – asked Lafleur for his advice on two thorny issues. The first was whether parliament could be assembled and conduct business before the receipt by the general returning officer of the armed forces' results overseas during the 1917 election, but following receipt of a telegram from the overseas returning officer stating the outcome. Lafleur advised the minister of justice that there was nothing illegal in summoning parliament before the actual returns were in hand. And, once the war ended, what, asked the minister of justice, was the status of all the orders-in-council passed under the War Measures Act? Lafleur's opinion was that they ceased to have effect once the peace treaty was signed. This very point was to be among the principal issues in the case of the deportation of Japanese Canadians after the Second World War, but in its decision on that matter the Privy Council did not agree with Lafleur.[7]

In 1924 Mackenzie King pleaded with Lafleur to accept the chief justiceship of Canada and indeed put immense pressure on him to take the appointment. That year had been one of the busiest in Lafleur's career; he had been heavily involved preparing for the Crow's Nest Pass proceedings before the Board of Railway Commissioners; he conducted a dozen or so appeals in the Supreme Court of Canada, and he was giving advice on the upcoming church union as well as on the myriad lesser matters constantly referred to him. It is not clear what personal contact there had been between King and Lafleur prior to 1924 but probably very little though King was thoroughly familiar with Lafleur's reputation in the country and valued him, notwithstanding Lafleur's involvement in the well-known 1911 case of *Morang v. LeSueur* in which, though not a named litigant, King had been very much a presence. The case is one of the few examples in Canada of attempted literary censorship by a high elected official. LeSeur, a reputable author of history, was commissioned by Morang, a well-known publisher, to write a biography of King's grandfather, William Lyon Mackenzie; Morang and LeSeur signed an author-publisher contract and Morang paid LeSeur a substantial advance. King and his family gave permission to LeSeur to examine family documents. When LeSeur submitted his manuscript, Morang showed it to King, who at the time was minister of labour in the Laurier government. He was horrified: LeSeur had not done justice to his ancestor and he persuaded Morang not to publish it. When LeSeur learned of this, he demanded the return of his manuscript but Morang would neither publish it nor give it back. After refunding the advance, LeSeur sued Morang for return of his manuscript. He won in the lower courts but Morang appealed to the Supreme Court of Canada, where Lafleur represented the author. King, in an ill-advised and totally unethical step, wrote personally to the judges who were to hear the appeal urging them not to return the manuscript to the author because of his 'unfair' use of the family material. Lafleur, of course, may not have been aware, probably was not, of King's extraordinary intervention, but King would certainly have been aware of Lafleur's advocacy on behalf of LeSeur. Lafleur, himself an author, persuaded a majority of the court to decide that failure to publish necessarily implied an obligation to return the manuscript.

There had always been speculation about Lafleur going to the bench – he was such an obvious candidate – but a correspondent to the Winnipeg *Free Press* identified only as 'citizen' wrote perceptively: 'The leader of the Canadian Bar, Mr. Lafleur K.C. of Montreal, was prepared to make personal and financial sacrifice, in a high sense of public duty, and accept a judgeship on Supreme Court bench, when each of the last two appointments of Quebec jurists were made. Whatever qualifications these gentlemen had for the appointment, neither of them nor their friends would claim that their qualifications in any way matched those of Mr. Lafleur. But at the last instance in any rate, the answer was that Mr. Lafleur was a Protestant and no Protestant could be appointed from Quebec.' The writer, deploring the influence of religion in the appointment of judges to the higher courts, must have been either a lawyer or a politician or both to have had apparent knowledge of the Laurier episode in 1907 and the debate within the Borden cabinet in 1918.

The second attempt to secure Lafleur's elevation to the Supreme Court was made immediately after Chief Justice Sir Louis Davies died on 1 May 1924; Davies had been incapacitated by illness for two months prior to his death, and during that period King began thinking about possible successors. Of current members of the court who might be promoted, Duff seemed the logical choice, but not to the prime minister. Less than a week after Davies's death, King obtained his cabinet's approval to Lafleur's appointment as chief justice. That same day King met with Lafleur, who happened to be in Ottawa. King records the event.

Attended meeting of Council at noon. It discussed apptmt of Chief Justice and got Council to agree to Lafleur being offered the position anew [no doubt this is a reference to the previous consideration of him by the Borden cabinet in 1918]. The Maritime province men agreeing to let their chance for nominee pass if Lafleur would accept. Quebec to wait re further nomination. Ont. to let chance go by – I sent for Mr. Lafleur at 5 & talked with him in my office, the tears came into his eyes as I spoke to him of the confidence of the Govt & the bar in his ability & of our desire to fill the position to strengthen the bench & uphold Br. conception of justice – he spoke of not being indifferent to a desire to be at public service but of getting on in years, that what the Supreme Court needed was younger men. I agreed except as regards the Chief Justice who must be of authority and experienced in his profession. I spoke of his going to imp. Privy Council to take part with Law Lords there. He promised to reconsider but did not give me any assurance. The M.P.C. [the membership of the Privy Council] may be the means of securing him.

A week later King went to see Lord Byng, the governor general, in an effort to get him to talk Lafleur into acceptance: 'In afternoon went for a walk with HIS EX. We talked of apptmt of chief Justice. I asked him to see Lafleur and urge him to accept – he said he wd. do so that he wd. like to have him to act in his absence. He spoke to Sir Louis' fuss over manner of appearance when acting as Govr., ADC's style of carriage, etc.'

Lafleur evidently did not change his mind. From May until September King mulled over the matter, considering various other candidates his political partisans put forward; chief among them were Mr Justice F.A. Anglin, a member of the court but junior to Duff, Sir Robert Borden, and Duff himself, who had many supporters. Yet King continued to favour Lafleur. On 8 September he wrote him the following letter:

My Dear Mr. Lafleur:

You will permit me, I am sure, to make one more appeal to you to accept the position of Chief Justice of the Supreme Court of Canada. I do so not only in the name of the government but as one whose duty it is to make secure to the extent of his power the foundation upon which the Government within the British Empire rests. I need not tell you of the need which exists in Canada today to place at the head of our judiciary a man whose pre-eminence in his profession would gain for the Supreme Court the place it should hold in the respect of the bench and bar. Not only of our own country but also of the British Isles. Nor need I assure you of the unanimity with which members of the profession, and all classes in Canada would welcome your appointment.

I realize the sacrifices, personal and otherwise, which acceptance of the position may mean to you, and I should be pleased in this connection to consider any suggestion you may wish to make which might serve to secure your services to the country. If you are in doubt about the wisdom of severing your Montreal associations not being sure how congenial the atmosphere of the Bench might be, let me suggest that you accept the position, with the understanding that it be held at your pleasure.

You are the one man in Canada who could meet what today is our country's most imperative need, and it is on this ground that I feel justified not only in urging upon you the acceptance of the post, but as going as far as may be possible in the meeting of your wishes to have you accept it.

I shall be in Ottawa on Friday and Saturday of this week and would be glad, if convenient to you, to talk the matter over again, or I would go to Montreal to see you at any time if by letter you can give me some hope of your final acceptance.

With kindest regards, believe me, dear Mr. Lafleur, yours very sincerely.

W.L. Mackenzie King

The next day Lafleur, in a handwritten letter to King, reiterated his decision:

Dear Mr. King:

Your letter of yesterday is so kind and so persuasive that it requires all the courage I can muster to persist in my previous decision. Let me assure you that since my last interview with you on the subject [there is no indication of just when that last interview was] I have given the most anxious consideration. But the more I think of it, the more I am convinced that I ought not to devote the declining years of my life to such an important and responsible position. I have long thought that what the court needs most is to be rejuvenated, and it is not by appointing men who are nearing the 70 mark that you will really strengthen it.

Thanking you again for your extremely amiable and almost irresistible persistence which I appreciate more than I can tell you, I remain very sincerely yours,

E. Lafleur.

King replied that very day in a typed letter in which he gave up the struggle:

Dear Mr. Lafleur:

I suppose I shall have to bow before your decision, though I confess that in so doing it is the first time since I have had to do with the administration of public affairs that I have been conscious of adopting an attitude quite clearly opposed to the public interest. However, there is such a thing as the inevitable, and your letter causes me to realize that I have reached that most formidable of all barriers.

I shall always continue to wish that you had found it possible to accept the position of Chief Justice of Canada for I know what your acceptance of the position would have meant to our country. On the other hand I can well appreciate many of the considerations of which you have had to take account, and I cannot too gratefully express my thanks for the patience with which you have endured my persistence and the care and concern with which you have viewed the whole matter.

With kindest personal regards believe me yours, very sincerely.

W.L. Mackenzie King

Three days later King named Anglin as chief justice. He did so with great reluctance because he disliked Anglin personally though not politically: 'Anglin is narrow, has not a pleasant manner, is very vain, but industrious, steady and honest, a true liberal at heart.'

In his efforts to persuade Lafleur to accept the appointment, King may even have gone to Montreal for a personal meeting with him. A.K. Hugessen, later a partner of Lafleur, recalls King showing up one day unannounced at Lafleur's office, though he does not say just when the visit took place. It may well have been on 9 September, the date of the two letters, which would explain how Lafleur's handwritten letter could reach King that very day, whereupon the prime minister may then have returned to Ottawa to write his letter of capitulation. In any case, Lafleur remarked to Hugessen once his irrevocable decision became known: 'Hugessen, I love the smell of powder.' One likes to believe that there lay the real reason for Lafleur's refusal – it was not age but a distaste for the judicial life and a love of courtroom battles that deterred him, though 'battles' may be too strong a word for so gentle a warrior.[8]

Lafleur's decision did not deny him important business from the King government. In 1925 he represented it in the Supreme Court of Canada on the reference concerning the League of Nations Convention respecting hours of labour for employees in member countries, and in 1927 he appeared successfully on behalf of Canada on a reference to the Supreme Court of Canada concerning the validity of federal legislation enacted to deal with separate school matters arising from Alberta's entry into confederation. A year later he represented Ottawa in still another constitutional reference, this time involving an attempt by the federal government to regulate fish canneries in British Columbia, whose opposition to the legislation was backed both by Quebec, for which Geoffrion acted, and by a group of Japanese-Canadian fishermen, for whom Geoffrion also acted. The Supreme Court struck down the legislation. In the last major constitutional case he argued in the Supreme Court, he represented the Proprietary Articles Trade Association in attacking the validity of the federal Combines Investigation Act. He succeeded in persuading the Supreme Court that the legislation did not fall within the federal jurisdiction over criminal law. The government then appealed to the Privy Council but Lafleur died before the hearing in London, at which no doubt he would have appeared. The Privy Council overturned the Supreme Court's ruling.

The last major case he did argue *for* the dominion was the famous 'Persons' case, which involved the eligibility of women for membership in the Senate. Lafleur's instructions from the government of Canada were to oppose female membership, which he did, both in the Supreme Court in

1928 and before the Privy Council in July 1929 on what proved to be his last appearance before that tribunal. A group of five determined women had petitioned the King government in 1927 demanding appointment of a woman to the Senate. Among the petitioners were Emily Murphy, an author, an advocate for women, and a stipendiary Juvenile Court judge, from Edmonton, and the well-known writer Nellie McClung. King submitted the question to the courts and Lafleur was retained to argue the case, joined by Lucien Cannon, the solicitor general, and C.P. Plaxton of the Department of Justice. But this was not Lafleur's first involvement with the issue. In 1921 Emily Murphy had consulted him (actually through her Edmonton lawyer) on whether the appointment of a woman to the Senate would be constitutionally valid. Lafleur, in a very long opinion, said that the courts would hold the appointment invalid. He reached his opinion without enthusiasm, indeed one can say with reluctance, divorcing his personal views from legalities, for Lafleur was no misogynist. He had actively championed the cause of women to become lawyers in Quebec and had appeared on their behalf before the bar council of that province. In his letter to Murphy's lawyer, Lafleur pointed out that in England a series of cases at the highest level, one recently in the House of Lords, had decided that the word 'man' when used in a statute defining qualifications for public office excluded women. Since decisions of the House of Lords – the highest court in the United Kingdom – were almost invariably followed in Canada, he 'feared' that the Supreme Court of Canada would, similarly, hold that 'person' was intended to apply to the male sex only.

Here was Lafleur giving an opinion to the woman whom, seven years later, he was to oppose in court, but there was nothing unethical in doing so. She chose not to engage him, the government of Canada did, and he put forward the same arguments on its behalf as he had given to Murphy's lawyer. Lafleur did not take the extreme view enunciated by Chief Justice Anglin and three of his colleagues, who said that the mediaeval common law rule still held true in Canada: women had never fought in battle, women were therefore unfit to govern, and therefore women were unqualified to hold public office. On the other hand, Lafleur could not bring himself to cast aside judicial precedents and embrace a bold new approach based on common sense. Even so, it was not up to Lafleur to play the role of the zealot (after all, he was obliged to follow the instructions of his client, the government of Canada). In the result the Supreme Court declared women ineligible. Not 'persons'? newspapers asked, with hoots of derision. The five women appealed to the Privy Council in 1929 and this time they succeeded. Lafleur's legalistic arguments could not prevail against the liberal outlook of Viscount Sankey, who in one sentence summed up the case for the women: 'The word 'person'... may include members of both sexes and those who ask why the word should include females, the obvious answer is why should it not?'

Quebec had been represented at the hearing in the Supreme Court of Canada, though one cannot tell from the published reports what position it took (presumably on the side of the government of Canada). Later, only one province, Alberta, bothered to support the women in the appeal to London. It is not known whether this provincial inaction resulted from indifference, parsimony, or a belief that to question the soundness of Lafleur's, and the Supreme Court's, reasoning would be futile.[9]

That summer of 1929 was a busy one. Lafleur had gone to England early in June for the Canadian appeals sessions of the Privy Council at which he had three cases: apart from the 'Persons' appeal in late July, he was successful in a case heard late in June and then, in mid-July, he was unsuccessful in the appeal from the British Columbia fish cannery decision. In the fish cannery appeal he was associated with Hugh Macmillan, the brilliant Scottish-born English barrister. The year previous, 1928, Macmillan and his charming wife had come to Canada as guests of the Canadian Bar Association, which asked Lafleur and his daughter to entertain them. Lafleur arranged a canoe trip. With four canoes, guides, a cook, and someone to set up camp, the Lafleurs and the Macmillans spent a week in idyllic weather exploring lakes in the Laurentians. They were not exactly roughing it, but, after all, Lafleur was seventy-two years old; Macmillan was fifteen years younger. He was a most agreeable man, very good company, and they all relished the experience, so much so that just a month before Lafleur died it had been arranged they would have a repeat holiday, this time in western Canada. The plans coincided with Macmillan's elevation to the House of Lords as a law lord (a mark of his talents – to go straight from the bar to one of the top judicial posts in the United Kingdom), and so Lafleur, had he lived, would have appeared before his friend at sittings of the Privy Council. But it was not to be. Writing many years after Lafleur's death, Macmillan described him as 'one of the most gifted lawyers' he had met. Macmillan has an important place in Canadian history, for he was to head the Royal Commission on Banking and Currency, whose report led to the creation of the Bank of Canada in 1935.

During the six months subsequent to his return from London Lafleur conducted only half a dozen cases in the Supreme Court, a workload far lighter than that of previous years. He concluded his final appeal to the

Supreme Court late in February 1930, although others were in preparation. The fact is that he was slowing down, feeling his age. On 22 April he left Montreal for Ottawa to work up another appeal to the Supreme Court. No sooner had he arrived in his customary suite at the Chateau Laurier where he had stayed hundreds of times than he came down with a heavy cold and was confined to his room, unable to work. His cold turned into pneumonia and his worried daughter Violette came up to be with him, followed later by her brother, Gilbert, and his wife. Lafleur was obviously a sick man but he was not believed to be at death's door. On the 29th he was cheerful and took nourishment, but he died suddenly at 6 p.m. The next day, his body was taken to Montreal.

On 30 April in the House of Commons the minister of justice, Ernest Lapointe, spoke of Lafleur's talents, concluding his tribute by describing him as 'a fine type of Canadian gentleman.' R.B. Bennett, then leader of the opposition, spoke more feelingly. It is sometimes forgotten that Bennett, regardless of what view is taken of his political achievements, had a distinguished legal career; he and Lafleur had had many an encounter in the courtroom. To him, Lafleur was a 'lovable friend' who will be 'long regarded as the standard by which eminence and worth in the legal profession will be judged,' a sentiment echoed by Louis St Laurent, another of Lafleur's frequent adversaries. On that day also the *Times* of London ran a lengthy obituary, noting that Lafleur was more than a great lawyer: 'He was one of Canada's most distinguished citizens and even his firm Protestantism did not prevent his Catholic compatriots in Quebec from holding him in honour and affection.' The obituary notes that Lafleur was a 'Liberal of an independent turn of mind' whose advice was sought not only by the leaders of his own party but by 'Conservative chieftains' as well. It is interesting to speculate on who wrote this perceptive obituary; it may have been someone in Canada well familiar with Lafleur who telegraphed the material to London, but more likely it was Hamar (later Lord) Greenwood, a Canadian-born lawyer who had a distinguished career in England, who knew Lafleur well, and who occasionally acted as Lafleur's junior in Privy Council appeals. In any event, the author of the obituary was accurate in describing Lafleur as an independent-minded Liberal. Though undoubtedly a Liberal in politics (if he had been anything else King would not have offered him the chief justiceship), Lafleur never engaged in political activity, never made political speeches, and never sought political office. Apart from his abiding interest in literature and other artistic pursuits, he gave his whole life to the practice of law.

The Privy Council was sitting in London, hearing Canadian appeals, when word reached it on 1 May of Lafleur's death. The eight law lords present, including Lord Macmillan, paid deserved tribute to the lawyer who had so often appeared before them. W.N. Tilley, who was present on an appeal, told the lords that Lafleur 'for many many years back ... has been distinctly regarded as the leader of our [Canadian] bar.' This was high praise from an unbiased adversary. Viscount Dunedin, as the senior law lord present, put his finger on what was perhaps Lafleur's salient characteristic: 'He was a model advocate ... he was eminently fair minded and quite incapable of seeking to sway the Tribunal towards error of misrepresentation or concealment.' On another occasion, Lord Dunedin, casting his mind back over fifty years of experience with the leading advocates in England, was to say that 'upon purely legal questions Lafleur was of a stature that you could compare him with any of them.'

Also on 1 May the *Times* printed a letter from Sir John Simon, the future lord chancellor, expressing his grief. Like Lord Dunedin, he identified one of Lafleur's admirable characteristics: 'I never finished a contest with him [Simon had indeed been a frequent adversary and a sometime colleague] without liking him better and respecting him more. To my mind he was one of the shining examples which Canada has produced of a really good lawyer who was all the better because he would not allow law to be the whole of his life [a reference to Lafleur's wide range of learning and interests].'

Lafleur's body lay at his home until May 2nd, when his funeral was conducted according to the rites of the Church of England at Christ Church Cathedral in Montreal. Among the many mourners were numerous lawyers and judges. The Quebec courts had adjourned so that the judiciary could attend the funeral but not one judge of the Supreme Court of Canada was present, only E.R. Cameron, the registrar. Some excuse may be made for Duff's absence; he abhorred funerals and, besides, he was unwell at the time. Ernest Lapointe attended, as did R.B. Bennett; the two of them walked into the cathedral together. Sir Arthur Currie, principal of McGill, was also there. Lafleur was buried in Mount Royal Cemetery. Also on May 2nd, Lord Macmillan's wife wrote Lafleur's daughter Violette and in a letter free of clichés expressed her and her husband's sorrow, telling Violette of the Privy Council session the day before. Lady Macmillan referred to Lafleur as 'Le Patron,' a delightful French phrase not easily translated into English but denoting primacy.

In 1933 a bust of Lafleur was unveiled at the Montreal courthouse and, a year later, a replica of it was unveiled at McGill. Both may still be seen.

Duff, when speaking at the McGill ceremony, observed that 'in a few years there will be none to remember his voice' but he consoled himself with the thought that 'beyond the life of this generation we may rightly believe that he will live [because of his] shining exemplification of the austere and lofty ideals of the profession of which he was the ornament and pride.'[10]

Fulsome praise? Fulsome certainly, but deserved because it reflected the sentiments of the legal profession across the country and, more important, of virtually every person who had had contact with Lafleur in whatever capacity. If one had to extract a single nugget from the lode-mine of funereal tribute to Lafleur, it would be his Canadianism, his straddling of the two principal cultures in Quebec, a Protestant French Canadian with a foot planted as strongly in the one culture as in the other: not for him the 'two solitudes.'

2

William Norman Tilley

Even the most eminent of counsel sometimes have to wait their turn and William Norman Tilley was no exception. One day he was seated at the back of a courtroom waiting for the case ahead of him in the Ontario Court of Appeal to finish. A young lawyer whom he had never met nor ever heard of was experiencing heavy weather from the three overbearing judges on the panel. The flustered lawyer soon capitulated and slunk out of the courtroom, obviously upset. Tilley's case was called, he came forward to the counsel table, laid his brief on it – and began to lecture the judges. They had been, he told them in calm and measured tones, disrespectful to the young barrister, who, though perhaps inexperienced, was doing his job and should not have been badgered. With that, he picked up his brief and began his argument before the subdued judges. This episode is of a piece with the incident involving Lafleur before the Supreme Court of Canada in the 1920s. Neither man would tolerate undue interference by judges with the independence of the bar. Of course, there were few, if any, other counsel who would have been brave enough to do what Tilley so rightly did. In the courtroom and out of it, Tilley was a powerful figure.[1]

In July 1934, in the last year of Tilley's treasurership of the Law Society of Upper Canada, Earl Smith was appointed secretary. Knowing Tilley's reputation for gruffness, Smith, who in later years was to achieve distinction as the Society's treasurer, attended his first meeting of the benchers presided over by Tilley. He did so with considerable trepidation, but the meeting went well enough. However, when the next meeting was scheduled, Smith realized that he had not presented the minutes of the earlier meeting to Tilley for his approval and signature. He searched Tilley out, found him in the law library of Osgoode Hall, put the unsigned minutes before him, and asked him to sign them. The treasurer scrutinized them, peered at Smith, looked again at the unsigned minutes, and asked Smith gruffly: 'What changes have you made to these minutes?' Smith, discomfited, made no reply. Was Tilley joking in a rather heavy-handed fashion, or was he serious? No one knows. Not even Smith, who often told the story. This was the enigma of Tilley: was he a genuine ogre or a seeming one? What is clear is that he was a lion of the legal profession almost from the day of his qualification in 1894 until his death in 1942. Any personal shortcomings did not impede his legal career – indeed, his single-mindedness of purpose, his inability to suffer fools gladly, his well-grounded confidence that he knew more law than anyone else – served him in good stead professionally – but they certainly gained him few close friends.

Through inadvertence or design, he undoubtedly could rub people the wrong way. For some reason not now known, he attracted the ire of R.R. Cromarty, publisher of the *Dominion Law Reports*, which printed and circulated those decisions of the courts thought by the editor to be of value. Cromarty, an ambitious man inclined to trade on his acquaintances, must have had a run-in with Tilley, who would have found Cromarty tiresome. In reporting decisions, the invariable practice of all law publishers is to show the names of the lawyers involved, but, over a period of about ten years, Cromarty refused to print Tilley's name in his series. A number of the cases in which Cromarty refused to acknowledge Tilley's presence concerned the CPR; it is possible that the peppery Cromarty had spoken ill of the railway, for which Tilley was then acting, and Tilley had taken him to task.

And yet his often stern appearance was belied by private acts of kindliness and generosity, as witnessed by his conduct towards Smith's predecessor, Holford Ardagh, a veteran of the First World War who came down with a serious war-related illness that incapacitated him. Tilley, as treasurer of the Law Society, did Ardagh's work for at least a year, handling correspondence, dictating letters, dealing with routine business so that Ardagh continued to draw his salary until his death. Fellow lawyers, such as John Robinette and the late J.C. McRuer, also attested to Tilley's essential kindliness and modesty. Unfortunately, however, these qualities were sometimes well disguised and the result was that others not so familiar with him thought him aloof and cold.

Tilley was not without a certain sardonic sense of humour: always refusing to sit for an official portrait as treasurer, he once, when pressed, conceded that he had heard of a certain artist by the name of Sherwin Williams – the well-known paint company. The painting of him now hanging at Osgoode Hall was painted posthumously, from photographs. Yet a quality he more frequently showed was stubbornness. Once an established client asked him for an immediate opinion on some supposedly urgent matter. Tilley refused; the client insisted. Tilley said that he himself would not offer an opinion on such short notice but there was someone else in his office who could and would help out. He showed the client the office to head for; on the client asking whose it was, Tilley said, 'It is my law student.' He was not going to be pushed into giving a hastily considered opinion. Similarly, Tilley could be difficult in his relations with his law students. One of them, David Walker, much later a cabinet minister in the Diefenbaker government, recalls an occasion when Tilley asked him to work up a point of law. He consulted an American encyclopaedic publication on the subject. Tilley complimented him on his work, but, on learning that Walker had drawn it from the American source, upbraided him. Walker stood his ground, saying that the entry in the American publication had been submitted by Tilley's own firm. There was not much Tilley could say in response. Many years later, in 1941, David Walker appeared in the Supreme Court of Canada in a case involving a claim by his client against the CPR. Walker, and his client, had earlier failed at the trial level and before the Court of Appeal. At the Supreme Court, Walker found himself in opposition to his mentor. It was not a happy occasion for Tilley. After the hearing, the two men retired to the barristers' room where they removed their legal accoutrements. According to Walker, Tilley was distinctly rude to him because he expected the court was going to rule in favour of Walker's client, which it did, and a subsequent appeal to the Privy Council by the CPR was unsuccessful.

Though not given to cracking jokes in the courtroom (he did occasionally), Tilley could see the humorous side of a situation. One day when arguing a case, he was interrupted by the presiding judge who asked, with a certain maliciousness, if his argument was not exactly opposite to what he had urged in another case only a week before. Tilley unblushingly agreed, commenting: 'Wasn't that a silly argument?' At his death, intimates spoke of his 'jovial laugh' and his 'human side' and his 'genial companionship.' He had a great fondness for the comic strips; he was once observed reading a newspaper in the courtroom just before his case was called; he was not reading the editorial page but the comic page.

(Dare one ask whether Tilley read one of the most popular comic strips of his day, 'Tillie the Toiler'?) As the clergyman put it at Tilley's funeral, he walked humbly with his God and 'over an apparently austere surface rippled a sunny humour which delighted his intimates.'

Tilley's absolute devotion to the practice of law isolated him not only from many fellow lawyers and from those whom he believed inferior but also from the community at large. Apart from his very happy family life, he displayed no interests in activities outside the sphere of the law. His tenure as bencher and treasurer were not really diversions from law but simply aspects of his career. Given his single-mindedness, it is not surprising that, during the debate within Osgoode Hall Law School in the 1930s as to the future direction of legal education in Ontario, Tilley stood on the conservative wing. He was one of the members of a special committee struck in 1933 to consider the issue, which, at the risk of gross oversimplification, involved deciding whether legal education was primarily a form of vocational training or an intellectual discipline that acknowledged the utility of practical instruction. The committee plumped for the practical: legal education was best left in the hands of practitioners who alone knew how to prepare law students for entry into the profession. As Jerome Bickenbach and Ian Kyer have put it, the recommendations of Tilley and his colleagues represented the views of the 'very conservative old-school practitioner' who 'held firmly to the view that the true lawyer was an experienced and successful practitioner.' Tilley, of course, would not have viewed his stance in that way: professional training should be left to the professionals – not the academics.

What talents was Tilley blessed with to bring him to the pinnacle of the profession? In 1930 he had gracefully acknowledged Lafleur as the undisputed leader of the Canadian bar, yet one could make an argument that Tilley, even then, was as much a leader of the profession as Lafleur. After the latter's death that year, Tilley stood alone at the top. Or did he? Did Geoffrion join him as a co-equal? Lawyers endlessly debate comparisons between lawyers: who are the most effective, the most eloquent, and so on. Comparisons are at best a poor guide in the case of lawyers for the style of successful lawyers differs so much that it is difficult to find a common denominator. So far as Tilley is concerned, he charged high fees, won more cases than he lost, and figured not only in many high-profile pieces of litigation which have had an impact on the country but also in various government inquiries and commissions.

It is difficult to single out any one talent that explains the success of a professional man, and, without denigrating other professions, the task is even more difficult with lawyers. A superb eye surgeon, for example, brings to bear many talents: concentration, a compendious knowledge of medicine and anatomy, particularly of the eye, and, of course, a steady hand. But a successful advocate, in addition to being well trained, must be a psychologist; he must be well informed (an eye surgeon can be a literary dolt without harming his patients), flexible, quick thinking, and political in the broad non-partisan sense; and, last but not least, he must possess an intuitive sense of what to do under urgent conditions. Tilley had those talents, in abundance, but the one single quality that was recognized by his contemporaries and more particularly by his adversaries was his powerful courtroom presence. Of medium height, and portly, he had a strong resonant voice and in the courtroom exuded utter confidence in his case. Though he was not ponderous, there was about him an unmistakable air of authority – a palpable *gravitas*. As Brendan O'Brien puts it: 'Tilley was the most forceful counsel that I have ever seen. If we visualize a counsel as a hammer driving in a nail, then Tilley would qualify as a sledgehammer. He not only rode roughshod over other counsel, but also over most judges.' John Robinette formed exactly the same impression using similar imagery: 'Tilley built his cases brick by brick and hammered home the mortar so that in the end he had built an unassailable structure.' Tilley had never been timorous and had always adopted the attitude that he knew as much law as, perhaps more than, any judges he appeared before and that it was up to him to inform the less well-informed. Of course, he had to do so in a fashion that would not prejudice his clients' interests in the eyes of the court. There, perhaps, is the true test of a great advocate: instruct the judge and incline him, to use the language of the Book of Common Prayer, to keep the law – as the lawyer interprets it. But he did not always succeed in this endeavour. In 1936 he argued a case in the Ontario Court of Appeal in which all the judges but one were over the age of eighty; the venerable chief justice, Sir William Mulock, presided. Tilley left the courtroom with his opponent, who remarked that his only criticism of Tilley's presentation was that he had said everything twice. Tilley retorted 'that with those judges' he should have said everything three times. He was right; the court ruled against him.

Tilley, unlike Lafleur but like Farris, was prepared to take trials throughout his career. Lafleur, after his early years at the bar, appeared only in the higher appellate courts and before the Board of Railway Commissioners. Geoffrion did occasional trial work but preferred to confine himself, like Lafleur, to the higher echelons of the court system. Tilley, however (and Farris), was not only a skilled lawyer on points of law in appellate courts but also a superb trial lawyer. It is true that he mostly concerned himself with the legal problems of the rich and influential, but he would take a case off the street with no or paltry fees if he believed a grave injustice was threatened. Thus he acted for the female proprietor of a small knitting shop on Yonge Street in Toronto which had been expropriated; the compensation offered was trifling and Tilley got proper value for her. With regard to the more socially exalted, one of the most noteworthy of Tilley's cases involved a libel action by Sir Arthur Currie against a newspaper publisher, who had alleged that Currie had been callously negligent in ordering Canadian troops into action at Mons on the last day of the First World War. The case was by no means cut and dried, and Tilley agreed to act only with considerable misgivings. Though a jury awarded Currie damages, they were not substantial and so the outcome was rather clouded – but Tilley's defence of Currie was stout-hearted. One of the last major cases Tilley took, in 1941, was another libel action, in which he successfully represented the Toronto *Globe and Mail* in a suit brought against it by the Toronto *Star*.

Tilley progressed to remarkable heights of achievement from an unremarkable background. He was born in 1868 in the village of Tyrone, in Durham County, Ontario, but because his birth was registered in nearby Bowmanville, east of Toronto, the latter became his official place of birth. Tilley's father was school inspector for the county and he encouraged his son to follow his profession, though Tilley always wanted to study law. At elementary school in Bowmanville his instruction followed guidelines applicable to all Ontario youngsters of the day. 'Every youth, whether in Town or Country should be able so to read that reading will be a pleasure and not a labour ... he should be able to write readily and well; he should know Arithmetic so as to perform readily and properly any financial business transactions, and be able to keep Accounts; he should be able to speak and write with correctness the language of the Country.' He attended high school in Lindsay, a town some distance east of Bowmanville where he must have boarded. The choice of Lindsay may be explained by the fact that it was in Victoria County and his father perhaps felt it was wise to send his obviously bright son to a school outside his jurisdiction. In any case, after graduation he did teach school for two years. He did not attend university but came to Toronto to study law, eking out his existence by working as a night librarian at Osgoode Hall for fifty cents a day. The library then was much the same as it is now, a stately room with handsome bookcases and desks positioned between colonnades. In the year of his call to the bar, 1894, he took the gold medal at Osgoode Hall. His fellow students included two men later to be prominent in the profession, A.E. Hoskin of Winnipeg and H.E. Rose (a future chief justice of Ontario). Although not an exact contemporary, for she was called to the bar three years after Tilley amid much controversy, Clara Brett Martin became the first female lawyer in Ontario. Not to be outdone by a lot of males, she applied in 1899 for one of the four positions as examiner at Osgoode Hall but lost out to Tilley and Rose and another pair.[2]

Tilley had articled to Daniel Thomson, in Toronto, a well-known lawyer who was regarded with disapproval by some members of the Toronto establishment because he was a Liberal and, worse still, a Baptist. Though not a Baptist, Tilley was certainly a Liberal and, after his call to the bar, stayed on with Thomson's firm, Thomson Henderson and Bell. The firm over the years added, and lost, partners, but Tilley stayed with it all his career. Chief among the additions was C.F.H. Carson, a formidable counsel and later, like his mentor Tilley, treasurer of the Law Society. The firm was never large; one suspects that Tilley would not have been comfortable among many nominally equal partners.

There was never any question of Tilley becoming office-bound as a solicitor; litigation was his choice and forte and he plunged into it. Within two years of his call he made his first appearance at the Supreme Court of Canada though only as junior counsel to a more senior man. They both were unsuccessful, but it was his maiden appearance in what proved to be a long successful career in that court. By 1906 he was conducting cases in Ottawa on his own as the lead counsel. He appeared in just under 200 cases which made their way into the published law reports and on many other unreported occasions involving motions or applications of various kinds. As for his reported cases, he was successful in just under 60 per cent of them but statistics are only a guide. Many of the cases he won were of the first importance and had permanent impact, and some of the ones he lost in Ottawa were reversed by the Privy Council. Before that tribunal he appeared at least seventy times that can be identified, but his track record was not quite so good in London as in Ottawa, his successes barely more than his losses. Yet, when he won, he won big! His introduction to that tribunal came in 1907 when he appeared as junior counsel on two appeals. In the first he was junior to the renowned Sir Edward Carson; they were opposed by Sir Robert Finlay who, representing the CPR, won the day. Tilley had better luck on the second occasion. The following year he also appeared twice as junior counsel, first with G.F. Shepley, also of Toronto, in a successful appearance and secondly with H.A. Lovett in opposition to a man equally as famous as Carson, Rufus Isaacs, later the Marquess of Reading, who triumphed.

Tilley, in those consecutive appearances, had made important contacts with Sir Robert Finlay and Shepley. And so there was no doubt a connection between Tilley's performance in London and his appearance, in 1910, with both those men in the much anticipated arbitration at The Hague of a North Atlantic coastal fishery dispute involving the United States, Great Britain, and Canada. Finlay was the leading counsel for Great Britain and Shepley one of the leading counsel for Canada. Tilley, like Geoffrion before him and Lafleur after him, found himself in the international spotlight. With Geoffrion it had been the Alaska Boundary Tribunal of 1903, with Lafleur the Chamizal arbitration in 1911. Tilley was hardly a neophyte at the time of the arbitration – he was then forty-two and had been a lawyer for fifteen years – but it was still heady stuff, high drama played on a world stage with top-calibre lawyers from the three countries playing their roles.

The arbitration had been invoked to settle various vexed questions arising from a treaty concluded in 1818 between Great Britain and the United States concerning the rights of Americans to fish in British territorial waters. Prior to the American revolution, residents of what became the New England states had, as British subjects, traditionally fished off the shores of Newfoundland and the North Atlantic coast. Although the treaty of 1783 ending the revolutionary war dealt in part with this historic fishery, the 1818 treaty was specifically intended to define post-revolutionary entitlement. That treaty itself had been later amended in certain respects but, as population increased and fishing fleets grew larger, regulation by Great Britain of the fishery led to heated disputes with the United States for many years. The eventual result was a convention, ratified in 1909, by which the two countries agreed to submit their differences to an international arbitration tribunal at The Hague.

The arbitration concerned the interpretation of Article I of the 1818 treaty, which gave Americans the right to fish on the south, western, and northern coasts of Newfoundland, and the south coast of Labrador, in common with the residents of Newfoundland and Labrador, with certain privileges to dry and cure fish in unsettled areas on those coasts. In return, the Americans renounced the right to fish within three marine miles of the coast although they could seek shelter within that zone to repair their vessels. There were two aspects of the problem, one relating to the fishery around Newfoundland and Labrador, and the other relating to the fishery off all other regions of the Canadian Atlantic coast.

Three principal issues emerged: first, to what extent could American fishermen be subjected, if at all, to unilateral fishery regulation by Great Britain designed to promote the conservation of fish stocks by, for example, fixing the times and dates of fishing and the size of nets not only around the Newfoundland and Labrador coasts but also around the Magdalen Islands; second, to what sort and size of 'bays' did the American right to fish extend and were the Americans excluded from all bays on the Newfoundland and Labrador coasts; and third, how was the three-marine-mile exclusionary zone to be measured in relation to 'bays,' a problem that affected the fishery off Canada as well as Newfoundland and Labrador. There were subsidiary questions as well, such as customs-clearance provisions and whether every member of the crew of an American vessel was required to be an 'inhabitant of the United States of America' or whether non-nationals could be employed. The 1909 convention provided for a five-member tribunal to be formed according to the rules of the Permanent Court of Arbitration at The Hague, which had been formulated in 1907. Canada, of course, was not a signatory to the treaty of 1818, nor, since it did not then conduct an independent foreign policy, was it a party to the convention. Newfoundland was in an even more subservient position for it was still a British crown colony. None the less, Canada had a vital stake in the proceedings because it had an indirect interest in any fishing that occurred off its shores in the region of Newfoundland and the Gulf of St Lawrence, and a direct interest in the delineation of the three-marine-mile exclusionary zone which would apply to all Canadian Atlantic shores. One worry for Canada had been the status of the Bay of Fundy, but, by an agreement between Great Britain and the United States reached before the arbitration began, that bay was closed to American fishing altogether.

Once the composition of the tribunal was settled, the treaty signatories, the United States and Great Britain, appointed their counsel. The two leading Americans were Elihu Root, then a United States senator and formerly secretary of war in the administration of Theodore Roosevelt, and George Turner, formerly a United States senator from the state of Washington. Both these men had been arbitrators on the Alaska Boundary Tribunal at which their objectivity had justifiably been called into question. The American nominee on The Hague tribunal, George Gray, a Circuit Court of Appeal judge, was a good deal more objective. Great Britain's nominee was Sir Charles Fitzpatrick, chief justice of Canada, who, while minister of justice, had been much involved with the Alaska Boundary Tribunal. The British and Canadian contingent of lawyers outnumbered the Americans by eleven to six. The nominal leader of the British group was the attorney general, Sir William Robson, but the actual leader was Sir Robert Finlay, the eminent English barrister who had led the British case before the Alaska Boundary Tribunal and later was to become lord chancellor, the top judicial post in the United Kingdom. Leading the Canadian contingent was J.S. Ewart, the great nationalist, who, alone of all the Canadian lawyers, presented arguments to the tribunal. Next came Shepley, who had a long history of court appearances at high levels, and, behind him in seniority, Tilley. But behind Tilley, in seniority, were three English lawyers also of future fame: Raymond Asquith and Geoffrey Lawrence, later both English law lords as Lords Asquith and Oaksey respectively, and the Canadian expatriate Hamar Greenwood. Tilley, equally as talented, was to work with and sometimes against all these men in the decades to follow; whatever subsequent directions their careers took, they remained a friendly brotherhood from their days at The Hague.

The tribunal convened on 1 June 1910 under the aegis of its chairman, H. Lammasch, professor of international law at the University of Vienna. The pomp and circumstance, the *politesse*, the civilities, the due obeisance to the 'laws of equity, justice and humanity' did not disguise from him the fact that the disputes between the contending powers, the United States and Great Britain, had been so severe as to bring them in one or two instances 'to the verge of the extremities of war,' as he expressed it in his opening statement to the tribunal. And so, he went on, the tribunal that met in 'modest provisional rooms' was called upon to settle matters of great international delicacy. He lauded the two contending parties for their desire to maintain 'the sublime cause of international justice and peace' by submitting to a decision of an arbitral body, thereby setting 'an example for the whole community of nations.' But in his modesty, Lammasch disclaimed any personal virtue in being chosen as the chairman of the tribunal; rather it was a tribute to the disinterestedness of the treaty powers which had deferred to the impartiality of international arbitration. Lammasch said that he had agreed to undertake the task of arbitration because of the 'experience' and 'tact' of his 'honoured colleagues,' which gave him 'courage to accept the functions so noble ... incumbent on me.' In his peroration, he reminded his listeners that the Permanent Court was a temple in which 'a new marble pillar [sustained] the ideal palace of Justice and Peace.' And then, turning his mind to the issue at hand, namely fishing in the high seas, he declared: 'Being conscious of our responsibilities, we should do our best to render justice to those "captains courageous" and hardy fishermen of both nations, who in the uproar of the sea and at the risk of their lives ply the treasures of the Ocean for the benefit of men. In doing our duty in that way, we hope to settle peacefully and definitely a difference which for so long a time has agitated the two branches of the Anglo-Saxon race.'

The opening formalities concluded, the tribunal adjourned a week, to reconvene on 6 June. In the meanwhile, evidently prodded by Lammasch's remarks about their 'modest' surroundings, the sessions had been moved to more commodious quarters. There, on the tribunal's reassembling, the chairman acknowledged the receipt from Wilhelmina, Queen of the Netherlands, of a letter in response to one from the tribunal expressing its 'respectful homage' to Her Majesty and expressing 'good wishes ... for the happiness of Your Majesty and Your August Family.' The Queen replied in similar vein, assuring the tribunal of 'her interest in and great sympathy with their task.' Today we may smile at these courtly, outmoded forms of dealing with highly contentious international disputes, but we have not improved upon them.

The submissions lasted forty days, ending on 12 August 1910. The evidence was not oral but documentary, though the legal arguments were oral. The documents put before the tribunal take up seven volumes of the twelve subsequently printed, and the oral arguments three. Four lawyers conducted the American case, Root, Turner, Samuel J. Elder, and Charles B. Warren. Tilley was one of a number of very bright people organizing the case for Canada and Great Britain; he helped prepare the ammunition but did not fire it. Working with the others as a team, he digested the masses of documents and correspondence accumulated through the decades and pored over maps of the Atlantic region, familiarizing himself with every bay and inlet on the Newfoundland and Canadian coasts. Analysing the formal arguments of the United States, he helped to develop the arguments eventually submitted to the tribunal on behalf of Canada and Newfoundland.

The argument by counsel went on for so long that the tribunal chairman suggested, in the mildest manner possible, that perhaps counsel could avoid repetition? And that other counsel still to follow could avoid treading paths already trodden? In spite of this plea, the hearings went on for another two weeks. When the legal arguments ended, Lammasch courteously paid tribute to the adversaries who, he said, had looked on the tribunal as a body designed to lend 'friendly assistance.' He commended them for the 'most valuable assistance we have had from your speeches, for the courtesy you have shown us and especially for the courtesy you have shown to one another. I am sure that the chivalrous spirit in which you have treated the grave controversies existing between your countries will facilitate us to come to a just and happy solution of them. It is with regret that we take leave of you, who have been our friends and our guides in this long and sometimes laborious journey.' He informed them that the tribunal, on four days notice, would announce its award.

Tilley had gone to Europe with his wife and with his two daughters, who during the months of preparation and the hearings themselves had resided in a boarding-school in London; Tilley and his wife stayed at The Hague throughout. The tribunal reassembled on 7 September. Considering the complexity of the issues, the fact that a conclusion had been reached only four weeks after the legal arguments ended seems astonishing by today's standards. Not all the lawyers who had been present when the case started three months earlier were there at the end. Tilley's presence is proof that he had played a significant role in the preparation of the Canadian and British case. Shepley, too, was there and so was Sir Allen Aylesworth, the minister of justice, who had also been present in June, not as an active participant but in his capacity as official agent. Although the two countries enjoyed divided success, on balance the British and Canadians gained greater advantage, a triumph of 'equity and justice' as Lammasch would have put it. The tribunal declared that Great Britain could indeed regulate unilaterally the common fishery provided the regulations did not give unfair advantage to one or other of the parties, and it spelled out in considerable detail housekeeping provisions designed to make the general award workable. As well, the tribunal ruled that non-Americans could be employed on American vessels without violating the treaty, and, as far as customs clearance was concerned, it was 'not unreasonable' to require compliance with local regulations so long as customs facilities were within 'convenient' reach of an American vessel.

The most troublesome issues, however, were the definitions of the extent of the 'liberty to fish' granted the Americans by the treaty of 1818 and the delineation and location of 'bays' and the measurement of the three-mile limit in relation to them. The British had argued that the Americans by the treaty had no right to fish in any of the bays along the treaty coasts of Newfoundland and Labrador because the word 'bays' was not used in conferring the right to fish. The tribunal decided, however, that the right to fish along the treaty coasts included by implication the right to fish in bays; the Americans succeeded in that part of the argument. But 'bays' presented difficulties in fixing the three-mile limit, not only on the treaty coasts but on all coastal areas, mainly Canadian, which lay outside the treaty coasts. The British (and Canadians) contended that the zone must be measured from 'a line drawn between the headlands' of the bays whereas the Americans argued that the three-mile zone must follow the 'sinuosities' of the shoreline so that they would be excluded only from waters of bays less than six miles in width. But what was to happen if a bay was greater than six miles in width? And when a body of water commonly known as a 'bay' narrowed to become a 'canal,' or 'channel' in common parlance, where was the line to be drawn? The tribunal took a common-sense view of the problem: seafarers know a bay when they see one even though experts may have trouble defining it. In the result, the tribunal decided that the three-mile limit in the case of bays should be measured from a straight line drawn across the bay at the point where it lost the configuration and characteristics of a bay. Recognizing, however, that that method might create future practical difficulties, the tribunal recommended, in accordance with a treaty provision, additional study of the problem and offered suggestions for drawing the line in many specific bays, including the Baie de Chaleur, Miramichi Bay, and Chedabucto Bay. With respect to bays not specifically described, the tribunal urged adoption of a ten-mile rule by which the three-mile zone would be measured from a straight line drawn across a bay when it narrowed to a width of ten miles.

Neither the United States nor Great Britain took any step to appeal the award and, in fact, two years later they adopted, with some variations, the recommendations of the tribunal, at the same time excluding Hudson Bay. This was a remarkable achievement and, as P.E. Corbett puts it, 'the almost universal unanimity [the Argentine member of the tribunal had dissented on one of the less important questions] in this important decision ... is a notable tribute to the personnel of the tribunal and to the provisions of The Hague Convention.' The arbitration was a significant event in the history of Canadian-American relations. The broad outlines of the settlement and the conduct of the fishery industry on the east coast remained pretty much intact until altered by global conventions such as the 1958 Convention on Fishing and Conservation of the Living Resources of the High Seas. From Canada's point of view, the result was satisfactory; from Tilley's, the experience had been rewarding and one that he valued all his life. While it would be too much to say that his role at the arbitration by itself propelled him to stardom, it was certainly influential. Within a year, no doubt on the recommendation of Shepley who had often represented railway clients, he was doing work both for the Canadian Northern Railway and for its subsidiary telegraph company, which he represented at the important Board of Railway Commissioners inquiry into telegraph tolls in Canada, an inquiry that proceeded by fits and starts between 1911 and 1914. Tilley's engagement by the Canadian Northern Telegraph Company in 1911 marked his entry into the lucrative but demanding field of railway tariffs, telegraph tolls, and express rates. He quickly became expert in all those areas and his talent was recognized by the CPR in 1914 when an initial engagement that year matured into a retainer which lasted until his death.

Early in 1910, when Tilley was preparing for the fishery arbitration, the Winnipeg Board of Trade and the Winnipeg Grain Exchange filed a complaint with the Board of Railway Commissioners alleging that the various telegraph companies charged rates in the west that were unjustifiably higher than those in eastern Canada. Although the charge was that 'western Canada' was being short-changed, the Winnipeg complainants did not visualize British Columbia; for many, the western boundary of 'western Canada' was the Rocky Mountains. The board converted what had been a specific complaint by particular bodies into a general inquiry into the structure of telegraph rates throughout Canada. In 1911 Isaac Pitblado of Winnipeg was appointed by the federal minister of justice to act as counsel to the inquiry and Tilley was retained at about the same time by the telegraph company, which operated almost entirely west of Fort William (Thunder Bay). The tolls charged by Tilley's client and the other companies in western Canada were indeed higher than those charged in the east for messages sent comparable distances, but, as he argued in his submission, the margins were explained by the different conditions obtaining in eastern Canada where a concentration of service among competing companies resulted in lower rates. In the west, the greater distances over which transmission lines had to be strung warranted higher service charges. To counter that argument, Pitblado, who was not at this time as in later cases allied with Tilley, pointed out that a message was not like a train: it was transmitted instantaneously and distances, apart from initial capital expenditures, had little to do with costs.

Tilley's written argument was typical of the man, blunt and to the point. Pitblado had suggested that the revenues of the telegraph company, the subsidiary, should be consolidated with the revenues of the railway and that the telegraph company was merely a handmaiden of the principal enterprise, an adjunct whose revenues were inconsequential and therefore could safely be reduced through reductions in telegraph rates, the railway picking up the slack. To this, Tilley said that it was 'difficult to conceive of a more unreasonable argument from counsel charged with a serious responsibility.' 'Why not, on that line of reasoning,' Tilley asked, 'compel his client to carry messages for nothing?' In the upshot, in a decision delayed by the outbreak of war, the board in an elaborate ruling sanctioned particular zones of the country in which specified rates would apply to transmission of messages originating in them; overall, the west (even including British Columbia) benefitted from modest reductions in telegraph rates.

Concurrently, the board launched a general inquiry into the freight structure throughout the country, the first held since creation of the board ten years earlier. This was a massive undertaking. Statistics of every kind imaginable were produced: numbers of boxcars loaded and hauled and numbers of engines; haulage volumes for commodities of all kinds and description; operating costs region by region, division by division, section by section; profit and loss statements, capital expenditures, rates in one region for haulage of specified goods compared to the rates in other regions for carriage of the same goods – all these were sifted through by senior railway staff in consultation with their lawyers for presentation to the board, and, of course, were scrutinized as closely by the various groups trying to achieve rate reductions. The resulting judgment in 1914, which came to be known as the western freight rates case, laid down a pattern of railway freight rates which in general remained in force for thirty-five years. There were many high-powered lawyers at the frequent hearings of the board, which convened in various centres across the country. Pitblado represented the city of Winnipeg and the Winnipeg Board of Trade, both of whom were on the side of rate reductions, and, among the others opposing him, were Eugene Lafleur representing the Grand Trunk and Grand Trunk Pacific Railway Company, and Tilley representing the CPR. Somehow he was able to steer between the shoals of a conflict of interest or, in a more appropriate metaphor, switch to a siding to avoid a main-line collision because, also in 1914, he had successfully represented a client in the Privy Council on an appeal brought by the CPR from a decision of the Supreme Court of Canada. Although the subject of the litigation involved a railway tariff, it bore no direct relation to the freight inquiry, having been launched two years before it started. It is entirely possible that the CPR raised no fuss about Tilley acting against it, particularly since he was not the leading counsel in the case. In any event, that was the last occasion on which he acted against the CPR.

Tilley and Lafleur achieved notable success for their clients. In its ruling the board accepted their arguments that it was impossible to equalize rates throughout the country, not even in some regions, and that the mountain-differential rate charged by the railways for haulage through the Rockies was justified. The foundation for each of these two important pronouncements was the provision in the Railway Act forbidding 'unjust discrimination' and 'undue preference' in fixing rates. The board agreed with Tilley and Lafleur that competition in central and eastern Canada from American carriers, and competition from water-borne carriers on the Great Lakes, explained and justified the lower rates charged in those areas and if that circumstance amounted to 'discrimination' it was neither 'undue' nor 'unjust.' The board viewed the mountain differential, which principally affected British Columbia, in the same light. The railways insisted that higher construction costs through the mountains and higher maintenance costs because of severe winter conditions justified a differential rate: a commodity hauled through the mountains for one mile could be hauled on the prairies at the same rate for a mile and a quarter. The differential was reiterated by the board time and again though hotly contested by British Columbia, which argued that if there was a cost difference it should be spread over the whole system rather than being applied solely to shipments bound for British Columbia. The rate persisted until after the Second World War; in fact, the mountain differential became as much a sacred cow of the railways as the Crow rate was of the prairie farmers.[3]

In 1918, two years after his appointment as King's Counsel, Tilley became standing counsel for the CPR in all high-echelon matters, a connection ending only with his death twenty-five years later. In 1919 he appeared for the CPR in the Privy Council on two cases, each of which involved a major shipping catastrophe to a CPR vessel. The *Empress of Ireland* had sunk in the St Lawrence River in 1914 with heavy of loss of life after being rammed by a vessel, the *Storstad*, which was found to be wholly at fault. After the vessel was sold for the payment of claims, the proceeds were far less than the total claims outstanding and a lower court had given priority to the claims for loss of life and injuries. The Privy Council agreed with Tilley that no priority should be given and all claims, including those of the CPR, should share *pro rata*. The other case arose from the sinking of the *Princess Sophia* in October 1918, in Lynn Canal, Alaska, one of the worst marine disasters on the Pacific coast. The vessel, with 343 passengers and crew aboard, crashed onto a reef in a blinding snowstorm and could not be dislodged. Heavy winds and high seas made it impossible to lower the lifeboats, nor could anyone be taken off by the small craft hovering nearby. Passengers and crew endured thirty-six hours of terror while waiting rescue by larger vessels dispatched to their aid: waves remorselessly pounded the ship, which shook and shuddered continuously, driving it gradually across the jagged reef and, finally, into the sea itself. There were no survivors. The crew, hired in British Columbia, had been covered by the recently established Workmen's Compensation Act. The CPR went to court in an attempt to prevent the compensation board from paying pensions to dependents of the drowned crew members, believing that such payments would impair its defence of any claims against it under the Merchant Shipping Act. The British Columbia Court of Appeal ruled in the company's favour, but the provincial government represented by J.W. de B. Farris appealed to the Privy Council, where Tilley unsuccessfully appeared for the company: Viscount Haldane, delivering the judgment, robustly demolished all his arguments. The apparently callous position taken by the company attracted much censure in Canada.

About the same time, Tilley conducted another case for the CPR which, like the *Princess Sophia* sinking, partly explained why many citizens held the railway company in low regard. Two engines and their tenders were coupled together. Proceeding in reverse, that is, with a tender in front, they approached a level crossing. The Railway Act provided that, in the case of a train not headed by an engine, there had to be a look-out man to warn people about to cross the track at the level crossing. There was no look-out to give warning and, as a consequence, two young boys were run down and killed. A jury awarded damages to the parents against the railway company, but the latter, represented by Tilley, later persuaded a majority of the Supreme Court of Canada that by whatever other term the moving cars could be described they were not a 'train' and so no look-out was required. The impecunious parents filed an appeal to the Privy Council in *forma pauperis* – a kind of legal aid of the time – and managed to engage a top-flight English lawyer, D.N. Pritt, to take the case for nothing. Pritt was on the extreme left of the political spectrum and relished the chance to overthrow a ridiculous ruling in favour of a rapacious railway company. (In later years he often acted on Canadian appeals to the Privy Council.) Tilley went over for the appeal. Just as the Privy Council was later to do in the 'Persons' case, it took a common-sense point of view: a tender was a tender, an engine was an engine, and, when one had an engine and a tender hooked together in whatever order to form an integral unit, one had a train. Because the tender was leading, the law lords ruled, a look-out should have been kept. They restored the jury's verdict.

A couple of months after the hearing in the Supreme Court of Canada on this case, Tilley turned to the Crow rate hearings before the Board of

Railway Commissioners and the ensuing appeal to the Supreme Court of Canada. A columnist for the Montreal *Daily Star* gave a spirited account of one of the sessions at which Tilley, Pitblado, and Lafleur were present along with a dozen or so other lawyers, including H.J. Symington of Winnipeg and G.G. McGeer from Vancouver. The columnist describes the scene as the lawyers joust and posture over whether certain rate tariffs should be filed as evidence with the board. 'He [Symington] seems very confident, too, despite the efforts of Mr. Tilley, the famous K.C. from Toronto, to rattle him. Mr. McGeer of Vancouver, a tall, keen legal gladiator, sits just around the corner, and Isaac Pitblado comes next. Eugene Lafleur, a short thin man whom you would never guess to be the greatest Canadian lawyer of the day, is next to Mr. Tilley. He speaks very seldom but his earnest blue eyes are fixed on whoever happens to be talking.' The columnist, after noting that Symington took a careful look at Tilley, continues: 'The Toronto K.C. is easy to look at anyway and rate hearings are not beauty shows. Finally everyone looks at Mr. Lafleur, who is tapping his forehead with the forefinger of one hand and gazing raptly at the ceiling. There is a long silence. Mr. Symington is nettled, but he goes on to say, a trifle bitterly, that he has a complete file of these tariffs.' According to the columnist, Symington finally declares that he will put the tariffs into the evidence 'as a last resort,' at which point Tilley says audibly, 'Oh, go on and file them.' When Symington indicates that he may call a rate expert to give evidence concerning those tariffs, the columnist records Tilley as interjecting 'jocosely': 'File him too.' The columnist then gives a humorous account of the ingenuity of railway lawyers such as Tilley in making distinctions so as to take a commodity out of the Crow rate and thus allow the railway to haul it at a higher rate. Wire and iron pipe were within the Crow rate but they could be transmogrified, as Pitblado sarcastically demonstrated:

Prior to July 7 all sorts of iron piping were carried under the same classification and at the same rate. Since then the railways have been discovering previous mistakes. Put a coat of paint on the inside of an iron pipe and it is an iron pipe no longer. Mr. Pitblado is lost in admiration of the delicate, fine distinctions the railways now make. What was, isn't. This round cylinder – he holds it in his hand – was a pipe before July 7th, and now it has become a conduit and is much more expensive for the railways to carry. Then he turns to wire. The Crow's Nest Agreement gives the lower rates to 'wire all kinds' yet, says Mr. Pitblado, since July 7 if you dare to take two strands of wire and twist them together, alas, they are wires no more. They have become cables. Mr. Commissioner Oliver takes an unholy glee in delving to the bottom of these curious cases, and so the hearing goes on. It is one of the first days of the struggle and the boys haven't really become warmed up yet.

The Maritimes did not enjoy the Crow rate as did the prairies and felt suitably aggrieved. As a Maritime lawyer put it, 'The Crow's Nest Agreement is well named as far as we are concerned. Not having the benefit of them, we have nothing else to do than to eat crow. The crow is now becoming a vulture eating out the vitals of the Maritime provinces.' He would have received scant sympathy from Tilley and his client.

Tilley's involvement at protracted hearings of major freight-rate matters on behalf of the CPR ended with the decision of the Supreme Court of Canada in 1925 in the Crow rate appeal. Unwilling to take a year off from everything else, he did not appear on the general rate inquiry of 1927 (though unquestionably he would have offered advice), which lasted for more than a year and was the last comprehensive examination of freight rates until following the Second World War. He did, however, appear from time to time in the Supreme Court of Canada on important cases involving the jurisdiction of, and rulings by, the Board of Railway Commissioners. As well, he appeared in the Privy Council on similar matters.

Tilley and Lafleur occasionally teamed up on matters other than freight rates. In addition to the water-power controversy, referred to in the preceding chapter, they were jointly consulted by the federal government on the delicate matter of disposing of alien German property confiscated during the First World War. The question was whether Canada, though a signatory to the League of Nations but not yet being fully sovereign, could dispose of the assets of a foreign power. Both Tilley and Lafleur argued that Canada could act on its own – thereby striking a blow for Canadian nationalism. A few years later, when the Commons and the Senate debated the Canada Grain Act, a knotty legal point arose on which Pitblado, Tilley, and Lafleur – the latter two acting jointly – gave the same opinion. The Liberal leader in the Senate, Leon Dandurand, advocated a contrary view, but in reply his Conservative counterpart, Sir George Foster, said that 'when eminent lawyers like Mr. Pitblado, Mr. Tilley and Mr. Lafleur hold an opinion which is absolutely opposite to the opinion of my honourable friend [Dandurand] I am not lacking in courtesy [when I have] a certain degree of confidence in relying upon the opinion of those three eminent counsel.'[4]

As suggested earlier, Tilley's involvement in the fishery arbitration at The Hague in 1910 and the connections he made there led to his engagement by the railway companies in important business and, in later years, to his emergence as one of the top lawyers in Canada. That same 'networking' led also to his retainer as one of the counsel for Thomas Kelly at a royal commission inquiry in Manitoba into the scandalous circumstances surrounding the construction of the legislative buildings by Kelly's contracting firm. He had been recommended by the prominent Toronto lawyer Zebulon Lash to F.H. Phippen, Kelly's lawyer, who was looking for an associate; Phippen was formerly a judge of the Manitoba Court of Appeal but had returned to practice law in Toronto. Tilley not only appeared as a lawyer at the commission but also was present as a witness at a second but related royal commission. The affair was extraordinarily convoluted: one government resigned while in office and was succeeded by that of another party; one royal commission was appointed and, before it finished its work, another commission was set up to inquire into additional allegations of corruption. It all amounted to one of the most turbulent episodes in Manitoba's history.

Students of Manitoba history are thoroughly familiar with the corruption that stigmatized the construction of the legislative buildings in Winnipeg with the resultant downfall of the government of Sir Rodmond Roblin, the Conservative premier, and his replacement by the Liberal leader, T.C. Norris. Roblin's government had authorized the new buildings. Controversy and hints of scandal were soon rampant but, notwithstanding, Roblin, to the surprise of many, was returned to office in the election of 1914, and construction proceeded apace. In the ensuing months, however, there were increasing reports of massive wrongdoing, indeed not merely wrongdoing but outright fraud and corruption. Roblin came under growing pressure to launch some kind of inquiry into the reports – which were a matter of common discussion on the streets – but he failed to respond until the lieutenant governor, D.C. Cameron, intervened by threatening to exercise the royal prerogative of removing him from office. On 21 April 1915 Roblin announced the appointment of a royal commission headed by the chief justice of the trial court, T.G. Mathers. The commission convened, and, representing Thomas Kelly, the contractor around whom allegations of corruption swirled, were Phippen and Tilley. The two men had been associated at the western freight rates case, at which Phippen represented the Canadian Northern Railway Company; Tilley, as recounted, had been one of the lawyers for the CPR. Among the other lawyers involved in the royal commission were H.J. Symington and J.B. Coyne, later a judge of the Manitoba Court of Appeal.

From the very start it was clear to Phippen and Tilley that their client was at the very least going to be sued by the government for refund of monies improperly paid and more likely was to be charged with fraud or theft. They were concerned that any inquiry by the commission into Kelly's conduct would be injurious to his defence in any later criminal proceedings and, accordingly, they were, to put it mildly, uncooperative in producing documents which would prejudice their client. Yet they realized that they could keep up the delay for only so long as the commission failed to subpoena the documents, and on 11 May, three weeks after the commission had been established, Phippen and Tilley started court action for an injunction to prevent the commission from carrying on its investigation; they also served copies of the initiating writ and statement of claim on Mathers and various others connected with the commission. By that date also it was apparent that the premier himself was highly suspect and could no longer carry on in office. The next day, 12 May 1915, he resigned and T.C. Norris was sworn in as head of a Liberal administration. The circumstances of the transfer of power gave rise to a second royal commission, this time appointed by Norris, to investigate accusations of corruption on his part in taking office; this circumstance formed the nexus between the two royal commissions. Both Tilley and Phippen testified before the second, headed by Mr Justice W.E. Perdue of the Manitoba Court of Appeal, as did Roblin, A.B. Hudson, the new attorney general (and later a judge of the Supreme Court of Canada), H.M. Howell, chief justice of the Court of Appeal, and John Wesley Dafoe, editor of the Winnipeg *Free Press*. It was quite a cast of characters and the tale they collectively told the Perdue commission was an extraordinary and often amusing example of parish pump politics, Manitoba style.

The appointment of the Perdue commission in June 1915 had followed allegations by a group of fourteen disgruntled Conservatives led by C.P. Fullerton, a prominent Winnipeg lawyer, that the transfer of power from Roblin to Norris on May 12th had been the result of a $50,000 bribe paid to Norris, partly to induce him to discontinue the Mathers commission and partly to persuade him to halt the petitioning by defeated Liberal candidates under the Manitoba Controverted Elections Act. Accordingly, the circumstances of the meeting on May 12th at which Roblin resigned and the events leading up to it became highly relevant, and it was to that issue that the evidence of Tilley and others was directed. But Tilley and Phippen's quite understandable attempts to extricate their client by negotiating either a suspension of the Mathers inquiry or, better still, its termination became bound up and confused with Roblin and Norris's plans to switch office. And that the senior judge of the province – Howell – should have become part of the process is, today, quite astonishing, although few at the time found it untoward, not even John Dafoe. One person who did was Fullerton, who in his final submission to the Perdue commission said that Howell 'had no business meddling between political parties.' When Perdue – a member of the court headed by Howell – admonished Fullerton for not speaking 'tactfully' and then noted that Howell had some rights as a private citizen, Fullerton left the hearing chamber in high dudgeon.

Dafoe, in the thick of events, testified that he, along with T.C. Norris, A.B. Hudson, and several other Liberal stalwarts had met in Hudson's office on May 7th 'to discuss and approve of the proposals of Frank H. Phippen, ex-judge and the chief counsel for Thomas Kelly touching the swapping of office between the old and present cabinets, and the suppression of the old [Mathers] royal commission.' Dafoe claimed that there was no impropriety whatever in these proceedings and 'that Mr. Hudson had assured them emphatically that there was no promise of immunity [that is, to Kelly] and that the new government would not only be at liberty but would be expected to prosecute persons civilly and criminally, whenever a case could be established.' Dafoe went on to say that the approval of the old commission was to be secured before it ceased its labours temporarily or permanently but the Liberals were to have nothing whatever to do with securing that consent.

Phippen testified that, prior to any discussion of arrangements to suspend the hearings of the Mathers commission, he had dissuaded Sir Rodmond Roblin from resigning. However, when it appeared that Roblin was going to resign, he then thought that he had negotiated a 'deal' with Hudson and others to suspend the commission and that this was achieved 'by the combined eloquence of myself and Tilley coupled with a few bottles of Apollinaris at the Manitoba Club'; they must have added some whisky to that fashionable mixer. There was also a later discussion at the Manitoba Club involving Chief Justice Howell and the lieutenant governor, who said that he had arranged everything with Mathers. Phippen testified that, before Tilley left for Ottawa on May 12th, he, Tilley, had phoned Hudson and was told by him that 'everything would take place as arranged.' Phippen went on to maintain that 'the arrangement was proper and was merely in the interests of his client to save him from the prejudice of the people and insure him a fair trial of any similar criminal actions that might be instituted.' Further, Phippen said, Hudson had insisted that the old government resign and the new government be sworn in before the old commission would be called off. Phippen then said that he had left everything in the 'hands of Chief Justice Howell who assured him that the old commission had approved the arrangement.' Phippen summed it all up by saying that the 'agreement was so absolutely proper that it could have been printed in the newspapers, but it was not made public "out of courtesy to the Lieutenant-Governor."'

Tilley testified before the Perdue commission on 6 July 1915 concerning the cessation of the Mathers commission. He said that, prior to leaving Toronto to come to Winnipeg to work on the Kelly case, he knew nothing at all about the affair. But, he continued, 'as soon as I arrived I realized what a very serious hardship was being put upon Mr. Kelly in having all the hearsay and gossiping that was being put in before the commission. That he [Kelly] must realize that he would be faced later on by another government with a civil action and I thought it was very important from his standpoint that matters should be arranged if they could be arranged so that the proceedings before the commission would stop and that the government would commence an action and have the case tried in the ordinary way.' Tilley testified that he had discussed the problem with Phippen and also with A.B. Hudson but he then noted (in this instance his story differed somewhat from Phippen's version of events): 'I don't remember what Mr. Phippen says that if anything unforeseen turned up that the Commission should go on, but my understanding was that if we made the arrangement, that Commission would put up its shutters and stop the business, and I thought that was the thing very desirable for Mr. Kelly.' Tilley confirmed that, before leaving for Ottawa 'on an important case,' he spoke to Hudson to discuss with him 'the language which would be used relating to the cessation of the Commission.' But Roblin at the time of this discussion was still premier and so it was necessary to consult him about the cessation. Tilley testified: 'The language of that document [that is, the one authorizing the cessation of the commission] was submitted to the Premier [Roblin] in my presence, and he raised no difficulty about the language that was used, and I had a thorough conviction that if anything had been warranted by way of change in that document, it could have been done.' It was here that the confusion originated. Phippen and Tilley's quite legitimate and ethical efforts to help their client by halting the Mathers commission was interpreted by Roblin's opponents as evidence of his corruption. It is also clear from Tilley's testimony that he was the architect of the arrangements intended to protect Kelly.

Tilley was cross-examined by Isaac Pitblado, who acted for Norris, though 'cross-examined' is hardly the right word since Tilley was, so to speak, on Norris's side; it was more a little chat between friends. Tilley reiterated that everything was 'above board,' which prompted Perdue to observe that 'there does not seem to have been anything wrong about it so far as I can see.' Tilley, under questioning by Pitblado, repeated that no improper arrangements had been made, no money had been paid. There was never any suggestion that money would be paid and, if such a suggestion had been made, 'he would never have been a party to such an arrangement.' Pitblado, in order to put Tilley in as good a light as possible (though it was hardly necessary to do so), reminded him of his long years of practice and referred to his work on the 'Alaska boundary tribunal.' Tilley, in correcting him, said that he had been on the 'fisheries case.' An illustrator for the Winnipeg *Free Press* drew a likeness of Tilley as he gave his evidence; it shows a handsome, well-built man, with a definite air of authority about him.

The combined evidence of Tilley and the others absolved Norris of any wrongdoing in the suggested dismantling of the Mathers commission but could not help him so far as the other allegation was concerned, namely that money had been paid to stifle the election petitions. Other witnesses, including Roblin himself, swore that no such bargain had been reached, and the Perdue commission in July found Norris, Hudson, Roblin, and all others involved innocent of any wrongdoing in the change of government. But Tilley and Phippen's efforts on Kelly's behalf were to no avail. Although Tilley himself had left the hearings by May 12th, the Mathers commission did continue. On May 20th, the Norris government launched a civil action against Kelly for return of moneys obtained through 'collusion and fraud,' whereupon Kelly and Phippen withdrew from the proceedings never to return. In August the Mathers commission brought down its report, in which it found that there had been systematic looting of public funds in the construction of the parliament buildings. Roblin eventually stood trial for theft and fraud; a jury could not reach a verdict and he was not retried. Kelly, in 1916, faced similar charges. Defending himself, he was convicted and sent to prison.

Tilley was to have one more experience as an active participant in a commission which, although not styled 'royal,' deserved the title – the commission set up in 1926 by federal order-in-council to divide the approximately $10,500,000 in assets of the newly founded United Church between it and the non-concurring Presbyterian congregations – that is, those that elected not to be part of church union. He had been retained by the United Church but was not able to take part in the initial stages of the commission's work because of appearances at the Privy Council – the life of a busy counsel: off the transatlantic ship one day and into church finances the next. With a plethora of statistics and tables, the task resembled freight-rate work. And during an adjournment of the commission he embarked for London to argue two more appeals before returning to the problem of distributing Mammon among men of God. The commission was headed by Mr Justice Duff, who with two 'neutral' colleagues had been chosen by the three men representing the non-concurring Presbyterians and the three nominees of the United Church, one of whom was Isaac Pitblado. Duff, at the opening session, posed the problem: 'Here you have two Churches, a United Church and a Continuing Church proceeding. The United Church requires funds for a certain purpose; a Continuing Church requires funds for precisely the same purpose. On what principle is the board to say that the Continuing Church may not require just as much in proportion to its membership, as the United Church, or even more, possibly.'

No witnesses were called but multitudes of documents were presented containing clergy lists, schedules of real estate and other property, balance sheets and statements of profit and loss, lists and descriptions of churches with estimates of the number of parishioners in each, endowment funds, and appraisals of all assets from the most rickety chair in a church hall to big items such as Knox College. And, of course, all these were prepared province by province. The hearings really were bargaining sessions among the lawyers who were frequently able to agree on apportionment of assets, with such agreements being then ratified by the commission in the form of orders. In matters of disagreement, as was the case with the three theological colleges – in Montreal, Toronto, and Winnipeg – Duff and his colleagues made the decision. The detail was meticulous: 'The History of St. Gabriel's Church and all other manuscripts prepared by the late Rev. Robert Campbell shall be returned to his son, George Campbell, K.C., of the City of Montreal.' The commission also had to deal with foreign missions and the funds endowed for their work in such places as British Guiana, North Formosa, and South Bhil, India; in the case of the last mission, the Bhil building fund of $305.84 was awarded to the trustees of the Presbyterian Church. But the most significant decisions were those that gave Presbyterian College in Montreal and Knox College in Toronto to the Presbyterians; the loss of Knox College was a particularly heavy blow to the new church, but it bore up, one might say, with Christian fortitude. Overall, the non-concurring congregations were awarded 31 per cent of the property and funds.

Matters religious were a fruitful source of litigation in the earlier years of this century, particularly where separate schools were concerned; a sig-

nificant part of the constitutional history of the country has been determined because of disputes between religious and secular educators, and
Tilley got his share of the work. In 1916 he made a wartime voyage to
London to argue before the Privy Council, back to back, two cases concerned with separate schools in Ontario. In the first, Sir John Simon represented Roman Catholic trustees who were appealing an edict of the
provincial Department of Education limiting the use of French as a language of instruction in all schools, public or separate. Tilley represented
the group in favour of the restriction and was joined in the same cause by
Sir Robert Finlay. The Privy Council held that the requirement was not an
invasion of the constitutional protection bestowed upon separate schools
by section 93(1) of the British North America Act because that protection
was based upon religious belief and not upon race or language. The other
case involved regulations made by the Ontario Department of Education
which, among other details, specified dates of school openings and laid
down requirements for the qualification of teachers. The Roman Catholic
school trustees objected to those provisions, whereupon Ontario wielded
a legislative sledgehammer by appointing commissioners to run the
schools if the Roman Catholic trustees refused to comply. They did
indeed fail to comply, and the commissioners did indeed take over the
schools. Again Simon acted for the Roman Catholic schools, opposed
once more by Tilley and Finlay, but this time the Privy Council found in
favour of the separate schools; the legislation clearly was prejudicial to
the guarantees given to them.

There was an interesting aftermath which illustrates the hazards of litigation. The commissioners ran the schools for roughly a year during
which they incurred liabilities incidental to the ordinary operation of any
school and also drew on the funds of the Roman Catholic trustees themselves as authorized by the heavy-handed legislation. In the wake of the
Privy Council decision invalidating the appointment of the commissioners, the Ontario legislature passed still another law declaring that all
expenditures made by the commissioners when in charge were deemed
to have been made on behalf of the Roman Catholic trustees. The validity
of that legislation also wound up in the Privy Council, where, once again,
Simon and Tilley squared off against each other. One would have thought
that, if the appointment of the commissioners in the first place was
invalid, as the Privy Council had ruled, their actions would also be
invalid – the tail going with the hide. But no, the Privy Council said that
the expenses incurred were a legitimate charge against the school funds
of the Roman Catholic trustees. Thus, in three successive encounters with

Simon concerning Ontario's separate schools, Tilley had emerged victorious in two.

However, Tilley's most notable triumph in separate school litigation came in 1928 when the Privy Council accepted his arguments in a decision that remained effective for sixty years, not only in Ontario where the case originated but in every other province with separate schools. The earlier cases chronicled here had been lively political issues of the day, but the 1928 case involving the Tiny Township school district, the 'Tiny' case as it came to be known, caused far greater controversy and stirred far deeper emotions. The Ontario legislature had passed various acts and regulations affecting all schools in the province and their funding. Although the Tiny case had been initiated by the Roman Catholic separate school trustees for Tiny Township, it was enlarged to include all Roman Catholic separate schools in Ontario. It became a test case to determine whether Ontario school legislation of general application would be constitutionally invalid if it adversely affected rights granted to denominational schools by the BNA Act. The Supreme Court of Canada upheld the measure as did the Privy Council, which, notwithstanding its earlier decision about the school commissioners, declared that the province had the power to control higher education in all schools. Tilley argued the case successfully for the Ontario government both in Ottawa and London, and the decision stood until 1987 when the Supreme Court of Canada overruled it in sanctioning Ontario's decision, again reached amid much public controversy, to provide full funding to Roman Catholic schools for instruction at all levels.

The Tiny case was probably the most important constitutional case Tilley had handled up to that time. In the 1930s, however, a number of other major cases came his way and together they put him in the front rank of constitutional lawyers, perhaps even at the head of the class. In the British coal case in 1935 Tilley acted for the federal government in the Privy Council, which upheld the power of the Canadian parliament to abolish appeals to it in criminal cases. As a matter of custom, the Privy Council had seldom heard criminal appeals from Canada and this decision officially closed the door (one noteworthy example of the council's position in this regard was its refusal to hear an appeal by Louis Riel in 1885). And in 1938 Tilley successfully acted for the Canadian chartered banks and for the Canadian Press in the references to the Supreme Court of Canada, and the subsequent appeal to the Privy Council, as to the validity of legislative attempts by the Aberhart government of Alberta to tax chartered banks, set up a provincial banking system, and muzzle the press. Although today any attempt to stifle free expression of the press would be challenged pursuant to the Charter of Rights rather than by reliance on British democratic tradition – as was the case in the references – the rulings on Aberhart's banking legislation remain valid since the regulation of banks continues to fall under federal jurisdiction.[5]

Two other cases that Tilley also successfully argued for the federal government in the Privy Council are still of fundamental importance. In each, he was opposed by, among other lawyers, Aimé Geoffrion, who appeared for the province of Quebec to argue against federal legislation that was seen to intrude into the right of a province to control all business conducted within its boundaries. The first case involved the new field of aeronautics. When the Fathers of Confederation had framed the BNA Act, airplanes were unknown. In the twentieth century, therefore, the question was whether the regulation of airplanes was a matter of 'property and civil rights,' over which the provinces had control, or of 'peace, order and good government,' which lay in the federal domain. The Supreme Court of Canada ruled in favour of the provinces, but the Privy Council reached a different conclusion; notwithstanding the customary eloquence of Geoffrion and his English associate, Sir John Simon, the law lords accepted Tilley's argument that the regulation of air traffic was of national interest and the federal government therefore had exclusive jurisdiction in this area. In the second case, the Supreme Court of Canada, no doubt prompted by the Privy Council decision regarding aeronautics, ruled that the federal government possessed exclusive jurisdiction over radio transmissions. At the appeal in London before the Privy Council, Geoffrion was joined by D.N. Pritt in an unsuccessful attempt to establish provincial control over radio signals. The radio case led directly to the establishment by the Bennett government of the Canadian Radio Broadcast Commission, now the Canadian Broadcasting Corporation. The continuing importance of these two decisions is obvious and Tilley's role in them deserves recognition. Had it not been for the Privy Council's decision in the aeronautics case, chaos would have resulted from the fragmentary control of such a critical area of technology. As for the radio case, the Privy Council's ruling paved the way for the birth of a national public radio system that has conferred innumerable benefits on the country.

Although there was a camaraderie among lawyers who regularly appeared before the Privy Council, it did not spring from constant association with certain lawyers always appearing on the same side. In one instance, they might be associated; in the next they might be opposed. The radio case affords an excellent example of how top-flight lawyers, allied one moment, might be opposed the next. In that case Geoffrion and Pritt argued against Tilley for three days – December 11th, the 14th, and the morning of the 15th, 1931 – in what proved to be a losing cause. Yet, on the afternoon of December 15th, argument started on an unrelated appeal from Alberta which lasted until December 18th. And who were the lawyers? Tilley and Geoffrion appeared for the attorney general of Alberta, successfully, and were opposed, astonishingly, by Pritt. The explanation, of course, for these seeming cross-overs is that on important cases where large sums of money or issues of great public interest were involved, leading lawyers in Canada such as Tilley and Geoffrion and, in England, Simon and Pritt would be called upon. As professionals, they would find nothing incongruous with being associated one day with a lawyer against whom on the day following, or even on the same day, they would be locked in combat.

There were diversions for Tilley from settling the affairs of the country. One of them was the litigation arising from the eccentric will of the eccentric lawyer Charles Millar, who left shares in breweries to known teetotollars and shares in a jockey club to known opponents of horseracing; odder still, the will set up a 'baby derby' which bequeathed a large sum of money to the woman in Toronto who gave birth to the greatest number of children over a ten-year period. Tilley acted for the executors of the estate and saw much action, including an appeal to the Supreme Court of Canada to decide if the word 'children' as used in the will included illegitimate children. The court declared that only children born in wedlock could qualify; it also declared that the baby-derby scheme itself was valid. Millar's blood relatives had challenged the scheme on the ground that to sanction it would necessarily encourage excessive copulation. Yet that argument did not find favour with the sober judges of the Supreme Court of Canada, who, having decided that entitlement depended upon children conceived and born in wedlock, implicitly ruled that any amount of copulation within the bonds of marriage was permissible.

The outbreak of war put a temporary stop to Privy Council appeals by Canadian lawyers – the journey overseas was too hazardous – and even major litigation in Canada declined. Tilley made what proved to be his last appearance in the Supreme Court of Canada late in 1941; perhaps he had not given it as much preparation as he would customarily have done in earlier times, for he lost the appeal, and Sir Lyman Duff, who was presiding, was heard to mutter to himself, 'arrant nonsense, Tilley, arrant nonsense.'[6]

As he neared the end of his life, Tilley was not much given to sentimental reflections on the past. He lived in the affluent section of Avenue Road in a fine stone house which he named 'Durham House' after the county of his birth. He enjoyed a large income but was frugal. Although he owned a car, neither he nor his wife drove; he went to his office by tram. He had no real vices unless one includes among them an appreciation of good whisky and a fondness for horseracing; for years he rented a track-side box at Woodbine. He was utterly devoted to his wife, who had also been born in Bowmanville, and to his daughters (a son had died in infancy of scarlet fever). They frequently accompanied him on his voyages to England, usually on the 'Duchess' liners of the CPR. In London they took a suite of rooms at Queen Anne's Mansions and attended high-society events such as the Lord Mayor's Ball. There were also glittering evenings at Gray's Inn, one of the London inns of court for English barristers and judges, where Tilley was an honorary master of the bench. Following the Privy Council sessions they would holiday in Scotland before sailing back home.

One of his neighbours on Avenue Road was Howard Ferguson, the former premier of the province and a good friend. According to David Walker, who recounts a conversation he had had with Ferguson, Tilley once remarked to Ferguson that he would have loved 'to have had your career and to have served in public life.' Upon Ferguson remonstrating that Tilley had done great service for the government over the years, Tilley replied: 'But what good has that done? What will I be remembered for? What have I done for my country?'

One 'service' that Ferguson unquestionably had in mind was Tilley's successful prosecution during Ferguson's premiership of Peter Smith and Aemilius Jarvis, an affair that had direct repercussions for more than a decade. Peter Smith had been the provincial treasurer in the Farmer-Labour government headed by E.C. Drury, elected in 1919 but defeated in 1923 by the Conservatives led by Ferguson. Jarvis was a wealthy stock-broker who moved in the upper strata of Toronto society – member of the Toronto and York clubs, the Hunt Club, a yachtsman, and president of the Navy League. He and Smith were charged with conspiracy to bilk the Ontario government of large sums of money by pocketing commissions from transactions involving the purchase and redemption of government of Ontario bonds from British investors – commissions which the prose-cution said were corruptly obtained but which Jarvis and Smith said were legitimate.

Smith and Jarvis (and two others) stood trial in October 1924 before Chief Justice R.M. Meredith and a jury. The case had a large dose of politics: the former premier, E.C. Drury, was the principal witness for the defence; there were allegations of misconduct by politicians in the earlier Conservative administration of William Hearst and innuendoes that Ferguson, a Conservative, had sought to divert attention from the alleged misdeeds of his fellow Conservatives by launching the prosecution against Smith and Jarvis. As if this were not enough, there was the spectacle of a former cabinet minister and a pillar of Toronto society seated together in the prisoner's dock and charged with a squalid crime. It all caused a sensation and drew enormous publicity. Tilley, for the crown, at his most formidable, demolished Drury on cross-examination; Smith and Jarvis did not testify, doubtless fearing that they would be no match for Tilley. They were both convicted and sentenced to heavy fines and terms of imprisonment. Smith appealed his conviction, unavailingly; Jarvis did not appeal. (At a later trial, Smith's deputy treasurer, Charles Matthews, was also convicted and sent to prison.)

Hardly was Jarvis released from prison in April 1925 than he began an unremitting campaign to clear his name which he kept up until his death in 1940. He bombarded the press, government officials, and anyone else who would listen with a litany of complaints that he had been, in effect, a sacrificial lamb. In the early stages of his campaign he received unexpected encouragement. In his bond dealings in London, Jarvis had been accompanied by one Andrew Pepall who also had made much money from the bond transactions – more, in fact, than Jarvis himself. By the time of Jarvis's trial, Pepall had fled to the United States. The crown wanted to try him also for conspiracy to defraud, but conspiracy was not an extraditable offence and Pepall remained in the United States for the entire length of Jarvis's trial. Eventually, he was charged with theft – which was an extraditable offence – and was returned to Toronto to face trial in November 1925 (because of the law relating to extradition offences, he could be charged only with the offence for which he had been extradited). Tilley once again represented the prosecution; Arthur Slaght, a highly skilled lawyer, defended Pepall. Much of the evidence of the Jarvis trial, but not all of it because of legal technicalities, came out at the Pepall trial; also, Jarvis himself testified for the defence even though he had not done so at his own trial.

The jury acquitted Pepall, who returned post-haste – the next day – to the United States. Jarvis immediately seized on his acquittal as vindication of himself. He enlisted the written support of fifty of the crème de la crème of the business, professional, and ecclesiastical community for a lengthy – and unsuccessful – petition to the federal Department of Justice seeking exercise of the royal prerogative to clear his name. Though Tilley did not himself prepare the written response to this petition by the Ontario attorney general, he would undoubtedly have been consulted. In 1926 a group of Jarvis supporters asked Ernest Lapointe, then the federal minister of justice, to investigate the circumstances of Jarvis's conviction. Nothing came of their request but, by the turn of the wheel of political fortune, Lapointe ten years later again became minister of justice and Jarvis and his supporters this time persuaded him to refer to the Ontario Court of Appeal the propriety of Jarvis's conviction and whether he should have a new trial. In a unanimous decision delivered by the chief justice, N.W. Rowell, the court ruled that he did not deserve one. (Peter Smith, who, unlike Jarvis did not have friends in high places, took his medicine and said nothing.) Tilley, understandably, remained convinced of Jarvis and Smith's guilt and also that of Pepall; one can visualize him shaking his head in disbelief when the jury returned a not guilty verdict against the man who had received more money out of the transactions than either of the other two. The affair is still part of the curriculum, so to speak, of students of the political history of Ontario.

Tilley's remarks to Ferguson concerning his lack of service to his country are curious because he did have the specific opportunity of entering public life as a cabinet minister in the Union government of 1917. In that year Borden, reacting to the conscription crisis, strove frantically to form a coalition government; he was even willing to cede the leadership to someone else, if that would do the trick, but he eventually decided to stay on as prime minister. In his attempts to lure prominent Liberals into a coalition, he approached Lyman Duff, then a puisne judge of the Supreme Court of Canada, who before going to the bench had been an active Liberal in British Columbia. Duff was interested but told Borden that he would join the cabinet only if Tilley came in as well. Duff, according to Borden, 'spoke in highest terms of Tilley's character and ability.' Borden discussed this possibility with Arthur Meighen, who approved of both Duff and Tilley as worthy candidates for office. Learning from Duff that Tilley had decided not to take a cabinet position, Borden interviewed Tilley himself and pleaded with him to accept office. He told Tilley that 'it was his duty to enlist in public life for the rest of the war and that his actions would create a profound impression.' But Tilley was adamant, prompting Borden to record in exasperation, 'Duff and Tilley have not idea of entering the government. They lack the spirit that prompted our young men to cross the seas and go over the parapet.' With Borden's retirement in 1920 (on medical advice), Tilley's name was one of several bandied about as a possible successor but his candidacy was dismissed because of political inexperience. Had he accepted the post offered to him in 1917 he would have been in a strong position to become prime minister in 1920. The conclusion seems inescapable, then, that he was not interested in a political career regardless of what he said to Ferguson, any more than he was interested in a judicial one. His remarks are typical of what many people successful in one sphere may utter, in an idle moment, about what they might have achieved in another. He made the right decision to stay where he was, at the top of the legal heap.

But for bad timing, he might have become the first head of the Canadian National Railways in 1921. He had had much experience with railway matters and, most recently, had acted as one of the government lawyers in the difficult arbitration arising from the amalgamation of the Grand Trunk system with other lines to form a national railway system. Meighen, who genuinely admired Tilley, temporized, however, and went out of office before making any appointments. Many years later, Meighen engaged Tilley to represent him on one of the frequent occasions when Mitchell Hepburn, after becoming premier of Ontario in 1934, hounded him with allegations of misconduct during his term as a commissioner of Ontario Hydro in the previous Conservative administration of George Henry. In 1936 the Hepburn government sued Meighen and a fellow commissioner for refund of money, which, it was alleged, had been paid out on Meighen's instructions without proper authorization. Mr Justice H.E. Rose dismissed the action, observing that the government case 'fails hopelessly and entirely.'

Tilley died on 10 June 1942; hardly a week earlier he had been on a case in the Court of Appeal. For years he had suffered from angina and he always carried digitalis with him when in the courtroom. His simple funeral at Timothy Eaton Memorial Church, just a few blocks from his home, was attended by over 600 people, from the high and mighty of the Canadian establishment down to ordinary mortals. At his death he had been a director of the Bank of Montreal, Canada Life, the Royal Trust Company, and, of course, the CPR. The president of the CPR, D.C. Coleman, spoke feelingly of the loss to the 'Canadian Pacific family,' and Aimé Geoffion came to grieve at the death of his frequent courtroom opponent and good friend. In London the Privy Council, sitting on a wartime Canadian appeal (no Canadian lawyers were present, however), assembled to voice regret at 'the grievous loss which the profession has suffered by the lamented death of Mr. Tilley.'

Tilley, who twelve years earlier had voiced similar sentiments on the occasion of Lafleur's death, would not have been unappreciative of the Privy Council's remarks. Yet the praise showered upon him by the law lords would not have changed his mind about the role of the Privy Council in Canadian affairs. Privy Council work had formed an extremely rewarding chapter in his life in all respects, but he was pragmatic enough to believe that Canadian appeals should eventually be abolished and he lived long enough to hear the Supreme Court of Canada agree with him. In 1924 he had told federal politicians, following the death of the chief justice, Sir Louis Davies, that Duff should be appointed to succeed him because only such a man as Duff could elevate the standard of that court 'as would justify the stopping of appeals to the Privy Council.'

Perhaps that was Tilley's principal characteristic: pragmatism. It was certainly the hallmark of his attitude towards legal education and indeed of his approach to advocacy: no flights of oratory, no trickery, no nonsense; hard work and impeccable character will get you everywhere.[7]

3

Aimé Geoffrion

In July 1945 Louis-Félix Aimé Geoffrion, known universally as Aimé, was seventy-two years old. The war having just ended, Canadian counsel could once again safely journey to London for sessions of the Privy Council which, notwithstanding the war, had continued to hear appeals from Canadian courts though they were not argued by Canadian lawyers. The government of Canada had retained Geoffrion to act on a case that month which it believed to be of such importance as to warrant elaborate arrangements for his transport: a special passport as well as special customs and immigration clearances from the American ambassador in Ottawa for Geoffrion's transit through the United States to Baltimore, Maryland, where he was to board an American military aircraft for the flight to England. Arriving in London on 10 July, Geoffrion, like Tilley, stayed at the Queen Anne's Mansions, a superior hostelry much favoured by Canadian lawyers who valued the spacious quarters. On the 19th he was before the Privy Council for the first time in almost exactly five years to argue that fines levied by courts in Toronto arising from combines offences belonged to the federal government by virtue of an earlier Privy Council ruling that only the federal government had jurisdiction over combines. The amount involved was $155,000, a not inconsiderable sum. D.N. Pritt acted for the city of Toronto; Geoffrion, who had not acted on the case in the Ontario courts, was assisted by the English barrister Frank Gahan, another familiar figure in Canadian appeals. He was successful.

Geoffrion returned home agreeably by ship but a few months later found himself called on by the federal minister of justice to conduct another appeal. This time the matter was far more significant than a crass argument over money; it was an important constitutional case stemming from the Canada Temperance Act first passed by parliament in 1878. Once more special arrangements were made for his journey; the clearances and permits and passport endorsement that he carried with him certified that he was travelling to represent the attorney general of Canada at hearings of the Privy Council in London. On this occasion, however, he flew in an unheated Lancaster bomber specially requisitioned. Quite apart from the discomfort of the flight itself, he felt physically wretched on arriving in England. But he gathered himself together and on 3 December and on the ensuing five days, unassisted by a junior lawyer, he persuaded the Privy Council to rule in Ottawa's favour in a dispute involving the redefinition of circumstances under which the federal government – acting under the authority of the peace, order, and good government clause of the BNA Act – could enact legislation in fields particularly reserved to the provinces by that act. The decision upholding the federal legislation, still relevant, was but the latest example of Canadian constitutional law being shaped by liquor legislation.

By an odd turn of events, Geoffrion, who had been flown to London at the federal government's expense to argue a case for Ottawa, applied unsuccessfully on 4 December on behalf of the province of Quebec – and in opposition to the federal government – for leave to appeal a decision of the Supreme Court of Canada. To illustrate further the cross-overs of counsel from one side to another almost at a moment's notice, he was opposed in this application by Frank Gahan, acting for Ottawa, who, a week later, joined with him, unsuccessfully, in opposing yet another petition for leave to appeal. Geoffrion became too ill to argue the resulting appeal, and so the occasion, though he did not realize it at the time, proved to be his last appearance at the Privy Council.

He stayed on in London for a week or so primarily to visit his son, Guillaume, still on active service as an officer with the Canadian army, but also to seek medical advice about his nagging constipation, which proved to be an early symptom of the cancer that killed him ten months later. He flew back to Canada on the same Lancaster aircraft, still unheated, and still very uncomfortable. His two trips to the United Kingdom illustrate that when a client wants the best no expense or trouble will be spared. By now, Lafleur was dead, and so was Tilley; only Geoffrion, the last of the trio, was still alive, though not for much longer.

Hardly was he back in Montreal than he began to prepare for what proved to be his last big case in the Supreme Court of Canada, argued in late January 1946 (his final case, a routine one, was a month later) on behalf, once again, of the attorney general of Canada. Late in 1945 the federal government, by three orders-in-council passed under the War Measures Act, had authorized the deportation of Japanese nationals and, in some circumstances, British subjects of Japanese ancestry, the second category including Canadian-born residents. The enactments drew the censure of many civil libertarians, who launched the Cooperative Committee on Japanese Canadians, and that committee proceeded to retain J.R. Cartwright (a future chief justice of Canada) to fight the deportation orders. The government directed a reference to the Supreme Court of Canada for an opinion as to the validity of the deportations. Before that court, Cartwright and F.A. Brewin led the attack and Geoffrion endeavoured to repel it. In the result, the court reiterated its ruling of twenty-five years earlier in the conscription case that an order-in-council under the War Measures Act had the unassailable force of an act of parliament and that the cabinet in passing the orders-in-council must be the best judge of whether the post-war condition of the country warranted them. The decision was appealed, unsuccessfully, to the Privy Council but Geoffrion, who by then had become seriously ill, was unable to argue the case in London.[1]

It was fitting that Geoffrion in the last year of his life handled two appeals in London and was involved in another case which was clearly headed for the Privy Council, for it was in England, in 1903, that he had emerged as a counsel of real stature. (His first appearance before the Privy Council had taken place in 1902.) In that year he joined a team of Canadian and English lawyers to prepare and argue the case for Canada before the Alaska Boundary Tribunal. That body had been established to settle the boundary of the Alaska panhandle, a narrow neck of land some 800 kilometres long running southeasterly from the mass of Alaska to a latitude of 54° 40'. A treaty between Great Britain and Russia in 1825 attempted to define the boundary in terms which at the very least were vague and at the worst impossible to construe. On purchasing Alaska in 1867, the Americans acquired whatever rights the Russians had to the panhandle, and Canada, on becoming a dominion that same year, inherited the British claims. Much bickering took place in ensuing years, marked by occasional ugly clashes between American and Canadian law-enforcement authorities attempting to assert jurisdiction over disputed ground. In January 1903 the Americans and British signed the Hay-Herbert Treaty referring the dispute to a tribunal of 'six impartial jurists of repute,' three from each country. The Americans, George Turner, Henry

Cabot Lodge, and Elihu Root, though legally trained, were more politicians than jurists and were anything but impartial. Sir Louis Jetté, formerly a judge but currently lieutenant governor of Quebec, and Allen B. Aylesworth, a distinguished Toronto lawyer, represented Canada, and Lord Alverstone, lord chief justice of England, rounded out the number.

In British Columbia there was a good deal of dissatisfaction among Liberals (the Laurier government was in power) that no one from the province had been selected as an arbitrator since, of all the provinces, its interests were most affected. Yet no amount of political pressure succeeded in altering the tribunal's composition. There was also a good deal of political jockeying in the formation of the Canadian legal team, appointments to which were regarded as rich plums. English lawyers were to be in charge, led by Sir Robert Finlay, the attorney general, with Edward Blake, then living in England, in close association. Blake fell ill at the last moment and was replaced by Sir Edward Carson, the solicitor general. Christopher Robinson, though in failing health, was the leading lawyer from Canada. Typical of the politics involved was a letter from Charles Fitzpatrick, minister of justice, to Clifford Sifton, who, as minister of the interior and official Canadian agent for the arbitration, was the person in charge of all appointments and arrangements: 'Would it be possible for you to profitably utilize the services of Mr. D.L. McCarthy ... His father was useful to me on one or two occasions and I would like to liquidate my obligations to his son.' Fitzpatrick's attempt to reverse the biblical injunction of visiting the sins and not the virtues of the father upon the son was unsuccessful. Sifton selected Geoffrion early in the process not only because of his political connections but also because of his knowledge of French. As he told Blake before the latter withdrew: 'I think of employing a couple of junior counsel here who will go over [to London], one of them being a son of the late Mr. Geoffrion [who had been briefly a member of the Laurier cabinet]. Needed to understand shades of meaning in French documents.' Many of the early Russian documents were in French, then the language of international diplomacy.

Geoffrion reached London on 10 July 1903. He had been provided with one thousand dollars for his initial travelling and other expenses and was to receive fifty dollars per diem as his remuneration, a handsome but not munificent sum. A stalwart Liberal lawyer from Vancouver, F.C. Wade, had been selected as one of the Canadian team but Senator William Templeman of Victoria, the grand panjandrum of the Liberal Party in British Columbia, who was still smarting that no one from the province had been appointed to the tribunal, put increasing pressure on Sifton to appoint an additional British Columbia lawyer, Lyman Duff, of Victoria. Sifton reluctantly agreed and Duff sailed from New York with Sifton early in August 1903. S.A.T. Rowlatt, an English barrister and later a judge, and John Simon completed the Canadian-British group, of which only three, Finlay, Carson, and Robinson, were to address the tribunal. Thus began a lifelong friendship between Geoffrion, Duff, and Simon, the latter two destined for the highest judicial posts in their respective countries. Their function, as Sifton defined it, was 'that of assisting to draw up the papers, drafting the case and counter-case, and the written arguments and preparing the brief for Senior Counsel.'

This painful episode in the history of Canadian boundary disputes has been much written about and need not be described here in detail.[2] The hearings, which took place at the Foreign Office in Whitehall between 15 September and 8 October 1903, were so much posturing because Theodore Roosevelt, the American president, had let it be known that he would never accept an adverse ruling. The American contention essentially was that the eastern boundary of the panhandle, that is, the eastern boundary of Alaska and the western boundary of Canada, should be drawn along a line that effectively shut out the Canadians from access to tide-water ports at the heads of inlets. The Canadians, on the other hand, relied on the 1825 treaty provision; it defined the boundary as being within ten marine leagues of such ranges of mountains as were 'parallel to the coast' and indicated that, where parallel ranges were beyond the ten-league limit, the line was to be drawn parallel to the 'sinuosities' of the coast at a distance of ten marine leagues. The fundamental difficulty with the Canadian position was that the framers of the 1825 treaty had never closely examined the mountain ranges intended to be boundary markers; they were a jumble of peaks with no discernible patterns, let alone one that ran parallel to the coast. In addition, evidence showed that even maps at the British Admiralty were drawn in accordance with the American contention; moreover, a Russian map of 1827 showed the boundary essentially in the same position. Geoffrion, Duff, and all the others struggled manfully but it must have been obvious to them that the cause was hopeless; even 'impartial jurists' would likely have ruled against Canada.

There were the usual civilities attendant upon such occasions. At the conclusion of the hearings Finlay and the official American agent exchanged pleasantries, employing such platitudes as 'friendly rivalry' and praising the absence of any 'harsh words ... or manipulation ... of disturbed or irritated feeling.' A few days later, the lord mayor, Sir Marcus

Samuel, entertained all those connected with the tribunal and a number of other distinguished guests at a lavish banquet at the Guild Hall, though, curiously, Geoffrion was not listed as a guest; he must have been ill. Among other banalities, Sir Marcus expressed confidence that the members of the tribunal 'would carefully and impartially follow the dictates of their consciences and be guided entirely by the evidence.' Fine words, but divorced from reality, for the American arbitrators privately told Alverstone, president of the tribunal, that unless he went along with the American contention Canada would wind up with nothing; in so saying they merely followed Roosevelt's instructions. Alverstone, virtually with a gun at his head, negotiated the best deal he could get from his American colleagues. The result was that the United States received a slightly narrower panhandle than it had asked for and Canada got two of the four islands at the entrance of the Portland Canal, which formed the east boundary of the panhandle; the south boundary was drawn westward through Dixon entrance along latitude 54°40'. The finding meant that Canada possessed indeed no salt-water ports at the heads of inlets within the panhandle, a severe blow. The ghosts of the arbitration still hover about, for the Americans today contend, for the purpose of defining fishery entitlement, that the line through Dixon entrance is not a fixed boundary but one subject to enlargement by three, ten, or two hundred miles or whatever territorial economic zones may be allowed by international conventions.

Two days after announcement of the decision, Geoffrion and his Canadian colleagues received a sort of consolation prize – an invitation to Buckingham Palace for an audience with the king. And then it was back home. Many years later, Duff, in recalling his work in London with Geoffrion, remarked that he had 'spent two months arguing with him, or perhaps conducting reciprocal slang matches with him would be a better description.' Geoffrion, understandably, treasured his part in the arbitration and in later life occasionally gave speeches on the subject. In 1943, on the occasion of Duff's retirement as chief justice, Geoffrion was one of those invited to the ceremony. Speaking extemporaneously, he recalled with emotion those momentous days he and Duff had spent in London. 'There were five juniors on that commission. One was Mr. F.C. Wade who has just died. Another was S.A.T. Rowlatt who has since been made a member of the Privy Council. The third was Mr. Simon, later Sir John Simon, who is now Lord Chancellor. The fourth was Mr. Duff who later became the chief justice of Canada and the fifth, myself – I am the only plain one left.'[3]

The 'Mr. Geoffrion' to whom Sifton referred when deciding to engage his son was Christophe-Antoine Geoffrion. Though a prominent Montreal lawyer and politician, C.-A. Geoffrion was of humble lineage; his father and earlier ancestors were farmers. But he had married into an illustrious Quebec family, for his wife, Eulalie Iphigénie, was a daughter of Antoine-Aimé Dorion (afterward Sir Antoine-Aimé), a well-known *Rouge* politician in Quebec in the pre-confederation era. Though he hotly opposed confederation, Dorion later became part of it by winning a seat in parliament and by serving briefly as minister of justice in the Alexander Mackenzie government of 1874 before being appointed that year as chief justice of the Court of Queen's Bench. He held that post until his death in 1891, nineteen years after the birth in Montreal of the grandson named for him, Louis-Félix Aimé Geoffrion. Dorion's wife, grandmother of Aimé Geoffrion, was the granddaughter of Johan Joseph Troestler (gallicized to Jean-Joseph Trestler), a native of Mannheim, Germany, who, after serving with the British army as a mercenary in the American revolutionary war, settled in Quebec. He built a splendid mansion in Dorion on the Ottawa River which still stands, Le Maison Trestler, though it is no longer in the family.

Young Geoffrion attended Collège Sainte-Marie, a Jesuit school in Montreal, first as a boarding student, a life that he detested, and later, on promising his father that he would continue to study hard despite the change, as a day student; he led his class in virtually every subject in every year of his attendance. He was to advise his own son, Guillaume, many years later that he should accept education by the Jesuits but not their religious teachings; he evidently was thinking of his own experience. At the college Aimé got a solid grounding in the classics, and he never lost his love for this subject – it was not unusual for him to stride up and down his home declaiming in Latin passages from the Roman historians Tacitus and Lucretius. So far as religious adherence was concerned, young Aimé was raised as a Roman Catholic but in later life attended church 'as little as possible,' as his son puts it. Also, his attitude towards the church may have been coloured by his early strong support for the Liberals – the *Rouges*. At a time when many of the Roman Catholic hierarchy were ultra-conservative *Bleus* – and when many a local curé told his flock that to vote for Liberals was sinful – Geoffrion may have found this attitude too much to stomach. None the less, he remained nominally a Roman Catholic. From 1917 until 1921 he was the secular head of the Roman Catholic separate schools in Montreal; at his death, he received a Roman Catholic funeral; and today he lies buried in the Roman Catholic Côte-des-Neiges cemetery.

As a boy, Geoffrion grew up with French as his first language and was taught English at the school by, oddly, a man named French. He developed a facility in English and soon spoke each language without a trace of accent of the other. His boyhood experience prompted him to make English the language of his household (his wife also spoke both languages flawlessly), but in his law office French was the working language though communication with clients who spoke only English (not many anglophone clients spoke fluent French in those days) was, of course, in English. Geoffrion took a degree in civil law at McGill in 1893, winning the gold medal, and after his articles he was called to the bar in 1894 and set up practice in Montreal. Somewhere he had caught the attention of F.E. Meredith, a partner in a large Montreal law firm (and one of those who attended the Shakespeare dinner described in chapter 1). Meredith perceived that Geoffrion was a very bright person but more comfortable with French-speaking clients than English-speaking ones. Accordingly, he generously referred English-speaking clients to the young advocate, who thereby established connections with the English-speaking community which later were to prove valuable. He quickly made his mark as counsel, though more in civil litigation than criminal law. Within a year of his call to the bar he won his first case in the Court of Appeal; his opponent had been one of his lecturers at McGill.

Geoffrion had not articled with his father – they decided that such an association would be unsatisfactory – but with Eugene Lafleur, fifteen years older, who was already a notable figure in the Montreal legal community. Thus began a long, respectful, and friendly connection between two lawyers who were to adorn the Quebec and Canadian bars for so long. Though they never practised in the same law firm, they were colleagues at McGill where Geoffrion also held a part-time professorship, in civil law from 1905 to 1920. Lafleur, who had started lecturing in 1890, retired from his professorship at virtually the same time as Geoffrion. Their association in the courts lasted for thirty-five years; most often they were adversaries but it was not uncommon for them to act for different clients in a common cause and sometimes they served as lawyers for the same client with pockets deep enough to afford the two of them. Occasionally, one would ask the other for advice. The two were on opposite sides of some highly significant litigation, perhaps the best-known being the *Ne Temere* case. In that instance, Geoffrion represented the province of Quebec in its successful bid to have the Supreme Court of Canada uphold the power of the church to regulate marriages between persons of different religions. Unlike Lafleur, he also acted on the subsequent appeal to the Privy Council, where he was again successful. On another occasion, in the well-known salmon-cannery case of 1928 in which the federal government attempted to impose licensing restrictions on salmon canneries in British Columbia, and fish canneries generally in other provinces, Geoffrion acted in the Supreme Court of Canada for a group of Japanese fishermen from British Columbia opposed to the legislation as well as for the province of Quebec. Lafleur again represented Ottawa in a vain attempt to uphold the enactment but he did not go to the Privy Council for the subsequent appeal, which was conducted by Hugh Macmillan (soon to go to the House of Lords); Geoffrion and Geoffrey Lawrence carried the day.

Until Lafleur's death many of the constitutional law cases Geoffrion took involved both of them; probably their most significant association in that field was in the famed Bonanza Creek mining case, which went to the Privy Council in 1915. The war did not deter Canadian lawyers from attending the appeal; there were at least a dozen of them present besides a few English lawyers, chief among whom was Sir Robert Finlay. The case was perhaps the most important among a flurry of constitutional cases heard before and during the First World War in which the power of Ottawa under the BNA Act to regulate trade and commerce collided with the provincial power under the same act to legislate in the field of property and civil rights. Generally, the disputes were resolved in favour of the provinces, and that was also true of the Bonanza case, which produced an important affirmation of the power of provincially incorporated companies to do business outside provincial borders. Geoffrion and Lafleur were on the losing side on this occasion, as they would also be in 1929. In that instance – the final important collaboration between Lafleur and Geoffrion in a constitutional case – the Supreme Court of Canada upheld the validity of the Combines Investigation Act as a valid exercise of the power to legislate over criminal law, a significant finding. Lafleur died before the subsequent unsuccessful appeal to the Privy Council and Geoffrion also, for some reason, did not argue the appeal. One case in which they did not collaborate but in which their paths definitely crossed involved the already mentioned attempt by Quebec to turn Jews into Protestants within the Protestant separate school system. Impetus for the legislation had been provided by Michael Hirsch, a philanthropist and educationist who was a highly regarded member of the Montreal, and Jewish, community. Geoffrion, acting for Quebec, succeeded in persuading the Supreme Court of Canada to validate the legislation but did not go to London for the Privy Council appeal brought by the Protestant school boards. Lafleur, however, who did not argue the case in Ottawa, did go to London where he obtained a reversal of the Ottawa ruling.

Early in 1918 Geoffrion and Lafleur were asked by the federal government to give a joint opinion on the legality of an order-in-council under the War Measures Act which forbade the sale of debentures by provincial governments without prior consent from Ottawa. Both lawyers believed that the measure would be declared invalid by the courts on the ground that it was an invasion of the rights of provinces, which by the BNA Act had exclusive jurisdiction over 'property and civil rights.' The matter seems to have ended there. Six months later Geoffrion unsuccessfully argued the case for one George Gray who tried to quash an order-in-council which took away his exemption from conscription; the Supreme Court of Canada decided that an order-in-council had the force of an act of parliament and could not be challenged. Geoffrion and Lafleur, with Tilley, collaborated in the monumental water-power case (referred to in more detail in chapter 1), which was heard in the Supreme Court of Canada in 1929. Digesting the judgments handed down by the members of the court must have taken Geoffrion almost as long as working up the case.

The final professional association of the two friends found them on opposite sides of the fence. The case was a gold mine for lawyers. Sir Mortimer Davis, the wealthy and well-known Montreal citizen and president of the Imperial Tobacco Company, had appointed A.M. Reaper and Lord Shaughnessy (son of the CPR magnate, and himself a lawyer) as trustees of his estate. The courts have power to remove trustees from their office in case of financial mismanagement or negligence and Davis's widow commenced proceedings to remove both Reaper and Shaughnessy. With the prominence of the people involved – dead and alive – and the amount of money at stake, both sides to the dispute hired the best, Lafleur by Shaughnessy and his colleague, and Geoffrion by the widow. Each was head of a carefully selected team; however, neither man spent every day at the protracted hearings, relying on competent underlings to do most of the detailed and often tedious work of going over financial statements. Lafleur died before the proceedings ended. Shaughnessy, who perhaps was more affected by that event than anyone else outside Lafleur's family, lamented: 'To me, apart from the loss of a friend, I have lost my senior counsel in an important case in which his indefatigability was most striking and his counsel most comforting.' But he need not have worried – Lafleur's groundwork paid off; Geoffrion's efforts proved of no avail for the court ruled against his client. It was said that the litigation had been among the 'longest and most costly actions in the history of Canadian jurisprudence.'[4]

In August 1929 the Canadian government appointed Eugene Lafleur as its nominee on a tribunal investigating the affair of the *I'm Alone*, a rum-running boat that was at the centre of an international controversy; it also appointed Geoffrion and W.N. Tilley as counsel to work up the case for Canada though it would not be presented by them but by John Read, the official Canadian agent. Thus the three most eminent lawyers in Canada were in one way or another involved in this fascinating episode. An editorial in the Ottawa *Evening Journal* on 9 August 1929 expressed confidence that Canada's interests would be 'safe in the hands of those eminent legal gentlemen.' Though the *I'm Alone* was of Canadian registry and was skippered by J.T. Randell, a retired Canadian officer, it was effectively owned by Americans – a crucial factor in the ensuing arbitration since a treaty of 1924 had given to the Americans the right to search and seize 'British vessels' only. Well known to the United States Coast Guard, which enforced the American prohibition laws, she loaded liquors at Caribbean ports, gaining port clearance by falsely declaring another Caribbean port as the destination when, in reality, as everyone well knew, she was headed for an American port or to an American vessel off-shore to unload the illicit cargo. In March 1929 she had taken aboard a cargo of assorted liquors at Belize, in British Honduras, and set sail. Although the fact was never stated in the subsequent hearings, the shipment was by the Bronfman family. One of the claims, subsequently rejected by the arbitrators, was for $27,000 paid to Lazarus Phillips, the Bronfman's lawyer in Montreal, for work done on behalf of Randell and the vessel owners. After being spotted by an American Coast Guard vessel just less than nineteen kilometres off the Louisiana shore, she set off towards the open seas. The American vessel gave chase, caught up with her and then, in an extraordinary episode, the two skippers held parley on the *I'm Alone*. Randell readily admitted that he had contraband liquor aboard but told his fellow skipper there was nothing the Americans could do about it since they were in international waters. The American skipper returned to his vessel and the *I'm Alone* headed into the Gulf of Mexico, pursued now by two Coast Guard vessels. The captain of one of these bellowed at Randell by megaphone, calling on him to surrender; Randell in effect told him to 'go to hell,' whereupon the Coast Guard skipper opened fire and sank the rum-runner. One crewman was drowned in the incident, which took place 320 kilometres off the nearest United States coastline. The fact that the *I'm Alone* was a rum-runner, though obviously the trigger for the affair, was of relatively little consequence in the subsequent arbitration; what was really at stake were the territorial limits within which customs laws could legally be enforced. The Canadian government put forward claims on behalf of the family of the dead man, for loss of possessions of all the crew, for loss of cargo, and for other matters, arguing that the sinking occurred on the high seas and could not be excused by the doctrine of hot pursuit which, since the *I'm Alone* when first spotted was probably within the territorial limits of the United States, allowed a chase for whatever distance might be necessary to capture her. 'Capture' is one thing, but to shoot the vessel out of the water was another.

Two years before the hearings, the Privy Council had handed down its decision in *Croft v. Dunphy*, in which Lord Macmillan not only confirmed Canada's right to exercise customs jurisdiction within a nineteen-kilometre limit but postulated circumstances when that limit might be extended even farther. Ironically, the successful appeal by the government of Canada in the *Dunphy* case now undercut its position in the *I'm Alone* affair: if a further enforcement zone existed, as Lord Macmillan had suggested, obviously this would help the Americans' case, and at the hearing they in fact made much of it. Tilley and Geoffrion were disconcerted by the *Dunphy* decision; Tilley, in fact, said that the two would 'go into the fight ... with one arm tied.' The Canadian government was so concerned about the implications of the *Dunphy* appeal for the *I'm Alone* hearings that it had taken the extraordinary step of trying to persuade Macmillan to water down his language. The attempt was ultimately abortive, not because Macmillan was unwilling to 'alter' a few words, but because Lord Sankey, the lord chancellor, got wind of the suggestion and absolutely forbade any tinkering with the judgment. The hearings took place in 1934. In the upshot, the arbitrators, Duff and Van Devanter, decided that the sinking could not be condoned but that the *I'm Alone* was an American vessel, a finding which barred any compensation for the loss of the vessel and its cargo. Randell and his crew were compensated, as was the widow of the drowned seaman. Also, the arbitrators recommended a lump sum payment to Canada, which had suffered an 'affront' in the deliberate sinking of a vessel under the Canadian flag even though that vessel was not of Canadian ownership.[5]

Lafleur's death in 1930 left Geoffrion and Tilley incontestably at the top of the litigation heap in Canada. Tilley, though four years older than Geoffrion, had been called to the bar the same year, 1894, and so in that sense the two were equal. There were, of course, other fine lawyers practising in the courts: N.W. Rowell, later the chief justice of Ontario, Louis St Laurent, whose political career still lay ahead, O.M. Biggar, S.B. Woods of Edmonton, and R.B. Bennett, who by the mid-1920s was becoming less and less a lawyer and more a politician, to name but a few; Farris in British Columbia was not quite in his prime. Yet none of these men, admirable lawyers though they were, could match the range and diversity of Geoffrion and Tilley. And, as between the two of them, their styles of advocacy were markedly different. The old cliché applies: one used the broad-sword, the other a rapier. Geoffrion's essential style resembled that of a debater with a flair for the dramatic – he revelled in the cut and thrust of courtroom jousting – but it was a skill grounded in wide learning. He read extensively in a varied array of subjects and kept up-to-date on current events both in Canada and abroad. Although urbane, he loved to poke fun at judges and other lawyers who, because of his consummate tact, good humour, and impeccable taste, were never offended. On one occasion, when arguing a case before Duff and his colleagues, Geoffrion thought that he was making headway. After the lunchtime adjournment, however, he sensed that Duff had changed his mind and had become unsympathetic to his argument, prompting him to observe that he was sorry 'His Lordship had suffered from an attack of indigestion over the lunch hour.' Duff laughed harder than anyone else. One is reminded of the fencer in the James Thurber cartoon who decapitates his opponent with such finesse that the poor man does not realize what has happened to him until his triumphant adversary cries, 'Touché.' Isaac Pitblado said that Geoffrion was 'the fastest speaker I ever listened to,' adding that his mind also 'worked very fast' and his tongue, too, 'moved like a rapier.' So rapid was his delivery that a slow-witted judge would be unable to keep up with him; once Mr Justice Mignault of the Supreme Court of Canada said plaintively to Geoffrion at the end of his opening argument, 'Before you sit down Mr. Geoffrion, would you mind telling me what this case is all about?' The Hon Willard Z. Estey saw Geoffrion in the Supreme Court of Canada only once. He says that he spoke 'about a hundred words a minute,' never repeating himself in spite of the fact he hardly ever referred to his notes. On that occasion he was being badgered by Duff to shorten his argument by not reading the relevant statutes to the court. Geoffrion, as Estey says, spoke to Duff 'as he [Geoffrion] would talk to one of his colleagues back at the office: polite, direct, but by no means retiring,' inquiring, 'Have all your Lordships read all these statutory references from this act?' Not hearing unanimous agreement, he said: 'Very well then, it would be mutually helpful if I now read those sections to you.' Estey believes that only Geoffrion could have got away with it.

Since Geoffrion during all his professional life was a member of a very small firm, usually with only one partner and the occasional junior lawyer, he met with a diversity of legal problems. He did not take jury trials – in murder or rape cases, for example – but he certainly did other forms of criminal work at the trial level. In 1932 T.B. MacAulay, president of Sun Life Assurance Company, was accused by one J.J. Harpell, publisher of the Garden City Press at Sainte-Anne-de-Bellevue, Quebec, of having, in effect, rifled the till of Sun Life. At a time when the prosecution of criminal cases was not so structured as today, private citizens, if able to afford it, could engage their own lawyer to prosecute a case on their behalf. (Even today, citizens occasionally hire their own lawyers to prosecute a criminal charge.) MacAulay hired Geoffrion to prosecute Harpell for criminal libel, then a rarely used section of the criminal code. Harpell was sentenced to prison. Geoffrion, an approachable man with the common touch, was willing to take any case that interested him even if there was the prospect of little money in it; in doing so he followed the best traditions of the bar. One day a mayor and his entire municipal council called on him for advice concerning some difficulty within their municipality. After the problem was described to him, Geoffrion said that he would like to check the applicable provisions of the municipal code, whereupon the mayor said, 'If you have to look up the code, Mr. Geoffrion, we don't want to consult you.' They then all trooped out of his office – much to Geoffrion's amusement. He often laughed over the incident. But, inevitably, generalist though he was, Geoffrion, because of his talents, attracted the wealthy in trouble.

In January 1935 Sam Bronfman and his brothers, Harry, Abe, and Allan, faced charges of having conspired to export liquor to the United States free of Canadian excise charges with the intention of smuggling it back into Canada, thus evading payment of customs and excise taxes estimated at five million dollars. They were also charged with exporting liquor to the United States for sale there in violation of American prohibition laws. In addition to the four Bronfmans, forty-seven other people were indicted on similar charges which had resulted from a lengthy investigation by the RCMP for the Department of National Revenue. Geoffrion was retained by the four Bronfmans as lead counsel, assisted by Lazarus Phillips who was more or less on permanent retainer to the Bronfman family. Geoffrion's son, Guillaume, says his father told him that the prosecution had originally planned to go straight to trial by direct indictment, thereby sidestepping a preliminary inquiry. A preliminary inquiry is a pre-trial procedure designed to ascertain if the prosecution has a case strong enough to warrant a full-blown jury trial; defence counsel have the chance of cross-examining witnesses in order to test their veracity and to establish firmly their stories so that they cannot change them at the trial without weakening their credibility. The attorney general can circumvent the process, however, by preferring a direct indictment, to use the correct term. When that happens defence lawyers cry, 'Foul,' because it deprives their client of having, in effect, two kicks at the can. Geoffrion, of course, realizing full well the benefits of having a preliminary inquiry, interceded, according to his son, with Prime Minister Bennett to persuade him to instruct the crown prosecutors to proceed in the more common manner by preliminary inquiry. Bennett, a Conservative, was no political friend of either Sam Bronfman or Geoffrion, both Liberals, nor, as far as Geoffrion was concerned, was he under any obligation to him. Quite the opposite, for Geoffrion had acted against Bennett on behalf of a Liberal candidate in the 1921 general election in the riding of Calgary West. Bennett had initially been declared the victor by a slender margin but on a recount the returning officer had rejected ballots marked with a pen and not a pencil as required by the Dominion Elections Act, with the result that Bennett lost the seat by sixteen votes, a decision affirmed by the Supreme Court of Canada; Lafleur had acted for Bennett. In any event, the Bronfman case did proceed by preliminary inquiry.[6] At the start it was very complex – there were thousands of documents as exhibits and many witnesses – but at the end it boiled down to a relatively simple issue: if Canadian distillers such as the Bronfmans make perfectly legal sales of liquor within Canada, paying all the excise taxes, for delivery at points outside Canada such as the French Islands of Saint Pierre and Miquelon (which figured so largely in the evidence as a distribution point), should they be found guilty of a criminal conspiracy against Canadian laws simply because they knew full well the liquor would be transshipped into the United States, a country that forbade importation of liquor? To put it another way, should Canadian distillers have to be guided in their legal commercial transactions within Canada by the knowledge that their liquor will wind up, illegally, in the United States? Geoffrion, throughout the proceedings, hammered this point home: it is not up to Canadian authorities to enforce in Canada laws promulgated in the United States forbidding traffic in liquor in that country.

The prosecution case against the Bronfmans rested on the evidence of a disreputable liquor dealer who had purchased on two occasions substantial quantities of liquor from Abe Bronfman to be shipped from Rimouski to Saint Pierre and Miquelon. But the prosecution had no evidence that such liquor, which everybody knew was going to the United States, was to be returned to Canada for illegal 'duty-free' sale. The preliminary inquiry dragged on for months. Not unexpectedly, tempers became frayed. Geoffrion had occasionally absented himself from the hearings, pleading the obligation to appear in a higher court, and had thereby secured adjournments in deference to his standing as senior counsel. On the final day of the hearings, Geoffrion asked for and was granted permission to offer rebuttal on behalf of the defence to the rebuttal by the prosecution of the defence submissions; the judge allowed Geoffrion one hour, in what technically is called surrebuttal. When the prosecutor objected to this leniency, accusing Geoffrion of being responsible for delays, Geoffrion replied that he had been absent only for six days whereas the prosecution had taken more than six months to present its case. Testy behaviour of this kind is not uncommon when cases go on much longer than anyone contemplated. Geoffrion, however, was not without fault. Having accepted the brief, he should have stayed on the case or, if other demands were paramount, he should have entrusted the conduct of the case to a reliable associate rather than by his own absence force an expensive and inconvenient adjournment. Geoffrion did not lie back in the weeds, so to speak, but conducted the case for the Bronfmans very aggressively since he was determined, if he could, to have the charges thrown out at the preliminary stage. He succeeded. The judge, Jules Desmarais, agreed that no crime had been committed by the sale of liquor in Canada, regardless of its ultimate destination, and since the crown had failed utterly to produce any evidence of liquor smuggled into Canada for illegal sale he dismissed all the charges.

By an odd circumstance, just two days before the hearings had started, the Duff-Van Devanter commission handed down its ruling in the *I'm Alone* affair. It will be recalled that the liquor on that rum-runner had been loaded in Belize, in British Honduras; the commissioners noted that it had been shipped by the Atlas Shipping Company Limited, a company run by Abe Bronfman. On the first day of the preliminary inquiry the crown put in formal evidence of banking documents linking Abe Bronfman to Atlas Shipping, but the *I'm Alone* affair does not seem to have come up at the preliminary inquiry. A grateful Sam Bronfman put Geoffrion on a handsome annual retainer; at his death he was still a director of Distillers Corporation Seagram's Limited. Moreover, the Bronfmans granted a block of share options to Geoffrion's wife, the rising value of which over time made her independently wealthy.

As observed elsewhere, religious matters brought a great deal of work for lawyers earlier this century. Though acting, in effect, for the Roman Catholic Church in two notable cases, the *Ne Temere* and *Hirsch* cases, and a Roman Catholic himself although not a particularly enthusiastic one, Geoffrion was chosen by the United Church to pilot through the Quebec legislature the bill amalgamating the physical assets of the Congregational and Methodist churches and such Presbyterian churches as stayed within union, all forming the new United Church. The church was created by federal legislation, but provincial legislation was also required since the physical assets, particularly land, were under provincial control. The irony of a Roman Catholic helping create a new Protestant church was not lost on Geoffrion, who used to joke about it.

A case in which Geoffrion acted for Quebec had important but unintended consequences. In the early 1920s, Quebec legislation passed as a consequence of an anti-prostitution campaign authorized the forcible closing of a dwelling if an occupant had been convicted under the criminal code of operating a bawdy house. The legislation was challenged on the ground that it related to criminal law and hence was beyond the jurisdiction of a provincial government since, by the BNA Act, only Ottawa could legislate on 'criminal law.' Rather surprisingly, the Supreme Court of Canada agreed with Geoffrion's submission in the *Bédard* case, as it was known, that the subject matter of the legislation related to the use of property and so was within provincial jurisdiction rather than related to criminal law. Thirty years later, the government of Maurice Duplessis started its vendetta against Jehovah's Witnesses by passing a series of enactments designed to stifle the propagation of their faith. A number of legal actions ensued. The first, in 1953, involved the constitutionality of a municipal by-law forbidding the distribution on streets of religious tracts, an enactment which, it was shown, was enforced only against the Witnesses. The second, in 1957, involved the imposition of the now infamous Padlock Law. Geoffrion was not alive at the time of these cases but, as a broad-minded man, he would have been distressed that in both of them the arguments put forth by the province of Quebec to support the validity of the measures relied heavily on his arguments in the *Bédard* case. In both cases, the judges of the Supreme Court of Canada had an instinctive feeling that the legislation was somehow wrong and, by tortuous reasoning, were able to get around the *Bédard* case without explicitly saying it was wrong. One court is loath to categorize the decision of another of equivalent or higher status as incorrect though now and then it does happen. Usually the later court will draw distinctions; still other courts will follow, and multiply those distinctions, until the original decision has been distinguished to the vanishing point where, like the smile of the Cheshire cat, it remains a mere image of its former self.

Geoffrion, however, did act for Quebec in two major cases with results of which he was undoubtedly proud. In the first, the Privy Council ruled that title to lands reserved for Indians and then surrendered to them by the crown belonged to the crown provincial – in this case Quebec – and not the federal government. Geoffrion's principal legal opposition in the case was his old friend Sir John Simon. The other related to the controversial decision in Nova Scotia in 1925 calling out the militia to quell civil disturbances and riots at New Waterford on Cape Breton Island. The litigation concerned the question of who was to pay the bill, Nova Scotia or Ottawa. Quebec, obviously, was not directly involved, but when constitutional questions arise in one province other provinces are notified and they can, if they wish, intervene so as to become a party to the litigation. Quebec did intervene and engaged Geoffrion as its champion. Under the federal Militia Act a provincial attorney general could requisition a military force to aid the civil power if the attorney general certified that it was necessary to maintain order. (In 1913, in British Columbia, there was a similar occurrence when the militia was called out to assist the police in the disturbances at the Nanaimo coal mines; Farris defended some of the miners at their ensuing trials.) In his requisition, the attorney general, W.F. O'Hearn, also stated that the Nova Scotia government would pay all expenses. Because there were insufficient troops in the active militia – the permanent force – in Halifax, reinforcements of troops, horses, and equipment were brought in from various centres in Ontario and Quebec and remained on duty for about ten weeks, at a total cost of over $133,000. One might wonder why Quebec would involve itself in an unseemly dispute over liability for this sum, but often Quebec zealously took a position on matters that, in the future, could affect its own interests, as was to happen, for example, five years later when it hired Geoffrion in an unsuccessful bid to void the federal government's legislation over combines, the Proprietary Articles Trade Association case. In the Cape Breton case, the Supreme Court of Canada decided that the attorney general of Nova Scotia had no legal authority to commit his government to paying the bill, and the ordinary rule applied: the federal government was responsible for the army, and militia, and was obliged to absorb the cost.[7]

Geoffrion led a happy married life. He and his wife, Marguerite, 'Rita,' who was the daughter of a prominent Quebec family – her father was a senator – had four children, two daughters and two sons, with whom he got on very well. Their oldest daughter, Renée (later Renée Vautelet), achieved fame as a crusader for women's suffrage in Quebec and as the founder and first president of the Canadian Association of Consumers, and she was awarded the CBE for her wartime activities. Geoffrion always enjoyed a large income which he spent freely. He was also generous, supporting ungrudgingly a number of impoverished relatives for many years, mostly on his wife's side of the family. Adelard Godbout, the leader of the Liberal Party in Quebec at Geoffrion's death, had in mind these acts of generosity when in his funeral tribute he spoke of Geoffrion's 'innumerable acts' of private charity.

His methods of gathering in his income were, to say the least, curious. To start with, he believed in billing clients annually. Since the majority of his clients were governments, business corporations, or wealthy individuals, once-yearly billings, though unusual, did not result in long outstanding accounts receivable. For the rest of his clientele, who were *ad hoc* so to speak and not permanent, he did bill on completion of work, though there might be a considerable lag between the actual end of the work and the arrival of the bill. In all instances, he set his fees in an amount that he reckoned would, at year-end, produce a total pre-determined by him sufficient to pay his staff, any junior lawyers, and other running expenses. Thus, if he decided that the sum of $100,000 in gross income was enough to pay all expenses and leave him with, say, $50,000 net, that was the figure that must be adhered to, and he would not countenance 'extra billing' which would push the gross beyond $100,000. These billing practices seem to us to be quirky if not antiquarian. Today, every time a lawyer utters a word to a client or scratches his nose while thinking about a problem, it goes on to the computer, which spews a printout showing exactly how much the client has to pay for his lawyer's thinking, or scratching. In Geoffrion's day, the lawyer's life was much simpler – and perhaps more sensible.

When Lafleur, Geoffrion's mentor, colleague, and friend, died in 1930, Geoffrion's most noteworthy and far-reaching cases lay ahead. Still, he had solidly established himself, financially and socially, as a member of the Montreal élite. He had not consciously set out to carve for himself that niche, and, having achieved it, never sought to capitalize on it for personal aggrandizement. Though a member of various clubs, including the Country Club in Ottawa and the St James in Montreal, he much preferred when in the latter city to go to the Mount Royal Club to meet his cronies. Significantly, he never joined the Saint-Denis Club, the one most frequented by successful French-Canadian businessmen and professionals, and, when he built his house, it was in Westmount on Upper Belmont

Avenue; it still stands, the site of a Roman Catholic girls' school. It is a splendid structure, Italian Renaissance in style. From the street, the ornate honey-coloured stonework, scrolls, arches, pillars, and balustrades carry the observer's eyes skyward, past the gargoyles at each corner to the crenellations of the upper of the three storeys. While the house was undoubtedly massive, there were surprisingly few rooms within it, only four bedrooms, but a very large entrance hall, a large dining-room, a large sitting-room, a large library, a very large playroom for the children on the third floor, and quarters for the staff, which included a nanny for the children, a cook, and a chauffeur, all hired year-round. Geoffrion, like many a professional who offers advice to others, took no precautions in his own interests in the building of the house, for the cost ran three times over the estimate. After her husband's death in 1946, his wife lived on alone in the mansion, cared for by her children, until her death in 1956.

But even before he moved into his palatial Westmount mansion, he had a substantial country home at Oka on the Ottawa River which he owned until his death, and where he spent as much time as possible. The background of the Oka property is fascinating. By two separate grants, in 1717 and 1735, the king of France granted to the clergy of the Seminary of Saint-Sulpice of Montreal a tract of land along the shore of the Ottawa River some fourteen kilometres long and of almost equal depth. It became known as the Seigniory of the Lake of Two Mountains and contained within it a 'common' – the name still used today – about four kilometres long and three and a half kilometres deep which was made available to the local Indians for pasturing their cattle and cutting firewood. These Indians, Mohawks, have not been occupants of the lands 'from time immemorial' – a legal requirement for establishing aboriginal ownership – but were settled there early in the eighteenth century. In 1909 the seminary, confident that it had exclusive and unquestioned ownership, decided to subdivide some of its lands and sell lots to prosperous citizens of Montreal. At that point the hereditary chiefs of the Mohawks at Oka went to court, alleging that they were the traditional and rightful owners of the land and the seminary had no legal right to sell it. The case went through the Quebec courts and wound up in the Privy Council where Geoffrion, with Sir Robert Finlay, successfully represented the seminary. The decision of the Privy Council, rendered by the redoubtable Lord Haldane, is a fine example of legal obfuscation. While agreeing that the Indians had no claim based upon aboriginal title (because their occupation was of relatively recent origin) and that, in any event, the grants of the king of France in the eighteenth century were conclusive and overrode any legal interests the Indians might have held, he went on to say: 'If in some different form of proceeding the Crown, as representing the interests of the public, puts the law in motion, if negotiations are initiated for the settlement of a question as to the location of these Indians which may be of importance to the general interests of Canada, their Lordships desire to make it clear that nothing they now have decided is intended to prejudice the questions which may then arise.' One of the questions that Haldane suggested might come up was whether there was a form of charitable trust for the benefit of the Indians which might confer upon them some right of use, if not of ownership, a notion akin to that postulated in the landmark *Delgamuukw* decision of the Supreme Court of British Columbia in 1991. The case is an early instance of the courts' grappling with aboriginal title, a concept that today is in the forefront of the Canadian legal and political debate. The Mohawks, meanwhile, pay no attention to Lord Haldane – they say that it's their land and that's all there is to it.

Because of Haldane's ruling, Geoffrion bought a tract of land roughly a half-kilometre long lying between a road and the river on which he built a substantial country home. In addition to a living-room, a dining-room, and other family rooms on the ground floor, there were playrooms for the children and staff quarters. On the second floor were six bedrooms, two sleeping porches, several dressing-rooms, and utility rooms. When the house was under construction a group of Mohawks performed a ritual dance around the building site with the intention of establishing their right of possession or ownership of the land, but there was no hostility. Geoffrion, in fact, got on extremely well with his Indian neighbours and had a high regard for them. In summer he was driven from Montreal to Oka and was met there by one of his three employees, who boated him across the river and back again the following morning. In winter he frequently made the trip, crossing the river by horse and sleigh if the ice was strong enough. He, his wife, and children often went out in their horse-drawn sleigh, wrapped in buffalo blankets with hot bricks at their feet. In winter, Geoffrion often tramped about in snowshoes, with easy grace. He was very fond of his delightful place at Oka and the life there suited him most agreeably for he had a deep love of the outdoors which, because of his ample income, he was well able to indulge. In his younger days, when travelling by himself to appear before the Privy Council, he would join friends on climbing parties in the Swiss Alps; once he and his party ascended Mont Blanc by a new route, an achievement that found its way into the *Encyclopaedia Britannica*, much to his pleasure. Later in life, when flying in Canada became common, if he spotted from the air a remote lake or unusual geographical feature he made a mental note and, when he was able, explored the area with a guide, often taking his young sons with him. Besides three men he employed permanently at Oka for gardening and transportation, he hired a cook who came out from the Indian village when the family was in summer residence, as well as two live-in maids. Meanwhile, of course, the staff at the Westmount house stayed on, but with not much to do. The Oka property was sold after Geoffrion's death. The house is about 270 metres from the part of the 'common' which, as this is written (1995), has been the scene of confrontation between the Indians, ostensibly seeking to enlarge a cemetery, and the municipality of Oka. In fact, during the dangerous confrontation in 1990 between police, army, and Mohawks, a group of the latter occupied the house (by then an alcoholic treatment centre).

The Oka affair is an excellent example of the relevance of history – in that case, ancient deeds – to the solution of current legal problems. Another is the use that can be made of historical writings that refer to the shifting boundaries of bodies of water. In two of these instances Geoffrion found himself on opposite sides of the same question. In 1925 he acted for the Quebec government in a suit brought against it by Price Brothers, the large forestry company. Its timber holdings in the region in question were defined with reference to a Lake Metis which had been the subject of an early grant by France. The province contended that Lake Metis must be given a restricted meaning confined to one particular body of water, a definition which, in turn, would have substantially reduced Price's timber limits. The company argued that 'lake' had always been understood by the local population to refer to a series of connected lakes known collectively as the 'lake' and that such usage was confirmed by historical writings. The courts in Canada, including the Supreme Court of Canada, adopted Geoffrion's submission that such evidence should be excluded, but the Privy Council disagreed, ruling in favour of Price Brothers. Twelve years later, Geoffrion appeared in the Privy Council, again on Quebec's behalf, to support the opposite point of view in a case involving riparian boundaries of a river. His contrary position is easily explained: the Privy Council had rejected his argument in the earlier case and he was now advancing a proposition sanctioned by it, namely that historical writings referring to the course and use of a river in times past was evidence relevant to proving the present state of the river. His opponent in that litigation was Louis St Laurent, the last occasion on which these two outstanding Quebec lawyers faced each other in the Privy Council, for St Laurent was soon to abandon the practice of law for politics. The decision was not reported in the published law reports, which is a pity because it is a valuable contribution to the subject of the use of historical evidence in the courts. (More difficult, however, is the use of oral tradition as evidence, a question that arises often in litigation involving claims for aboriginal title).[8]

But by far the most important of Geoffrion's cases in which historical evidence was paramount occurred in 1926. That year he, with his family, sailed to London where he spent the next two months working with a legal team assembled to conduct the case in the Privy Council for Canada in its dispute with Newfoundland over the location of the boundary with Quebec; the issue, in effect, was how to apportion Labrador. The dispute, which had festered for decades, was exacerbated by Newfoundland issuing timber licences along the Hamilton River in an area considered by Quebec to be within its borders. Eventually Canada and Newfoundland (though a colony, it was self-governing) agreed to submit the problem to the Privy Council by way of a 'reference.' Normally, the Privy Council sat on appeals in litigation but occasionally it heard such references; another instance was the Irish boundary dispute in 1922. There was rather a touchy matter to be settled at the outset. Quebec, which of all provinces was most affected, thought that it should have a voice at the hearings in London separate from or in addition to that of the Canadian legal group. Though the Privy Council normally allowed only two lawyers to speak for a contending party, and Quebec obviously being part of Canada was not entitled to separate representation, the Privy Council none the less granted special dispensation and was prepared to hear three lawyers. Geoffrion, who had been retained by the province, was to be allowed to put forward Quebec's point of view. In the result, the additional voice was unnecessary as one of the lawyers for Canada deferred to Geoffrion, who addressed the tribunal for Canada – as well as for Quebec. Geoffrion was sensitive to the ambiguities of his position, however, for he told the tribunal that the interests of Canada had become merged with those of Quebec. This concern over representation was one of the underlying reasons for Quebec's objections to the eventual ruling by the Privy Council.

Since the Newfoundland-Canada dispute was regarded as delicate, more than usual care was taken in the selection of the members of the tribunal. The lord chancellor, Viscount Cave, presided, joined by lords Haldane and Finlay, both former lord chancellors who were familiar with Canadian issues, Lord Sumner, and Lord Warrington. (By an odd turn of events, Warrington was 'Sir Thomas' Warrington when the hearings commenced but midway through them he was elevated as a law lord to become Lord Warrington of Clyffe.) The legal teams were equally renowned. Sir John Simon was the lead counsel for Newfoundland; his principal assistant was an English barrister, F.J. Barrington-Ward, joined by the Newfoundland attorney general, W.J. Higgins, and Walter Monckton, an English barrister who ten years later came to public prominence as legal adviser to King Edward VIII. Heading the Canadian team was Hugh Macmillan, again a lawyer with much experience in Canadian matters, assisted by C.J. Doherty, the former minister of justice in the Borden government, and a Quebecker, and by Geoffrion and several others. The bulk of the evidence consisted of historic documents, proclamations, and statutes together with affidavits from a great many persons knowledgeable about Labrador, among whom was Sir Wilfrid Grenfell, the famed medical missionary.

The precise question presented to the Privy Council by agreement between Canada and Newfoundland was, 'What is the location and definition of the boundary as between Canada and Newfoundland in the Labrador Peninsula under the statutes, orders-in-council and proclamations?' In all this, the Privy Council did not act as a kind of boundary commission seeking to establish a line to accommodate opposing points of view without reference to historical guidelines. Macmillan defined the problem succinctly. 'Your Lordships' task is not to create a new boundary between the Colony of Newfoundland and the Dominion of Canada, but to declare an existing boundary between the Dominion and the Colony. That is, of course, a very broad and important distinction with regard to the task imposed upon your Lordships. It leaves the matter not at your arbitrement as to what you think would be the best boundary, but you are charged with the task of ascertaining what is the existing boundary which exists as a legal entity at the moment, and we are all engaged in the search for that line.' That point of view was accepted by the board itself, which agreed that its role was that of an interpreter not an arbitrator and that it was to declare the boundary as deduced from written records and historical events.

There were two sharply divergent points of view at the hearing; both Newfoundland and Canada agreed that there was no middle ground. Canada argued that Newfoundland's entitlement to Labrador should be limited to a kilometre-wide littoral strip following the sinuosities of the coast from Ance Blanc, the point at which the north shore of the Gulf of St Lawrence ends and the Atlantic Ocean begins, to Cape Chidley on the south edge of Hudson Strait. Newfoundland, on the other hand, contended that the south boundary of Labrador should commence at Ance

Blanc, but its western extremity should be fixed according to the watersheds, the heights of land, of the various rivers which flowed into the Atlantic Ocean. The difference between the two positions was substantial, a trifling shoreline strip compared to a region comprising 285,000 square kilometres.

All the lawyers – and the judges – agreed that resolution of the controversy largely depended on how the words 'coast' or 'coasts' used in historic documents in reference to Labrador should be interpreted. Was 'coast' or 'coasts' – the words were used interchangeably – to be given an extended meaning in the sense of embracing a country or region, an example being the 'Gold Coast'? Or were they to be limited to a narrow shoreline? In solving that problem everyone concurred that the fundamental documents in which 'coast' or 'coasts' appeared were a proclamation of 1763 appointing a governor of Newfoundland, followed in the same year by the famous Royal Proclamation of King George III dealing with the conquered territory of New France, and a statute of 1825 which established the boundaries of Lower Canada. Geoffrion said at the outset of his submission that 'this is primarily and one might also say exclusively a question of construction of the relevant documents of 1763' and only 'to a lesser degree' were later statutes, such as that of 1825, helpful.

The Newfoundland proclamation in 1763 was couched in such wide phraseology with reference to the 'coasts of Labrador' that it could hardly be taken as referring to a mere coastal strip. It contemplated the establishment of forts and garrisons as well as of a judicial system to administer justice for the king's subjects 'inhabiting there,' that is, the coasts of Labrador, to supervise the fisheries, and so on. The whole tenor of the document was to provide for governance of a region. The later proclamation came into existence in the aftermath of the Treaty of Paris and is the very one which is now at the heart of every claim for aboriginal title in this country because of its references to lands 'reserved' for Indians and its prohibition of alienation of these lands without their consent. This exceedingly significant document also defined the boundaries of four distinct governments, Quebec, East Florida, West Florida, and Grenada. So far as Quebec was concerned, the proclamation fixed the east boundary 'on the Labrador coast' at a point well inland from the Atlantic Ocean. The judges, differing with Geoffrion and the other lawyers, thought that the 1825 statute which re-annexed to Quebec certain 'parts of the ... Coasts of Labrador' was the most important document of all for it left as part of Newfoundland a very large region. After a detailed examination of all the documents and other historical evidence, such as the grant of privileges to Moravian missionaries over a wide area, the Privy Council fixed the boundary in what is now its current location, which, generally, embraces the territory east of the watersheds of the rivers flowing into the Atlantic Ocean, the most important of which is the Churchill, formerly the Hamilton. Although the province of Quebec lost territorial entitlement to that river by the ruling of the Privy Council, it later gained a substantial measure of compensation resulting from the deal made by Newfoundland, highly advantageous to Quebec and highly injurious to Newfoundland, to sell cheap power to Quebec from the Churchill Falls hydro installation.

An impartial examination of the evidence and proceedings makes clear that Newfoundland had a very strong case indeed, and it is not therefore surprising that both Macmillan and Geoffrion had an uphill struggle throughout. In the face of the historic evidence, to argue that the 'coasts of Labrador' were no more than a kilometre-wide littoral took considerable nerve and ingenuity, and sometimes the credulity of the judges was strained. When Geoffrion severely criticized an argument of Simon, Lord Finlay interjected: 'I understand your position to be that your opponent's argument is bad, but that is no particular reason for your deducing another argument equally bad.' And when Geoffrion, speaking of a grant of up to 100,000 acres of land to the Moravians, suggested that the tract was to be strung out along the shoreline rather than constituting an inland territory, Lord Cave interjected, 'Would any sensible mission have extended 100,000 acres into a long strip along the coast?' Even so, there was much politesse, and diversions to take one's mind off boundaries, such as the discussion of the fly-fishing characteristics of Scottish streams well known to Finlay and Macmillan, both Scotsmen. Lord Sumner inquired at one point if Macmillan knew of any good streams in Lancashire; Macmillan did not, adding, 'But that is my misfortune.' One may well ask what Scottish fishing streams have to do with rivers rising in the mountainous headlands of Labrador and flowing into the Atlantic Ocean; the answer, of course, is nothing, but such was the civilized atmosphere in which hearings before the Privy Council were conducted that lawyers, and the judges, all gentlemen, found that such digressions relieved the pressure of more urgent questions.

There are interesting parallels and contrasts between the Canada-Newfoundland dispute and the United States-Canada dispute over the Alaska panhandle in which, of course, Geoffrion had also been involved. In the Alaska case the Canadian legal team had argued in London in 1903 for a boundary along the shoreline or, at least, one close to the shoreline, as

Geoffrion did in London in 1926, but in each instance the tribunal fixed the boundary at the watershed or height of land, denying Canada access to salt-water ports in the panhandle and cutting Quebec off from rivers north of the St Lawrence. The disputed Labrador territory did become part of Canada upon Newfoundland joining confederation in 1949, so in that sense the dispute is perhaps of academic interest only, whereas the Alaska panhandle remains a painful example of American realpolitik. Quebec has never accepted the ruling of 1926. Canada has resigned itself to the loss of the panhandle though it has failed to take the opportunities occasionally presented to it of softening the consequences of the arbitration by controlling or developing the waters of the panhandle rivers, all of which have their sources and main flows in Canada, and, as this is written, the question of fish spawning within the Canadian sections of rivers flowing through the panhandle is very much an issue between Canada and the United States. Finally, the historical record in the Newfoundland dispute was a good deal more complete than that available in the Alaska negotiations, in which only one treaty was in question and that so vague as to be of little use.

Geoffrion, after the hearings, holidayed in Europe with his family and sailed home from Naples in comfort on an Italian liner. He told his son Guillaume in later years that the decision was 'unfounded' and had been reached for 'purely political reasons – in the hope that Canada would buy Labrador and thus solve the financial problems of Britain with Newfoundland.' This rather tortuous theory would seem to indicate that the decision rankled with Geoffrion, but, in view of the strength of the evidence against his client, he could not have had much expectation of success.[9]

Although Geoffrion's national reputation had been well established earlier by various appearances in the Supreme Court of Canada and the Privy Council, it was in the 1930s that a series of constitutional cases brought his illustrious career to its peak. As we have seen, in the immensely important aeronautics case – did the provincial governments or Ottawa have regulatory control over aviation? – he represented Quebec and was successful in the Supreme Court of Canada, but the Privy Council overturned that decision by holding that the federal government occupied the 'whole field of legislation in relation to aerial navigation in Canada.' W.N. Tilley, who had not argued the case for the attorney general of Canada in Ottawa, showed up in London where he triumphed over the combined opposition of Geoffrion and Sir John Simon. As also recounted, a similar problem came to the courts hardly a year later –

which government controlled radio transmissions? The question had been submitted by the newly elected Bennett government to the courts for an opinion. In the Supreme Court of Canada, Tilley, a Liberal, was engaged by the Conservative government to defend its proposals to legislate on the subject. Again, Geoffrion represented Quebec, unavailingly, because the Supreme Court of Canada upheld the jurisdiction of Ottawa. That is hardly surprising in view of the aeronautics decision. However, Quebec decided to appeal to the Privy Council and, on that occasion, Geoffrion and D.N. Pritt did their best in unsuccessful opposition to Tilley, who appeared for the government of Canada.

In the first several years of the 1930s Geoffrion often appeared before the Supreme Court of Canada on unremarkable but handsomely remunerated appeals; he was successful in just over 60 per cent of the cases that found their way into the published reports; there were other, unpublished, results which cannot be tabulated. Of course, a statistical analysis of Supreme Court results takes no account of the successes that Geoffrion achieved in the lower courts, the Court of Queen's Bench (appeal side) and, of course, the Quebec Superior Court. The statistics at the highest level, however, are what really count and Geoffrion's – both in the Supreme Court of Canada and in the Privy Council – are superior to those of his contemporaries. Any lawyer would be pleased to boast a record such as his, for the result of litigation is unpredictable.

In October 1935 the Bennett government was defeated in a general election and Mackenzie King took office. In the dying stages of his administration Bennett, desperately grappling with the effects of the Depression in an attempt to regain the confidence of voters, had put through parliament six pieces of social legislation; inspired by Roosevelt's example in the United States, they became known as the 'New Deal.' Bennett campaigned on them, to no avail. King, in a quandary, decided to refer all six acts to the Supreme Court of Canada for an opinion as to their constitutionality. On 15 January 1936 an impressive array of lawyers (including Farris) from across the country assembled to start the submissions, which continued until February 5th. Geoffrion acted for Quebec; with him was the provincial deputy attorney general, Charles Lanctot. Geoffrion's role was a bit out of the usual because, six months before the hearings in Ottawa, he had been asked by the Bennett government to give an opinion on one of the acts, the Trade and Industry Commission Act. He said that it was clearly *ultra vires*. That was the position Quebec took on the Bennett New Deal – it claimed that the legislation intruded upon provincial jurisdiction over 'property and civil rights' – and so, Geoffrion, in appearing for Quebec, was consistent. N.W. Rowell acted for the federal government throughout all six cases, of which two were far and away the most important. The labour conventions case was concerned with whether the government of Canada could enact legislation pursuant to conventions of the International Labour Office providing for a maximum work week of forty-eight hours, a weekly day off, and minimum wages in some occupations. Each of the judges of the court hearing the case wrote a lengthy judgment but the court split three to three on whether the legislation was valid. The other case concerned a scheme for unemployment insurance, probably a more significant subject than the labour conventions. The court by a majority declared the scheme invalid. Both cases went to the Privy Council, which also ruled them invalid; Geoffrion was not involved in the appeal. King personally favoured the scheme for unemployment insurance but had to secure an amendment to the BNA Act before it could be implemented.

Almost two years to the day after the commencement of argument in the New Deal cases, Geoffrion led off the argument in the Supreme of Canada for the government of Canada in the first of a batch of cases arising from the Social Credit legislation of Premier William Aberhart in Alberta. Geoffrion was to achieve great distinction in these cases; one in particular, the newspaper case, was probably the second most important of his career. After taking office Aberhart had sought to usher in a new economic order, founded on principles of Social Credit as he envisaged them, by the passage of a blizzard of legislation; of more than twenty enactments, three were disallowed by the governor general. Later, the Alberta legislature passed the three acts which were eventually to come to the Supreme Court of Canada, one providing for the regulation of credit, another for the taxation of banks, and the third requiring newspapers to publish the government point of view on any matter of public debate. When these bills were presented to the Alberta lieutenant governor, John Bowen, for royal assent, he declined to give it and instead referred them formally to the governor general for possible disallowance. In doing so he relied on advice clandestinely given him by the noted Edmonton lawyer S.B. Woods. Aberhart was so angry at Bowen that he ordered Government House closed up, forcing Bowen to move out; he also was infuriated at the prospect of disallowance, and Mackenzie King, hardly an admirer of Aberhart, agreed to refer the validity of the three acts to the Supreme Court of Canada. But O.M. Biggar, counsel for Alberta, questioned whether the power of disallowance by the governor general even existed, arguing that only the sovereign personally and not his viceroy could disallow legislation. That threshold question was also submitted to the court for an opinion; the argument on it took only one day, the court giving short shrift to Biggar's contention.

The court then turned to the three specific acts. By the first, Alberta sought to license financial institutions which were to dispense credit, Social Credit style. By the second, a provincial tax was imposed upon chartered banks, calculated on the size of their paid-up capital reserves and retained earnings. By the third, the Accurate News and Information Act, newspapers could be ordered to print defences of government policy prepared by government officials; further, these articles were to be given prominence equal to that given to those critical of government policy, and newspapers were to be forced to disclose their sources for any article critical of the government. Aberhart and his policies, especially 'funny money,' had been the butt of many jokes and cartoons in Alberta newspapers, and he was not amused; passage of the bill was legislative revenge. At the hearings the occasional bit of banter lightened the rather dreary proceedings. Once, Geoffrion, when referring to a case naming the Esquimalt and Nanaimo Railway Company on Vancouver Island, mispronounced those names and was corrected by Duff; Geoffrion replied, 'Your Lordship comes from that country. I would not argue with you on that, but I might on the pronunciation of some Quebec names,' prompting Duff to retort, 'British Columbia is *in* Canada, you know.' The court handed down its decision with astonishing speed, hardly a month after the conclusion of the hearings. It ruled that all three acts were unconstitutional. The first two were invalidated because their essential purpose was to control banking, a field in which only Ottawa could legislate. The newspaper bill failed also, because it was an integral part of a Social Credit scheme which, taken as a whole, was unconstitutional. Even had this bill stood alone, it probably would have been invalidated for, as Geoffrion said in his argument, 'free exchange of news [was] necessary to [the] Canadian political setup.' Geoffrion was suggesting that Canadian parliamentary institutions, derived from the British parliamentary system, would be jeopardized by unreasonable limitations on free expression and freedom of the press. Duff picked up on this argument and adopted it in his judgment, which, until the advent of the Charter of Rights in 1982, formed the legal basis for press freedom and free speech in this country. The province of Alberta appealed to the Privy Council in only one of the three cases, the bill to tax chartered banks. Geoffrion went over to London for the appeal, with Tilley, who was acting for the banks; the Privy Council affirmed the rulings of the Supreme Court of Canada.[10]

Just a year later, in June 1939, Geoffrion appeared on his most significant constitutional case. He once again represented the government of
Canada, this time in support of an amendment to the Supreme Court Act
which would constitute that court the final tribunal for all Canadian lawsuits and which would, by necessary implication, abolish appeals to the
Privy Council. Those who favoured abolition were convinced that parliament could abolish appeals from the Supreme Court of Canada, but there
was far more uncertainty about the ability of parliament to abolish the *per
saltum* appeals from the provinces. Of all the provinces, Quebec was the
most nervous about losing those appeals. Though the Privy Council was
in a sense a relic of detested British colonialism, many Quebeckers saw it
as a bulwark against any future attempts by Ottawa to intrude into Quebec language and culture. Oddly, Quebec was not represented at the hearings in Ottawa but most of the other provinces sent strong contingents of
lawyers with instructions to retain intact the *per saltum* appeals.

For twenty years there had been heated debate about the wisdom of
making the Supreme Court of Canada the final arbiter of litigation in
Canada. Many scholars and practitioners said that appeals to the Privy
Council should continue until the Supreme Court became stronger; others said that one could not have a strong court so long as there were such
appeals. This circular argument only delayed matters. Under Duff's leadership, the court had attained judicial respectability and Ottawa began to
give serious thought to abolition. The subject came up in parliament in
rather a back-door way. C.H. Cahan, a former cabinet minister in the Bennett government, introduced in January 1939 a private member's bill
declaring the Supreme Court of Canada to be the court of last resort. Officials in the Department of Justice suggested certain amendments which
Cahan agreed to; he then moved second reading of his bill. The minister
of justice, Ernest Lapointe, endorsed it, but, doubtful of parliament's ability to abolish the *per saltum* appeals, said that he would refer the entire
question to the Supreme Court of Canada for an opinion. Geoffrion must
have approached his task with mixed feelings. His role was eminently fitting for he and Tilley, along with D'Alton McCarthy, had been instrumental in persuading Duff not to resign in 1924 when he was denied the chief
justiceship in favour of Anglin precisely because, by staying, he would in
their view strengthen the court to the point where appeals to London
could safely be eliminated. As a Quebecker, however, Geoffrion would
have been aware of strong provincial opposition to the measure and he
also must have thought his engagement by Ottawa rather ironic given
that he had been its constitutional opponent on so many other occasions.

On top of all this, he was personally attached to the Privy Council. He had had many an enjoyable time on his frequent visits to London for appeals. Although he usually journeyed alone – his wife did not like travel – there were the occasional trips as a family accompanied by a nanny, with comfortable lodging at Queen Anne's Mansions and invitations to Ascot and from old legal comrades to spend weekends in the country. And now, all that might end.

In spite of all the lawyers present, the arguments took up only three days, but six months elapsed before the decision. Duff, who had presided and rightly seen the case as the most important of his career, laboured over his judgment. In it he upheld Ottawa's power on several grounds; essentially, however he had decided that Canada's nationhood demanded judicial sovereignty, and he tailored his stated reasons to fit that view, a most uncharacteristic method for him. By the time of the judgment, the war was on and it was agreed on all sides that an appeal to the Privy Council itself, intended by the provinces, should be delayed until the war was over so that Canadian lawyers would have the opportunity to appear on a case of the first importance. Geoffrion undoubtedly would have conducted the appeal if he had been well. He became seriously ill early in 1946 with liver cancer, which, although it caused him no pain, incapacitated him physically and affected his mental powers. He died on 15 October 1946. Eight days later the appeal started but before it did Lord Jowitt, the lord chancellor, noting Geoffrion's recent death and referring to him as 'our old friend,' praised him 'as a great and profound constitutional lawyer and a distinguished Canadian' whose work was 'enriched by his own personality and his own enthusiasm.' The province of Quebec, although it had not participated in the Ottawa hearing, applied for leave to intervene in the Privy Council, where it argued that Ottawa had no power to abolish the *per saltum* appeals because they formed an integral part of the 'administration of justice,' a subject reserved to the exclusive jurisdiction of the provinces. Other provinces made the same argument, but all to no avail; the Privy Council dismissed the appeal. The ramifications of Geoffrion's submissions and Duff's decision, affirmed by the Privy Council, are still with us. Canada ventured on a new constitutional course which culminated in the unilateral patriation by Ottawa of the constitution in the face of protests by Quebec and the adoption of an American-style Charter of Rights. Because of Quebec's resentment, and the Americanization of our judicial and political systems, one cannot but feel that Geoffrion and Duff, both loyal to the British tradition, would have disapproved of the train of events they set in motion.

Geoffrion's body lay in his residence until October 17th, two days after his death, and was then carried in a cortège to the Roman Catholic Church of Saint-Leon de Westmount. Following the solemn requiem mass offered by four prelates, his body was interred in Côte-des-Neiges cemetery under a simple headstone inscribed only with his name and dates of birth and death. His wife, to whom he was devoted, lies beside him. It is always interesting to examine the names of those who attend the funeral of a prominent citizen and to note those who did not. Such an occasion is a combination of social ritual, affection, protocol, and grief. No judge of the Supreme Court of Canada attended, nor did any person designated as a representative of the court, but, on the other hand, many Quebec judges and numbers of lawyers were present. St Laurent, the minister of justice, was there; his attendance would have been more than mere courtesy to a respected adversary. There were representatives from the various large corporations on whose boards of directors Geoffrion sat, among them the CPR, the Aluminum Company of Canada (of which he had also been vice-president), the Canada Life Insurance Company, and, of course, Distillers Corporation Seagram's. Sam Bronfman, his brother Allan, and Lazarus Phillips all were present. Again, their attendance was likely more than obligatory.

Running through all the tributes to Geoffrion printed in the Montreal newspapers was the same theme as that noted when Lafleur died – the lamented loss of a great 'Canadian.' Writing to a friend in 1918, Geoffrion had cautioned him not to be swayed by a 'Francophone group which has always existed and should not be given undue importance. It is a noisy minority which has not forced us out of the Confederation in the past and which should not make us do so now.' He went on to deplore the notion that Quebec should quit Confederation because of a 'temporary crisis' and stressed that it should 'go on fighting' in the interests of Canada as a whole. Yet, despite his strong views on national questions, Geoffrion made a conscious decision early in his life not to seek political or judicial office. He was certainly 'political,' often making campaign speeches for the Liberal Party in rural ridings in Quebec where his common touch served him in good stead, but he was never a candidate though often asked to be. Nor was he a 'joiner': he never became involved in community activities except for his stint on the Roman Catholic school board. There is no evidence that he was ever formally offered a judicial appointment, probably because his aversion to judicial life was well known. Partly his reasons were financial – he would have been quite unable to keep up his two substantial properties on the relatively meagre stipend of a judge, even of one on the Supreme Court of Canada. Moreover, he felt an obligation to his wife and children. Geoffrion was nearly fifty and his wife was forty-four when their youngest child, Guillaume, was born, and the father felt that he should continue his practice until his youngest son and a slightly older brother, Antoine, became old enough to take it over should they choose to do so. Both sons, in fact, became lawyers though only Guillaume survives.

Geoffrion was a Canadian nationalist in the best sense. He had a foot both in the English culture and in the French, favouring neither one nor the other. Of ancient Quebec lineage, he attended a Jesuit school but studied at McGill. He had his city residence at Westmount but his summer home in rural Quebec. He was as familiar with the English common law as he was with the Napoleonic code embodied in the Quebec civil code. A 'clubbable' man, he tended to frequent English-speaking clubs rather than French ones, but he delighted in giving campaign speeches on behalf of some local worthy seeking political office in a French-speaking riding in the country. When for the first time Canadian bank notes were printed in both English and French, Geoffrion thought that it was a silly demonstration of bilingualism. Better stick with the English language, an attitude that today would hardly bring him commendation in Quebec. When on trips to the Privy Council, he would hob-nob on the weekends with his English counterparts at their country homes, yet when the case ended, he went over to Paris. As pointed out earlier, Geoffrion was identified by his fellow citizens of Quebec as French, and outside Quebec he was seen as English. This is a great tribute: for him Canada was neither French nor English – but one country.[11]

4

Isaac Pitblado

On 10 March 1930 a group of men and women gathered for a seance at the house of Dr Thomas Glendinning Hamilton in Winnipeg. Hamilton, a reputable medical doctor and, variously, president of the Manitoba Medical Association and a member of the Faculty of Medicine at the University of Manitoba, was more widely known as a spiritualist; his correspondents included Sir Arthur Conan Doyle and Sir Oliver Lodge in England, and, in Canada, Mackenzie King. He had spent months of meticulous planning for this particular seance, which would be conducted under very strict controls. Not a charlatan, he was convinced that one could reach out to the *other side* and be able to prove it. Those attending would be the regular members of his circle, but in addition he arranged for an official court reporter to record in shorthand, and later transcribe, the events of the evening and he invited Isaac Pitblado to be *scrutineer*. Pitblado was not one of the regular circle members but certainly, at the very least, he was a believer, having attended several earlier seances. Years later, in 1950, Pitblado recalled those days in a letter to Mrs Hamilton: 'I have very happy memories of the occasions when I was privileged to attend the seances at your home and of the great kindnesses of your dear husband and yourself to us all. I note that you have been re-reading one of Lodge's books. I must try and get it. It is a great comfort to believe in personal immortality as you and I do.' Pitblado's wife had just died and Mrs Hamilton, whose husband had died in 1935, had written him a letter of condolence.

Pitblado was well known to Hamilton, who, on the occasion of Conan Doyle's visit to Winnipeg in 1923, had asked Pitblado and his wife to entertain the great man and his family. Doyle was not on a tour promoting his latest Sherlock Holmes mystery but on a spiritualist trip. The Pitblados took the Doyles to lunch at the Fort Garry Hotel and afterward drove them around Winnipeg to see the sights. At the seance in question in March 1930, Hamilton clearly believed that Pitblado's stature as a lawyer, renowned throughout the land, would lend maximum credibility to the event by ensuring that there would be no hanky-panky and everything would be above board. Hamilton's purpose in this seance was to obtain photographic proof of psychic phenomena, if such occurred, and to that end elaborate precautions were taken to ensure that the room where the group gathered could not be tampered with and was, as we would say today, secure. Pitblado himself wrote a detailed description of the occurrences which conformed to the running account kept by the official reporter and by Hamilton himself.

The group had already assembled by the time Pitblado arrived at 9 p.m. He saw to it that everyone, men and women, discarded their outer garments, which, with purses and handbags and any other loose items, were placed in a hallway. Pitblado frisked all the men, who were left wearing nothing but shirts and trousers. The women were searched by the wife of a Dr Creighton; the female medium was completely disrobed by Mrs Creighton (in an upstairs bedroom), who supplied her with loose-fitting clothes to wear during the seance. Pitblado then examined the seance room itself. The door into it had been padlocked the night before by Dr Creighton, who, as he told Pitblado, had sealed the hasps of the padlock with cord. Anyone who had gained entry overnight would either have had to break the string or cut it. It was undamaged. Creighton, in Pitblado's presence, cut the string and unlocked the door. Pitblado, alone, went into the room, which was in pitch darkness; aided by a pocket flashlight with a red glass, he thoroughly inspected it, finding nothing more than a table, chairs and couches, and, in a side room, a closet which was also empty. Returning to the hall, he admitted the circle to the room one by one, doing a head count which accorded with the tally he had made on arrival. The medium was the last to arrive and took her position at the centre of the circle. At her left was an empty chair. The door was shut and Dr Creighton, who remained in the hall throughout, padlocked it and stood guard until the seance ended. The only objects in the seance room out of the ordinary were a tripod camera, flash apparatus, and photographic plates, all belonging to Hamilton. Pitblado sat in front of the medium during the proceedings, holding her hands continuously; others placed their hands on his. The reporter sat at the back of the room. He wrote shorthand by instinct and habit because the room remained in total darkness.

There then ensued three hours of what to an unbeliever seems a bizarre episode. The group sang many hymns, sea shanties, and ditties, two of the latter being *Solomon Levi* and *My Bonnie Lies over the Ocean*. There was some point in singing *Bonnie* because for years the group had been trying to reach Robert Louis Stevenson and David Livingstone. This night, however, the object was to contact *Sister Lucy*. It is difficult to tell from the material just who she was or was thought to be, but it seems that she was a departed loved one of a member of the circle. At 10:37 p.m. she spoke to the circle through the medium, who was in a deep trance: 'Good evening. You can sing your Te Deums and shout your Hosannas for everything is all right – wonderful!' Through the medium she was introduced to Pitblado; she expressed pleasure at meeting 'one who is not afraid to speak,' a sentiment drawing thanks from him. A little later, when asked by Hamilton if they spoke Latin *over there*, she replied that it was spoken only *under earth conditions*, prompting Pitblado to ask, 'Are there languages on the other side?' Lucy replied, 'No, my friend, just thought. You think of me and you bring me.'

At what proved to be a critical juncture Pitblado remarked that he thought he could see a 'whitish light' around the medium. Hamilton fired the flash on the camera and several times at later stages. During the three-hour session there was a good deal of light-hearted banter and some gentle ribaldry, which is hardly surprising given that men and women were seated close together in a dark room with persons not their spouses. When the seance ended and with the group still locked in the room, Pitblado once more searched it with his flashlight and found nothing untoward. Dr Creighton unlocked the door and the group filed out. Pitblado helped Hamilton with the camera equipment; they carried five exposed plates to the darkroom where Hamilton developed them. In each photograph, in the chair next to the medium, there appeared the ghostly figure, almost childlike, of *Lucy*. The figure was surrounded with what appears to be a corporeal substance, but Dr Hamilton said that it was *teleplasm*. The figure had not been observed when the group filed out of the seance room.

Pitblado, in recalling this manifestation, told Hamilton that it would have been impossible for the medium or anyone else for that matter to have arranged its appearance. Writing his account two days after the event, Pitblado said, 'I am convinced that the phenomenon of a figure seated in the chair was genuinely produced without the aid of any known physical or mechanical means, process or apparatus and that there is no "fake" or "trickery."' Hamilton, in his own recollection, stated that several who were present (whom he does not name) saw by the light of the photographic flash the form seated in what had been a vacant chair; they thought the form, though girlish, was that of an adult. Hamilton made much of this episode in the remaining years of his life, pointing to it as incontrovertible proof not only of life after death but of the ability of a spirit under the right circumstances to return briefly to earthy conditions. When Mackenzie King visited Winnipeg in 1933, he called on Hamilton, who showed him photographs of psychic phenomena. Though King, in his recollection of the visit, does not specifically refer to it, the *Lucy* photograph would unquestionably have been one of them. King described his afternoon with Hamilton as 'quite the most remarkable one – save the direct voice experiences with Mrs. Wriedt – I have had in my life ... I believe absolutely in all that Hamilton & his wife & daughter have told me.'[1]

At the time of that seance in 1930, Pitblado was sixty-three years old and at the height of his powers. He had practised law for forty years and was to do so for another thirty-four. He was the senior partner in a Winnipeg law firm which, if not the premier firm in the city, certainly held second place, and he himself was the most prominent lawyer in the city, the province, and the prairies and indeed stood among the legal élite of the country. He had come to Winnipeg as a boy of fifteen and had quite literally grown up with the city. As his life and career proved, he had arrived in the fledgling city just at the right time. He witnessed the arrival of the CPR train carrying troops to the North-West rebellion and, later, stood on the platform to greet the first transcontinental passenger train on its westward journey to the Pacific coast. The opening of the west, the flood of immigrants to the prairies, the growth of agriculture, and the rise of the prosperous grain trade all contributed to Winnipeg's prosperity in the late nineteenth and early twentieth century. Businessmen and clever lawyers such as Pitblado thrived in this environment, and they were to continue to do so for many years. Between the First World War and the second, grain still dominated but increasingly there were differences of opinion about how it should be marketed, whether by state agencies, private enterprise, or farm co-ops. Conflicts on such issues provided a fertile and lucrative field for lawyers. Simultaneous, of course, with the burgeoning of the farm economy was the expansion of railway systems to serve the farm producers – the proliferation of branch lines to reach country elevators owned by grain companies headquartered in Winnipeg whose shrine was the Winnipeg Grain Exchange. If the prairie economy was firmly centred on grain, the grain industry was just as firmly centred on Winnipeg, where the two railways, the CPR and the CNR, had their western headquarters. Lawyers became identified with the farm producers, or the elevator operators, or the railways, or the Grain Exchange, or the Winnipeg Board of Trade. Sometimes lawyers would act for one group and, soon after, for another.

Pitblado was in the thick of all this, initially for the producers, then for the Grain Exchange, and, later in his career, as counsel for the railways. He was not a traitor to any cause nor was he unethical – far from it. By the late 1940s he was the acknowledged master in Canada of the right relationship that ought to obtain between farm producers and manufacturers on the one hand and the railways on the other. Indeed, he had achieved that mastery long before 1947, when, as will be seen, his greatest achievement occurred. Thereafter – he was now eighty years old – he began to slow down or, perhaps more accurately, a change in the economic climate of the prairies reduced the available work. The advent of the Canadian Wheat Board, the state marketing agency, the disappearance of the Board of Railway Commissioners as a regulatory body and its replacement by the Board of Transport Commissioners – in short, the increasing role of government in the prairie economy – resulted in less work for old warhorses such as Pitblado and the economic decline overlapped with his own aging. Just as his arrival in Winnipeg in 1882 had occurred at the threshold of the city's prosperity, so his death eighty-two years later coincided with its diminished importance as a commercial hub.

His name, Pitblado, was always a bit of a puzzle to new acquaintances. It was Scottish. His revered father, Charles Bruce Pitblado, a Scottish Presbyterian clergyman, had come to minister in Nova Scotia where in 1867, the year of confederation, his son Isaac was born, in Guysborough County, in the village of Glenelg. (Is there another Canadian community whose name is a palindrome?) Young Pitblado completed his schooling in Nova Scotia and one year at Dalhousie (which in 1919 granted him an honorary doctor of laws degree) before his father accepted a call to Winnipeg. Various descriptions have been given of Winnipeg at that period but young Isaac remembered it as a sort of shanty town on a mud plain. The houses had no running water or flush toilets; privies served the purpose. There was no piped water; in summer it was sold by the barrel and in winter it was obtained by melting blocks of ice. Pitblado had a weekly bath in the kitchen, after melting ice and heating the water on the stove. To stay clear of the muddy streets, pedestrians walked on board side-walks. Yet the community of 8,500 was vibrant, at least for its younger members. Pitblado took up competitive cycling, soccer, and foot racing but it was as a lacrosse player and curler that he is chiefly recalled in the annals of Winnipeg sports history. Between 1889 and 1892 he was a star of the premier men's lacrosse team. His prowess was recognized in 1957 by the Manitoba Lacrosse Association, which invited him to participate in the official face-off at the opening game of the senior league, describing him as 'one of Winnipeg's greatest athletes in early days of sport.' Pit-blado gladly accepted the invitation and later turned over to the associa-tion the Drewry trophy which he and his teammates had won sixty-five years earlier. With members of his rink, he won the men's curling champi-onship in the city five times, and he played the sport competitively until he was nearly forty. Later in life, in recognition of his achievements, he would be asked to throw the first rock at big bonspiels. He said that his skill at curling came naturally to him – he was, after all, Scottish. And indeed he was interested all his life in matters Scottish; he was an active member of the St Andrews Society and various other Scottish organiza-tions, attending Burns dinners regularly and enthusiastically. He became a keen hunter and a good shot, going duck-hunting until he was ninety-two. But he was also committed to wildlife conservation and preservation of wetlands; two years before his death a large bird sanctuary northwest of Winnipeg was named in his honour by Ducks Unlimited (Canada). Last but not least, he was a keen football fan. In 1959, at the age of ninety-two, he flew to Toronto to see the Grey Cup game between the Winnipeg Blue Bombers and the Hamilton Tiger Cats. In an interview, he said that he could not recall how many Grey Cups he had seen, but he did say that football was not so exciting as formerly when individual players such as Indian Jack Jacobs were more in the limelight.

In 1885 Pitblado's father served as a chaplain to the troops sent to quell the North-West rebellion and, after Louis Riel's surrender at Batoche, was one of those chosen to accompany Riel on his fateful journey to Regina. Isaac retained vivid memories of the stories told him by his father of that occasion: Pitblado, the Presbyterian, and Riel, still an apostate Roman Catholic, got on famously; Pitblado was called as a witness at Riel's trial to testify that he did not believe Riel was mentally deranged.[2] After the rebellion, the elder Pitblado resumed his ministry in Winnipeg and was gratified to mark the progress of his obviously talented son, Isaac. (There was another son, John, who, though clever, never achieved the eminence of his brother; he became a stockbroker and financier in Montreal.) In 1884 young Isaac enrolled in Manitoba College, one of the affiliated colleges of the University of Manitoba, thereby beginning a long and illustrious connection with the institution, one which, however, was to bring him much distress in 1932. He received a BA with honours in classics in 1886, standing at the head of his class. He then applied for a position as headmaster in the Brandon Public School but was not accepted.[3] After articling to J.A.M. Aikins (afterwards the eminent Sir James Aikins) in 1886, he took his LLB in 1889 and was called to the Manitoba bar in 1890. Though he started to practise law with Aikins, he left after a year to join A.J. Andrews. In 1891 he was elected as a convocation representative on the council of the University of Manitoba and remained one until 1917 when, with the university becoming a teaching institution rather than merely a degree-granting body, he became the first chairman of the board of governors. After being awarded an MA in 1893, he was named college registrar and served in that position until 1900. At his death in 1964 he was the oldest living graduate of the University of Manitoba, both by date of birth and by year of graduation.

His early years in practice were spent mainly in general civil litigation; he excelled at this work – he did little criminal law – and was created King's Counsel in 1909. Gradually, however, he was drawn into freight-rate litigation, the fixing of charges by railways for hauling commodities which, after passage of the Railway Act by parliament in 1903, fell within the purview of the Board of Railway Commissioners, the powerful regulatory body set up under the act. Its jurisdiction was extended in later years to related matters such as rates for express shipments and tolls for telegraph messages. A whole new field or body of law grew out of the functioning of the board, which, as noted earlier, enjoyed a status almost equal to that of the highest court in the land and superior to that of many lower courts. A crucial feature of the board's jurisdiction was its responsibility to maintain, so far as possible, equal rates for haulage of the same commodities over the same distance by different rail systems in all regions of the country. Yet – and the qualification was highly significant – it was recognized that the ideal could not always be attained and hence, if there were differences in charges for rail shipments, such discrimination was to be neither *undue* nor *unjust*. It was this element of discretion vested in the board which gave rise over the years to major battles between the rail carriers and their customers on the one hand and the carriers and regional interests on the other. But while the board's major influence lay with large general issues that involved the country as a whole, it had to deal with a plethora of minor matters because by law only parliament, as expressed in the Railway Act, had jurisdiction over questions, however trivial, which affected nationally chartered or interprovincial railways. Thus, if a small farm community complained about the actions of a local station master, demanding his removal, the board would consider the matter. If a landowner wished to have a private rail crossing to reach his land, he had to apply to the board for permission. There were endless arguments over the description and nature of goods and which particular railway tariff applied: was a steel bed-frame subject to a tariff for the haulage of metal goods or to one for furniture? In all these matters the board as a whole, or designated members, travelled across the country to conduct hearings.[4]

In 1916 Pitblado appeared before the board at a hearing in Winnipeg on behalf of livestock producers complaining of charges by the railways for hauling cattle from western to eastern Canada. The railways in calculating their rates added in, over and above the standard tariff being objected to, a charge of 75 cents for disinfecting each cattle car prior to animals being loaded. Pitblado protested, 'The railway has no more right to charge for the disinfectants used on cars than they had to charge the shipper for the oil necessary to the locomotion of the trains.' The board chairman, Sir Henry Drayton, disagreed, ruling that disinfectant was a necessary charge, to which Pitblado replied unavailingly that if that was so the cost should be included in the general rate – spread over the system as a whole – rather than being placed on particular shippers. Such were the minutiae of the freight rate business. And such were the civilities among the participants in the rate wars that, only four months after Pitblado had lambasted the CPR for its disinfectant charges, he entertained the enemy – the head of the western division of the CPR, D.C. Coleman – and his wife at dinner. When acting for the railways in later years, Pitblado would take a position opposite to the one he had adopted in 1916 – and in doing so he would argue against the claim of British Columbia and Alberta that, even if a special charge was warranted for haulage through the Rocky Mountains, it should not be applied to goods destined for those provinces but included in a general rate spread over the whole system. Lawyers, however, do not adopt contradictory positions out of contrariness but on instructions from their clients.

Illustrative in this regard was the litigation in 1916 over an issue that is still topical: direct democracy. In that year the T.C. Norris government of Manitoba passed the Initiative and Referendum Act. The object was to allow initiatives and referenda by voters so as to free the province from

the supposed evils of a party system of politics. Opponents of the legislation attacked its constitutionality on the grounds that it violated ministerial responsibility, a tenet of the British parliamentary system, and that
the legislature could not delegate its authority. The legislation stipulated
that, on receipt of a petition from 8 per cent of the electorate, a bill, or
piece of legislation, would have to be submitted to a general vote and, if
passed, would become law regardless of what the legislative assembly
thought of it. This was controversial enough, but perhaps the most
extraordinary feature of the legislation was the manner of its testing in
the courts. The bill had been drafted by a well-known Winnipeg lawyer,
W.H. Trueman, on behalf of the Direct Legislation League. Yet, when the
constitutional question came before the court, the Manitoba government,
acting like a school debating society, retained Trueman to argue against
constitutionality and engaged Pitblado to argue for it. It was a sort of
Alice-in-Wonderland situation – the man responsible for drafting the legislation was being paid to argue that his handiwork was worthless. The
Manitoba Court of Appeal agreed with Trueman the debater that the legislation was invalid. This ruling was upheld by the Privy Council, which
concluded that the legislation amounted to interference with the lieutenant governor's power of disallowance and therefore infringed the BNA
Act.

Pitblado's first important foray into the railway business and board
hearings was in 1910 and it happened in rather a curious fashion. Shortly
after the board had been granted jurisdiction over telegraph tolls, the
Winnipeg Grain Exchange and the Board of Trade, both represented by
Pitblado, applied for a reduction in rates throughout western Canada,
more particularly those applicable to messages transmitted to Winnipeg
and the province of Manitoba. On an early appearance before the board,
Pitblado argued that section 315 of the Railway Act (the non-discrimina-
tion section) should apply to telegraph tolls. To accede to this argument
the board would have had to expand the inquiry beyond a merely local
concern by examining regional or perhaps national tolls, which it was
reluctant to do. However, it agreed to recommend to Ottawa that counsel
be appointed to conduct a general inquiry, with the result that Pitblado
and a colleague, W.S. Buell, were appointed to act for the government of
Canada in a broader inquiry. And so Pitblado, initially representing local
interests who advocated rate reductions, found himself, in effect, acting
as counsel to the board. He was very conscious of his delicate and ambig-
uous position, partisan one moment and neutral the next. At the conclusion of the hearings, the board asked him what he, as counsel to the

government, regarded as a 'fair schedule of rates to be put in force.' Pitblado was not required to give an immediate answer since he, and all the
other lawyers, had been told to submit their arguments in printed form –
written arguments as lawyers say. In his, Pitblado, after expressing hesitation in making any recommendations since he had only been appointed
'to assist the Board in bringing out the facts,' offered a rate schedule
which he thought would be 'fair to the telegraph companies and allow
them a reasonable return' while at the same time being 'reasonably fair to
the public.' The rates he proposed were in fact significantly less than
those currently charged, particularly in the west. The board, in a decision
delayed by the outbreak of the First World War, did indeed order reductions and the west did indeed benefit. This unusual, not to say extraordinary, change in Pitblado's status tempts one to speculate whether there
was something Machiavellian about it – he gained for his initial clients
essentially what they wanted, under the guise of neutrality.

Contemporaneously with the telegraph inquiry, the board conducted
its first general inquiry into country-wide freight rates and, though these
hearings began later than those on telegraph tolls, the decision was
handed down earlier, in 1914, in what became known as the western
freight rates case. Indubitably the most far-reaching piece of commercial
litigation heard in Canada up to that time, this case – which has been
described in chapter 2 – saw Pitblado acting for the city of Winnipeg and
again for the Winnipeg Board of Trade in what proved to be an unsuccessful attempt to resist rate increases granted the railways. Among other rulings, the case entrenched the mountain differential as an essential element
of the general rate structure of the country; the board held that it did not
violate the anti-discriminatory section 315 of the Railway Act. To that
extent, therefore, Pitblado was successful since the differential tended to
discourage westbound shipments of goods and to encourage their shipment eastward – through Winnipeg. Thus, on the strength of the western
freight rates case and the telegraph tolls case, Pitblado emerged as one of
the Canadian lawyers pre-eminent in the field of railway and telegraph
regulation, a rank he maintained for another forty years until the infirmi-
ties of age set in. During the First World War he appeared before the
board on various cases to balance the wartime financial needs of the railways with the national wartime interest of shipping goods at the lowest
cost.[5]

Almost at the same time as he was working on these major rate cases,
political events were brewing in Manitoba which led to Pitblado's
retainer by Premier T.C. Norris in 1915 to defend him on corruption

charges, a case which, thirty-five years later, Pitblado was to describe as one of the two or three most significant pieces of work he had done, apart from freight-rate litigation. The story has already been told in the chapter on Tilley, but, given its complexity, the main points should be repeated here. In June 1914 the premier, Sir Rodmond Roblin, was returned to office in a general election in spite of arousing suspicions of criminality in the awarding of contracts for construction of the legislative buildings. Following the election, ten defeated Conservative candidates and seven defeated Liberal ones filed petitions under the Controverted Elections Act seeking to overturn the election results in those seventeen ridings. Such petitions were a common feature of elections in the early years of this century, based as they often were on bribery of voters with free food and liquor and on ballot-box stuffing, and Manitoba was no exception. In that province it was common practice to do 'saw-offs,' that is, one petition would be dropped in return for another being withdrawn. Any remaining petitions, as would have been the case in 1914, would be negotiated in some political deal or might possibly even wind up in court. Everyone deplored the practice, but it was entrenched. Roblin started negotiations for 'saw-offs' and these were still continuing in April 1915 when, under severe public pressure, he was forced to appoint a royal commission, headed by Chief Justice T.G. Mathers, to investigate the scandal charges swirling around the new legislative buildings. The negotiations were still unresolved a month later when he abruptly resigned in favour of T.C. Norris, the Liberal leader of the opposition who became premier. Allegations soon followed that $50,000 had been paid to Norris to induce him first to 'stifle' the Mathers commission, whose work was under way, and, second, to ensure that the election petitions would all be withdrawn and that any by-elections made necessary by fresh cabinet appointments would be unopposed by the Conservatives. Norris immediately appointed a second royal commission headed by Mr Justice W.E. Perdue of the Manitoba Court of Appeal to examine those charges and engaged Pitblado to defend him personally.

There was some smoke but, as it turned out, no fire. The reader will recall the arrangements designed to suspend the Mathers commission so as to ensure a fair trial for the principal contractor, Thomas Kelly; none of these arrangements involved Norris and so the first of the two allegations against him collapsed. The Mathers commission continued in tandem with the Perdue commission at which, among many others, J.H. Howden, the former Conservative attorney general, testified to events prior to Roblin's resignation. Howden's own role in the building scandal had been, to say the least, questionable. He readily admitted the discussions about 'saw-offs' but then described a cloak-and-dagger drop-off of $25,000 in a coat rack at the Carleton Club; he retrieved the money and handed it over to a fellow Conservative who then handed it over to a Liberal stalwart, the latter boasting that for another $25,000 he could 'stifle' the Mathers commission and get the election petitions out of the way. The accusation that Norris received this cash rested on statements made outside the courtroom by shadowy figures, as Pitblado effectively demonstrated by his questioning of the witnesses. The new attorney general, A.B. Hudson, swore that there never had been any deal for saw-offs or for the suppression of the Mathers commission, let alone for the payment of money to achieve those objects. Norris testified to the same effect, as did Roblin at a time when he was under grave suspicion of fraud. He denied all suggestions of a corrupt deal with Norris or the new government, going on to say, moreover, that Norris was simply not the sort of man to enter into such criminal arrangements. Though they had long been political opponents, Roblin said, he had 'never known him [Norris] to do, or even to suggest, a dishonourable thing.' This testimony was drawn from Roblin by Pitblado's cross-examination, which, according to the Winnipeg *Free Press* on 3 July 1915, was conducted with 'great tact and brilliancy.' In the result, Norris and his government were completely exonerated and not just on a mere balance of doubt – the Perdue commission declared all the charges to be 'unfounded.' Norris's political career was saved by Pitblado's skilful performance; Pitblado once said of the occasion that it was the only case in his entire career that had made him nervous.

Pitblado, of course, had been asked by Norris to defend him not only because he was a good lawyer but because he was a staunch Liberal. In 1905 he had been elected president of the Winnipeg Liberal Association and had given unwavering support to the party ever since, though he never ran for office. Like many other prominent Liberals in 1917, he became caught up in the ferment of a proposed union government in the belief that only a coalition could effectively conduct Canada's war effort. On August 22nd Pitblado and a number of Liberal stalwarts met to condemn a recent decision reached by other Liberals to oppose any coalition government, more particularly one headed by Borden. Pitblado's group, while not wholeheartedly in favour of Borden, criticized Laurier for his anti-conscription, and anti-union government, stance. This condemnation of Laurier led to no animosity between him and Pitblado – indeed Laurier was inclined to make light of it for a year later he wrote cordially: 'How I would like to see you. Are you sometime coming East? How I would like to exchange views with you, to compare notes, to discuss the points where we differ, and to try to unveil the future, as to the principles and aspirations which at one time you and I held in common!' Laurier signed this letter, 'Believe me, ever my dear Isaac, your old friend Wilfrid Laurier.'

Speculation grew that Pitblado might be invited into a union cabinet, but there were four other western Liberals who were even more likely candidates, A.L. Sifton, the premier of Alberta, J.A. Calder, the minister of railways in Saskatchewan, T.A. Crerar, the minister of agriculture in Manitoba, and A.B. Hudson, the Manitoba attorney general. Borden was in touch with these four men either personally or through Arthur Meighen, and indirectly with Pitblado through the latter's brother John, in Montreal. On September 26th Meighen wrote Pitblado a long fervent letter, pleading with him to enter the war cabinet and guaranteeing him virtually any portfolio he wished. Meighen referred to the perhaps higher claims of Calder *et al.* (because they were politicians in office) by saying they had been invited to join but had so far declined to serve under a government headed by Borden. Therefore, Meighen went on, if Pitblado came in notwithstanding any diffidence he might feel about ousting his four fellow Liberals, should they later agree to join they could be accommodated and Meighen himself would willingly stand aside to facilitate their entry, a magnanimous gesture not lost on Pitblado; national unity and winning the war were far more important than personal ambitions. On the same day Borden telegraphed Pitblado to the same effect.

Pitblado replied to both in letters of October 1st. In essence he told Meighen that because he was not really part of the Liberal party apparatus he ought not to step in while the other four were undecided. He pointed out that for someone in his position – a relative upstart – to enter government ahead of those four or any of them would be bound to create disaffection among western Liberals generally and might even prompt them to withdraw their support from a union government. If it should turn out that none of them went into the government he might well agree, so he said, to enter the cabinet, assuring Meighen that he too was motivated not by partisan politics but by a wish to do his duty for the good of the country. In a brief letter to Borden, Pitblado said much the same thing. Borden responded on October 4th, telling Pitblado that the western four were coming to Ottawa for a conference and he appreciated 'the considerations which made it undesirable in your judgment to come to an immediate decision.' Obviously Borden saw some hope with the Calder group and, in the end, Calder, Sifton, and Crerar did enter the cabinet and Pitblado stayed out. He never had another chance at political office, even if he had been interested. He did, however, become a partisan of Meighen, whose disinterestedness he much admired and for whom he actively campaigned during the 1921 federal election. He remained a loyal defender of Meighen until the latter's death in 1960. One day in 1950 Pitblado lunched with Grant Dexter, then the managing editor of the *Free Press*, who cast aspersions upon Meighen's character. This did not sit well with Pitblado, who sent Dexter in confidence (for Meighen was still alive) a copy of Meighen's letter to him in 1917, underlining those passages in which Meighen offered to resign if that was necessary to fashion a union government. One cannot tell if Dexter replied; he probably remained unrepentant.[6]

The Winnipeg General Strike began on 15 May 1919 and ended on 26 June. This extremely well-known episode needs no description here, but several interesting aspects of Pitblado's involvement in the ensuing trials are worth noting. Arthur Meighen, then the acting minister of justice, made A.J. Andrews his agent in Winnipeg and lead counsel, and, balancing the prosecutorial team between Liberals and Conservatives, appointed to it Pitblado, W. Travers Sweatman, and two others. Andrews, a busy Winnipeg lawyer with much courtroom experience, was a Conservative, and, incidentally, the man with whom Pitblado in his early career had practised for eight years; he later gave much of the credit for the successful outcome of the prosecutions to Pitblado. By today's rules of legal ethics, neither Andrews nor Pitblado nor Sweatman could have been crown prosecutors for all three had been active in the Citizens Committee of 1000 formed by Winnipeg business and professional citizens to combat the strike – and strikers. In a speech he prepared for the convocation at which Dalhousie granted him an honorary degree in 1919, Pitblado said, 'I believe that in fighting the uprising in Winnipeg we citizens were doing so not merely for our own local benefit but for the benefit of all Canada.' He and the others viewed their jobs as prosecutors simply as an extension of their work on the Citizens Committee. Conflicts of interest, as we would now call them, were of much less significance in 1919 than now. Still, while the dual role of the three lawyers seems not to have caused much remark by lawyers defending the accused strikers, one of the latter, John Queen, conducting his own defence, commented on it bitterly.

The prosecution alleged that nine strike leaders were bent on overthrowing the government and establishing the rule of the working man and hence were guilty of seditious conspiracy, a charge akin to that of treason. Of the nine, seven were convicted; one R.B. Russell, said to be the ringleader, was sentenced to two years in prison; six (including John Queen) served one year each and the seventh served six months. Notwithstanding their convictions, all went on to useful careers and one, Queen, became a long-serving mayor of Winnipeg. Of those acquitted, one, A.A. Heaps, attributed his success to the fact that he had no lawyer defending him, thereby casting some aspersion upon the defence team, one of whom, J.E. Bird, had been prominent in the defence of the coal miners in the violent strikes in the Nanaimo coal fields in 1913. J.S. Woodsworth, though arrested on a charge of seditious libel arising from his editorial comments on the strike, never faced trial. Between them, the five lawyers acting for the crown received a total of $127,000 in fees; Andrews and Pitblado received the largest amounts, $33,000 and $27,000 respectively, considerable sums for those days.

Pitblado was not yet finished with the strike trials when he launched himself into a series of cases before the Board of Railway Commissioners and the Supreme Court of Canada which were to take up the bulk of his professional time for the next ten years. The series commenced with a case begun early in 1919 in which he represented grain-elevator companies in a heated dispute with the CPR over charges by the railway for stop-over of cars in transit and for switching them at rail terminals. Pitblado's arguments were reminiscent of those in the disinfectant case and were equally unavailing: the charges should be part of a general rate and not levied on a specific shipper. In 1921 Pitblado for the first time acted for the Canadian National Railways as its representative on a board of conciliation in a wage dispute with the railway running trades, but it was not the first time he had been retained by a railway. After the western freight rate case of 1914, in which he had been 'harshly critical' of the Canadian Northern Railway, the latter had retained him in a dispute with its running trades; a few months later, the CPR asked him to serve as its nominee on a conciliation board set up to resolve a similar dispute, the first occasion on which he acted for the CPR. And it was two years after that engagement by the railway company that, as we have seen, Pitblado was locking horns with it over disinfectants in cattle cars. Also in 1921 he was allied with the railways, though not formally representing them, in a claim made by British Columbia shippers for 'equalization of freight rates,' in effect, for removal of the mountain differential. Not only the railways looked on the surcharge as a sacred cow; so did the city of Winnipeg and its Board of Trade, both of which were represented, successfully, by Pitblado. His argument for retention of the differential was really a plea for interprovincial trade barriers, an issue that, though in a different context, is still with us. He argued that the differential 'did not prevent any-body from doing business but merely prevented them from expanding in the rapid manner they wished.' He then extolled British Columbia as a sort of paradise which justified charging higher freight rates on goods shipped to it since, he said, 'it enjoyed so many natural advantages for being a seaport that equalization of freight rates would enable British Columbia manufacturers to come into the prairie provinces and take away trade that rightfully belonged to businessmen east of the moun-tains.' By Pitblado's lights, it was British Columbia, not Winnipeg, that was acting selfishly.

That same year, Pitblado, acting for the Winnipeg Grain Exchange, appeared before the Hyndman Royal Grain Inquiry Commission in an important investigation concerning the grading of wheat. A few months later, as the representative of both major railways, he sat on another con-ciliation board to settle a wage dispute with the railway-shop employees. And a few months after that, Pitblado, along with Lafleur and Geoffrion, was at the royal commission to consider rail charges for commodity haul-age by land compared with charges for water-borne transportation across the Great Lakes. Less than a month later, in March 1923, Pitblado appeared at a session of a committee of the federal cabinet convened to hear a last-ditch appeal by British Columbia, represented by the feisty Gerry McGeer, from the decision of the Board of Railway Commissioners refusing to remove the mountain differential. In the run-up to the hear-ings themselves, Pitblado addressed a packed meeting in Winnipeg orga-nized by the Board of Trade on the virtue of the mountain differential and the absolute necessity – from Winnipeg's point of view – to maintain it. Just as water 'cannot be made to run up hill,' so railways should not be expected to run their main line through mountain ranges without being compensated for the additional expense of maintenance and operating costs. The cabinet, sensitive to the politics of the situation and unwilling to pit one of the western provinces against another, pusillanimously refused to make a ruling, sending the issue back to the board where it died; Winnipeg and Pitblado had triumphed once again. Six months later, in November 1923, the province of Manitoba engaged him to oppose an application by the railway companies for an increase in express rates, that is, the charges for consigned shipments of parcels. The railways' applica-tion remained dormant until 1927 when it was renewed. Surprisingly, the British Columbia government then appointed Pitblado to act for it, infuri-ating McGeer who for so long had been the doughty champion of the province. That the province should have engaged a lawyer who had so often argued against its interests was a tribute to the man and his skills in the field.

But these encounters paled in significance when compared to the excitement and importance of the Crow rate hearings in 1924 and 1925. Pitblado was involved throughout these hearings, opposing the railways and advancing or attempting to advance the commercial interests of the Winnipeg Grain Exchange, the grain-elevator companies, and the Winnipeg Board of Trade by ensuring maximum volumes of goods shipped through Winnipeg not just from points in Manitoba but from Saskatchewan and Alberta. At the same time, he opposed any diversion of traffic by the railways across the Great Lakes or via the Soo Line (in the case of the CPR) to the United States.

The Board of Railway Commissioners found itself almost in an impossible situation in trying to balance competing interests advanced by highly articulate and well-informed lawyers such as Lafleur and Tilley, and, more particularly, Pitblado, and in attempting to do so it sometimes created artificial barriers. Nowhere was this more vividly illustrated than at a general freight inquiry held by the board in 1927. In the western freight rates case in 1914, the board had decreed that, though the actual distance between the Lakehead and Winnipeg was 420 miles, the mileage for calculating freight rates between the two points was to be 290. This ruling obviously favoured companies shipping goods from eastern Canada to the prairies over those firms in Alberta or British Columbia that shipped to the east where a mile was a mile, not a 'constructive mile.' Moreover, it also favoured distributors in Winnipeg who, to bring goods from eastern Canada, had only to pay haulage on 290 miles instead of 420, whereas shippers in Vancouver were given no such advantage. The logical basis for chopping 130 miles from the distance actually hauled is hard to ascertain but it is not difficult to understand either the displeasure of shippers from Vancouver whose freight charges were calculated upon geography or the satisfaction of the merchants of Winnipeg at the disparity. Yet the board, in trying to make a complicated situation less complicated, sometimes achieved the opposite. When it ruled that export grain shipped to British Columbia must be at the Crow rate proportioned for distance, in the case of Edmonton 766 miles and from Calgary 640 miles, the CPR fixed a rate from Calgary to Vancouver equal to that charged by the CNR from Edmonton; since the haul from Calgary was shorter than that from Edmonton by 126 miles, the CPR had added a non-existent 126 miles to its Calgary-Vancouver haul and gained in effect a higher rate. In spite of protests, the board refused to intervene and British Columbia was unable to rectify what seemed an obviously unfair situation. Pitblado, like any lawyer worth his salt, tried valiantly to defend the interests of his client even though they seemed indefensible. He claimed that the constructive mileage between the Lakehead and Winnipeg was an advantage to the prairie provinces which should be continued since the merchants of British Columbia and manufacturers there could ship their goods through the Panama Canal to eastern Canada at vastly cheaper rates than the same shipments could be carried by rail from the Pacific Coast to eastern Canada. Any attempt to establish parity among goods shipped between the two regions, that is, the prairies and British Columbia, would be bound to lead to regional discontent and economic hardship on the prairies. The board agreed with him.[7]

Interspersed with these appearances in railway matters was his work with the commission set up to apportion physical and monetary assets between the newly created United Church and those Presbyterian congregations that chose not to unite; one of his other colleagues was Walter C. Murray, president of the University of Saskatchewan. Pitblado had been raised as a Presbyterian; his father, from 1893, was first pastor of Westminster Church in Winnipeg. That parish, in 1912, built a new church on Maryland Street, a large edifice which still stands. The Reverend C.B. Pitblado officiated at its opening but died a year later. Its congregation elected to join church union and the parish became Westminster United Church; Isaac remained a parishioner. He was a logical choice for commissioner, with his long history of church affiliation and his reputation as a fair-minded man. It seems that he and Mr Justice Lyman Duff, the chairman of the commission, shouldered the burden of its work, for Duff wrote to him: 'To me, one of the gratifying incidents, if not the most gratifying of all, has been the opportunity of getting into closer personal relations with yourself. I can never forget what a tower of strength you were at critical moments. I believe you have not the remotest notion what relief I owed to you at times when the situation seemed to be almost hopeless.' It was not only Duff who was grateful, for the church itself told Pitblado: 'To you personally we owe much for we are aware that you threw into this most difficult task not only your fine legal powers but a vigor, a self-restraint and a mastery of the problem which are beyond price.'

In 1929 Pitblado found himself defending still another Manitoba premier on allegations of corruption. John Bracken's government had awarded a concession to the Winnipeg Electric Company to develop a hydro installation at Seven Sisters Falls. In a political speech at Oak Lake, Manitoba, F.G. Taylor, the Conservative leader, alleged that the company had paid $50,000 to Bracken to secure the concession. (By an odd coincidence this was the same amount allegedly involved in the 1915 payoff to Premier Norris.) Bracken, as premier, was forced to respond to the accusation, which he did by appointing a three-man royal commission and engaging Pitblado and A.E. Johnston to represent him. Pitblado's old mentor and colleague, A.J. Andrews, represented the company. The circumstances were far less complicated than those in 1915 and also differed in that only a few people (among whom were the editors of the Winnipeg *Tribune*) believed Bracken was a 'bribable' man – unlike Roblin. Pitblado's defence of Bracken was vigorous and skilled. He established beyond doubt that the statements made by Taylor were based on second-hand information at best, perhaps even third-hand, and fell into the realm of rumour and conjecture. There are not many contemporary accounts of Pitblado in action but the *Tribune* had this to say of his appearance before the commission: 'He is of lighter build than his learned friends and opponents; his dark hair is tinged with grey above the ears. He has an air of unlawyerly shrewdness, and his manner and speech are almost conversationally argumentative.' This description of Pitblado's speaking style accords with an amusing description of him in the Winnipeg *Free Press* which spoke of 'his charming, pleasant, expensive baritone which has flowed in its time into the ears of the very gods – railway commissioners and such like.'

There was an interesting aftermath. In 1951 Pitblado appeared before a Manitoba legislative committee which was considering a bill to expropriate the power-generating assets of the Winnipeg Electric Company, including its hydro installation at Seven Sisters Falls. The company in 1928 had been granted (and this was of course the basis for the accusations against Bracken) the right of power development until 1962, with the proviso that, if the provincial government decided to acquire the generating station, compensation would be paid to the company based on the Water Powers Act; that legislation, briefly, allowed for a proper appraised value, including loss of future profits, and, in case of dispute, provided for arbitration. The Manitoba government instead proposed to pay only the original capital cost less depreciation. This was not expropriation but confiscation, as Pitblado pointed out to the committee on behalf of the company. In a submission lasting four and one-half hours he expressed dismay that a provincial government would acquire assets by 'unjust' methods. Though he was eighty-four at the time, as the *Tribune* noted, 'he acted like a man of 55. The mechanism of mind and body was unchilled by age. His gestures teemed with punch and fire.' When a committee member deferentially suggested that Pitblado might prefer to sit, he retorted, 'I'll do this job standing up.' But the legislation went through. Some years later in an identical situation, the British Columbia government took over the assets of the principal power-generating company in that province but, unlike Manitoba, provided for arbitration of the value of assets. Perhaps a lesson had been learned.[8]

Pitblado, having extricated successfully a second premier from potentially ruinous allegations, was himself to face embarrassing allegations three years later, in 1932, not of fraud or corruption but of negligent performance of his duties as chairman of the board of governors of the University of Manitoba. The circumstances of the affair and the subsequent royal commission before which he testified in self-defence formed the most painful episode of his professional career. In August 1932 John A. Machray was arrested and charged with the theft from the University of Manitoba of just under one million dollars. He had been a pillar of the Winnipeg establishment for thirty years, a highly respected member of the legal profession in whose office two distinguished lawyers had worked, R.A. Dennistoun, later a judge of the Manitoba Court of Appeal, and C.H. Locke, later a judge of the Supreme Court of Canada. Machray was a nephew of a former archbishop of Rupert's Land and he himself was chancellor of the diocese, and his firm was the investment agent both for the diocese and for the university. He was bursar for the university and in 1925 had become chairman of the board of governors. Thus he wore three hats: investment manager, bursar, and chairman of the board. No one questioned the propriety of multiple positions – until the defalcations were discovered. He lived comfortably but not ostentatiously and was regarded on all sides as a man of the utmost probity. After his arraignment on the charges of theft from the university it emerged that there were also roughly a million dollars missing from diocesan funds; although he was never formally charged with their theft he had undoubtedly embezzled them and in doing so had bankrupted the diocese. Not just the diocese; the retired and saintly Archbishop S.P. Matheson had entrusted his paltry funds to Machray for investment, and lost everything.

Machray, suffering from terminal cancer, pleaded guilty to the charges of theft and was sentenced to seven years in Stony Mountain Penitentiary, where he died a few months later. Everything about the affair was tragic; all the endowment funds of the university gone, all the diocesan funds, all poor old Archbishop Matheson's mite, the shock to the parishes of the diocese, the shock to the academic community of the university, the dis-

belief of Machray's friends and legal colleagues, and Machray's own dis-
grace and early death after going to prison. 'How could it have
happened?' was the question universally asked and to answer it the
Bracken government appointed a three-man royal commission headed by
Mr Justice W.F.A. Turgeon of Saskatchewan. Pitblado's involvement in
the debacle began during the period between 1917 and 1924, when he
served as chairman of the university's board of governers (the first person
to hold this post after the reconstitution of the university in 1917). Though
as a member of the council he had possessed no authority over finances,
he certainly had such authority as chairman. Unknown to him, however,
was the fact that Machray, as the university's manager for investment of
its endowment funds, had already been for many years engaged in systematic embezzlement. By far the largest sums taken were after Machray
became chairman of the board of governors in 1925, but those taken in
prior years were by no means trifling.

In retrospect, as the commission subsequently determined, there were
many factors that Machray took advantage of to carry out his criminal
schemes – most importantly, the acquiescence and connivance of his partner and law clerk in devising false financial statements and reporting
non-existent stocks and bonds as part of the university portfolio. But how
was this possible when there was a requirement for an annual audit of
accounts? Pitblado found himself accused of negligence or, possibly, of
turning a blind eye to Machray's larceny. Soon after Pitblado assumed the
chairmanship of the board, it had received an audited statement from the
university's auditors that all funds and securities were intact (the Turgeon
commission did not explain how this could be, but the answer undoubtedly is that Machray disclosed to the auditor securities and deposits
which in reality belonged to other people). A year later, a change in government policy played into Machray's hands. In 1918 the province
decided as a cost-cutting measure that the university could no longer hire
its own auditors and that the function would be taken over by the provincial comptroller general; in each of the next two years, this official certified that all was in order. There was a delay in the preparation of the 1921
audit, about which Pitblado had complained in writing, but eventually it
was provided. All was in order. Astonishingly, for the next three years, no
audit was completed in spite of attempts by Pitblado and his board to
secure them. Various bureaucratic excuses were made: a strike by print-
ers, changes in accounting records, delay pure and simple, but, eventually, in August 1924, the comptroller general certified that all endowment
funds were intact and that all securities were in order.

By that date, however, Pitblado and all his other board members had resigned in a dispute over selection of a new campus, Pitblado and his colleagues favouring a site in Tuxedo while the university administration preferred one at the Agricultural College at St Vital – which was eventually chosen. Machray was appointed as Pitblado's successor, whereupon the fox indeed had been let loose in the chicken run. Although the comptroller general in January 1925 again certified the soundness of the university funds, there was no further audit during Machray's tenure. He found it easier to hoodwink provincial bureaucrats than chartered accountants in private practice because for seven years the board never received a financial statement audited in accordance with generally accepted accounting principles, as the chartered accounting profession would phrase it. In May 1932 the comptroller general, suddenly coming to life, told the attorney general that there was something radically wrong with the university accounts, which showed that Machray's investment firm owed the university just less than $600,000. Bracken was campaigning for re-election and this sort of information, if it became public, would not be conducive to his re-election hopes. Unbelievably, on 13 July 1932, even in the face of the comptroller general's report, Machray was reappointed as a member of the board of governors. Bracken, through Pitblado's skills, had earlier escaped ruin from unjustified accusations; he should more logically have been called to account for this decision; three days after Machray's reappointment to the board, Bracken was re-elected. And a month later Machray was in jail.

As might have been expected, in all this there was much finger-pointing and very little *mea culpa*. Pitblado was one of those against whom fingers were pointed, a circumstance that caused him great distress. (Two others against whom fingers were also pointed were Dennistoun and Locke, both of whom were partners of Machray until they joined the armed forces in the First World War. As former partners, they might well have been held liable for Machray's embezzlements conducted through the law firm. Yet they both testified that they were completely unaware of what was happening, and were exonerated.) Pitblado spent long hours preparing a brief – hardly 'brief' because it ran to thirty-eight typed pages – outlining the course of events, weighing their importance, and citing court decisions supporting his position, which essentially was that the board of governors was justified in relying upon certificates from auditors, even if delayed, and, moreover, had repeatedly tried to secure audited statements from the comptroller general.

He showed up at the Turgeon commission with all guns firing. Describing his appearance as a witness, the Winnipeg *Tribune* reported: 'For two hours he poured devastating volleys into the leading counsel's arguments [that Pitblado was in some way responsible for what had happened]. He was merciless in his treatment and did not mince words in conveying his meaning.' And, still on the stand two days later, he invoked scripture, in which he had been well versed by his father, when arguing that innocent people such as himself were being made scapegoats: 'Now a word or two about scapegoats. Do you remember how in the Old Testament the High Priest Aaron put upon the goat all the sins of the children of Israel and sent it off into the wilderness. That is what Mr. McWilliams [the lawyer acting as commission counsel] is trying to do. Well here is one goat that is not going to take on its head all the iniquities of the children of Israel. I am a pretty lively old goat yet [he was sixty-six] and I am not going off into the wilderness dishonoured if I can help it.' The Turgeon commission unreservedly exonerated Pitblado. During his tenure as chairman of the board of governors he had done all he could to ensure that the board received proper audited statements and, moreover, the commission declared that had Pitblado remained as chairman of the board the large-scale defalcations by Machray would never have occurred. Pitblado, immensely relieved by the finding, was even more gratified by the letters that poured in from friends, legal colleagues, and opponents expressing satisfaction at the outcome. Clearly, however, many of those people had had nagging doubts before the commission reported. It took a long time before Pitblado's anger against McWilliams cooled. In 1940, on hearing rumours that McWilliams might be appointed lieutenant governor, Pitblado wrote his old lawyer friend Leonard W. Brockington, then chairman of the Canadian Broadcasting Commission, to urge him to do what he could to prevent the appointment since McWilliams was 'very unpopular and lacks qualifications for the position.' Brockington spoke to the prime minister, Mackenzie King, who told Brockington that he had thought of Pitblado himself as a possible appointment but did not think he 'would consider it.' McWilliams did eventually become lieutenant governor and in that capacity was a head-table guest at the lavish dinner in 1950 to mark Pitblado's sixtieth anniversary as a lawyer.[9]

Through the 1930s Pitblado kept up his very busy practice in railway-related matters, such as conciliation boards and wage disputes, but he was busier in matters related to the Winnipeg Grain Exchange. The Exchange was coming under increasing pressure from the 'pools,' the farmer cooperatives, and from the public to discontinue the grain-futures market and to leave to the producers through their pools the sale of grain on domestic and international markets. Pitblado, on behalf of the Exchange, appeared before two important royal commissions examining these issues, the first in 1931 headed by Sir Josiah Stamp (the English economist) and the second in 1936 under Mr Justice Turgeon. The latter commission was lengthy, extending well over a year and not bringing down its report until 1938. During the course of its hearings it travelled to Europe to examine the international marketing of grain. One of the witnesses called by Pitblado was H.R. MacMillan of Vancouver, the lumberman, whose export lumber business thrived in the international market; he deplored any notion of a government board to sell grain – or lumber. Pitblado was involved throughout the hearings of the two royal commissions and did a good job for his client, for both commissions decided not to recommend radical changes in grain marketing. The Grain Exchange remained alive, but perhaps not well, because it had become obvious that its control over the grain trade was likely to be weakened. Indeed, the outbreak of war eighteen months after the Turgeon report brought radical changes, which led ultimately to the establishment of the Canadian Wheat Board as the principal marketing agency for prairie grain producers.

Pitblado's journey to Europe with the Turgeon commission was his second within the year for late in 1936 he made his one and only appearance in the Privy Council. The province of Manitoba had imposed a levy on earnings of all employed persons in the province and the legislation was challenged by Ottawa, which argued that the tax, really a form of income tax, could not be applied to members of the military or to the federal civil service. Pitblado acted for the province in the Supreme Court of Canada, where he was successful, and also in the Privy Council, again successfully. Incidentally, although Pitblado appeared in the Supreme Court of Canada only five times, he was successful in four of those appearances. Yet the sampling, as pollsters say, is too small for the drawing of any conclusions.

The Second World War caused no lessening of Pitblado's work, though some of it may have been done without fees. He and all the members of his firm wrote J.L. Ralston, a familiar legal opponent who had become minister of national defence, offering to do any government work in Manitoba without charge as a 'contribution to the war effort.' Ralston said that he would call on them without hesitation as he knew their 'readiness to serve can be taken at one hundred percent.' Thus, in 1944, Pitblado was retained by Ottawa to represent it in test cases before the Exchequer Court to determine the income-tax liability of farmer cooperatives, but the issue was eventually handed over to a royal commission. As before, there was ample fee-paying work from grain and elevator companies and from railways having problems with their unions over wartime regulation of wages. However, the war brought more serious problems than the nuisance of regulated wages. Though operation of the rail systems was an essential wartime service, shortage of supplies and labour had made maintenance of the physical plant – road-bed, rolling stock, shops – very difficult and wartime taxation of earnings had prevented the railways from building capital reserves to finance post-war renovations and replacements. Accordingly, the two principal rail systems, the CPR and the CNR, along with other smaller lines, decided at the end of the war to apply for a general rate increase and hired Pitblado as chief counsel to act for them. It was the most important piece of freight-rate business since the Crow rate hearings in the 1920s and the most arduous that Pitblado himself had undertaken. The hearings before the Board of Transport Commissioners (which had replaced the Board of Railway Commissioners) began in February 1947 and ended a year later with publication of the report. In that time the commissioners criss-crossed the country hearing evidence and submissions; not all the horde of lawyers involved trooped along, nor was it necessary for them to do so, but Pitblado had to. The sessions opened in Union Station at Ottawa on February 15th. The Ottawa *Evening Journal* described the event as 'probably the most glittering galaxy of legal talent ever gathered together under a Canadian ceiling ... This array of ... bombardiers is drawn up into battle lines in what promises to be the mightiest tussle of the law books that the Dominion has ever seen. The stakes are perhaps the biggest too, running into potential billions of dollars.'

Among the opponents of the increase was Pitblado's own province. After years of representing its interests in freight matters, was he now on the wrong side of the tracks? The strategy of the opponents was to try to convert the application for a specific increase – 30 per cent across the board – into a general inquiry into the rate structure country-wide and thereby delay any increase to the railways. The railways, through Pitblado, strenuously opposed any such tactic, arguing that cash was needed immediately to rebuild systems worn down by neglect forced by wartime conditions. The board, recognizing the urgency of the railways' position though not pre-judging the extent of any increase, decided that the hearing should be confined to considering the economic necessities of the railroads in the post-war era; a general inquiry could come later if thought appropriate. The application for a percentage increase was unusual; hitherto, applications had been for increases or decreases in published tariffs or rates in particular regions of the country. This application was all-encompassing but there were some exemptions. The railways agreed that any increase awarded should not be applied to prairie grain shipments covered by the Crow rate or to grain shipped to the Pacific coast for export. Presumably by design, and perhaps on Pitblado's advice, this was a very shrewd move because it tended to defuse opposition from the prairie provinces to a general increase by ensuring that the principal commodity of the region would be unaffected, and even opposition from British Columbia was muted since the export grain that filled the port terminals and provided longshoring jobs would also be exempted. As well, the board itself, in light of the railways' decision, could be expected to take a more sympathetic view of their case. The railways also softened their demand in the case of coal and coke shipments, requesting less than a 30 per cent increase for each commodity – which benefited not only Alberta and British Columbia but also the Maritimes. Pitblado, in his closing arguments to the board, made much of these concessions by the railways. British Columbia had argued that if an increase was granted the rate on shipments from the province eastward should be lower than the general rate. Pitblado poured withering scorn on this argument. As the result of a decision of the Board of Railway Commissioners in the 1920s lowering the export rate to British Columbia to the level of the Crow rate, the business of the port of Vancouver had burgeoned; even Gerry McGeer, whose efforts as special counsel to the British Columbia government in the 1920s had brought significant commercial benefit to the province, had himself agreed in the 1930s that Vancouver had prospered under the rulings of the board. For the present government of British Columbia to plead discrimination, Pitblado proclaimed, was hypocrisy.

On 15 March 1947 Pitblado celebrated his eightieth birthday while the commission was still sitting in Ottawa. That day, J.L. Ralston, acting for the Maritimes (like Pitblado, he was a Maritimer), took to his feet to tell the commissioners that his principal opponent had reached that milestone. The chief commissioner, J.A. Cross, and all the lawyers present, rose one by one to pay tribute to a very spry old man. The occasion made its way into the proceedings of the Senate, which in July debated a bill to force civil servants to retire at age sixty-five. Senator J.T. Haig observed that there was not much sense in fixing sixty-five as the arbitrary age for retirement when men such as Isaac Pitblado, aged eighty, could conduct an important case like the rate inquiry. And later in the year, Ralston again alluded to Pitblado's vigour notwithstanding his age, describing him as 'that great young man' and complimenting him on his presentation even though, as he hastened to add, he disagreed with most of what Pitblado had said. This was lawyer talk, between friendly rivals.

After reviewing the 19,000 pages of evidence, the Board of Transport Commissioners handed down its decision on 30 March 1948; the railways were given a 21 per cent general rate increase on all goods, except for the specific exemptions which the railways had agreed to at the outset. Though less than they had asked for, the railways were content but not so their opponents; seven of the provinces initiated an appeal to the federal cabinet, which convened a committee – the Canadian equivalent of the Privy Council – to hear the appeal. On the committee, which convened in October 1948, were Louis St Laurent, C.D. Howe, Brooke Claxton, Paul Martin, and Lester B. Pearson – an impressive group. Pitblado again represented the railways. The Ottawa *Journal*, in the breezy journalistic style of the day, gave a full report of the opening session. Some members of the cabinet who were still 'in diapers' when Pitblado started his practice got 'an eyeful and earful as this spry oldster laid down the law to them. The 81-year-old "Mr. Pit" who still rates as the Dominion's top legal expert on freight rates headed the battery of legal talent ... He was really bossman too. Built like a low slung middle weight fighter and with an agile mind to go with an amazing physical endurance.' In its account of the afternoon session, the *Journal* kept up its vivid style: Pitblado 'rattled off a two hour rejoinder, much of it right off the cuff and delivered at machine gun pace. Some of the cabinet members' eyes bulged at this forensic display, for few of them had seen the nimble Mr. Pitblado in action before ... Although this is old stuff to the Winnipegger, all of his previous cabinet appearances were made before most of the present ministers were in politics.'

Pitblado and his clients carried the day: the cabinet committee upheld the 21 per cent award. For their part, the railways, as a sort of counter-appeal, asked the cabinet to grant them an additional 20 per cent by way of emergency relief. The cabinet declined to adjudicate on that application, sending it back to the Board of Transport Commissioners; a year later, the board granted an additional sum of 8 per cent, afterwards increasing it to 20 per cent. Pitblado, however, did not participate in that application – the earlier application of 1947–8 was his last engagement in a major rate case. Yet it was not his final appearance. There were several matters he handled, including representation for the railways on a federal conciliation board in 1950 to deal with wage claims by a total of 142,000 employees. His last documented appearance in a freight-related matter was before the Board of Grain Commissioners in Winnipeg in 1955, when he represented the Lakehead Terminal Elevators Association; he was then eighty-eight years old.[10]

Why was he so skilled at freight rates and related matters? There are the obvious answers – brains, a good memory (perhaps a more important ingredient for a successful lawyer than brain power), the ability to concentrate, and, of course, sheer hard work. But in his case there was a more important reason. The work was terribly complicated: experts would troop into his office laden with volumes of records on every conceivable aspect of operating a railway, or a grain terminal, or a chain of country elevators, or the Winnipeg Grain Exchange – so that it was easy to become hopelessly mired in detail. Alan Sweatman (son of W. Travers Sweatman, one of the crown prosecutors associated with Pitblado at the strike trials in 1919) worked in the Pitblado firm and observed Pitblado at close hand for nearly twenty years. To start with, Pitblado was a 'clean desk' lawyer – no clutter in his office; the floor was not an auxiliary filing cabinet. When the experts arrived with their array of statistics Pitblado would not allow himself to become bogged down in them. What am I to get out of these? What is there in them that is helpful to our cause? Or unhelpful? What does it all mean? He had the knack of quickly grasping the nub of a complex problem and, once prepared, presented the case before the appropriate tribunal – the Board of Railway Commissioners or the courts – effectively. He had a good instinct for courtroom advocacy. With his strong but pleasing voice he worked the judges well, as lawyers say, and never needed to repeat himself. On the other hand, he could easily lapse into pleasant banter with the other lawyers or the judges if the atmosphere got a bit heated.

On 23 February 1950 the Manitoba Bar Association sponsored a gala black-tie dinner to honour Pitblado on the sixtieth anniversary of his call to the bar. Countless members of the Canadian élite were present or, if absent, sent messages, from Prime Minister W.L. Mackenzie King down. The association later bound in two fat volumes all the letters and telegrams that had poured in and presented them to Pitblado, who, greatly touched, treasured them and frequently showed them to visitors and friends. It was, of course, one of those occasions prompting reminiscenses, stories and anecdotes, and recollections of departed legal colleagues and adversaries, the sort of evening that marks the end of an era. Pitblado's labours on behalf of the organized bar over many years were warmly acknowledged. In Manitoba he had become a bencher (that is, a member of the governing body) of the Law Society in 1901 and was regularly re-elected until 1934, when he became a life – non-elected – bencher;

he continued in that capacity until his death – a tenure without parallel in Manitoba. Undoubtedly, his continued re-election as a representative of the profession was largely due to his unfailing courtesy towards, and encouragement of, younger members of the profession, combined with a warm manner and great charm. There was never any 'side' to Isaac Pitblado. He never forgot the advantages bestowed on him by older members of the profession, such as Aikins and Colin Campbell. A Winnipeg lawyer, Ivan Deacon, recalled that as a junior lawyer he had attended a meeting of creditors of a large commercial concern without correct documentation. When it seemed that his client might suffer through his oversight, he went for help to Pitblado, who dropped what he was doing and quickly offered a solution to the young lawyer; Deacon was eternally grateful for his rescue by a man he had never previously met but had heard of as one willing to help younger lawyers.

In 1915 he had become president of the Manitoba Bar Association and in 1918 was appointed to represent the province at the conference of commissioners of uniformity of legislation, an unheralded and unsung but practical organization formed by the provinces in an attempt to achieve uniformity of statutes – for example, those relating to debt enforcement – so that dealings between provinces would be predictable and simpler. During the course of his long career, there were many pleasant bar-association gatherings, outstanding among which was the joint meeting in London in 1924 of the American Bar Association and the Canadian Bar Association, of which Pitblado was then a vice-president. He and his wife were presented to the king and queen and, at one of the many dinners hosted by the several inns of court, Pitblado spoke on behalf of Canadian lawyers in response to the speech by the lord chief justice of England, Lord Hewart. He capped his career of service to the profession by election as president of the Canadian Bar Association in 1934. It meant taking virtually a year out of his practice. As president, he travelled to every province to meet the local bar associations, and on those occasions he enjoyed cracking jokes at the expense of the profession. As a matter of fact, he enjoyed cracking jokes on any occasion because he had a great sense of humour. Several times he told the same story, one of the better examples of a lowly genre. During the Napoleonic wars, a group of lawyers in London raised a regiment which was reviewed by the king. When the latter inquired what the regiment's name was, the honorary colonel said that no name had yet been picked because the regiment had only recently been formed, whereupon the king suggested, 'The Devil's Own.' A fairly witty response, but at Pitblado's anniversary dinner real wit and wisdom were displayed by his old pal, Leonard Brockington, perhaps the finest orator Canada has produced, who paid a brief but jolly tribute. Arthur Meighen, nearly as eloquent an orator as Brockington, also spoke feelingly. Pitblado himself spoke. One can forgive him, but he spoke too long – nostalgia got the better of him. He might have taken his cue from Lear: 'We'll ... tell old tales and laugh/ at gilded butterflies, and hear poor rogues/ talk of court news; and will talk with them too:/ who loses and who wins; who's in, who's out.'[11]

Pitblado's first marriage had ended with unpleasant divorce proceedings, in which he was the petitioner; there had been a son of the marriage, Edward, who served in the First World War and then, after studying at Oxford on a Rhodes Scholarship, joined his father's firm.[12] Pitblado's second wife, May, whom he had married in 1907, died in 1950 and afterwards he lived on in his comfortable apartment on Wellington Crescent. Trite though it sounds, he grew old, and older, gracefully. In February 1960 he observed his seventieth anniversary as a practising lawyer, which made him the senior practising lawyer in Canada if not in the entire commonwealth. With his final appearance before the Board of Grain Commissioners in 1955, his litigation practice had ended; thereafter he was purely a solicitor, advising clients on business and personal difficulties. He had good business sense, an instinct for what was commercially important, and this ability led to directorships of large Canadian corporations, banks, and trust companies; at one time he was chairman of Winnipeg-based Investors' Syndicate, the large financial concern, which is still going strong. In March 1964 he reached his ninety-seventh birthday; he had always held a firm belief that work keeps a man alive, and he followed his own advice, maintaining regular hours at his office until the last two years of his life when he tended to stay at home. He enjoyed seeing friends such as Alan Sweatman but wished to know beforehand of any intended visit so that he could in the interval catch up on current affairs and local goings-on and then share this information with his guest. He made a conscious effort to remain alert and in this regard succeeded admirably. After June 1964 he no longer went to his office, nor did he see clients, but he kept in touch by reading the law and business reports as well as innumerable magazines. One of the last people to visit him, just a few days before his death, was his old friend Brockington.

But his internal mechanism just ran down – old age killed him. On 6 December 1964, alert almost to the end, he became unconscious and died a few hours later. As the newspapers noted, the dean of the Canadian legal profession had died. But he was also lauded as a 'bonny fighter'

who was 'always scrupulously fair' and invariably even-tempered. After
an elaborate funeral at his, and his father's, church, Westminster United,
Pitblado was buried in the family plot at Elmwood Cemetery. His divorce
from his first wife, the Machray scandal and the resulting Turgeon commission, and the death of his second wife were really the only events that
marred an otherwise astonishingly happy and satisfying life. He had
never been interested in being anything but a lawyer. His stature always
gave rise to speculation about his going to the bench, but there is no indication that any formal offer was made; if it was, he refused it. In 1932 Mr
Justice L.A. Cannon of the Supreme Court of Canada and a good friend of
Pitblado urged him to accept an appointment to that court, where his
'clear mind and ... talent for compromise' would 'help us in our work.'
Cannon told Pitblado that he would personally intercede with the prime
minister, R.B. Bennett, and Hugh Guthrie, the minister of justice, if Pitblado would but give the word. Pitblado did not give the word.

   In an editorial on the occasion of Pitblado's anniversary dinner in 1950,
the Winnipeg *Free Press* had said: 'Mr. Pitblado will be ranked as one of a
small and notable company some of whom have passed on but others like
Mr. Pitblado still hold the cords: Eugene Lafleur, W.N. Tilley, Aimé Geoffrion ...' That editorial may have been written by the renowned journalist
Bruce Hutchison, who was then the associate editor of the *Free Press*.
Whoever the author was, however, he was remarkably perceptive in asso-
ciating those four men; all in their lifetimes were gratified to be linked
with the others in the brotherhood of the law.[13]

Eugene Lafleur *c.* 1924 (McCarthy Tétrault, Montreal)

The Privy Council in session, July 1920. Left to right: Lord Atkinson, Viscount Cave, Viscount Haldane, Viscount Dunedin, Mr Justice Lyman Duff. All these faces were familiar to Lafleur, Tilley, Geoffrion, and Farris (National Archives of Canada)

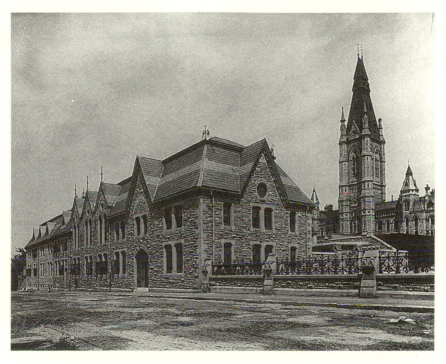

The original Supreme Court of Canada building. It was torn down to make way for the present Supreme Court of Canada building, which opened in January 1946 (National Archives of Canada)

W.N. Tilley as depicted in a newspaper sketch at the Perdue commission hearings, Winnipeg, 1915 (Provincial Archives of Manitoba)

W.N. Tilley – painted posthumously from photographs (The Law Society of Upper Canada Archives, Photograph Collection)

Aimé Geoffrion – the fledgling barrister (Guillaume Geoffrion)

Alaska boundary tribunal in session, Foreign Office, Whitehall, London, October 1903. Tribunal, left to right (seated): Senator George Turner (U.S.A.), Louis Jetté (Canada), Elihu Root (U.S.A.), Lord Alverstone, Henry Cabot Lodge (U.S.A.), Allen B. Aylesworth (Canada). Counsel for United States of America (on left), counsel for Britain, at right facing left to right: Sir Robert Finlay, Christopher Robinson (back to camera), Lyman P. Duff (with beard), Aimé Geoffrion, S.A.T. Rowlatt, F.C. Wade (behind Rowlatt), and John Simon (behind Wade) (Vancouver Public Library)

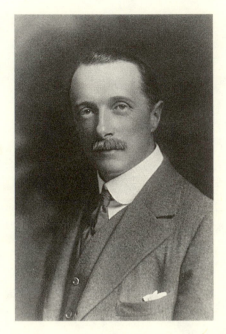

Aimé Geoffrion in his prime (Guillaume Geoffrion)

The young athlete Isaac Pitblado, standing at right, 1889 (University of Manitoba, Department of Archives and Special Collections)

The old athlete Isaac Pitblado, age eighty-eight, still in good form (University of Manitoba, Department of Archives and Special Collections)

Sixty years a lawyer: Arthur Meighen on left, Isaac Pitblado, Chief Justice E.K. Williams on right (University of Manitoba, Department of Archives and Special Collections)

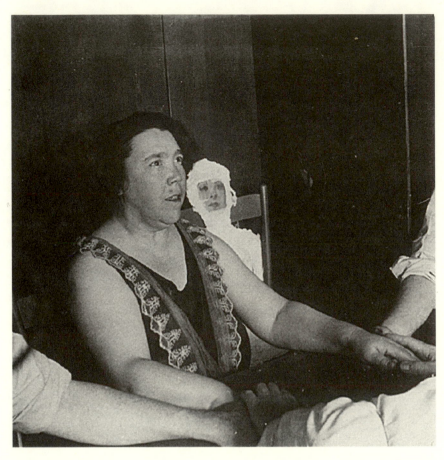

One of the 'Lucy' photographs: Pitblado's hands are in lower right holding the hands of the medium in her trance (University of Manitoba, Department of Archives and Special Collections)

J.W. De'B FARRIS
- City Prosecutor, 1903 - 1905
- Attorney General of B.C. - May, 23, 1917-Jan. 22, 1922
- King's Counsel, May, 23, 1917
- Bencher, Law Society of B.C. - 1933 - 1948
- Treasurer, Law Society of B.C. - 1934 - 1938
- President, Canadian Bar Assoc. - 1937-1938
- Senator of Canada, Jan. 11, 1947 - Feb. 25, 1970

J.W. de B. Farris as he appeared in 1903 on arrival in Vancouver; the *curriculum vitae* was added by the staff of the Vancouver City Prosecutor's Office after his death (Kerr Clark Regional Crown Counsel Office, Vancouver)

J.W. de B. Farris the politician, in foreground; to his right the premier, John Oliver; T.D. Pattullo at top right, *c.* 1921 (University of British Columbia, Special Collections Library)

J.W. de B. Farris (head discernible at upper left) watches with others the administration of the chicken oath to a Chinese witness during the Nanaimo strike trials; the decapitated chicken bound the non-Christian Chinese oath-taker to tell the truth (Farris and Company, Vancouver)

Pilot Officer F.M. Covert, 1944 – the navigator (Covert family)

J.W. de B. Farris – leading counsel (Mrs J.L. Farris)

F.M. Covert – the deal maker (Covert family)

The heavy hitters arrive: J.W.E. Mingo and F.M. Covert (Stewart McKelvey
Stirling Scales)

F.M. Covert (on right): the wise counsellor (Covert family)

Gordon Henderson – the graduate, University of Toronto (Joan Henderson)

Gordon Henderson as he appeared when president of the Canadian Bar
Association, 1979 (Joan Henderson; John Evans Photography)

Gordon Henderson – the chancellor, 1992 (Joan Henderson; John Evans Photography)

5

John Wallace de Beque Farris

Early in 1954 a lawyer stood trial at Duncan, British Columbia, a small town on southern Vancouver Island, charged with obstructing or perverting the course of justice. The charge arose from a case also heard in Duncan. The lawyer had defended an accused man at whose trial the central issue was the identity of the perpetrator of the crime. Could the prosecution prove it was the accused? The presiding magistrate allowed the accused to sit in the public gallery and not in the prisoner's dock when the prosecution's chief witness to prove identification was called to the stand. The witness looked round the courtroom and pointed out the accused. The lawyer then startled the court by revealing that the 'accused' was in fact a look-alike. The magistrate concluded that he was compelled to dismiss the charge but, outraged at what he considered a fraud inflicted on his court, reported the matter both to the Law Society of British Columbia, which exercised disciplinary control over the professional conduct of lawyers, and to the attorney general, who authorized criminal proceedings against the lawyer; if convicted, he would almost certainly have been disbarred. A loyal worker for the Liberal Party, he turned in his hour of need to one of the most powerful Liberals in British Columbia and, indeed, in Canada, and one of the country's most widely known lawyers. J.W. de B. Farris, a former provincial attorney general and minister of labour and now a senator, agreed to defend him. The county court judge, who would normally have heard the case, disqualified himself because of his long-standing friendship with the accused lawyer, and a judge from the lower mainland of British Columbia was deputed in his place. Both judges owed their appointments to Farris's recommendations. Farris and the judge travelled on the same ferry to Nanaimo but then drove separately to Duncan, some forty-eight kilometres south.

The crown's case was conducted by an inept prosecutor and, at the conclusion of the prosecution evidence, Farris rose to make a 'no-evidence' motion: while reserving the right to submit defence evidence, if called upon, he argued that the crown had failed to prove that the lawyer had engineered the deception, which might well have been concocted by his client, and thus its case was so weak that the charge should be dismissed out of hand. After speaking a few minutes in support of his motion, Farris paused and, with a theatrical gesture, pulled his watch on its chain from his waistcoat pocket. Like the White Rabbit, he studied it a moment. Then, replacing it, he went on to say that he had intended making a further submission but it was necessary for him to conclude immediately since he had to depart for London the next day from Vancouver for an appeal in the Privy Council; that appeal, he explained, might prove to be the last British Columbia case before the council and, unless he caught the next and last ferry to Vancouver which was scheduled to leave within an hour or so, his departure for London would be jeopardized. Therefore, he urged the judge, the charge against his client should be thrown out forthwith to enable Farris to make his connections. The prosecutor made a feeble response. The judge quickly agreed that there was no case to answer, dismissed the charge, and freed the lawyer. Farris caught the ferry and made it to the Privy Council on time.

The episode is instructive for in it are found the principal elements of Farris's long career: his success and stature as a lawyer; his willingness to take a case in any genre and in any forum, a drab courtroom in Duncan, British Columbia, on a rather grubby criminal case one day and the elegant chamber of the Privy Council in London the next; his lifelong devotion to the Liberal Party; and his influential role in the appointment of judges in British Columbia.

John Wallace de Beque Farris was born in White's Cove, New Brunswick, not far from Fredericton, in 1878, a scion of a family of Huguenot, Scottish, and United Empire Loyalist stock and one well entrenched in New Brunswick political life on the Liberal side. His grandfather had been the Liberal member of the confederation parliament for Queen's County, and his father was at one time both attorney general of New Brunswick and minister of agriculture. Farris Sr, a lawyer, owned a 240-hectare farm on which young Wallace, with his three brothers, grew up.

Wallace was always proud of his farming background. In 1949 there was a good deal of controversy over proposals to allow margarine manufacturers to colour their product yellow, to resemble butter. Farris was on the side of the dairy industry. In a speech on the subject he said, 'Tomatoes are red, lettuce is green and margarine is white ... Yellow is not the natural colour of margarine. It's the colour of butter. Being yellow doesn't make it taste any better. Squash is yellow. It's not coloured white.' These comments got wide coverage in the newspapers, prompting a woman in Saskatchewan to ask the following pointed question: 'Have you ever made butter?' She noted that except when there is lots of green grass the natural colour of butter is white. Just as people use cosmetics, she said, or, in the case of men, just as shaving hair and whiskers improves their appearance, so does yellow colouring improve the appearance of margarine. 'Same argument isn't it?' Farris replied cordially, telling her that of course he knew something about making butter, but it made no difference whether butter was coloured yellow naturally or artificially: what counted was that the colour yellow had become synonymous in the minds of consumers with butter. He concluded: 'If butter had always been white the producer of margarine would now be anxious to use that colour for his product.'

The youngest Farris son, Wendell, practised law with his brother for many years and ultimately became chief justice of the Supreme Court of British Columbia. He was not noted for hard work. Wallace, who as a lawyer worked extremely hard, used to say of his brother, 'That damn Wendell. I used to chase him around the barn with a horse whip. Too bad I didn't catch him more often.' After attending the local school, Wallace went to a preparatory school, St Martin's Academy (one of his fellow matriculants was Walter Pidgeon, the actor) and thence to Acadia University in Wolfville, Nova Scotia, from which he graduated in 1899 with a BA. During these formative years he displayed those characteristics which so distinguished him in later life: cleverness, a capacity for hard work, a ready wit, loyalty to the Liberal Party of the intensity that one encounters in the polarized politics of the Maritimes, and, above all, a 'gift of the gab.' It was inevitable that he become a lawyer and his family decided that he should go to the University of Pennsylvania, which then had – still does have – one of the premier law schools in the United States. In Philadelphia he lived in comfortable surroundings with an uncle who had a prosperous medical practice. Wallace early established himself as a prominent debater for the university, not just the law school, and he was particularly proud when he led his team to victory over the University of

Michigan. After taking his degree in 1902, he was admitted to the New Brunswick bar and hung out his shingle in Saint John, where he practised for six months with a notable lack of success. With free time on his hands, he was able, even eager, to go on the campaign trail with his father, who, though capable and well respected, did not set the heather afire with his speeches from the hustings; Wallace helped him out. On one occasion in the small town of Jemseg, Wallace attacked the Tories for having too many planks in their platform: 'Now you know this is a cure-all they have got, going to cure everything. Reminds me of the fellow with a patent medicine who displayed a testimonial [to the efficacy of the medicine]. The grateful patient said: "Before taking your medicine my wife was so nervous I couldn't sleep with her. She took two bottles of your medicine. Now anybody can sleep with her."' After the laughter from the audience subsided, someone shouted, 'Wallace, what's the name of that medicine?'

Farris's ability to tell humorous but appropriate stories lasted all his life, in and out of the courtroom. His rhetorical skills also endured. During his lifetime he made countless speeches across Canada and frequently in the United States. Usually he would be invited to address legal bodies in both countries on specialized topics but many times he spoke to non-legal organizations which simply wanted a skilled speaker and left the choice of subject to him. In such cases he would talk about Canadian-American relations, the desirability of Canada remaining within the commonwealth, the value of the monarchy, and, after the end of the Second World War, the need to be vigilant against the perfidy of the Russians. Before the Second World War, one of his favourite topics before an American audience was the need for an Alaska Highway, not so much from the standpoint of military advantage but as a means of opening up northern British Columbia and Alaska. In an unusual appearance he stepped in on two days notice, replacing the scheduled speaker, the formidable Gerry McGeer, who had died suddenly. His role was that of narrator in Aaron Copeland's 'Lincoln Portrait,' performed in Stanley Park by the British Columbia Electric Symphony before an audience of 10,000. He received rave reviews.

As a young lawyer, Farris, with virtually no clientele in Saint John, decided to relocate to Regina; there he became a member of the territorial bar (Saskatchewan not then being a province). He thought he might try his hand in Moose Jaw and a Regina friend accompanied him on a trip to that town to introduce Farris to a solicitor who was looking for an associate. However, his friend got drunk for forty-eight hours and Farris never did meet the solicitor. He returned to Regina and stayed there until 1903, when he moved to Vancouver and was called to the British Columbia bar. Farris would later say that 'sometimes liquor does have beneficial results. This is not intended as a reflection on Moose Jaw, but an appreciation of Vancouver.' Not long after his call, and with the help of friends, he became the city prosecutor in police court. This was a position he was to hold until 1907 but it did not preclude him from carrying on a general civil practice. He was on his way.

While studying at Acadia he had met Evelyn Keirstead, daughter of an Acadia professor. The two of them reached an 'understanding' and then embarked on a six-year engagement. After she graduated from Acadia – a year before Wallace – she went on to teach at a high school in Connecticut during the time he was studying at the University of Pennsylvania. There was one possible impediment to their relationship – her family was Tory. The differing political loyalties were not, however, the reason for the extended courtship. The two had agreed to delay any union until Wallace had established himself and that did not occur until 1905 in Vancouver. Evelyn, like Wallace, was an exceptional student, intelligent and, unlike him, endowed with a great deal of practical common sense. The two were married in 1905 in Wolfville by Evelyn's father who, in addition to being a professor, was also a Baptist minister. Wallace, who still did not have much money, travelled to the wedding as a guard on a train carrying Chinese labourers to eastern Canada; the CPR hired guards to accompany the Chinese from Vancouver and the guard was paid with a return Pullman ticket. Evelyn, for her part, was given as a wedding present a special one-way Pullman ticket to Vancouver issued by the minister of railways. Farris used to joke about the conductor who, when the two showed up for the journey, found that one had a pass as guard for the Chinese train and the other had a ticket from the minister of railways himself. The train trip was their honeymoon. The marriage was eminently successful, and happy. Evelyn fulfilled a role of community service. She became the founder of the University Women's Club in Vancouver; she was the first female to serve on the senate of the University of British Columbia; and she was the first woman to serve on the board of governors of the university, a post she held for thirty years. As will be seen, she played a vital role at various stages of her husband's career; 'steady as she goes' might well have been her motto.

But Evelyn had not been Farris's first love. At his death in 1970 all his papers and correspondence were, most commendably, preserved and presented to the Special Collections Library of the University of British Columbia. It is a rich collection. Farris, or more usually his secretary, had kept virtually every piece of paper that came across his desk or a copy that went out over it. In the collection is a charming letter from a young girl, written in 1888 when Wallace was ten, from Chipman, New Brunswick:

Dear Wallace:

I received your very welcome letter on the 6th inst. and had I not been so busy I should have written before for I suppose you will be anxiously waiting for assurance. Freddy and Mary have been sick with scarlet rash but they are better now. I suppose our house is nearly finished. Do your men work well? [A reference to the farm labour on Wallace's father's farm.] I am expecting you up soon with your pa and ma and brothers. Freddy talks a great deal about you. He calls you my fellow and tries to tease me about you. Well Wallace I guess I shall have to make my letter very short at this time as the mail will soon be going. I remain your loving friend, Nell King.

By any standard, this is a fascinating letter. It obviously meant something to him for he kept it. Nell, presumably about the same age as Wallace, says that she is his 'loving friend.' Were ten-year-olds in the 1880s more ardent than they are now? And, most tantalizing, what became of that delightful girl?[1]

From the outset of his career Farris was a courtroom man. He had no interest whatever in being an office lawyer – a solicitor – and remained an advocate all his days. Similarly, he had no interest in law-office management and was fortunate at most stages of his career to have a partner or an associate to look after that important aspect of legal practice. He did not hire staff or engage lawyers or attend partners' meetings or make business decisions – all these were done by others. At a time in the early 1960s the Farris firm became the first major Vancouver law firm to engage a Jewish lawyer. John Farris told his father the man had been hired and was Jewish and what did he think of it? Farris Sr replied, 'Is he honest?' His son said that there was no doubt on that score. 'Is he capable?' There was no doubt on that score either. 'Well, then, what's the argument about?' the father asked.

In the thirty years or so during which his son practised with him, Farris himself never sent out a bill – someone else sent it out and put a fee on it. On an occasion when Farris had won a big case for the British Columbia government in the Supreme Court of Canada in the 1930s, his brother Wendell went to Victoria to settle the account with the attorney general.

After the two agreed on a fee of $25,000 Wendell phoned his brother. Wallace told him: 'You ought to be ashamed of yourself. You know damn well that case isn't worth $25,000!' Wendell replied, 'Well, I'm sorry Wallace that you feel that way but there's nothing I can do about it because I have agreed to it.' The division of that large fee and others among the partners would not have concerned Wallace; as with every other aspect of the practice, he let others decide the profit sharing. At his peak, in the 1950s, he earned between $100,000 and $125,000 annually, a substantial but by no means astronomic income. He was fond of saying that he didn't earn much money but spent lots of it and indeed his investments at his death were valued at roughly $400,000, again not a trifling sum but not one reflecting great wealth either. For most of his active career Farris's law offices were the most sumptuous in Vancouver, located in what had been built as a residential penthouse atop a tall office building: rich panelling throughout, heavy pile carpets, crackling fireplace, and a handsome grandfather clock ticking and chiming sedately. Farris's large private office commanded a splendid view of Vancouver harbour and the North Shore mountains. The generally hushed atmosphere was occasionally punctuated by loud cuss words which Farris was wont to utter when displeased.

In his early years of practice, that is before the First World War, he was known as a 'labour lawyer' and considered to be quite radical. Before the days of the Workmen's Compensation Board he often represented injured workmen and trade unions, and it was because of that background that he acted – in his first really high-profile case – for a group of miners charged with various crimes in the aftermath of the violent strikes of 1913 on Vancouver Island. Beginning in 1912, miners from Cumberland to Ladysmith had picketed various mine operations in response to a call for a general strike by the United Mine Workers of America, which was seeking to gain recognition as the bargaining agent. The companies took retaliatory action, such as evicting families from company-owned houses, and hired large numbers of strike-breakers, or 'scabs,' to defy the picketing and to continue operations. The strike dragged on through the winter of 1912 and by the summer of 1913 tension had escalated as if in conjunction with the rising temperatures. In July there were riots in Cumberland followed by even worse riots around Nanaimo early in August, marked by property damage, assaults, and looting of company property. The regular police, augmented by 'specials' – civilians sworn in as temporary peace officers – were quite unable to cope with what really was a state of anarchy and, on 13 August 1913, Attorney General W.J. Bowser called out the militia to aid the civil power, just as was to happen fifteen years later on Cape Breton Island. Simultaneously, he hired a Pinkerton agent to work undercover among the miners; one of the men he reported on was Joshua Taylor, whom Farris later defended. Units of militia from Victoria and Vancouver were dispatched forthwith to Vancouver Island to take up positions to contain the violence. (One of the militia officers was A.W. Currie, later famous as commanding officer of the First Canadian Corps in France.) The militia, though in reduced numbers, remained in the mid-island area until the following year when, but for the outbreak of the Great War, further violence might well have erupted. Oscar Orr, who died in November 1992 at the age of 100, may have been the oldest survivor of this military operation at the time of his interview with the author. One of about 500 'week-end soldiers' sent from Vancouver, he recalled being issued with ten rounds of 'gallery ammunition' designed for use on shooting ranges and much less lethal than ordinary rounds; he also remembered the armoured railway car, which ran as far north as Cumberland. The arrival of the militia was followed by wholesale arrests of striking miners, who then faced a variety of charges under the criminal code. Farris, along with other counsel, showed up in court to defend many of them.

The first trials in which he was involved started in Nanaimo on 6 October 1913 before Judge F.W. Howay, a far better historian than judge. Two Nanaimo lawyers, J.E. Bird and Arthur Leighton, also appeared as defence counsel. (Bird, six years later, was to appear as one of the several defence counsel at the trials of the strike leaders in the Winnipeg General Strike.) Most of the miners either pleaded guilty or were found guilty but Farris and his colleagues did gain some acquittals. Two of those convicted were Joshua Taylor, vice-president of the British Columbia Federation of Labour, and Sam Guthrie, later a well-known politician. Some of the jury trials for men still in custody were scheduled for hearing at a special assize in New Westminster and the remainder were shifted there as the result of intemperate and ill-advised remarks made by Judge Howay in a newspaper interview following the trials conducted by him. Farris had more success in the jury trials than before Howay, gaining occasional outright acquittals and, in cases of multiple charges, acquittals in some of them. One of those convicted, however, was Joe Angelo, the organizer for the United Mine Workers of America, who had come to Vancouver Island to assist the local branches of the union in their attempts to organize; he was sentenced to four years' imprisonment for rioting and destruction of property. Of the miners convicted of various offences, and sentenced to prison, most were in fact freed soon after the conclusion of the special assize on 26 March 1914. Interestingly, when serving in 1919 as attorney general, Farris introduced legislation to compensate mining companies and householders for damages caused by the rioters, as recommended by a judicial inquiry; in all, $56,000 was paid out to claimants 'in the public interest' without any acknowledgment of legal liability falling upon the government.

One of the labour leaders Farris became acquainted with at this time was Parker Williams, a renowned advocate in British Columbia of the working man, whom Farris always held in high admiration though he was anything but a Liberal in politics. Williams had never been charged in the strikes of 1912–13, but he had been under surveillance by the Pinkerton detective.[2] In later years, Farris, as attorney general and minister of labour, was to work closely with Williams in the implementation of the Workmen's Compensation Act. By then Williams was serving as a member of the first Workmen's Compensation Board.

Although the ethics of the time allowed an attorney general to continue in private practice, Farris did not do so, leaving his Vancouver law office in charge of a partner. With his family he moved to Victoria and lived in a large handsome house at 515 Foul Bay Road, designed by the renowned architect Samuel Maclure. In his capacity as attorney general he made his first appearance, in fact his first two appearances, before the Privy Council in 1919, in both of which he was successful. In the first case his legal opponent was Sir John Simon acting for the government of Canada, which sought to establish federal jurisdiction over English Bay as a 'public harbour.' Those familiar with English Bay, an integral part of the waters adjacent to Vancouver, can understand the continuing significance of the Privy Council's ruling that Ottawa had no say in the management of the bay as a recreational resource. In the other important case, described in the chapter on Tilley, Farris successfully argued that claimants who were employees of the Canadian Pacific Railway were entitled to benefits under the Workmen's Compensation Act arising from the sinking of the vessel *Princess Sophia*.

Thus began a long and affectionate, though sometimes ambivalent, relationship between Farris and the Privy Council. He appeared before it on twenty-nine identifiable occasions, but there may have been more. Of those recorded, he won fourteen and lost fifteen. Unlike some of his contemporaries, he preferred the quiet dignity of the Grosvenor House Hotel in Park Lane to Queen Anne's Mansions, though after the Second World War he tended to stay at the Dorchester. Once when staying at the Gros-

venor House, he and his wife entertained a guest at dinner, perhaps Geoffrey Lawrence, later Lord Oaksey, one of his closest English friends.
Covers were laid for three at 8 shillings sixpence each; the wine from Bin
222 was 9 shillings sixpence. This all totalled one pound fifteen shillings
yet the waiter presented a bill for one pound five shillings, which Farris
charged to his room. The error was discovered by the hotel after Farris's
return to Canada; a flurry of correspondence followed; management was
exceedingly embarrassed but would Farris send another ten shillings?
Which of course he did. Not only was he enamoured of the virtues of the
hotel, he requested a room attended to by a particular valet whose services had impressed him. He used the opportunity of visiting London to
outfit himself from Savile Row with new legal regalia and other clothing
and, more mundanely, with golf shoes about which he was very particular – there must be no metal cleats but only rubber ones. And on one gala
occasion he attended the 'Grand Day' at Gray's Inn to mark the opening
of Michaelmas term in the courts. These elaborate ceremonial occasions,
mounted by all the London inns of court, followed an unvarying format.
At Gray's, one sat at dinner with certain companions and, when dessert
was to be served, changed positions, as in a game of musical chairs. Farris
was seated at dinner between Master [of the inn] R.E. Dummett and Master the Hon. Mr Justice Greaves-Lord. Opposite him was the ubiquitous
Canadian expatriate, the Rt Hon. Lord Hamar Greenwood. At dessert,
Farris had opposite him Sir Arnold Wilson and Master R. Storry Deans.
Seated next to him, both quaffing various wines including an 1826
Madeira, was the Reverend Canon F.B. Ottley, who preached a sermon to
close the proceedings. The question is whether anyone was still awake to
hear it.

In 1949, at the Privy Council, Farris argued what he considered to be
the most important case of his career, one that led to his most noteworthy
triumph. In the 1880s, as part of the arrangements between the federal
and provincial governments and the railway contractors leading to construction of the Esquimalt and Nanaimo Railway on Vancouver Island,
from Victoria to Courtenay, the provincial government ceded to the railway company a swath of valuable timberlands lying on either side of the
projected route. The railway company, later acquired by the CPR, made a
great deal of money by selling off parcels of timber free of any provincial
tax. In 1945 a royal commission on forestry headed by Chief Justice
Gordon Sloan recommended imposition of a provincial tax on the
unalienated portions of the railway's land grant, estimated at roughly
800,000 acres on which stood five to six billion board feet of valuable tim-

ber. The coalition government of the day came under pressure to pass enabling legislation – the CPR was not popular and was perceived as having got a bonanza from the timberlands. But the government was reluctant to proceed because it felt that such a tax, which had never been imposed before, violated the spirit if not the letter of the agreement reached sixty years earlier. Farris was consulted. There were two difficulties: first, in devising a tax that lay within the constitutional power of the province, which constitutionally could levy only direct taxes; and, secondly, whether such a tax would in effect violate the original agreement, which forbade taxation until the lands were 'leased, sold or otherwise alienated.' Sloan had proposed a tax on the timber levied when sold, but Farris realized that that was a tax which would be passed on to the ultimate consumer of the lumber cut from the timber and hence would be unconstitutional since it amounted to an indirect tax which only the federal government could levy. On his advice, the government drafted the Esquimalt and Nanaimo Railway Belt Land Grant Tax Act, which imposed a 25 per cent land tax – by definition a direct tax – on the timberlands. The CPR protested and its views had some sympathy in government circles; in fact, Attorney General R.L. Maitland remarked when retaining Farris, only half in jest, that he hoped he would lose the case. The effect of the legislation was obvious: the value of the remaining timberlands dropped instantly by 25 per cent. The validity of the legislation was referred to the provincial Court of Appeal, which upheld it; the Supreme Court of Canada unanimously reversed the judgment and British Columbia, represented by Farris, took the case to the Privy Council. By the time the case reached London the principal hurdle faced by Farris was the feeling that the provincial government was indeed playing a dirty trick by violating an implied contract of long duration. Farris hammered home his argument that that was irrelevant even if true. What really mattered was whether the province had the constitutional power to levy the tax even if the financial consequences were disagreeable to the CPR. The Privy Council agreed with him and the case was won. Estimates of the amount of money collected by the provincial government as a result of the decision are uncertain but definitely ran to many millions of dollars. The CPR was so incensed by the decision that it made a last-ditch appeal to the federal government to disallow the legislation. Farris again represented British Columbia, and the cabinet declined to interfere.

By the time of the Esquimalt and Nanaimo decision, the Privy Council had already ruled that Canada could abolish all appeals to it. Farris had mainly been a retentionist during the years of debate on the issue but over time he seemed to shift his position. When the decision of the Privy Council was announced, Farris, in a newspaper interview, accepted it as 'reasonable and practicable' and in conformity with the Statute of Westminster. Yet, now that the *right* to abolish appeals had been established, he personally favoured their continuance at least in some cases, perhaps constitutional ones, because judgments of the Privy Council were a 'useful contribution to Canada's jurisprudence and because the Privy Council was one of the last remaining links of Empire, promoted better understanding and would continue to be a beneficial influence in maintaining high legal standards and ideals of justice.' There spoke the monarchist and United Empire Loyalist. He had made much the same point in a *Canadian Bar Review* 'symposium' that also included the views of D.M. Gordon, the eminent lawyer-scholar from Victoria, and F.R. Scott of McGill. Gordon thought that the decision was bad in law and based solely on policy; Scott enthusiastically supported the decision both as policy and as law; and Farris was sandwiched between them. But of course his views were simply impractical, as he himself came to realize.[3]

The three largest commonwealth countries, India, Pakistan, and Canada, cut the judicial knot to the Privy Council within a year of each other, India and Pakistan in 1949 and 1950 respectively and Canada in 1950. The governments of India and Pakistan each sent gracious messages to the lord chancellor as the presiding officer of the Privy Council, formally advising him of the discontinuance of appeals but paying tribute to the Privy Council for its function in the administration of law in what had become the two separate countries. On each occasion, the lord chancellor sat on the board to read aloud the messages and to read his own responses, which also were very civilized and appropriate to the occasion. And Canada? In the final stages of debate in the House of Commons on the bill to adopt the legislation ending appeals, Stuart Garson, the minister of justice, remarked: 'If we no longer wish to have the United Kingdom Privy Council hear the final appeals of our Canadian law suits ... it is not because the Privy Council is not today perhaps the strongest law court in the world. We shall always be grateful for the massive judicial services which the Privy Council has performed for this country.' He went on to predict that, as the final court, the Supreme Court of Canada would acquire 'the same greatness as a court of ultimate jurisdiction.' This brief expression of gratitude, however, was never transmitted in any formal way to the Privy Council.

In 1951 Farris appeared before the Privy Council in two cases in what proved to be the last occasion he argued appeals (the legislation abolishing appeals effective 1 Jan. 1950 preserved the right of appeal in lawsuits commenced before that date). At the conclusion of the second appeal, he asked permission, and was allowed, to make a statement about the abolition of appeals. After recounting his many appearances before the board, and noting that this one was likely to be the last, he felt that he had to 'express my personal feelings of deepest regret that this most intimate tie between the lawyers of Canada and Your Lordships of the Judicial Committee is coming to an end.' Abolition was not occurring, he assured them, because of any dissatisfaction on the part of Canada; rather, it was more like a coming of age – 'A boy grows up and at the pride of his young manhood he is not content to dwell forever in the house of his father, no matter how welcome he is or how well he is treated.' He commented on the valuable unifying effect on the British commonwealth of the jurisprudence laid down by the Privy Council and, in the case of Canada in particular, he lauded it for its role in protecting 'the autonomy, authority and status of the Lieutenant Governors [which] should be maintained as well as the Central Power.' Here he was positioning himself as a provincial-rights man, in line with the interpretation of the BNA Act by the likes of Lords Watson and Haldane. He concluded by reiterating his 'deep personal regret' at a turn of events which would deny to his son (who was with him as junior counsel) and his contemporaries 'the invaluable associations which I, and my contemporaries, have enjoyed and the unrivalled experience of appearing before this great tribunal, the greatest of its kind in the world.'

Lord Simon, who was presiding that day, responded in kind to Farris's dignified remarks, voicing no recriminations but a 'complete full understanding of the decision that Canada has taken.' As a distinguished lawyer, Simon had often been involved in Canadian cases, starting with the Alaska Boundary Tribunal when he was junior counsel along with Geoffrion and Duff; later, after becoming lord chancellor, he had often sat on Canadian appeals. On this occasion he referred to an idea he had long held for reforming the Privy Council – namely, that the judges should be appointed not only by the British government but by the 'Dominion governments.' His notion was 'that we should consider whether it was not possible for the Judicial Committee to go circuit throughout the Commonwealth and sit in Ottawa and in other Capitals just as much as it sits here.' But now, of course, it was too late for such a reform. Simon reflected that 'it may have been that had those ideas prevailed in time that we should have recreated a new kind of Supreme Commonwealth Tribunal and there would have been no feeling that by coming to London, Canada in some way was travelling outside its natural judicial orbit.' He concluded by thanking Farris warmly and paying tribute to the 'capability and skill of Canadian counsel.' Here he undoubtedly had in mind, among others, Lafleur, Tilley, and Geoffrion as well as Farris. And Lafleur and the others would, from the grave, have heartily applauded Farris and Simon's sentiments. The *Times* ran a long editorial, noting that the appearance of a distinguished Canadian lawyer was appropriate to the occasion. Like Simon, the editorialist regretted the lost opportunity of reconstructing the Privy Council so as to adapt it to legitimate national aspirations.

There are several fascinating aspects of this episode. Simon's concept of a travelling court was never, so far as the author is aware, put forward in any concrete fashion and remains one of those 'what if' propositions. The existence of such a court would probably have had no effect on the decisions taken by India and Pakistan, but Canada? The great Canadian constitutional lawyers such as Tilley and the others (and Duff on the bench) espoused the views of Watson and Haldane and saw the Privy Council – as did Quebec – as a bulwark against the intrusion of a federal government into the affairs of the provinces. And, finally, one is struck by the lack of politesse by the government of Canada on the cessation of appeals: not one word (apart from Garson's remarks in the House of Commons), let alone a formal message from the prime minister, or the minister of justice, or even from the high commissioner in London. This was colonial gaucherie, akin to that of a guest who had come to dinner over a period of many years and, when the association ended, failed to give thanks to his long-time host. It was left to Farris to repair the omission by making a personal statement. Reading between the lines of this statement, one feels that he was embarrassed by the behaviour of his government.

The Canadian government's insensitivity went even farther. Farris thought in 1951 that he had made his last appearance but in fact he travelled once more to London, in 1954, to make an application for special leave to appeal, unsuccessfully as it turned out. The government of Canada had always kept within the Privy Council library a comprehensive collection of law reports from all parts of the country and many Canadian texts as well. Farris, knowing of this collection, was disconcerted to learn on arrival that the government had broken up the collection and sold it, over the protests of Privy Council officials and notwithstanding that Canadian appeals were still being heard. His agents had to scurry around to other libraries to find the materials he needed.[4]

Those who saw Farris in action in his hey-day believe that he was most effective as a trial lawyer, particularly before juries where his wit and aplomb served him in good stead. Often Chief Justice Aulay Morrison of the Supreme Court of British Columbia presided at these trials. In one, a litigant was named 'Bury.' Farris referred to him as Mr 'Bury' and Morrison would pronounce it 'Berry.' Finally, Morrison said, 'Mr. Farris, I was always taught to pronounce the name "Bury" as "Berry."' 'Well that's alright, my Lord,' Farris quickly retorted, 'but you wouldn't say these eight men here were sitting on the "jerry"?' Morrison once remarked to Farris – they lived across the road from each other – that he spoke Gaelic. 'It's useful,' he said, 'because it conceals your ignorance when you know little about the subject.' Straight-faced, Farris asked, 'Why don't you write your judgments in Gaelic?' Once, when defending the CPR for having caused a fire to a warehouse, his legal opponents produced a bushel of photographs showing the progress of the fire. The judge asked Farris if he too was going to produce a sheaf of pictures. 'No, my Lord,' Farris replied, 'we did not know there was going to be a fire.' And in addressing a jury in a libel case in which William Sloan, a former mines minister and a former cabinet colleague of Farris, sued the well-known Conservative politician Senator A.D. McCrae, who from the witness stand had professed on cross-examination not to remember certain vital details, Farris asked the jury to award 'an amount which is so large that when Senator McCrae is asked what it was he will not be able to say "I don't remember."' The jury complied, awarding $40,000, then the largest sum awarded for libel in British Columbia.

But he did not win all his jury trials, as an episode in Prince Rupert – one that Farris often laughingly cited as an instance of juries' unpredictability – well illustrates. A logger rolling into town from the woods spent his time, and money, in a sporting house. When he ran out of funds, he asked the madame to do business on credit. Naturally she refused, he grew ugly, she pulled a gun, there was a struggle, she shot him and was charged with murder. Her friends banded together to hire Farris to defend her. The day before the trial, Farris went over the jury list with Liberal acquaintances in Prince Rupert who identified any 'sport' on the list who would presumably be sympathetic to the woman and any religious type presumably unsympathetic. Farris picked a jury much to his satisfaction, comprised of well-known 'sports,' and was confident he would gain an acquittal. To his astonishment, the jury convicted the woman, though not of murder but of manslaughter. The next day as he was leaving, Farris bumped into the foreman and could not resist asking why they had not acquitted the woman. (Under the criminal code jurors may not be asked such questions and Farris himself was breaking the law in doing so.) 'What,' the foreman said, 'let a girl pack a gun in a whore-house, none of us would be safe.' Farris, a Baptist himself, later would remark that he should have picked a Baptist jury and talked about out-raged womanhood.[5]

By the early 1920s, after he had left the provincial cabinet, Farris acquired a notable reputation for winning jury trials against British Columbia Electric Railway Company, then the major power and transpor-tation utility. In the view of the general public, it was only slightly less unpopular than the CPR. The company decided as a sort of self-defence that it had better have Farris on its side; he agreed to act for it and to start at a date some months away to allow the company as gracefully as possi-ble to terminate the services of its present lawyers. In the interval, Farris had a case scheduled against the company; he phoned the company, which, believing that it had an iron-clad case, consented to him acting. He won it. The president phoned Farris to say, 'No more cases against us!' Thereafter Farris or members of his firm were standing counsel for the company. On one celebrated occasion Farris appeared in the Vancouver small debts court on behalf of the company. Following an increase in the price of streetcar fares in Vancouver, Effie Jones, a well-known local socialist, had climbed aboard a car, tendering a ticket issued at the old rate. The conductor refused to take it. She paid the difference, a few pen-nies, and then sued B.C. Electric to recover them. Appearing for her was another well-known socialist, the formidable lawyer Harry Rankin. The judge dismissed the suit. It cost B.C. Electric a large sum of money on a matter of principle.

Another instance of Farris's ability as counsel to gain important clients occurred in 1929. The Bank of Toronto (later the Toronto-Dominion), despite having Farris on its side, had lost an important case in the British Columbia Court of Appeal involving repayment of a large loan. It then sought an opinion from W.N. Tilley, in Toronto, as to the advisability of an appeal to the Supreme Court of Canada. He told the bank that there was no hope and it should settle at any price. Not yet prepared to give up the fight, the bank again consulted Farris, who told it, 'Tilley's a great lawyer but he doesn't know this case and he doesn't know what the hell he is talking about. I will win this case.' And he did. His chief opponent in the Supreme Court was, incidentally, Aimé Geoffrion. Farris encountered Geoffrion on two other occasions in the Supreme Court of Canada, and each time Geoffrion triumphed. In one of these cases, involving the

Alberta Debt Adjustment Act, Farris was asked to apply to the Privy Council for special leave to appeal but restrictions on wartime travel prevented him from doing so. However, the prospect of wartime travel to London did not daunt him. In 1941 he acted successfully in a case in the Supreme Court of Canada, from whose decision the opposite party appealed to the Privy Council. Farris's client wanted him to argue the appeal. Farris asked his friend, Ian Mackenzie, then the minister of national defence, if he could arrange a 'Bomber' to fly him over, but nothing came of it.

Though Farris never completely gave up trial work, increasingly he confined himself to the appellate courts, the Court of Appeal of British Columbia and, of course, the Supreme Court of Canada. Sometimes he appeared at royal commissions, including, in the 1930s, the Rowell-Sirois commission on the state of confederation and the Davis commission of inquiry into a violent longshoreman's strike in Vancouver. At the hearings of the latter, Farris represented the employers. H.H. Davis, a judge of the Supreme Court of Canada was, notwithstanding his Tory background, a good friend of Farris, having met him through the Canadian Bar Association. Once at a cocktail party in Ottawa, Davis remarked to Farris that they (the judges of the Supreme Court) had not seen much of him lately. 'No,' Farris told him bluntly, 'I prefer to take my cases to the Privy Council.' This sentiment explained a remark he made when exasperated by the unsympathetic view taken of his client's case by the judges of the Supreme Court. As he sat down he was heard to remark audibly (with his stentorian voice it was difficult for him to be inaudible), 'And to think we've abolished appeals to the Privy Council.' However, his record in the Supreme Court was really quite good. Of the seventy-two cases in which he appeared that reached the published law reports, he was successful in 60 per cent of them, a record that puts him on a par with Tilley and Geoffrion. On the two occasions when he and Tilley were opponents the verdict was split; each was victorious in one case. And similarly with Lafleur: two cases with divided success. On his first appearance in the Supreme Court, in 1915, when he was thirty-seven years old, he was successful; remarkably, he argued his last case forty-eight years later when he was eighty-five and he won that also, with John Robinette opposing him. Thereafter his court appearances dwindled noticeably. Talk about going out with a flourish![6]

Apart from the Esquimalt and Nanaimo case, Farris was involved in a number of other important constitutional cases, chief among them perhaps the references concerning the Bennett New Deal legislation in which he represented British Columbia throughout in a largely successful assault on the validity of the federal legislation. Farris also appeared in a constitutional case of continuing significance, the attempt by British Columbia in 1921 to prevent the employment of Chinese and Japanese on crown property. The intended legislation was in direct conflict with a treaty negotiated in 1911 between Great Britain and Japan by which nationals of one country would have the same right of employment as nationals of the other. The dominion government in 1913 declared this treaty to have the force of law in Canada. Farris represented British Columbia in the subsequent challenge to the legislation both in the Supreme Court of Canada and in the Privy Council. Before the latter body he had as colleagues Sir John Simon and Geoffrey Lawrence, but all three heavyweights were unsuccessful; the Privy Council agreed with the Supreme Court that the provincial legislation was invalid because of its conflict with a valid federal treaty. Farris may have had more than a merely professional interest in this litigation. British Columbia could not, as the result of the decision of the Privy Council, prevent Japanese from working on crown lands (though it could prevent Chinese from occupying them, a policy to last many years), but it could and did prevent them from voting, a policy with which Farris heartily agreed. At the end of the Second World War, when the question arose of returning Japanese displaced in 1942 to the Pacific coast, Farris was opposed. When it was also suggested that the franchise be extended to the Japanese, he was even more hotly opposed.[7]

In 1959 he acted on two notable cases. In the first he represented the city of Vancouver in a challenge brought by the Lord's Day Alliance of Canada against provincial legislation permitting that city to sanction paid spectator sports on Sunday afternoons. At the time, Sunday sports was a burning issue and the case is of continuing interest to constitutional scholars since Sunday observance laws crop up from time to time. The Supreme Court of Canada declared itself in favour of Sunday afternoon sports. A few months later Farris was again in the Supreme Court of Canada to defend, successfully, provincial legislation setting up milk-marketing boards; his principal opponent was John Robinette. The case is still relevant. All his working life Farris did a lot of criminal work, both at trials and on appeals, and two of his successful appearances in the Supreme Court of Canada resulted in what lawyers term leading cases. The first was *Ungaro v. The King*. Prior to it, a person found in possession of stolen goods was presumed to be the thief and the prosecution needed no other evidence of guilt. In *Ungaro*, the court, extending the concept of reasonable doubt in the criminal law, decided that if such a person gave an explanation for possession of stolen property that 'might reasonably be true' a jury would be entitled to acquit. And in the other case, the court applied the rule against self-incrimination to civil litigation, with the result that a witness giving evidence could be offered protection against prosecution.

After his appointment to the Senate in 1937, Farris endeavoured to schedule his Supreme Court appearances in Ottawa to coincide with parliamentary sessions so as to save the wear and tear on himself and also to reduce travel expense for his clients. He invariably stayed at the Chateau Laurier, generally in the same suite but, occasionally, through mishap, he would find himself in unfamiliar rooms, which would make him angry. Just as his office staff and partners relieved him of all concern for the tedious details of running a law office, so his wife relieved him of the tedious details of travel. If she was not going to Ottawa with him she would pack and send in advance of his arrival at the Chateau – this in the days before air travel – a trunk with socks, shirts, underwear, ties, and other garments with explicit instructions to the valet to place the socks in such and such a drawer of the dresser, shirts in another section, ties in still another, and so on, as the senator expected on arrival to find his accoutrements in their usual place. On Farris's return to Vancouver, the valet would do the packing. If his wife accompanied him, which she often did because she enjoyed visiting her many friends in Ottawa, she would do the packing. He was thoroughly pampered. At home and at the Chateau he invariably took breakfast in bed and became furious at any interruption in this habit. The Farrises employed a Chinese cook who, one night while indulging his passion for fantan in a Chinese gambling house in Vancouver, was arrested in a police raid and locked up. He phoned Farris from the jail to explain his predicament. Farris told the cook to get the police sergeant on the phone. 'What the hell do you mean by putting my Chinaman in jail?' Farris exploded. 'Who do you think,' he went on, 'is going to cook my breakfast in the morning? You put him in a taxi and send him home right away.' The sergeant complied. Farris could be authoritative, if not imperious.

What were the essential ingredients of his success as a courtroom lawyer? They were various, as is always the case with outstanding advocates. Farris was honest towards his opponents and would never take unfair advantage. If he won a case, he won it on its merits and not because of devious or tricky behaviour. If he appeared against a younger, less experienced lawyer, he would never bully him; on the contrary, he encouraged him. A former partner, Frank Murphy, said of him, 'He had an ability to look for what would be the kernel of the case and stick to it. He was not one to have 150 cases cited, he would concentrate on a few and take that as the core he would work on. In court he was a person that was a good judge of the many [judges] he was appearing before. He knew that he was dealing with personalities and those personalities had to be addressed and he dealt with that very well.' Farris had a superb working library at home where he did much of his work at night. Murphy says that he had an extraordinary capacity to drink a few 'slugs of rye' in the evening and work later, apparently unaffected.

Farris was fond of saying – the cliché is well known – that as a young lawyer he lost cases he should have won, but as an older lawyer he won cases that he should have lost. The point of the remark is that the older lawyer is more familiar with the judges before whom he appears, is aware of their foibles, and avoids striking a familiar raw nerve in a particular judge. Since many of the judges before whom Farris appeared in the last twenty or thirty years of his life owed their appointments to him, his attitude towards them on the bench was understandably different from that of other lawyers, as the episode recounted in the opening of the chapter well illustrates. Similarly, Farris's demeanour before British Columbia judges, who were indebted to him, was quite different from his demeanour before the judges of the Supreme Court of Canada, in whose appointment he had had no hand whatever; whereas with British Columbia judges he tended to be avuncular, and sometimes hectored them, he was wise enough never to adopt such tactics in Ottawa. Gordon Henderson, who often observed Farris in action in the Supreme Court, agreed that he was 'very able' and cut a distinguished figure with his shock of white hair and piercing eyes superimposed on a burly frame. But Henderson thought that Farris was too pedantic: 'He was a man who would grab a point ... and would wrestle it to death.' He also says that Farris was 'so full of himself,' that he was 'all business,' unable to relieve the seriousness of his presentation by some light-hearted sally. This description portrays a far different person from the jocular, self-confident Farris who had performed so adeptly on British Columbia's legal stage.

It is an undeniable fact that as lawyers grow older and more experienced in their profession they do have greater clout than younger lawyers (the same is probably true of all professions). This raises the question whether the familiarity of particular lawyers with particular judges before whom they appear gives their arguments greater weight than those of lawyers not so familiar with the judges or with the court itself. It is obviously not right that a lawyer such as Farris should benefit in the courtroom from his influence. To be fair to him, he did not always enjoy the benefits of undue influence because often the judges before whom he appeared leaned over backwards to give the appearance of impartiality, and in fact it can seldom be demonstrated that a client obtained any direct advantage from Farris's standing and his role in appointments to the bench. In his time, the bench and bar formed a smaller and more cohesive unit of judicial mechanism than it is now; personality traits both of judge and of lawyer were more obvious and more easily discerned and rudeness from judges and corresponding sparks from lawyers were common experiences. Today, the question of personal relationships between lawyers and judges is more subtle. To what extent should a lawyer appear before a judge who for many years was a partner? To what extent should a lawyer appear before a judge with whom he went to law school and has always remained very good friends? Conversely, should a judge decline to sit on a case in such circumstances?

Farris's remarks about confining one's citation of legal precedent to only a few cases reflects a long-held view. Writing in 1953, he observed that in his first speech as president of the Canadian Bar Association he had said that judges were 'too prone to seek authority [that is, legal precedents] rather than base their judgments on reason and common sense.' 'Nothing,' he said, 'was more irritating to a lawyer who had presented a well-reasoned argument than to have the judge enquire "Have you any authorities to support you?" as if there could be a higher authority than a conclusion based on the principle of justice and sound reasoning.' But he admired judges and their role, pointing out that the public will give laws public sanction only when satisfied they are just. 'That law which is unjust is tyranny and no people will submit to tyranny ... if our laws were unjust or if they were unjustly administered we would not be a law-abiding people.' Thus, he said, it is 'remarkable' that when persons were appointed as judges they usually 'become possessed of the highest sense of public duty.' The 'single-mindedness of fair play of our judges is the most outstanding achievement of our social organization.' The reader may well ask how these lofty views accorded with his sometimes less than respectful attitude towards some judges; not everyone is perfect in the heat of battle, but there is no reason to doubt the sincerity of his views. And what he said was right: lawyers, political partisans one day (as was always the case in Farris's time), became even-handed administrators of the law the next, at least as far as the frailties of human nature would allow. It was, as Farris correctly observed, an extraordinary transition. The explanation lies in the ethos of the British legal and judicial tradition which all lawyers and judges acknowledged as the historic mainspring for the preservation of the rights of citizens; the courts were historically the bulwark against injustice and every judge, even one at the lowest level, was conscious of this tradition and, in spite of personal limitations, sought to uphold it. Appointment of a judge ended any partisanship and launched a journey to justice. All the subjects of these portraits believed that a judge should be accompanied on that journey by advocates equally dedicated to the attainment of justice however that rather nebulous term might be interpreted from era to era.

In Farris's day, the big law firms were built around counsel; now, they are built around corporate lawyers with counsel somewhere on the sidelines. The change is also reflected in the Canadian Bar Association and the provincial law societies. A person became president of the Canadian Bar Association, as Farris did in 1937, as the result of an approach by a former president to see if the man, always a noted counsel (there were no female presidents in Farris's time), would become vice-president with the expectation of rising to president the year following. Today, presidents, who are not always leading counsel, come up through the ranks in a long progression. One system is not better than the other; they are just different. Similarly with treasurers [presidents] of law societies – they were always top-flight counsel, as Farris was when he became treasurer of the Law Society of British Columbia in 1934; that system has also changed.[8]

Law and politics were so intermingled in Farris's life that one can hardly tell if he practised law to indulge his political interests or whether he engaged in political activity to further his legal career. Whichever motive was paramount, he became one of the most influential Liberal politicians in the country and one of its most talented advocates. Raised in the hot-house atmosphere of the Maritimes where Liberals and Conservatives never changed their spots, Farris, not surprisingly, remained fiercely partisan all his life: the Liberals could do no wrong, Mackenzie King was the saviour of the country, and his critics were, in Farris's eyes, consigned to outer darkness. And when St Laurent succeeded King and Pearson came along later, Farris granted them equal adulation. But when John Diefenbaker became prime minister, Farris dismissed him as a charlatan 'whose wattles shook' when he spoke. Farris enjoyed raunchy jokes at the expense of the Tories. His son, John, wrote him, 'Did you hear about the dyed-in-the-wool Tory who was complaining about the trend toward paternalism and particularly with proposals such as the Beveridge Plan [which reshaped Great Britain's post-war society] which covers people from the cradle to the grave. He (the Tory) said, "Now they want to protect everyone from the womb to the tomb. The next step will be from erection to resurrection."'

But, of course, as with every rule there are exceptions. Farris, though he had a philosophical dislike of Conservative partisans in principle, yet admired many adherents of the party. Indeed, at one time in an unguarded moment he conceded that there really was not much difference between a Liberal and a Conservative: the true enemy was the socialist. Arthur Meighen, with his towering intellect, was the Conservative chieftain whom Farris most admired. When the two men were in the Senate, though on opposite sides, they became fast friends. He had many good lawyer friends in the Conservative Party, men such as R.L. Maitland and C.H. Locke (the latter became a judge of the Supreme Court of Canada). It was Maitland, a Conservative attorney general, who retained Farris in the Esquimalt and Nanaimo Railway case. Maitland was a fine man, admired by every person of whatever political stripe, including Farris, who in 1944 told him that he, Farris, could obtain a judgeship for him if he wished. Maitland graciously declined the invitation; sadly, he died not long afterward. Farris was among the principal mourners at the funeral, representing the government of Canada.

Farris did not allow his political loyalties to cloud his ethical standards. In 1925 R.H. Pooley, who later became a British Columbia attorney general, was about to be sued and Farris was asked to represent the plaintiff. Farris, who liked Pooley, refused to act. On learning of this Pooley wrote him, 'I have already told you personally how much I appreciate your kindly feelings in declining to take the brief against me personally, and I now again want to reiterate the statement ... I have opposed you politically in the past and no doubt will do so in the future, but I will always remember that I am dealing with a number one good sportsman – although a damned Liberal, nevertheless with a Kloosh Tum-Tum [Chinook lingo meaning a good fellow].' Another Conservative Farris much admired was T.G. Norris, who before the Second World War had practised in the interior of British Columbia, and, after a stint as judge advocate general during the war, had resumed his legal career in Vancouver. He and Farris were old friends, cut of the same cloth, pugnacious, honourable, at each other's throats during a case but the warmest of friends afterwards, in the best tradition of the bar. In 1955 a Liberal stalwart, Thomas Braidwood, wrote Farris to recommend Norris for judicial appointment: 'I hear from mutual friends there is some question of going beyond our own people in the appointment of new judges on the

Supreme Court Bench ... I want to be clear that I am not advocating we go beyond our own people but [a singular confession] it must be agreed that there is a great shortage of people of high calibre amongst our own.' He cited Norris as 'one who is the most friendly towards us as well as the most able.' Farris agreed, telling Braidwood, 'I think it is unhealthy to have all the Judges in the superior courts selected from the Liberal Party. If a Conservative is to be selected, I know no one who would make a better appointment than Tom Norris; in fact that applies not only for a Conservative appointment but a Liberal as well.' Norris did go to the bench four years later – appointed by a Conservative government.

Within three years of his arrival in Vancouver, Farris established a reputation as an accomplished public speaker and became a member of the Liberal riding association for Vancouver. On the strength of these credentials, he ran as one of the five Liberal candidates in Vancouver in the provincial general election of 1907. A publicity photo showed a serious-looking dark-haired man with a strong jaw and high forehead, although he was anything but subdued on the hustings; according to one newspaper, his lambasting of the Tories demonstrated 'with complete success' the 'unscrupulousness with which [Conservative] candidates endeavoured to distract popular attention from their own dereliction of duty.' And the same newspaper, in reporting Farris's appearance at a rally, proclaimed, 'Mass Meeting of Citizens Enthusiastically Sets Seal of Certain Triumph on Liberal campaign.' But, alas, it was not to be: all five Liberals were defeated. Two years later Farris had another run at a legislative seat, in a by-election for Richmond, but again was unsuccessful. In the general election of 1916 he ran once more in Vancouver and was elected in a Liberal sweep. He did not at first hold a cabinet portfolio, but in 1917 he unexpectedly became attorney general and minister of labour (the first in British Columbia to hold the just-created portfolio) on the resignation from the attorney general's post of M.A. Macdonald as the result of a scandal. It was alleged that in a by-election in 1916 a sum of $15,000 paid to Macdonald by the Canadian Northern Railway had wound up in his pockets and not in the hands of the Liberal Party for which it was intended as a campaign donation. A subsequent judicial inquiry cleared Macdonald of corruption but his undoubted careless handling of the funds was enough to force his resignation from cabinet, though he continued to sit as a private member. (This was the same man who later became chief justice of British Columbia.) The rule of the day required Farris as a new appointee to cabinet to stand again in a by-election and he was returned by acclamation in Vancouver.

His tenure as attorney general was marked by a number of progressive pieces of legislation, much of it aimed at improving the lot of working women; amendments to the Marriage Act prevented teenagers from marrying below a certain age without the consent of a judge; a comprehensive system of foster homes helped the plight of wayward or orphaned young children. As well, a scheme of industrial schools was established to which young offenders would be sent rather than be exposed to hardened criminals in the common jails. Women were given the vote in municipal elections and minimum wage levels were set for them, accompanied by increases in paid holidays. Although, as already observed, Farris had not been directly responsible for the creation of the Workmen's Compensation Act, he did sponsor increased benefits for injured workers. And the stigma of illegitimacy was removed from a child born out of wedlock. This list is impressive but in addition there were five measures of greater importance, all sponsored by Farris. Wives deserted by their husbands were given an expeditious method of collecting support and of enforcing court orders for payment. Mothers in real need, whether deserted or not, were given a monthly payment. The Testators Family Maintenance Act gave to a close relative, wife or husband or child, the right to claim a share of the estate of a deceased person who by a will arbitrarily excluded such relatives from deserved benefits, and a comprehensive, orderly method of adopting children was established. Finally, the whole system of juvenile courts was revamped and as part of the process Farris took the opportunity to appoint a remarkable woman, Helen Gregory Macgill, as the first female juvenile court judge in British Columbia in July 1917 (not, however, the first in Canada; that honour belonged to Emily Murphy in Edmonton). Though she had no formal legal training, Macgill had common sense, compassion, and the respect of Vancouverites. She would today probably be described as a feminist, a description she might have accepted; she was a social thinker with the ability to influence others – one of whom was Farris. Unquestionably much of the reform legislation he introduced was with her advice, which, he acknowledged in a letter to Premier J.D. MacLean, was 'of the greatest assistance.' For her part, Macgill saw Farris's resignation as attorney general in 1921 as a severe 'loss to the women and children of this province.' She went on, 'With so splendid a record of service even those who have opposed you must recognize the great advance made by the province in the care of its weaker and more dependent citizens during your tenure.' When a Conservative government came into power in 1929 her appointment was revoked. Farris was outraged but could do nothing about it. The Liberals, on resuming office in 1933, reappointed her. Farris may well have had a hand in that for the new attorney general was his former partner, Gordon Sloan. On Macgill's retirement, Farris was one of those who persuaded R.L. Maitland, then the attorney general, to augment her small pension with a special increment.

In October 1917 the provincial government had introduced prohibition. Though Farris as attorney general obviously bore some responsibility for the measure, he personally would not have paid much attention to it. Anyone with money or connections – and he had both – could skirt its restrictions by obtaining a prescription from a friendly family doctor for alcohol as a necessary treatment or by buying bootlegged liquor from men such as Henry Reifel, the Sam Bronfman of the Pacific coast (and a friend of Farris) who, if he had set foot in the United States, would have been arrested on the spot for shipping liquor in defiance of American prohibition laws. Soon after the law took effect, Farris applied for membership in the prestigious Vancouver Club and, because of his role in introducing prohibition, was black-balled. The lieutenant governor, a member, was so incensed that he put Farris up again for membership and let it be known that if Farris was turned down a second time there would be trouble.[9] The threat worked: Farris was elected.

One of the more interesting pieces of legislation Farris introduced was the Direct Legislation Act of 1919. Though inspired by the Initiative and Referendum Act of Manitoba, which had been declared invalid by the Privy Council (see chapter 4), the British Columbia act sought to avoid the pitfalls of the Manitoba measure. So far as a referendum was concerned, the British Columbia act treated it as a sort of straw vote. In 1956 Farris told an inquiring correspondent that he personally had been opposed to the legislation but was required to support it because of cabinet solidarity. He believed that the duty of a government was to govern 'and not pass the buck to the voters. The only exception to this in my opinion is legislation involving moral issues in which a division of opinion is not possible along party lines. On this basis I think submitting the question of prohibition to the electorate is justifiable.' He likely would have felt the same way about such issues as euthanasia and assisted suicides. In any event, the legislation of 1919 was not proclaimed, and so it never became law. At the time of writing, the British Columbia government has just proclaimed similar legislation but it has not yet been tested in the courts.

Farris was re-elected in the general election of 1920. Early in 1921, after a plebiscite that favoured ending prohibition, Farris introduced the Government Liquor Act, which created a provincial monopoly for the sale of beer and spirits in liquor stores run by the newly created Liquor Control Board. That year the board took an option to purchase a warehouse in Vancouver. The property, owned by a prominent Liberal and good friend of Farris, Charles Campbell, was assessed at $58,000 but sold for $150,000. There was a row in the legislature, with Farris defending the transaction. A few months later, to everyone's astonishment, he resigned from cabinet though retaining his seat. There had been no inkling of his intention to resign and a good deal of speculation ensued. He was probably the strongest member of the cabinet, not even excluding the premier, John Oliver, and had he remained in office would no doubt have succeeded Oliver in 1927; instead the lacklustre J.D. MacLean became premier that year. Farris's son says that his reason for resigning was simple: his law firm was unravelling in his absence and he was going broke. Also, Farris's wife may well have influenced him. However, the author of a book about the connection between liquor and politics in British Columbia suggests that his resignation 'had more to do with the warehouse controversy than with his alleged desire to concentrate on his law practice.' Whatever the case, Farris appears to have contemplated moving from British Columbia back to New Brunswick. Immediately after his resignation he wrote a New Brunswick lawyer friend to tell him that he had resumed practice, adding rather mysteriously: 'I will be greatly interested to know if, in your opinion, the situation offers any possibilities. I appreciate very much your kind interest on my behalf.'[10]

Farris's resignation from the cabinet did not mark the end of his association with liquor questions. In 1925 the provincial government authorized the sale of beer by the glass in licensed establishments on a local-option basis. In an era when political patronage extended to every facet of government activity it was no surprise that allegations of bribery, corruption, and political influence in the acquisition of beer licences and in the sale of liquor by distillers to the Liquor Control Board were rampant. An excellent example of how the system worked is found in a letter from J.G. Turgeon, a leading Liberal (and later a senator), to Farris. A man named Carmichael, a Liberal supporter, asked Turgeon's help in securing a beer licence in Burnaby. Carmichael had the assurance of being able to borrow the money to build a beer parlour if he could get a commitment in writing that a licence would be issued to him in which case he could be 'of great support to [Liberal] party.' Turgeon sent a copy of the Carmichael letter to Farris and observed: 'I do not know whether anything can be done in this regard for Mr. Carmichael but if you think it worthwhile I should be glad to give you any assistance possible.'

In 1926 and 1927 there were five royal commissions on the liquor traffic; Farris represented his distiller friend, Henry Reifel, in three of them and the provincial government in the other two. The first was set up by the federal government to investigate charges that liquor produced in Canada supposedly for export was in fact being illegally sold in British Columbia at prices lower than the same product on the shelves of the government liquor stores, precisely the type of allegation that was to be made against Sam Bronfman seven years later (see chapter 3). Reifel, testifying before the commission, said that he had made contributions of nearly $100,000 in the last year and a half, some of it to the Liberal Vancouver patronage committee. Having written off these sums as a business expense, he complained that he never got 'any return' on his money and boldly asked the commission in effect to protect him from himself by outlawing all campaign funds. This candid testimony provoked such a controversy that the provincial government was forced to investigate charges of corruption by Liquor Control Board employees. Again, Reifel, supported by Farris, gave remarkably frank evidence. He admitted employing a man to contact Liquor Control Board officials to promote his products, but the man was out of the country at the time of the hearing managing a Reifel brewery in Japan; since he could not be compelled to return to testify, conveniently for Reifel, the commissioner, Mr Justice Dennis Murphy, had no firm evidence on which to make a finding of corrupt behaviour against Reifel. Soon afterward Mr Justice Aulay Morrison embarked on the first of three connected commissions. The first involved allegations of kickbacks by brewers to finance the 1924 provincial Liberal election campaign. Again Reifel testified freely that he had made campaign contributions to all parties, mostly to Liberals, but it was for federal and not provincial electioneering. Because the commission's mandate was to consider only improper provincial and not federal campaign funds, Mr Justice Morrison found no blame attached to anyone. The two remaining commissions in which Farris represented the provincial government were concerned with other forms of fraud and, in each case, government members, all Liberals and employees, were cleared of all charges of wrongdoing.[11]

In the provincial general election of 1924 Farris once again ran in the Vancouver riding but was defeated. The premier, John Oliver, also lost his seat in Victoria, though the Liberal majority survived. Farris rather ruefully wrote Oliver to commiserate with him, saying, 'Sorry I have no seat to offer you.' Although the election occurred before the notorious royal commissions, there had been much adverse publicity for the Liberal government arising from the machinations of the Liquor Control Board and it is probable that the publicity caused Farris's defeat. There was no doubt in the mind of the *Daily Province*, a supporter of the Conservatives, which in a thinly veiled reference to Farris said that as a supporter 'of the old machine [he had] been left at home.' The fact that Farris ran at all suggests that perhaps there was indeed more to his resignation as attorney general than a desire to resume his law practice; yet, on the other hand, the practice of law could more easily be accommodated to the life of a private member than to that of a cabinet minister. He would not hold elected office again though he planned to run in the 1930 federal election, in Vancouver Centre, and was confident he would win because of having built up a strong organization. His wife, however, laid down the law that she wouldn't put up with his being a candidate and he bowed to her vehement opposition and did not stand. His friend, Ian Mackenzie, ran in the riding and, bucking the Conservative tide elsewhere, took it. Many years later, after the Second World War, Farris was encouraged to resign his Senate seat and run against Howard Green, the Conservative member for Vancouver Quadra, who was considered, correctly, to be unbeatable. Farris told one of his associates that he could not win but there was always an outside chance of success; he added, however, that winning, not losing, would be the real disaster.

Farris's career as a Liberal panjandrum falls easily into two stages. In the first, his political influence was felt mainly in British Columbia; in the second, after his appointment to the Senate in 1937, he became a potent influence across the country. So far as British Columbia was concerned, his tenure as attorney general, which qualified him for admission to the inner sanctum of the provincial Liberal hierarchy, his wide circle of acquaintances – he knew everybody who was anybody and they knew him – and his role in the patronage system resulted in his being consulted on every matter of importance to his party, and on many unimportant matters as well. In what became his last significant involvement in provincial politics, he was a member of the Liberal cabal which, in a palace revolution early in December 1941, forced Premier T.D. Pattullo to resign. In the general election in October, Pattullo had won only twenty-one seats, the CCF (now the NDP) fourteen, and the Conservatives twelve. Pattullo, who had become premier in 1933, often sought political advice from Farris but privately Farris had a rather low opinion of him; he told Ian Mackenzie in a letter of 17 November 1941 that 'everything he has done has been wrong and indicates a mentality not normal.' That letter was prompted by the resignation of John Hart as minister of finance, an event that led directly to Pattullo's resignation and his replacement by Hart as premier of a coalition of Liberals and Conservatives designed to forestall formation of a socialist administration. Pattullo left office a bitter man, complaining (correctly) of a conspiracy. But he did not harbour a grudge against Farris, with whom he subsequently corresponded on non-political matters.[12]

While still in the British Columbia cabinet, Farris together with his wife and T.D. Pattullo, then another cabinet member, talked John Oliver, who was not much interested in matters of the intellect, into establishing the University of British Columbia campus at Point Grey, a decision of immense significance. More specifically, beginning as early as 1937, Farris began promoting the creation of a law school at the university. When he became president of the Canadian Bar Association, he approached L.S. Klinck, president of the university, on the subject. At the time, there was no university program of legal education in the province: an aspiring law student either enrolled in the five-year program of the Vancouver law school, run by the profession, or went off to university elsewhere. Klinck was sympathetic, and Farris and others met with him on several occasions until the outbreak of war ended all plans. In 1938 Cecil 'Caesar' Wright, dean of the Osgoode Hall Law School, came out to Vancouver for the sessions of the bar association over which Farris, as outgoing president, presided. Farris approached him informally with a view to his heading a law faculty at the University of British Columbia. Wright and Farris were not able to discuss the matter at length – they were at a function – because of garrulous interruptions by Chief Justice Morrison. However, Wright was much interested because at the time he was becoming uncomfortable at Osgoode. He later wrote to Farris: 'I do not know, of course, what you contemplate in the way of staff, nor plans for possible expansion but I thought I should write you this note to let you know – in confidence naturally – that if I were to remain in academic work in this country I might be personally interested in the possibility of new fields of endeavour outside Ontario.' Farris replied that he 'was much interested in your letter and will pass along the idea to the proper quarters.' Which he did, for a meeting took place at the university in October to discuss Wright's obvious interest in coming to British Columbia. Yet, in the end, nothing came of it. After the war, Farris renewed his efforts to establish a law school and, with a small group that included his brother, Wendell (by then the chief justice), was instrumental in its founding in 1945, in time to enrol the first group of returning veterans. He taught constitutional law at the school until 1947.

But Farris's interest in the university went beyond the law school. He and G.G. Sedgwick, renowned head of the department of English, an eminent Shakespearean scholar and wordsmith, traded friendly insults and debated such philological questions as the differences in usage of the words 'power, capacity, right.' This relationship does each man great credit. Sedgwick, a fellow Maritimer who has become legendary, was no sycophant, loathed pretentiousness, and believed in the cultivation of the intellect as the most important thing in life. He obviously enjoyed Farris's company, and the latter, for his part, found in Sedgwick the sort of person whom he did not meet in his workaday life. (The author was privileged to have been one of Sedgwick's students.)[13]

Farris's intellectual interests always went hand in hand with matters more mundane and, to some, less edifying – such as patronage. The patronage system in British Columbia was ingrained and Farris was involved in it at least until 1937 when he went to the Senate; afterwards he mainly confined himself to recommendations for judicial preferment. He made a really significant patronage appointment in 1921. The British Columbia government had decided to go on the offensive against the Board of Railway Commissioners to secure removal of the mountain differential from freight rates and to win the same benefits enjoyed by the prairie provinces with the Crow Rate. Farris's appointment of G.G. 'Gerry' McGeer, a Liberal zealot but a comparatively junior lawyer, as the province's general counsel proved an excellent one since McGeer was a doughty champion whose efforts brought significant gains to British Columbia. The subject of freight rates in the 1924 provincial election was a popular one. Charles Woodward, the merchant, and a Liberal, campaigned on the issue and led the polls in Vancouver; the Vancouver *Sun* attributed the party's overall success to its espousal of the issue, though neither Oliver nor Farris benefited.

Farris was fond of deluding himself that he played little part in low-level appointments. According to his son, John, Farris, on returning to practice after his resignation from cabinet, put up a large sign on his office door designed to keep out people pestering him for jobs: 'This is a law office. I do not have any jobs. I do not know how you get into the Post Office. I do not know how you get into the Liquor Store. If you have law business, you're welcome, otherwise keep out.' Yet in 1934 he wrote the acting attorney general in the Liberal government offering an ingenious justification for patronage: 'So far as possible I endeavour to keep my hands off the question of government jobs. Occasionally, however, when some of my old friends speak to me I feel they would misunderstand a refusal to speak for them.' There were evidently many such occasions. Typical of several letters received by Farris after he left the cabinet was one from Dr J.H. Carson, superintendent of the provincial home for incurables, who asked Farris to intercede on behalf of a man whom Carson wished to hire as a clerk, describing him as a 'dyed-in-the-wool Liberal, and a man of influence among his circle of friends.' Farris wrote the premier recommending the man. Similarly, in 1937 he interceded with the postmaster general, in Ottawa, on behalf of a young man connected to the Liberal Party for a job as postman. With the advent in British Columbia of a coalition government of Liberals and Conservatives in 1941, low-level patronage appointments became more difficult and, by the time W.A.C. Bennett formed a Social Credit government in 1952, had virtually disappeared.[14]

As a provincial attorney general Farris had had a direct hand in the appointment of the lesser judiciary, magistrates, stipendiary magistrates, coroners, and the like as well as in the appointments of lawyers to prosecute at criminal assizes; for all of such jobs, political affiliation was important. Beginning in the 1920s, after he went out of office, he gradually acquired some influence in the appointment of federal judges, and this influence expanded significantly following his senatorial appointment. He never appointed himself, so to speak, though in 1926 he toyed with the idea of going to the bench. He exercised his influence in concert with his brother Wendell until the latter's appointment as chief justice of the Supreme Court of British Columbia in 1942, and thereafter Farris alone was either consulted about, or initiated, recommendations. The prime minister himself would be consulted before appointments of judges to the Supreme Court of Canada or of the provincial chief justiceships but only rarely would he be concerned with appointments to other positions, all of which would be made by the minister of justice; the latter would not make appointments until he heard from political allies who, in the case of British Columbia in the 1940s and 1950s, was Farris. Farris's recommendations were not always followed; one Liberal was often chosen over another whom Farris preferred. Yet he would be consulted and, for appointments that went contrary to his wishes, advised of the reasons. As with conferring patronage jobs, so with judicial appointments; he disingenuously claimed to have no influence. In 1942, writing to H.I. Bird (who did eventually become chief justice) about a pending appointment to which Bird aspired, Farris said, 'I have been asked by so many of my friends for support [in opposition to Bird's claim] that I have decided to make no recommendation, unless I am asked by Mr. Mackenzie [the ranking British Columbia cabinet minister in Ottawa] for one. I am fortified in this position by the fact that practically not one of my recommendations has been acted on in the past.' And in 1955 he made a similar statement to a well-known Roman Catholic lawyer in Victoria who had asked Farris for support in his efforts to succeed another Roman Catholic whose departure from the Supreme Court of British Columbia for the Court of Appeal had opened a vacancy: 'My experience has been that the Minister of Justice and the members of the cabinet from this province pay no attention to my opinions or recommendations and I have decided to make no more.' These observations by Farris are simply not true; he made them and other remarks like them to avoid offending applicants whom he did not favour or, as in the case of Bird, to avoid being drawn into a campaign among competing Liberals.

Examples of his role in appointments could be multiplied but three are typical. In 1937 the position of chief justice of the Court of Appeal for British Columbia became vacant. There were two contenders for the position, and both had been Liberal appointments: the senior judge on the court, seventy-two-year-old Mr Justice Archer Martin, a sound jurist but a thoroughly disagreeable man, and M.A. Macdonald, a younger man, also a judge of the court but with less seniority than Martin; he was the man whom Farris had succeeded as attorney general. At the time, there was no requirement that a judge must retire at the age of seventy-five. Farris brokered a deal, subsequently implemented by Ottawa, by which Martin would become chief justice but give an undertaking that he would in fact retire at seventy-five, whereupon Macdonald would succeed him. Before Martin reached seventy-five, a general election loomed and Macdonald, worried that if the Liberals should lose it to the Conservatives he would not be appointed, regardless of the gentleman's agreement, requested Farris to ask Martin to retire before the election so that his appointment would be assured. Farris refused. Macdonald was furious. The Liberals won the general election on 26 March 1940 and Martin kept his word, resigning in May; Macdonald was appointed though he died barely a year later. During that time he never spoke to Farris or rendered a judgment in favour of a Farris client. Such were the hazards of judge-making. When word got out that Macdonald was to be appointed, a partner of Farris, then in Ottawa, wrote Farris urging him to do all in his power to prevent the appointment; he warned that, though Macdonald was a Liberal, his 'liberality' consisted in ignoring 'law and all principles and precedents.'

The second example concerns Farris's brother Wendell. The late Oscar

Orr, for years a highly regarded magistrate in Vancouver, recalled speaking to Farris about his brother's appointment as chief justice of the Supreme Court of British Columbia in 1942. Farris told him, 'If I didn't promote him who would?' Then there was the matter of a replacement for Chief Justice A.C. DesBrisay of the Court of Appeal (and of British Columbia). Though he was a Conservative appointee, Farris held him in high regard. When he resigned in 1963, jockeying for his position began immediately. A senior member of the court was H.I. Bird; another judge of the same court was J.O. Wilson; the chief justice of the Supreme Court of British Columbia was Sherwood Lett. All these men had backgrounds in the Liberal Party though Wilson was less overt in his political beliefs than the other two. It was generally believed that Wilson and Bird were the front runners for the chief justiceship. On 29 May 1963 Farris wrote Arthur Laing, the senior cabinet minister for British Columbia, urging Bird's appointment rather than Wilson's. This was not because Wilson was not an admirable man – he was – but because his appointment as chief justice would not, Farris said, sit well with the remaining members of the court. On 10 July Laing wrote Farris to tell him that the government had decided to appoint Lett as chief justice of British Columbia and to move Wilson from the Court of Appeal to succeed Lett as chief justice. Farris, covering all the bases, immediately wrote Lett and Wilson to congratulate them. Lett, also an admirable man, died less than a year after his appointment. In July 1964 Mr Justice Davey of the Court of Appeal (later to be a chief justice himself) telephoned Farris on his own behalf and that of his brother judges on the Court of Appeal, so he said, asking Farris to do what he could to ensure the appointment of H.I. Bird as chief justice. Farris accordingly wrote J.R. Nicholson, by this time the reigning cabinet minister from British Columbia, and two weeks later Bird was appointed. Wilson went on to a distinguished career as chief justice of the Supreme Court of British Columbia, a position he adorned.

Manoeuvring for position among the judges in Farris's era was not uncommon and was sometimes nasty. When Chief Justice Gordon Hunter (a man whom Farris considered to be one of the best judges the country had produced, equal to Sir Lyman Duff) died in 1929, Mr Justice Aulay Morrison, the senior member of the Supreme Court of British Columbia, wrote Farris. Feeling entitled to be Hunter's successor, he expressed dismay at rumours that Archer Martin was to be appointed chief justice. Morrison, as much a Liberal partisan as Martin, said of him: 'If such a calamity as his appointment were to happen, then there is no use in anyone holding office under the Crown being decent, honourable or loyal anymore.' In the result, Morrison became chief justice and Martin remained on the Court of Appeal. Two observations are in order here: Morrison's strictures are an echo of a bygone age; and, more pertinently, his and other judicial appointments underline Farris's central role as judge-maker within British Columbia.[15]

In October 1936 Farris wrote Mackenzie King to say that he would like to fill a Senate vacancy in British Columbia. Another suppliant was Brenton S. Brown of Vancouver who, on learning of Farris's aspirations, withdrew from the lists; Farris was eternally grateful, and on 9 January 1937 King sent a telegram to advise him that, by an order-in-council approved by the governor general, he had been appointed a member of the Senate for British Columbia. Farris was comfortable in the Senate. He enjoyed the badinage and the give-and-take of debate; in a way it was a return to his old debating days at the university. He was occasionally highly partisan, a notable instance being his vociferous attack on John Bracken in 1944 for his failure to secure a seat in parliament while leader of the Progressive Conservative Party, an attack that drew much adverse editorial comment from around the country. But generally he was not provocative. Though his fellow senators often called on his legal expertise, he displayed a wide range of interests as a senator. His speeches had an air of spontaneity about them; he never read from a prepared text but spoke from notes with an easy form of delivery. In his very first debate he (and also Arthur Meighen) spoke in favour of federal legislation conferring on provincial courts of appeal the jurisdiction to hear appeals from rulings in divorce cases. The issue was an old one – did the legislation relate to marriage and divorce, areas within federal competence, or was it an intrusion into provincial jurisdiction over the administration of law? Farris thought that the federal government had the power to legislate but in the course of the debate informed the Senate that British Columbia's attorney general had assured him the province would legislate, if necessary, and indeed that is what happened. And in 1948 he carried the debate on the important amendment to the Canada Evidence Act relaxing the common law rule compelling a spouse to testify against the other in cases of certain sexual offences. Farris's common-sense argument was that the sanctity of the rule should be altered from time to time as circumstances changed. And at that same session, harking back to his days as attorney general, he supported legislation that imposed on young offenders an indeterminate sentence to be served in special detention homes and not among hardened criminals in the common jails.

Firmly convinced as he was of the utility of the Senate within the Canadian parliamentary system, he took his duties very seriously, attending sessions regularly (although there were occasional unavoidable absences) until he was ninety though by that time he debated very little. But he was pragmatic enough to recognize that some Senate reform was desirable, suggesting that the provinces be given the right to choose one-third of the membership of the body, thus broadening the political spectrum of the chamber. As a provincial-rights man, he was sometimes at odds with the leaders of his own party. For example, he was opposed, as early as 1943, to any suggestion that the Canadian constitution be repatriated without the consent of the provinces, a view that he reiterated from time to time in the Senate. Similarly, though he did not live to see it, he would have been deeply suspicious of the Charter of Rights, because under it British parliamentary supremacy has given way to the courts as the ultimate constitutional authority.

Two of Farris's activities in the Red Chamber should be singled out. The first harked back to the fall of Hong Kong in the Second World War. Late in 1941 the Canadian military had assembled a force, which after brief training embarked for the British colony; tragically, it arrived on the eve of its invasion by, and capitulation to, the Japanese. In 1942 Mackenzie King, under severe political pressure because of reports of atrocities by the Japanese committed against badly trained Canadian troops, persuaded the then chief justice, Sir Lyman Duff, to conduct a one-man enquiry into the circumstances of the manning, training, and transport of the Canadian units. In his report, Duff absolved the military establishment of any negligence in mounting the force. Then, in 1946, the Hong Kong garrison commander wrote his official report of the debacle for the British War Office. It contained scathing comments on the performance of the Canadian troops; a copy was routinely sent to Canadian Defence Headquarters which, worried about the effect of the comments, persuaded the British to tone them down. Both Brooke Claxton, the minister of national defence, and Lieutenant-General Charles Foulkes, chief of the General Staff, were privy to the editing (Foulkes, incidentally, thought that the expedition had been so badly handled that had he been in charge he would have court-marshalled all those responsible; still, he was opposed to reopening old wounds and favoured suppression of the unedited report).

Publication of the watered-down version early in 1948 provoked fresh debate. Claxton, when asked by a suspicious John Diefenbaker whether he had been aware of the contents of the report prior to its release in January 1948, brazenly said that he knew nothing about it. George Drew, who in 1942 had led the attack on the Duff report, now, as premier of Ontario, resumed his onslaught, aided and abetted by the *Globe and Mail*. King, anxious to deflect criticism of the military and of the Duff report, asked Farris to defend the government in the Senate, which Farris was only too eager to do. In fairness to him, he could not have known of the revisions about which Claxton had lied, or of Foulkes's opinion. In a heated speech, he lashed out at Drew, lauded King, praised Duff, and castigated the *Globe* and anyone else who dared suggest that there had been shortcomings in the planning of the expedition. King was delighted with Farris's performance, saying that it was 'the kind of thing that every Member of Parliament should be doing for all he is worth.'

Then, late in his career, when Farris was eighty-six, Premier W.A.C. Bennett of British Columbia asked him to sponsor in the Senate the federal bill for the incorporation of the Bank of British Columbia. Bennett, like Farris, had been born in New Brunswick and despite the differences in their politics – Bennett was head of a Social Credit Government which had a conservative tinge – the two liked and admired each other. In the Senate debates Farris emphasized the argument that no Canadian chartered bank had its headquarters west of Toronto and there should be a bank based in western Canada. He also told critics of the bill who attacked Bennett personally as unreliable because of his government's takeover of the British Columbia Electric Railway Company that that matter had been settled by the courts and fair compensation had been paid. When asked point-blank by one senator whether he, Farris, approved of the takeover, he said that he did not but 'the people of British Columbia by a majority of 41-5 did approve' (a reference to Bennett's massive victory in the last provincial election). The Senate gave its approval to the bill, and Bennett remained grateful to Farris for his effective support. On Farris's death in 1970, Bennett interrupted the proceedings of the legislature to pay tribute to him.

On 3 December 1968 Senator Farris observed his ninetieth birthday – 'celebrated' would not quite be the right word – and the sixty-fifth anniversary of his membership in the British Columbia bar. Since 1964 he had not been in the courtroom. That year he had acted on a case which he lost, and he had the nagging feeling that he had somehow missed the essential point. And indeed he had, as was pointed out to him by his concerned son, John. (Three years after his father's death, John was appointed chief justice of British Columbia, resigning in 1978.) The senator faced up to his failing powers and vowed never again to set foot in a courtroom. It was a tough and sad decision for the old warrior but he was not one to sulk.

About the same time, his beloved wife began to lose her memory and progressively became unable to converse in any meaningful way. They continued to live in their spacious home on South Granville Street which they had occupied for nearly fifty years, their needs attended to by a cook, housekeeper, housemaids, and a chauffeur-gardener.

Until the last six months of his life the senator was chauffeured to his office several times a week in his Packard sedan. At one time the Packard was the car of choice of the well-to-do but by the 1960s it had become old-fashioned. Once ensconced in his comfortable private office, he held court as the elder legal statesman of the firm. But he was always approachable; he enjoyed having people drop in for a chat; he used to say of these occasions that he was 'in his anecdotage.' He would go through his mail and willingly offer advice to any member of the firm who sought it. A piece of advice he was fond of tendering was that, if a lawyer had a case weak in its facts, he should pound the law; if the case was weak in the law, pound the facts; if the case was weak both in the facts and the law, he should pound the table. Occasionally he went out for lunch with an old friend. If not, just before noon, he would have a few nips of the bottle either by himself or with anyone who cared to join him. He would then have a snooze on the sofa in his office and in mid-afternoon his chauffeur came to take him home. This pleasant form of dotage ended about six months before his death when he no longer ventured downtown.

Late in February 1970 he fell out of his bed and in doing so knocked over an electric lamp still switched on which fell onto him. Unconscious, he was badly burnt and was not discovered for some hours later. He was rushed to hospital but his system could not withstand the shock and he died soon after, on February 25th. When his wife, whose mind by then was a complete blank, was told of his death she said, 'Isn't that too bad.'[16]

6

Frank Manning Covert

Frank Manning Covert was named a King's Counsel by the attorney general of Nova Scotia in March 1944. The appointment was unusual, not only because of his relative youth – he was only thirty-six – but because at the time he was in England with the RCAF, training for combat duty with Bomber Command. In August that year he flew on his first raid over Europe and by the following March had completed thirty-six bombing missions, a full 'tour.' By the rules of the day a crew after a full tour was 'screened' – grounded – for six months. In Covert's case, the war's ending precluded any possibility of a second tour. He was the only KC to have flown on combat operations with the RCAF during the Second World War and may possibly have been the only KC to have been on combat duty with any branch of the Canadian armed forces. That he was in Europe at all is in itself remarkable, a result of his courage and of his ability to pull political strings.

Covert had practised law for ten years with the firm in Halifax he was later to lead when in 1940 he was summoned to Ottawa to become a wartime bureaucrat in the Department of Munitions and Supply, headed by the formidable C.D. Howe. Covert served as assistant general counsel to Henry Borden, who had talked him into going to Ottawa, and for two years he negotiated contracts within Canada and the United States for the supply of war materiel. The job was well paid and interesting besides. It was also demanding: Covert recorded in his diaries that in 1941 he worked 287 nights. He was not office-bound and frequently appeared for the government before wartime regulatory bodies. After the war he was invested with the Order of the British Empire for his work in the department. Yet, though he established a close rapport with Howe, he soon began to think of making a more direct contribution to the war effort. In doing so, he was spurred by two events: Howe and Covert's friend Gordon Scott were torpedoed on a wartime voyage to England, and, while Howe survived, Scott did not; and Covert's brother-in-law was killed in a military training accident.

He told Howe that he wanted to enlist in the air force but Howe would not hear of it. One day in Howe's absence, Covert went to the RCAF recruiting centre, without his wife's knowledge, to join up. Informed he was too old, Covert phoned the office of C.G. Power, minister for air, which arranged a medical. His age, thirty-four, precluded any combat duty, but Power's office at Covert's insistence arranged an interview for him with Air Vice-Marshall L.S. Breadner, who for fifteen minutes suspended regulations by allowing Covert to enlist in an air-crew program as a navigator. Covert readily agreed and Breadner swore him on the spot as an aircraftsman second class. With his political connections he could easily have obtained some cushy service job and lived, as the poet Siegfried Sassoon put it, 'With scarlet majors at the base,' sending 'glum heroes up the line to death.' Instead, Covert was the guest of honour at a gala farewell party given by his colleagues at Munitions and Supply, presided over by Howe himself, who had relented in his opposition to the departure of his colleague. Following the presentation of a Rolex watch, Covert immediately left for the depot at the Exhibition grounds in Toronto to join thousands of other air-force recruits.

The next year he spent training for his navigator's wings. Although he was not intimidated by applied mathematics, he found the training course very difficult and at times despaired of his ability to learn how to navigate an aircraft by day, let alone by night. But he did well, attaining high marks, and received his sergeant's wings (of which he was immensely proud) on 14 October 1943. A day later he was commissioned as Pilot Officer F.M. Covert and not long after was promoted to Flying Officer, a rank he held until the end of the war. The head instructor at his training school asked him to stay on as an instructor. Covert told him that, if he did not get an immediate overseas posting, he would ask C.D. Howe to take him out of the air force altogether. Less than a month later, Covert, after farewells from his mother and wife and young son, Michael, marched through the streets of Halifax with 7,000 other servicemen to board the troop ship *Mauretania* on its voyage to the United Kingdom.

After some preliminary training under wartime conditions, he arrived in April 1944 at an operational training unit where crews were formed in a process that at first blush seems quaint, if not archaic. Pilots, navigators, bomb aimers, wireless operators, gunners, and other air crew from the various training schools were herded together in a large room so that all milled about eyeing each other rather like dealers at a cattle auction. A young pilot, Wib Pierce, aged twenty-two, spotted Covert and, as Covert later recalled, the following brief conversation ensued. After exchanging their names Pierce asked:

'How about being my navigator?'

'Sure,' Covert replied.

'Do you know anybody here?'

'No,' Covert responded.

Then, between the two of them, they picked a crew. Pierce's version is much the same – it all depended on the cut of a man's jib. His job was to get the best navigator and crew he could. He spotted Covert, who 'actually looked younger than I did,' with 'ample black hair, fair complexion and flashing eyes.' He explains that 'I picked Frank out of perhaps 30 navigators by sight alone. He was alert, casual, confident and struck me as my kind of man. I approached him and invited him to be my navigator. He said he had met a bomb aimer that seemed a good type so I said, "Bring him in." He knew two gunners that wanted to fly together so they came in. They knew a wireless operator & he came in. Such was what turned out to be a first-class crew formed.'

The crew trained on heavy bombers for operational duties, Covert having to master, like any other navigator of the time, the intricacies of the new and still relatively untried radar systems. Covert and his crew-mates flew their first operational mission on 2 August 1944, a flight that he later recalled as the most harrowing of all. One engine failed, and a second gave serious trouble, resulting in a severe loss of altitude. Pierce managed to limp back to an emergency landing in England but, as Covert wryly remarked, because they had not dropped their bombs the mission did not count as a flight; so, in effect, he did thirty-seven missions, not thirty-six as officially recorded. Between that date and 15 March 1945 the crew, mostly on Halifax aircraft but latterly on Lancasters, completed its tour. The crew's reputation was such that on occasion it had as passengers on operations various senior officers, including Wing Commander Sharpe, who was later to head the RCAF, and the station commander, Group Captain Rutledge. Ted Hutton, the bomb aimer, recalls that on the return flight with Rutledge, Covert warned the skipper three times on the intercom that he was flying off course, much to the surprise of the crew for Pierce was the last person to be guilty of such an error. On the third occasion, Rutledge came on the intercom to admit that he had been at the controls but was handing them back to the pilot. Covert rejoined: 'You'd better, if you want to get home today.' Covert, a flying officer, rebuking the group captain: it was the mark of a man confident of his own ability.

One of the missions, over Grevenbroich in Germany, was particularly hazardous, for constant changes in position because of enemy action made the calculation of the moment of the bomb drop very difficult. Pierce as pilot, Covert as navigator, and the bomb aimer were principally involved in this challenging operation and its success resulted in Covert being recommended for the Distinguished Flying Cross, which was awarded him in May 1945. Covert tersely recorded in his diary his final trip: 'March 15. No.36 op. Night – Hagen – HOT TARGET – Home trip Bad. 7:30 [time of return]. Seven planes shot down on way home.' Two weeks later the ground crew invited Covert and his crew-mates to a celebratory party in the sergeants' mess. After exacting a promise that his hosts would see him, and his bicycle, safely home, Covert spent the evening drinking large quantities of scotch whisky while telling endless stories and toasting missing comrades. He later observed of the end of his tour: 'It was really a great relief for me – I'd done what I set out to do, I was desperately tired and I had reached the stage where I feared that the extra trips would be our downfall. That was terribly bad for morale.'

On 13 May 1945, with thousands of other Canadian and American servicemen including his crew-mate Ted Hutton, Covert embarked for home on the *Île de France*. According to Hutton, Covert spent twenty-three hours of each day playing high-stakes bridge with American officers from whom he won large sums of money, not dishonestly, like a Mississippi river boat gambler, but by skill, for he was an expert. He was fascinated by the game, playing out hands in newspaper bridge columns and reading widely about it. There was obviously something about the game that appealed to his analytical and mathematical mind, and when on station whiling away the tedious days between operations (the waiting was more stressful than the flights), he played incessantly. Some years after the war he wrote a book on bridge, not for beginners, but for competent players interested in tactics. He does not seem to have sought a commercial publisher for he had it privately printed and circulated.

Forty years after the war Covert summed up his combat service in typical fashion:

1. It was a magnificent experience.
2. We had a great crew of wonderfully fine young men.
3. Had I known what it would really be like I wouldn't have had the guts to join.
4. Having come through it all I wouldn't have missed it for the world.

For their part, Covert's skipper, Wib Pierce, and bomb aimer, Ted Hutton, speak of Covert with enormous admiration. Discounting the camaraderie of shared combat experience, they are astonished that a man fifteen years older than any of the other crew should have been flying over Germany at all. But they both say that Covert was the smartest man they ever met. In this early evaluation, they were absolutely correct: most of Covert's legal colleagues, and opponents, would have agreed with them.

Covert kept in touch with all his comrades by correspondence and visits both in Canada and the United Kingdom (the flight engineer had been an Englishman), but apart from these contacts and the occasional crew reunion – the last in 1984 – he avoided general service functions and never attended Remembrance Day Services. Though not given to sentimental observances he remained justly proud of his own record and that of his fellow crew members.

A war hero, though he would have disclaimed any such pretensions, Covert returned to his wife, his ten-year-old son, and his law firm. He was thirty-seven years old. For a few months he suffered from what the medical people described as 'operational fatigue' but he soon recovered and for the next forty years worked as intensely as he had during the war, the enemy now being not a German night fighter but perhaps a hot-shot lawyer from Montreal or Boston or New York. Just as he repelled attacks in Europe, so he did with his law practice: he would take on the best and defeat them. Hardly had he disembarked before he was in his old office – there was no lengthy holiday, as one might have expected. His revered partner, James McGregor Stewart, had written a year earlier to assure him that a seat was being kept warm for him. And Covert responded in characteristic fashion by plunging into work at once as if to make up for his five-year absence. Within days of his return he collaborated with his other senior partner, Harry McKeen, in a jury trial in Yarmouth at which their client was acquitted. At the end of the year, his name was added to the firm masthead, which henceforth read as Stewart McKeen and Covert. That Covert understood the virtues of hard work was not accidental or acquired but ingrained, a product of his family background, of a boyhood spent in a small rural community and of an education provided by dedicated teachers in one-room country schools.

He was born in 1908 at Canning, in King's County, a village near the Minas Basin on the Nova Scotia north shore only a short distance from Kentville and Wolfville. His father, son of an Anglican parson on Grand Manan Island, was a country doctor who, after service overseas with the Canadian Medical Corps, returned to Canning to practise until his untimely death in 1922, leaving an impoverished wife to support four children and somehow maintain the large family home. Covert recalled his father, whom he often accompanied because of his mother's concern for her husband's health, driving out at all times of the day or night in all conditions of weather to treat patients and deliver babies for a pittance, often with no payment but gratitude and perhaps some farm produce. His mother was a farmer's daughter, an industrious and resourceful woman who, after her husband's death, studied pharmacy and opened a drugstore to raise her young family, the oldest of whom was aged seventeen and the youngest, Frank, aged fourteen, at the time of their father's death.

Frank retained vivid memories of a bucolic boyhood: watching shipwrights build three-masted vessels, from the laying of the keel until launching into the river basin; observing the grimy blacksmith at the village smithy unshoeing a horse, heating the old shoes, bending them, and refitting them by holding the horse's leg steady in an opening of his leather apron, all in a cloud of smoke and sparks; packing apples in barrels, the apples squeezed into every inch of space; savouring the pungent odors at the local cider and vinegar factory; admiring the skill of the men in the town's axe factories; fishing for tommy cod and eels and sometimes flounders off the sand beach of the Minas Basin; and hunting and trapping weasels, rabbits, skunks, raccoons, and muskrats – all indelible impressions on an impressionable boy. But young Frank did more than watch others labour. Besides working in his mother's drugstore he shovelled coal from rail cars onto a dray and shovelled it into customers' cellars; he worked in the post office in the summer months for eleven hours each day six days a week, earning eight dollars per week. He picked strawberries and apples and hoed and dug potatoes. Even at his young age he kept a diary recording that on one occasion he and three other boys had picked forty-five boxes [crates] of strawberries in one hour and twelve minutes. Sixty years later he purchased his seaside property at Hunt's Point on the south shore, where he built his comfortable and treasured house. There, he revelled in his vegetable garden, recording in the most meticulous detail imaginable the crops he garnered: six buckets of tomatoes, seventeen pumpkins, seventy-one squash, and so on. He spent hours on the patio, which faced Port Mouton and the open Atlantic, shelling peas, shucking corn (ninety-six ears one day), and preparing thousands of beets, broccoli, brussels sprouts, carrots, and other vegetables for freezing. The lovely but homely Hunt's Point property, with its well-tilled vegetable garden (not much in the way of flowers), was Covert's haven, the only place where he could unwind. It became his permanent home from which he commuted to his office and he grudged the many times he was obliged by work to stay over in his apartment in Halifax.

He valued his schooling at all levels, describing his teachers as 'magnificent,' even the one, a staunch United Empire Loyalist, who during a geography lesson cut out the pages from a textbook containing the geography of the United States. His father, infuriated on learning of this, said that he thought only the English could be capable of such a desecration. He completed high school in Kentville, where he continued to demonstrate his aptitude for learning. In his graduating year, he wrote the provincial exams. Though he did creditably in classics and French, he distinguished himself in algebra and trigonometry by achieving a 100 per cent mark in each, good preparation for his wartime training as navigator. A few years before his death in 1987 one of his old teachers at the primer school in Canning spotted an article about her former student and, although she must have known about him earlier, was emboldened to write him to congratulate him on his various attainments. Thus began an affectionate correspondence between the student and his teacher, who could have been only a few years older. 'Miss Chase,' as Covert dutifully called her at first (she had never married), lived in Kentville, and after the exchange of a few letters he presumed to call her Gertrude and visited her at least once. In one of his letters Covert recalled that he had received from her a volume of poems by Robert Service which she had inscribed 'For Best Progress of the Year' and which he still had on his bookshelf. It is easy for bright pupils to become sentimental about their early schooling and Covert is no exception. At the time contact between teacher and student was renewed, he was the most influential lawyer in the Atlantic region, yet, clearly, he was moved by her interest in his achievements.

After he completed high school, his mother, in consultation with her brother-in-law, W.H. Covert, a prominent Halifax lawyer, decided on Frank's future: instead of studying engineering, as her husband had wished, he would study law. To that end, Frank went to Halifax to enrol at Dalhousie. His uncle and his family, one of whom was a daughter, Mollie, lived in a splendid house in Dartmouth where Frank became *en famille*. He later recalled his first appearance on the Dalhousie campus in

1924, a country bumpkin aged sixteen wearing short pants, the only student so clothed; his aunt rescued him from his mortification by buying him a suit with long pants. Covert was eternally grateful to his aunt, not just because of that episode, but for her loving spirit. After finishing his pre-law courses, Covert was enrolled in the law school where he was taught by, among others, Dean John E. Read, later of the department of external affairs and a noted scholar of international law, and Angus L. Macdonald, later premier of Nova Scotia. To support himself he worked during the summers as a bellhop at the Hackmatack Inn in Chester where, as he recalled, he made more money from tips in summer than he did in each of the first seven years of his practice as a lawyer. He received many offers of employment from guests but resolutely decided to stick to the law, graduating from Dalhousie at the top of his class as gold medalist in 1929. When the subject of articling came up, his uncle discouraged him, rightly, from articling in his firm because, as he said, if his nephew did well, people would attribute his success to his uncle's influence. Instead, he articled with the Stewart McKeen firm, which, after his term of articles was finished, took him on as a junior lawyer; he was called to the Nova Scotia bar in February 1930 and became a partner in the firm in 1936.

For the remainder of his life, Covert maintained a close and harmonious relationship with his alma mater. In 1955 he became a member of Dalhousie's board of governors and for over twenty years he contributed his considerable financial and legal skills in a variety of ways: member of the executive and budget committees, chairman of the pension and investment committees, honorary treasurer in 1973. In 1976, after appointment as chairman of the board of governors of the Nova Scotia Technical Institute (later named the Technical University of Nova Scotia), he resigned from the Dalhousie board to avoid any suggestion of conflict of interest but remained on the investment committee to the end of his life. As well, Covert had a long connection with the law school. For a number of years he lectured on labour law, company law, and income tax. For many years, too, he was a member of the law faculty committee responsible for awarding the Sir James Dunn scholarships, a duty he took very seriously, attending all the meetings and interviewing the short-listed candidates. Ron Macdonald, now of the University of Toronto law school but dean at Dalhousie from 1972 to 1979, remembers Covert well during that period, describing him as a 'giver' not a 'taker,' a man who 'was a Canadian of that generation which wanted to contribute to the building of Canada' by fostering the education of the younger generation. Dalhousie's only tangible expression of gratitude for Covert's many years of devoted service was a 'certificate of thanks' bestowed in 1984; many believed that he should have been awarded many years earlier an honorary LLD.

Covert's legal career falls easily into two stages, the ten years before his wartime service (though he was in effect practising law with the Department of Munitions and Supply) and the forty-two years after the war during which he not only established himself as the leading lawyer in the Atlantic region but also acquired a national reputation. It was in this period that he became a powerful figure in the Liberal Party, an adviser to premiers and lesser politicians of the party and sometimes to Conservative politicians as well, such as Robert Stanfield. During these same years he acquired his acknowledged expertise as a corporate lawyer and, what is less generally known, as a labour lawyer.

During the period of his practice before the war, he laid the foundations for his later renown and developed the work and personal habits which set him so far apart from his contemporaries. In all his pursuits he was driven by a fear of failure. He had to achieve mastery over every problem presented to him, he had to know everything there was to be known about it, he had to be in control, and, accordingly, he went to extraordinary lengths to prepare himself so that he would never be caught out; he had to be right and almost invariably he was. Sometimes his confidence in the correctness of any position he took was mistaken for arrogance; when he knew he was right he never hesitated to say so and tended to be impatient with people who doubted him. As his son, Michael, put it, his father worked hard to be the best, constantly competing against himself 'in his exercise of self-improvement,' and this way of life left little time for his family. The struggle for self-improvement, moreover, was a feature not just of his professional career but of all aspects of his life. When playing pool at his house at Hunt's Point he had an imaginary opponent, Aylmer (one recalls Christopher Robin helping himself to an extra portion of food for his imaginary friend, Binker). Covert's daughter, Susan, said that the 'child living in him was quite healthy.' And the same with golf, at which he became really quite proficient, sometimes shooting his age. He would hit two or three balls off the tee and play each as if it were a separate round. To keep track of matters he used balls of a different colour or make and when the round (or rounds) was completed, he would record in his diary the best score of a particular ball as the official score of the day. Thus he was sometimes playing against not one imaginary opponent but two and was able in good conscience to record, a few months before he died, that he had played 3,140 games since 1970. But he never fudged his scores nor broke club rules about such things as the lie of the ball in winter or summer conditions. When he joined the Liverpool Golf Club, not far from his Hunt's Point house, the other members disapproved of what they viewed as his eccentric methods for he much preferred playing against himself than against others. To stay out of their way, he took early tee times, but when other members caught up to him he would willingly let them play through.[1]

It was partly because of this commitment to improvement that he did not enjoy attending social functions, which he saw as a frivolous waste of time, but he did attend when he could not decently avoid them. His aversion to cocktail parties and the like, unless attended by intimates, was due also, surprisingly, to a certain shyness, for he found it difficult to engage in small talk with unfamiliar companions not because of any belief in his intellectual or personal superiority but because of a natural diffidence. In fact, he got on extremely well with common folk, such as carpenters, postmen, gas-station attendants, and his office staff liked him because he was unfailingly courteous and respectful of their feelings. For a number of years he could not bring himself to discharge a secretary who had a serious drinking problem and even lent her a substantial sum of money at a nominal rate of interest, a loan she never repaid.

His native intelligence was considerable, undoubtedly a useful attribute, but he added an extra dimension to his activities. Besides being a Liberal in politics, he had a strong social conscience and was determined always to act in a manner consistent with his basic beliefs. So, rather than being motivated by a mere sense of duty, he bent his efforts to do things that he genuinely liked doing and that – the all-important factor – would also benefit the community. In this sense he had a civilizing effect on his clients, who recognized that the advice he gave them was of a very high order and based on moral principles. The most striking example was his marked sympathy for trade unions, which he repeatedly encouraged his corporate clients to accept as institutions indispensable to a free economy. He was also racially tolerant, as evidenced by his successful campaign to have the popular mayor of Halifax, Leonard Kitz, admitted to the Halifax Club. Kitz became the club's first Jewish member.

He was frugal in his personal spending habits. While he lived in comfortable houses, they were not mansions though after the war he could well afford one. Even his spacious house at Hunt's Point was unostentatious. (Though it had nothing to do with frugality he would not have curtains over the windows facing seaward: he wanted to be able to watch unimpeded the Atlantic surf.) He owned inexpensive cars and drove them into the ground before buying a replacement. After he built his home at Hunt's Point he spent less and less time in the Halifax Club, where in earlier days he had regularly played bridge at noon with his cronies. He applied for non-resident status to be eligible for the club's lower fees, but the club ruled that he was still a resident member because his law office was in the city. Covert resigned. He was equally sparing of his clients' resources, invariably flying economy class even when working for wealthy clients who would gladly have paid for first-class seats. On one occasion he found himself on the same flight as his partner, Bill Mingo, who was flying first class; Covert noted they did not have much chance to talk.

He had an astonishing capacity for hard work over long periods. In 1940 he recorded working 220 nights in the course of the year as well as nearly every holiday and virtually all Saturday and Sunday afternoons. In 1958, when he was approaching the peak of his career, he worked 337 nights (of the 365 in the year!), 47 Sundays, and 50 Saturdays. Small wonder his family life suffered. That he was able to maintain such a punishing pace was due largely to his abstemious habits. Until 1967 he smoked at least two packs of cigarettes a day and had a cigarette cough. Feeling wretched, he then quit cold turkey. For eight months he suffered the tortures of the damned but never smoked again. Similarly with liquor. He quit hard liquor on 28 February 1949, as he recorded, and thereafter drank only wine and then in moderation. In 1960 he took up the 5BX (air force) physical-training program of skipping and stationary-bicycle exercise, which he performed unfailingly each day for thirty-two minutes, not thirty-one or thirty-three but thirty-two. He continued this regimen until a few months before his death, when his medical condition made continuous exercise impossible. On his numerous trips to Montreal on purely legal business or for directors' meetings of the Royal Bank or Sun Life, he took his skipping rope with him and, it not being practicable to take his stationary bicycle, spent the thirty-two minutes skipping.

Another characteristic of Covert – and perhaps his most distinguishing one – was his sound judgment not just in legal matters but in a wide range of subjects. It was because he had such acumen in so many fields that he was constantly being asked to render advice and give assistance to charitable groups. Covert found it difficult to refuse assistance to a worthy community group and once he took on a commitment he stayed with it. Of course, it was because of his excellent judgment and sense of balance in the conduct of clients' affairs that he reached the pinnacle of the profession in the Atlantic region.

Covert, in the first decade of his practice, cut his teeth on cases in the magistrates courts not just in Halifax but elsewhere in Nova Scotia and, like many young lawyers starting out, he revelled in a victory in an unpromising case. One such instance involved a medical doctor who, addicted to drugs, was accused of breaking and entering a drugstore to steal morphine. What gave piquancy to the case was that the man was a nephew of a prominent Ontario legal figure and future chief justice of Canada. Covert got him off. He went on to do a great deal of civil and criminal litigation at all levels of the courts in Nova Scotia. He was particularly effective in criminal trials before both juries and judges and frequently appeared on cases before administrative tribunals such as the Public Utilities Board and the Workmen's Compensation Board. He developed a particular skill in expropriation cases; in 1931, only a year after his call to the bar, he represented Eastern Telephone and Telegraph on sixty-four arbitrations arising from the acquisition by the company of rights-of-way for its transatlantic cable. It is difficult to say just which sort of case chiefly appealed to him: he seemed to love all kinds of litigation, which formed the bulk of his work in his first decade of practice. Yet, as will be seen, he also developed his skills as a corporate lawyer, doing work for very large corporations from the earliest stages of his career. After the war he did much less litigation but enough to keep his hand in.

To Covert, however, the principal event of the decade was his marriage in 1934 to his cousin Mollie, the daughter of W.H. Covert, who by that year had become lieutenant governor of Nova Scotia. Following the wedding in St Paul's, the historic Anglican church in downtown Halifax, there was a splashy reception at Government House. For once, Covert was at a loss for words, stumbling through his response to the toast to his bride. Their marriage was unquestionably a happy one but often made difficult for the long-suffering Mollie by her husband's total immersion in his work. Just two months before he died, Covert acknowledged his debt to the woman who had 'really guided my life,' paying tribute to her for bringing up their family – they had four children (a fifth had died in infancy) 'almost single-handed because I was so busy or away.' This was the essence of what he had written seven years earlier, that he had neglected his wife and children 'in the pursuit of the law.' His oldest son, Michael, recalls his father saying that he had told Mollie he would look after the income and she was to look after everything else.[2]

Covert's diaries are extraordinarily revealing of the character of the man. They show a person driving himself to achieve, and succeed, convinced that the orderly recording of recent events is a valid pointer to future action. It was this proposition that governed him in all his dealings. Shortly before his death, he remembered his father emphasizing how important it was to develop the habits of punctuality and adherence to schedules. To this end, the father required his son to record various observations in scribblers and, before he went to bed, to plan his activities for the following day. Both activities became life-long habits. Covert was twelve years old when he first started to record events and he kept up his entries almost to the day of his death. A month before he died, he asked his loyal secretary, Beulah Mosher, to order the diary volume for 1988, telling her, however, 'I will not be here to use it.'

The diary volumes, produced by the English publisher Collins, had a substantial-sized page for each day's entry and contained numbers of tables of information which Covert found useful: phases of the moon, tables of weights and measures and metric conversion, red-letter days and holidays (English style not American), and perpetual calendars. He assiduously made entries every day, almost always filling the page in his neat concise handwriting. If he ran out of space, which he often did, he would dictate the remainder of an entry to his secretary (except of course when he was overseas), who typed it out and affixed it to the page. Everything that could be measured or counted, was measured and counted, all facets of his busy life logged and recorded. When flying whether in wartime or peace time he noted the exact hour of departure and arrival, or, in the case of his wartime entries, the time of return to base. After he acquired his Hunt's Point property in 1972, all diary entries made there were in red ink – a vivid colour – whereas those made elsewhere were in a subdued blue. One can trace the time he spent at work and on his myriad charitable activities. In 1954 he noted he had worked – in the broad sense – 3,646 hours, a figure that by 1959, probably his peak year, had risen to 4,369 hours, which works out to a daily average of 12 hours. Thereafter the hours gradually declined. In 1977 Covert wrote that he had worked 2,800 hours, spent 269 days at Hunt's Point, and attended 61 meetings of boards of directors. Two years later he recorded 2,645 hours at work, but he had somehow found time to spend 287 days at Hunt's Point ('a new record'), for a total of 2,326 days since he had bought the property. On 16 March 1987 he flew on what proved to be his last commercial flight, the 2,672nd of his career.

He was always intensely loyal to his law firm, which had been established in the 1860s. He became its head in 1963 and occupied that position until his death nearly twenty-five years later. Throughout his career, he was generous towards his staff and the junior lawyers; when at the peak of his earnings, he reduced his percentage share of profits so as to increase the available income for others. He was not known for billing at a high hourly rate, and in fact, not long after the war a complaint was made to the Law Society that he was billing less than the fees set out in a bar association tariff for particular services. He worked in a very organized manner. At the outset of each day when in Halifax he met with his secretary to schedule the day's events and to consider the correspondence that had just come in, dutifully answering every letter of consequence. He kept track of his billable hours to individual clients in a day diary; his secretary transcribed these into a docket from which bills were ultimately sent out. He worked in a tidy office: the only papers or files lying about were the ones he was actually working on that day. He did all his own filing, believing it was easier that way to keep up with matters (though he once told his secretary jocularly that her time was more valuable than his) and could lay his hands on a file at a moment's notice. Sometime during the day he would peruse the latest law reports and periodicals the firm's librarian sent up to him, often making marginal notes for the edification of other firm members. In the last few years of his life he lived exclusively at Hunt's Point, dictating tapes which were delivered to his secretary. She in turn would send back any necessary material.

Covert, in the course of his career, was involved in an enormous number of commercial and financial transactions and, at a time when there was much less concern about conflicts of interest, saw nothing wrong in acting for two sides, provided full disclosure was made. A good example occurred in 1955 when an important client, Fred Manning, sold his business, United Service Corporation Limited, the operator of a string of service stations, a bus company, and various other enterprises, to Canadian Petrofina Limited, the Canadian subsidiary of the big Belgian firm. Covert was recommended to the head of the Canadian operation, Alfredo Campo, who agreed that he would be the sole lawyer involved. Covert produced a memorandum of intent free of legalese, the parties signed it, and the deal went ahead. Thereafter, Covert continued to act for Petrofina and accepted appointment to the boards of directors of some twenty-six of the companies that Petrofina had purchased from United Service. When Petrofina later sold all those enterprises except the service stations, Covert was involved in the sales. He often acted for underwriters in public share or bond issues as well as for the issuing or borrowing company. Though recognizing that in many jurisdictions such a practice would be frowned upon, he stoutly maintained that two sets of solicitors would more than double the time required to complete a transaction and increase the cost as well and that once the parties were agreed on the terms of a transaction their interests became identical, requiring only one lawyer to complete the mechanics of documentation.

After the war his commercial corporate work and labour negotiations occupied most of his time, but until the 1950s he did a surprising amount of litigation, divorces, admiralty (marine law) cases, personal injury and medical malpractice suits, and tax appeals. He successfully claimed on behalf of the YMCA a trust fund set up by a victim of the *Titanic* to keep young people off the street. One of his most interesting cases never got to trial, being settled beforehand. In 1944 a Russian vessel, the *Kolkohznik*, carrying lend-lease materials from the United States to Russia, was torpe-doed off Sambro Light, near the entrance to Halifax harbour. A British sal-vage firm set out to recover the cargo, which was still intact and valuable. But who owned it, Russia or the United States? Covert was retained by the American government. After making many trips to Washington and examining the correspondence between Roosevelt and Stalin, he con-cluded that title had not passed to the Russians because the cargo was lend-leased. The Americans, after paying the salvage company, retrieved the cargo. Covert's bill was paid by the Americans in United States funds, which were then – the good old days! – trading at a discount. Covert good-naturedly remonstrated with his client but to no effect.

Much of the legal work done by Covert both before and after the war was generated by two clients and close friends – Fred Manning and R.A. Jodrey – perhaps the two leading industrialists of Nova Scotia. Jodrey, in Covert's appraisal, did more for the economy of the province than any other entrepreneur, but Manning was not far behind. Both men had been born poor and received little formal education but each had vast talents for business. Manning, who died in 1959, became Covert's client in 1933; Jodrey, who died in 1973, first consulted Covert in 1936. That year Covert became a director of Minas Basin Pulp and Paper Mills Limited, a Jodrey enterprise in Hantsport which manufactured ground wood pulp. Jodrey valued Covert's services so highly that during the war he literally saved work for Covert until his return.

Manning was sufficiently impressed by Covert's business ability that he asked him to give up the law and join him in business. Having exten-sive business interests in Venezuela which were ailing, he persuaded Covert to spend two months there to see what could be done. While engaged in this work, Covert had an unpleasant experience on a flight in Venezuela: he was working on a crossword puzzle and a bridge hand when the plane went into a steep dive, coming up sharply with a terrific jolt; the American pilots later confessed to him that they had fallen asleep. Covert himself was more alert in the pursuit of his task, reorganizing some of Manning's ventures during his brief visit. Still, when reporting to Manning, he advised him bluntly that the operations were a 'sink hole' and he should get out before losing any more money. Manning did not follow his advice and did indeed lose a great deal more money. So did other investors, including Covert's then senior partner, Stewart, who lost $150,000. Manning, none the less, was grateful to Covert for an honest appraisal. Covert, for his part, valued his exposure to Jodrey and Manning as much as they valued his services. Studying them, he once said, was an education in itself and something of their skills rubbed off on him.

Covert did legal work for a large number of corporations and held directorships in many of them; they included not only relatively small local companies but also large provincial enterprises as well as major national firms such as Trizec Corporation, Canadian Petrofina, the Molson companies, Industrial Acceptance Corporation, Royal Bank of Canada, and the Sun Life Assurance Company of Canada. Mersey Paper Company Limited (now Bowater-Mersey), the owners of a large paper plant at Liverpool, Nova Scotia, provides a typical example of Covert's involvement with an important provincial enterprise and the contributions he could make. He had actually assisted, as a law student, in drawing the incorporating documents for the controlling shareholder, Izaak Walton Killam. On Killam's death the company was sold to the Bowater group of Great Britain. Covert's firm acted for the company and Covert personally did the legal work in what was an extremely complicated transaction made more difficult by the fact that a significant portion of the purchase price came from a bond issue floated in the United States, so that Covert was dealing with various American lawyers in Boston and New York as well as with lawyers in Montreal representing the underwriters of a preferred share issue in Canada, the proceeds of which were also to help pay the purchase price of $53 million. He had a disagreement with the Montreal lawyers who had advised Bowater that it need not sign the Mersey prospectus. Covert told them that the Mersey company was a Nova Scotia one governed by the laws of that province and that its definition of 'promoter' included Bowater, which must sign. On the Montreal lawyers' balking at this argument, Covert suggested that they consult Bowater's solicitors in London; the London lawyers agreed with Covert and the Montreal bunch was cowed. It was no doubt this episode that persuaded Bowater to retain Covert as its solicitor following completion of the transaction; he became a director of the company in 1962 and remained one until his death. In 1963 Bowater sold a 49 per cent interest in Mersey to the owners of the *Washington Post* newspaper.

According to a retired president and general manager of Bowater-Mersey, Robert Weary, Covert made three pivotal contributions which assured the continuance of the plant at Liverpool. In the 1970s the Liberal government of Nova Scotia decided to legislate an end to long-term power contracts negotiated by the Nova Scotia Power Commission with companies such as Mersey. The Mersey contract of 1929, with Izaak Killam, was one of these. Any cancellation would undoubtedly have resulted in higher costs, which in turn would have threatened the economic viability of the mill. Covert persuaded the Public Utilities Board that the Mersey contract could not be revoked even by legislation because the Power Commission and the company were in effect joint venturers. Mersey was the only one of a number of companies to escape. Early in the 1980s Bowater wished to expand its operations in Quebec by acquiring a plant there but the Foreign Investment Review Agency – FIRA, the body despised by Covert and many businessmen but instituted by his idol, Pierre Trudeau – would not approve the acquisition. Stunned by this ruling, Bowater resolved to get out of Canada altogether by selling all its assets, including its 51 per cent interest in Mersey. Covert, alarmed at the implications such a decision might have for Liverpool and the province, talked Bowater out of it and indeed persuaded it and the *Washington Post* to spend a total of $200 million to upgrade the mill by changing its operation from a chemical to an environmentally friendly thermal-mechanical one which also had the additional advantage of lowering production costs. This large investment anchored the mill in Liverpool, and Weary considers Covert's role as one of the great triumphs of his career; in doing what he did for Bowater-Mersey, he also did it for Nova Scotia. Covert's final contribution resulted from the conversion of the mill to the thermal-mechanical process, for the change required much additional electric power at rates which had to be negotiated with the Power Commission and approved by the Public Utilities Board. These were highly technical and complex negotiations. Weary recalls Covert, who in 1986 had been hospitalized for leukemia, coming to hearings still wearing his identification bracelet and hospital coat. The hearings were successfully concluded the year following but Covert was too ill to be involved in the final stages, which were handled by his partner, Bill Mingo.

When author Peter Newman chronicled the twenty most powerful men in Canada based upon directorships of companies which controlled substantial assets, Covert was one of them. He disclaimed the honour, disenguously telling Newman that he had no real power. Covert's mother had read the article in *Maclean*'s magazine and sent it to her son with a note: 'Frankie I don't believe a word of it. Love, Mother.' Covert sent a copy of this to Newman with a delightful note of his own: 'You may fool some people but you can't fool Mother.' Covert underestimated himself: he could not have remained a member of the board of directors of an institution such as the Royal Bank of Canada for decades if he had been a mere cipher. Nothing exemplifies more vividly his influential role with major corporations of which he was both legal adviser and director than his connection with Sun Life Assurance Company of Canada. In his later years, Covert recalled with amusement that, when he bought his first house thirty years earlier, he had applied to Sun Life for a mortgage loan of $5,300 – and had been turned down. It was the largest insurance company in Canada, with head office in Montreal, and Covert sat on its board of directors from 1966. In 1967 and 1968 Sun Life became increasingly concerned about the activities of the Front de liberation du Québec, activities which, the company believed, were responsible for loss of business in the province. Jacques Parizeau, even then an influential advocate of Quebec sovereignty though not yet in government, had joined the Parti Québécois in 1968 and his nationalistic statements indicated the possibility of restrictions being placed on anglophone businesses. The directors engaged Covert to examine whether, and how, a corporate move could be effected without interference by government, or policy holders. Covert, working in secret, spent weeks in preparing a thick brief in which he maintained that the company could safely move if it decided to do so; he thought it should and, though a move would be bound to be controversial, any delay would make a future decision even more difficult. The directors decided not to act, and shelved the report.

By 1978 Parizeau had become finance minister in the Parti Québécois government headed by René Lévesque, and the separatist cause seemed to be gaining strength. The insurance business is based on confidence by policy holders and the possibility of Quebec's separation eroded that confidence, so the company believed. When the Quebec legislature passed the so-called Language Act – Bill 101 – encouraging the conduct of business in French, it was the last straw; Sun Life conducted virtually all its vast international business from Montreal in English. Covert's report was dusted off; early in 1978 he and fellow members of the executive committee recommended the move, a decision ratified by the full board. One of the many procedural problems to be resolved arose from the fact that Sun Life was a mutual company, that is, the million or so policy holders around the world were in effect the voting shareholders. At the previous annual general meeting, the policy holders had authorized the directors to conduct business for a three-year period – that is, for a period beyond the date of the proposed move; however, the question arose whether they must be consulted and, if not, whether it was fair to proceed without their consent. It was decided to call a special meeting to consider the move, in April 1978 in Toronto. Meanwhile, public notice had to be given of the company's intentions and a predictable fire-storm broke out, fueled by inflammatory statements from Parizeau and much adverse comment by the Quebec press. None the less, the move was sanctioned by an 84 per cent majority. Although in the short run the company lost much business in Quebec – the PQ government, for example, cancelled large group poli- cies – the move caused no long-term harm; in fact, the company has bene- fitted from the change. The real losers were Montreal and Quebec.

Because of his association with Jodrey and the latter's confidence in him, Covert played a role unusual in Atlantic Canada and probably unique elsewhere in Canada by becoming the president and the general manager (today we would say the chief executive officer) of substantial businesses in combination with his work as a lawyer and director (Geof- frion had been the president of several large companies but never man- aged them). In the 1950s, when Covert first operated a business, there were few trained management people: business experience or basic know-how was sufficient equipment for a manager. He operated three companies in the Jodrey group, the largest of which, Moir's Limited, the chocolate manufacturer, employed over 1,200 people, a number reduced by Covert to roughly 600. In addition to the Jodrey companies he oper- ated several other enterprises in Nova Scotia. Moir's, however, is the best example of his managerial career. Jodrey bought the business in 1956 because it was a major customer of another Jodrey enterprise, Canadian Keyes Fibre, a manufacturer of moulded paper products, such as candy boxes. As with everything else Covert did, he learned as much about the business at hand as could be learned. He had an innate ability to pick the best men for his management team and to delegate to them wide respon- sibilities. He might spend two days a week at the plant but, as his confi- dence in his deputies increased, he tended to manage by telephone except when it came to labour negotiations, which he personally conducted. As a corporate executive, Covert had good business sense and a feel for organization of the workforce, for mechanization – as an example, 'machining' chocolates instead of hand dipping them – and for plant maintenance. In 1968 Covert persuaded Jodrey to sell Moir's since he believed that there was no future in boxed chocolates, and the enterprise was sold to Standard Brands which seven years later closed the plant.

In 1961 the Jodrey Group bought the Halifax bakery business, Ben's Limited, which then had about 100 employees. Though Covert was the president, he had much less to do with the management than he had had with Moir's, leaving the day-to-day operation to a manager, Douglas Sawyer; Covert's role was principally financial supervision and labour relations. The business prospered and the workforce grew to over 300. Some years after R.A. Jodrey's death in 1973, Covert had a disagreement with some members of the Jodrey group (though not with Jodrey's son, John) over policy and resigned his management position in 1982, staying on as president of the holding company. The Jodrey family still owns the business.[3]

It may come as a considerable surprise to anyone familiar with Covert's stature as a corporate-commercial lawyer that he was a pioneer, if not *the* pioneer, of labour law in the Maritimes and, moreover, was genuinely sympathetic to the trade union movement. He was a staunch supporter of free enterprise, holding that entrepreneurial skills and not government intervention create wealth. Yet he also believed that the creation of wealth was possible only if the welfare of the employees was protected and promoted – a goal that was the *raison d'être* of trade unions. He invariably told his corporate clients that they should recognize trade unions as an indispensable and desirable element in running a business, profitable not only for the owners in a financial sense but for the community in social terms. In this view he was far ahead of his time and it was especially remarkable that one of the leading corporate lawyers in Canada should have taken such a progressive position from the 1940s onward. Though he occasionally represented unions in labour disputes, he was more often on the side of management and achieved what must certainly be a Canadian record: for thirty-five years, from 1945 to 1979, he personally negotiated 440 wage contracts (he recorded them in his diaries), only six of which were reached as the result of strikes. This is an extraordinary achievement. His expertise was such that he negotiated contracts in Prince Edward Island and New Brunswick; as well, he was frequently called upon in labour disputes to act as an arbitrator and also as a conciliator, especially in the coal industry. Moreover, he occasionally negotiated for unions, among them the International Union of Operating Engineers and the Eastern Woodworkers. Towards the end of his life he summarized his beliefs: 'Unions can be good; workers are the salt of the earth,' and 'labour agreements are one of the most important parts of a successful business operation.'

Covert became interested in labour law as a fruitful field for a lawyer immediately after his return from the war. At the time there was no comprehensive trade union legislation in Nova Scotia, labour relations being governed by rules enunciated in England for the regulation of trade disputes and 'combinations' of workers. In 1935, as part of the New Deal legislation, the United States enacted the Wagner Act, the first comprehensive trade union legislation in North America which, in essence, recognized the legitimacy of unions in an industrial plant; after a vote by a stipulated majority, union certification followed and thereafter a union became a bargaining agent free of intimidation by an employer, who was obliged to negotiate with it. In wartime Canada, in 1943, Mackenzie King, who in his earlier life had been a deputy minister of labour, introduced by order-in-council similar measures but the effectiveness of these ended with the war. Covert recalled that on his return from overseas he studied American materials on labour law – which must inevitably have included the Wagner Act – and became convinced that such a scheme should be adopted in Canada. Nova Scotia in 1937 had enacted similar legislation but it was never proclaimed; however, a new bill was passed and came into effect in 1947. Still, it was some time before academics and politicians took up the cause of labour relations: Dalhousie University did not teach labour law as a discipline until 1955, and not until 1957 was there a separate department of labour in Nova Scotia. (In contrast, Farris had become British Columbia's first minister of labour in 1917). Covert was years ahead of Dalhousie and the provincial government.

From the outset of his career as a labour lawyer, Covert was a 'final offer' disciple and his views on this score served him in good stead, as witnessed by his remarkable ability to arrive at settlements of labour disputes. In his day the concept was original and effective; at present it has fallen into some disfavour because labour relations boards tend to view inflexibility as evidence of bargaining in bad faith: a party to a labour dispute should be prepared to change position, so the reasoning goes, to demonstrate a willingness to engage in free collective bargaining. Thus, on wages, a company will start low and a union high, each hoping to arrive at a negotiated settlement somewhere in between. Covert's reasoning and methodology are cogent. He studied his client's working conditions and fringe benefits, those of competitors and of businesses generally in the community, so as eventually to arrive at a contract proposal which was financially the best the client could, and would, make. The real work in negotiations, he always maintained, should take place beforehand.

Once at the negotiating table Covert produced the company's offer, fully explaining its basis, and then adhered to it unless the union could demonstrate some fundamental flaw or basic unfairness. Covert constantly counselled his clients never to yield on a matter of principle simply for the sake of getting a settlement, but, once a contract was reached, he also urged them to ensure that it be fairly administered. An amusing example of his approach occurred when R.A. Jodrey phoned him from Hantsport one day to tell him that an application was being made to certify a union in his paper plant and that he was not going to have any union tell him how to run his business. When Covert responded that the law of the land permitted certification and that, in any case, unions were not bad, Jodrey hung up on him. Covert eventually negotiated a first contract. A few years later, after Jodrey had grown accustomed to labour contracts, he and Covert lunched at the Halifax Club. Sitting next to them was a group of Halifax businessmen complaining about unions and strikes. Jodrey proclaimed in a loud voice that he would not do without a union in his plant, going on to say, 'It gives you industrial peace, you can plan ahead and you treat everyone fair.' Covert recalled the 'shocked look' on the men's faces as they heard this heresy from the province's leading industrialist.

That Covert was successful so often in labour negotiations was largely due to the respect he enjoyed among union officials. He was widely known as a skilled negotiator who encouraged unions and the fair administration of labour contracts, and when he took a position on behalf of a client it was understood that he held it honestly and was in fact bargaining in good faith. What is more, Covert was recognized in the union movement as a man of his word; if he said 'yes' to something he stuck by it and never tried later to fudge or weasel out of a commitment. At the bargaining sessions themselves, no matter how long they lasted, Covert always remained collected and disciplined, though he would occasionally speak sharply. The manager of Ben's watched Covert in action at several lengthy bargaining sessions. Covert had a melodious voice which he used with the skill of an actor. He never lost his temper, was always polite, never made disparaging remarks about a stubborn or fractious union negotiator, and was always in control of himself. If something angered him, he spoke privately to the negotiator or wrote a confidential letter. In the few instances in which strikes did occur, in spite of his efforts, he never hurried a settlement; he thought that strikes were an aberration and a long strike would be a lesson to both sides not to let one happen again.

But Covert's involvement in labour relations went well beyond settlement of particular disputes for he was one of the original members of a non-statutory but influential committee which shaped labour legislation in Nova Scotia. As a result of a long strike in the gypsum industry, Judge A.H. MacKinnon was named chairman of a royal commission to study labour relations in Nova Scotia. In his report, handed down in 1962, he recommended that labour and management settle differences between themselves without running to government for legislated solutions, and that a committee be formed with representatives from both sides chaired by a neutral party to study contentious issues. The guiding principle was consultation by labour and management on specific contentious problems and, if legislation was believed desirable, a bi-partisan recommendation to government would be made. Guy Henson, the director of the Institute of Public Affairs at Dalhousie, agreed to become chairman of the committee, which came to be known as the Dalhousie joint labour management committee. Modelled on a system operating in Sweden which Judge MacKinnon observed in action, the committee was the only one of its kind in North America. Covert, an obvious choice for management, and Lloyd Shaw, a prosperous businessman but a utopian socialist, on the labour side, were, with Henson, the key members of the committee. The membership fluctuated but Covert remained an active member until its disbandment in 1979. During the course of its life, the government let it be known that it would not enact legislation without a committee recommendation. Thus the committee recommended giving the right to strike to firemen and police officers (Covert had serious reservations about the wisdom of letting police go on strike), and the government legislated accordingly. The government also acted on another important recommendation, that firing an employee for union activities be made illegal. As the result of recommendations that followed lengthy study by the committee, the government in 1971 completely revamped the labour legislation of the province.

The committee's disbandment in 1979 occurred in a blaze of controversy. That year the provincial government passed legislation allowing the Michelin Tire Company to operate a non-union plant. At a meeting with the minister of labour, the labour members of the committee urged the government not to proceed with the legislation; if it did, they warned, the committee would be destroyed. The government did proceed, the union representatives on the committee resigned, and the committee disintegrated. Covert, in writing of the events, recalled that the management representatives on the committee prompted the resignation of the labour members by refusing to condemn the legislation (though he does not reveal whether he was one of them). He regretted being absent at the time of a critical session of the committee, feeling that he might have struck some compromise. In recalling the work of the committee over almost two decades, Leo McKay, for more than thirty years executive secretary of the Nova Scotia Federation of Labour, cites Covert as a hard-working, effective member who had great influence on management people in Nova Scotia. Like Covert, McKay regrets the disappearance of a unique and valuable institution. Covert himself believed that, during the eighteen years of the committee's existence, labour-management relations were better in Nova Scotia than anywhere else in Canada.[4]

Though Covert was very much a political animal and a Liberal zealot, politics were never enmeshed with his legal practice as they were with Farris. Politics was not a factor in his hiring members of his firm and, according to Covert, in securing government work. It is difficult to accept that latter statement at face value. On the other hand, the firm was by no means dependent on government work and, as we have seen with the Bowater-Mersey mill, Covert was sometimes at loggerheads with his own party. Covert did, however, make an exception to his no-patronage rule in the case of the Royal Commission on Transportation established by Ottawa late in 1948 and headed by W.F.A. Turgeon, a veteran royal commissioner, the same man who had conducted the inquiry into the Machray affair in Manitoba. Originally, J.L. Ilsley, the wartime minister of finance, had been appointed commission counsel, but, with his appointment pending as chief justice of Nova Scotia, he recommended Covert to succeed him. Covert spent the best part of two years with the commission, which handed down its report in February 1951. The commission was an offshoot of the general rate increase ordered by the Board of Transport Commissioners in 1948. When eight provinces appealed to cabinet regarding the increase, they coupled their appeal with a request that a royal commission be set up to find a solution to the 'larger problem of establishing proper principles for equalization in rate making.' The government initially rejected the request but then relented, in effect creating the commission in order to placate the disaffected provinces.

The commission sat for 138 days in every province, heard over 200 witnesses, received about 150 formal submissions, and amassed 24,000 pages of evidence and argument. After the conclusion of hearings in May 1950, the commissioners, aided by Covert with his assistant counsel and other staff, attempted to digest the well-nigh indigestible mass of material. The two academic commissioners, Henry Angus (another veteran royal commissioner) of the University of British Columbia and H.A. Innis of the University of Toronto, wrote reports, which Covert described as a 'shambles' and which Turgeon wished completely to disregard since none of their recommendations lent themselves to remedial legislation. Turgeon, in fact, told Covert that he wanted the academics' reports 'destroyed page by page,' and the two men started all over again. In the course of redrafting, Prime Minister Louis St Laurent called Covert into his office to encourage him to stick it out and 'keep a balance wheel on the commissioners.' When the report was finally handed in, Turgeon remarked to Covert that nothing would ever come of it. He was unduly pessimistic though he was right in the sense that the long-term benefits of his labours, and those of everyone else associated with the commission, have been modest. This was partly, if not mainly, because the commission was specifically enjoined by its terms of reference from intruding into the jurisdiction of the Board of Transport Commissioners. It is hard to see how any discussion of railway transport in Canada, with which the commission was chiefly concerned, could avoid treading on the toes of the board, and it is probable that this state of affairs explains the difficulties in drafting the report.

The report was tabled in parliament in February 1951 and the ensuing debate lasted from April until the end of the year. In principle, the report advocated legislation to achieve freight-rate parity, not merely among the regions, but also for the shipment of goods based on weight and distance hauled rather than on the types of commodity. This was a laudable object in theory (the Board of Transport Commissioners could permit discrimination in rates that was not 'undue'), but in practice, particularly with regard to political realities, one very difficult to achieve. Thus the commission, though breathing undying devotion to equalization, recommended continuance of the Crow's Nest Pass rates and the Maritime Freight Rates Act, both grossly discriminatory measures, and payment by Ottawa of a subsidy to the two major railways to help defray maintenance costs of trackage through the muskeg of northern Ontario. The government did act upon some of the recommendations: the powers of the board to equalize rates were set out at greater length than previously, and the board was given the power to ignore equalization if it thought an exception should be made. The commission essentially had been an exercise in futility. The railways were given their recommended subsidies; there was an attempt to base rates on volume and not on the type of commodity, and there were a number of other, largely cosmetic, changes.[5]

Covert had no interest in becoming a judge. None of his family or associates can recall any specific offer to him but all agree that he would have found the judicial life too confining. Bill Mingo, his partner, goes so far as to say that Covert, a public-spirited man with a wide range of interests, made a far greater contribution to his province than he could have done as a judge. Nor was he interested in holding elected office. His Liberal credentials, certainly, were impeccable. He actively stumped in numerous campaigns in both provincial and federal elections from 1937 to 1953 (apart from the war years), and he became secretary of the Nova Scotia Liberal Association in 1952. He enjoyed the rough and tumble of an election campaign – even the heckling – but resisted all attempts by the Liberal hierarchy to lure him into politics. He was twice promised a portfolio in the Nova Scotia cabinet by Premier Angus Macdonald, and each time he refused to run. In 1949 the newly elected leader of the federal Liberals, Louis St Laurent, attended a gathering of prominent Halifax Liberals in an attempt to persuade Covert to stand for parliament. Covert told St Laurent that he had been five years at war, had a family of three, and wanted to stay home. St Laurent instructed the gathering to leave Covert alone because he was 'entitled to say no.' Yet within a month Covert was to embark on the royal commission which probably kept him more away from home than if he had been a member of parliament.

His political beliefs were grounded in his father's teachings. Every intelligent person, he thought, should join a party and remain loyal to it through thick and thin. Though his father's party was Liberal, his father was 'liberal' enough to recognize that good people could be Conservatives and they should be equally loyal to that party. His father – speaking in 1922 – told his son, aged fourteen, that the day would come when every province west of Ontario would elect a government neither Liberal nor Conservative and that Quebec, which did not have the disdain for the Maritimes that 'Upper Canada' had, would want to secede, just as Joseph Howe had wanted Nova Scotia to do. Covert, who did not hold the same benign view of Quebec as his father, lived to see his father's predictions come true. As far as he himself was concerned, though he never ran for office, he became prominent in Nova Scotia as an unelected Liberal of great influence with both provincial and federal politicians. Ron Macdonald says that Covert was constantly consulted by federal politicians about development in the Atlantic region and in the country as a whole.

A good example of the confidence placed in him by politicians occurred in 1970. Premier 'Ike' Smith, a Conservative, consulted him about difficulties in the heavy-water plant in Glace Bay, an enterprise that Covert privately believed was one of the greatest disasters in the province's history. Smith's government wanted to dispose of the plant to Atomic Energy of Canada Limited; however, the latter feared that if it operated the plant it might become involved in litigation with the inventor of the process, an American named Spevak from White Plains, New York, who, on the development of the plant, had been given a long-term contract by the Nova Scotia government for payment of a substantial sum of money. Smith asked Covert to get the government out of the contract, if he could, or get Spevak to give some form of release so that the plant could be sold and thereby allow the province to recoup at least some of its losses. Spevak had been asked to sign a release freeing a purchaser of any obligation to him though the government's obligation to pay him would be continued. He refused. Covert's account of the subsequent events is entertaining and cannot be bettered; it is also an excellent example of his *modus operandi*:

Spevak knew the Province's predicament and would not grant a release. After I was retained and had done some study, I called Spevak and said I wanted to talk to him about a release enabling people to examine the plant and to take it over. He said he wouldn't see me or even discuss it until he was paid all the payments set out in the contract and payable over a period of time. He was quite violent and abusive over the phone so finally I said, 'Well Mr. Spevak, I thought we could at least get together to discuss it, but if we can't I'm afraid I'll have to advise the Government to introduce legislation cancelling your contract without payment.' He told me that was impossible, so I said: 'You engage an independent N.S. lawyer and ask him if that can be done and when you find out that it can be done, call me back – I'll give you four days.' He went into a long tirade and again said he wouldn't do anything until he got paid. So I said: 'Mr. Spevak, you have four days and if you have nothing to say other than these tirades, I propose to hang up, but I'll give you the first chance to hang up so that it can't be said that I was rude.' When Spevak didn't hang up, I knew I had him – he talked for 1 1/2 hours, but he agreed he'd see me. I got David Chipman in our office to work on the Release and afterwards because of the complicated problems of 'know how' and patents involved, I got some help from Thomas Montgomery of a leading law firm in Montreal who eventually came with me for our negotiations with Spevak in White Plains, New York.

Four days after our first telephone call, Montgomery and I went to see Spevak in his offices in White Plains. Spevak's wife, Ruth, was a very clever woman and she was present during the negotiations. We finally settled on the terms of the Release subject to approval by his attorney. All the while for two days Spevak kept insisting he would not sign the Release until the contract amount was paid.

Whenever he got on that vein I would say – 'I guess I may as well go home and get the legislation passed.'

Finally we left for the plane and Ruth drove us.

A while later Spevak and his wife came to see me in Halifax.

Spevak started all over again! I asked Ruth if she would like a cup of tea or coffee and then she replied 'Yes' and that her husband would too. So Spevak continued on the attack until the tea arrived.

After I had the tea in my cup half gone, I said to Spevak, 'Mr. Spevak, I have half a cup of tea left. It will take not more than five sips, and when I have finished, the interview is over, there will be no second chance; so you have very little time left.' At the end of one sip I said, '4 more' then '3 more' and 2 more.' Ruth then said, 'Darling, you'd better sign.' He signed and I delivered the notes payable and spread over the years.

I then delivered the Release to the Premier with a covering letter and received a nice letter of thanks from him.

This enabled the Atomic Energy of Canada Ltd. (AECL) to take over the plant and 'rebuild it.'

I enjoyed the negotiations![6]

Smith was not the only Conservative premier to whom Covert offered advice. In 1957 Premier Robert Stanfield was planning the creation of a crown corporation to encourage industries to locate in Nova Scotia and he asked Covert to head it up. Covert declined but agreed to work on formation of the company; he incorporated it and suggested names of prominent businessmen around the province as potential directors. Thereafter, though he declined another invitation to become president, he gave advice to the board from time to time.

Prior to the Second World War Covert was making his way professionally and spent relatively little time in community activites, but afterwards, perhaps spurred by his wartime experience, he determined to assist so far as he could organizations that asked for his help; he did so not because he thought there would be a spin-off in new clients but because he believed it was the right thing to do. Before his time, it was unusual to find a leading barrister with a heavy commitment to community service. Of course, there were exceptions, such as Pitblado, who devotedly served the University of Manitoba for decades; his unfortunate connection with the Machray scandal apparently soured him, for subsequently he made little contribution to outside activities. And other leading lawyers, such as St Laurent and Diefenbaker, went into politics. By and large, however, leaders of the bar stuck to their profession and allied interests. Lafleur, Tilley, and Farris were not the slightest bit interested in involving themselves in extra-curricular activities, though Geoffrion, as we have seen, did serve as chairman of the Roman Catholic separate school board in Montreal for several years. Covert was different. Threaded through his legal career were contributions to a wide range of charitable and public institutions. At Premier Stanfield's request, he served on the executive of Neptune Theatre in the 1960s; he was chairman of the Izaak Walton Killam Hospital for Children, again, a rather fitting association in view of his work for the Killam interests in the Mersey plant at Liverpool; and he was a member of the boards of a host of other Halifax charities. His connection with Dalhousie has already been described, but he did much work for other universities.

As noted earlier, in 1976 Covert became involved with the Nova Scotia Technical Institute, which, though in Halifax, was a regional institution that accepted engineering students from various universities in the Atlantic region. Representatives from those universities sat on the board of the college, but their interests were far from identical and led to difficulties. For the previous five years, the college had been in a state of turmoil caused partly by the resignation of its president and the failure to appoint a successor and partly by the proposal to amalgamate the school with Dalhousie – a proposal that had been approved by the boards of both institutions but then defeated in the legislature because of opposition from the other Atlantic Canada universities, which were loath to increase Dalhousie's powers. This turmoil had badly affected the morale of the teachers at the college, all of whom favoured amalgamation with Dalhousie. It was against this background that the Gerald Regan government asked Covert to take on the chairmanship of the board of the college, to find a new president, and generally to rebuild the school and smooth over the difficulties with the associated Atlantic universities. Covert agreed to serve, but only for two years; in fact, he served longer. The first two years entailed a lot of hard work. To limit the powers of the associated universities, he proposed restricting their representation to an advisory board and creating a fresh board with full administrative powers. As part of the process, he agreed that the college would abandon any thought of amalgamation with Dalhousie and stand firmly on its own feet. To accomplish all this, the government passed the necessary legislation despite protests from those universities unwilling to yield their powers. Covert spent innumerable hours meeting with the constituents of the college: faculty, administrators, and alumni. A new president was appointed and a new name chosen, 'Technical University of Nova Scotia'

('TUNS'). In a way, Covert's involvement was fitting: his father had wanted him to study engineering. Covert did get an engineering degree, however, an honorary doctorate from TUNS in 1980.

Beginning in 1953, Covert was closely associated with the Roman Catholic Order of the Sisters of Charity. He did more work for this charitable organization than any other, and it was the one closest to his heart. In adulthood he did not attend church regularly though, as an Anglican, he gave financial support to the cathedral in Halifax for a long time, discontinuing it only after the diocesan journal published a series of articles which Covert believed condoned strikes as a valuable economic tool; Covert thought that the church should stick to matters of faith and not become involved in social issues such as labour relations, and thereafter he confined his financial support to the Anglican church at Hunt's Point. But he was a religious man with a belief in God, and no doubt his faith explains the warmth of his relationship with the Sisters of Charity and the respect, indeed affection, they held for him.

The Sisters of Charity had come to Halifax from New York in 1849 and in the 1870s the order established itself on property at the head of Bedford Basin; today, that property is the site of Mount Saint Vincent University, founded by the order in 1925, and of the order's own mother house, located on a magnificent hilltop looking across the basin to Halifax harbour beyond. Initially the order concentrated exclusively on teaching but soon it branched out into hospital work, eventually owning five hospitals in Nova Scotia, the largest of which was the Halifax Infirmary, a general hospital established in 1887 which at the time Covert became chairman of its board in 1968 had about 500 beds. A year earlier, the order had pondered how best to finance a pension scheme for its sisters, many of whom worked at the hospitals. It was reckoned that ten million dollars would be needed to fund the scheme, and at the same time the order received the disagreeable news that there was an accumulated debt of $10 million stemming from operating losses in the maintenance of its various properties and hospitals. Covert addressed a conclave (as he termed it) of the sisters on the state of their finances and, as chairman of the infirmary, he agreed also to head an advisory board to tackle the problem of finding ways to fund the pension scheme and retire the debt. The order was in fact land rich but cash poor. Covert devised an orderly scheme for the prudent sale of most of the properties in Nova Scotia, British Columbia, Bermuda, and the United States, which entailed much travelling and the expenditure of much time, all without remuneration of course. (For none of his charitable work did he receive remuneration – only travelling expenses.) In 1970, as part of the broad plan to dispose of assets to raise cash, the order decided to relinquish its control – indeed its ownership – of Mount Saint Vincent University by turning it over to a newly constituted public university. Covert was chiefly responsible for drafting a multitude of legal documents – and legislation – to accomplish the transition, which resulted in the order gaining approximately $2 million; he later reflected that, although he had been responsible for many commercial sales, this was the first and only time he had ever sold a university. The order divested itself of its hospitals in Nova Scotia, including the infirmary, which was sold to the provincial government in 1973. (The order still operates one hospital in Canada, at Westlock, Alberta.) To mark the occasion the medical staff threw a dinner for Covert and presented him with gifts. The government appointed a fresh board for the infirmary but Covert was not part of it, although he remained as chairman of the order's financial advisory board until the day of his death. By 1974 the pension scheme was fully funded and all debts paid. The order still owns a few properties in Canada and a valuable one in Wellesley, Massachusetts, but the mother house and its surrounding land is its principal asset. The sisters of the order with whom Covert chiefly dealt, the treasurers general and the superior, sing his praises; he was competent, patient, unstinting of his time, always available at the end of the telephone. They fondly recall little things about him: his habit of doodling, placing his glasses on paper and drawing around the frame, and his thrill at shooting his age in golf.

On 11 January 1986, two days before his seventy-eighth birthday, Covert went into Liverpool hospital for treatment of a kidney stone. Apart from that ailment he seemed to be in vigorous health. Then, two days after his birthday, he was told that he had leukemia. A day or two later he came up to Halifax. In his customary fashion he met with Beulah Mosher, his longtime secretary; swearing her to secrecy, he told her of his condition. Shocked by this news, particularly since he looked so well, she found difficulty in replying and could only say that it could be treated. He said, 'To hell with it anyway,' and went on with his work as if nothing had happened. It was at this very time that he was working extremely hard on the problems of the Bowater-Mersey plant with the Nova Scotia Power Commission. A week later he went to New York for removal of his kidney stone by laser therapy, a method not yet available in Halifax, and on his return he started a lengthy regime of chemotherapy and bone-marrow tests, which lasted until the following June. During this period his physical appearance did not alter much – he lost a bit of hair but continued to work and play golf. He had been told that he had a 70 per cent chance of recovery and indeed for a few months he went into remission. But in September 1987 the disease recurred; this time the chance of successful treatment was put at 30 per cent. According to Bill Mingo, Covert was prepared to carry on working and playing golf for as long as possible without active treatment but his family prevailed on him to return to hospital – the Halifax Infirmary – for treatment and he was admitted early in October. There he continued to work, dictating material for Beulah and talking on the phone until a week before his death. She recalls that he was worried he would be unable to make his diary entries. She saw him every day until two days before his death; in the last ten days his physical appearance radically deteriorated. One of the few people Covert saw outside his family was Robert Petite, the priest of the Anglican Church of St George's, Halifax, the so-called Round Church. At first Covert was angry about dying. Petite, who had often visited socially disadvantaged men dying of AIDS, observed to Covert's daughter, Susan, that he found it somewhat awkward ministering to a man who had had such a fortunate life as Covert. Susan forthrightly told him that notwithstanding 'his wonderful life he had as much right to be angry about leaving it as anybody else.'

In any case, Covert lost his anger. Bill Mingo visited him just five days before his death. Covert was in quite good cheer, Mingo says; in fact, he was in far better cheer than Mingo himself. Covert knew he was dying and said he could handle it. Another who visited him that same day was Wib Pierce, his old air force skipper who had flown down from Hamilton. He also flew down for the funeral the following week. The day before he died, Covert asked Susan, 'How long do I have to put up with this?,' obviously referring to the radical treatment he was receiving. At any one time four bottles were hooked up to him. She spoke to her mother; they instructed the hospital and doctor to discontinue treatment; she told her father she had done so and he squeezed her hand in response. He lapsed into a coma and died the next day.

Covert's funeral service at St George's was conducted by Robert Petite according to the rites of the Anglican Church. His body was cremated. A portion of the ashes was placed in a coffin for burial in the White Point Cemetery, on the very edge of the Liverpool Golf Club between the fairways and the Atlantic. (The remainder was scattered by members of his family in some of his favourite spots in Hunt's Point.) Somehow two of his grandchildren were able surreptitiously to place in his coffin a golf club and the collar of one of his favourite dogs. The headstone bears a simple inscription:

Covert
Frank Manning
1908 – 1987.

Covert was a complex man, admirable undoubtedly but often viewed by his contemporaries as someone who thought himself omniscient. He was unquestionably a superior lawyer and, also unquestionably, he did not always try to dispel his image as an abrasive and arrogant person. Fundamentally, however, he was characterized not so much by arrogance as by a quiet confidence in his own ability. His partner, Bill Mingo, acknowledges that Covert, to use the modern jargon, had an image problem, but he adds that in the last two decades of his life Covert was in reality far more benign than the perception of him by some of his fellow practitioners suggests. For Covert was sentimental. At his beloved Hunt's Point property, he flew the air force flag alongside the Canadian flag, and when a close canine companion was killed by a passing truck he flew the air force flag at half mast. Over a period of days, he went to the bottom of the property on the ocean shore where the dog was buried, and wept.

Like the other subjects of these portraits, Covert was a true Canadian patriot; he thoroughly approved of the patriation of the constitution though his views on the Charter of Rights which accompanied it are not known. How would he have wished to be remembered? Though he never troubled himself with such a question, had he turned his mind to it he would have responded: 'I served my country in war and in peace, and I did the best I could.'[7]

7

Gordon Fripp Henderson

Gordon Henderson, who knew Frank Covert well, admired his professional skills and acknowledged 'his enormous connection with the business community,' particularly in Nova Scotia. Beyond Covert's eminence,
however, Henderson discerned his true character: 'I think he illustrates
my point about [lawyers] getting along well with people. He related to
people extremely well. He was never full of himself. You would never
know that he was a man of such qualities, in other words, he never
paraded his brilliance. He was very human with everybody. He was a
gentleman. He was at ease with the lower as well as the upper strata of
society.' Such remarks reveal as much about Henderson as they do about
Covert. Henderson's professional skills were widely admired, and his
personal qualities were the same ones he identified in Covert. Like
Covert, too, Henderson was that breed of lawyer who, from a sense of
responsibility, devoted significant amounts of time to community causes,
particularly universities and hospitals.

He was born in Ottawa, and died there. He had no desire to live or
practise anywhere else in Canada, though his legal work and other activities entailed frequent journeys across the country. One of his earliest
cross-Canada trips occurred when as a young boy he accompanied his
father (also named Gordon) to Victoria to visit his grandfather, William
Henderson, a Scottish architect who had come to Ottawa to practise (he
worked on the parliament buildings there) and ultimately moved to Victoria to become a provincial government architect. Two of William Hend-

erson's sons, Gordon and Stuart, became lawyers. These two had much in common: each practised exclusively in the criminal courts and each was somewhat unorthodox; each was a rabid Liberal to whom there was no such creature as a good Conservative; both were for the little man, the underdog, and against the 'establishment' and big government. More than anyone else in British Columbia, Stuart was responsible, in 1905, for the abolition of wigs worn by lawyers in the courtrooms, a blow against the establishment. Some of his father's antipathy to big government rubbed off on Gordon Henderson Jr: he was seldom retained by government and far more often retained in cases against it. But, unlike his father, or perhaps because of him, Gordon Jr was apolitical – he never became involved in partisan politics. To Liberals he was a Conservative; to Conservatives he was a Liberal. There was another important influence: because of his father's example, Gordon never smoked and never drank hard liquor though he would take the occasional glass of wine.

Stuart, who graduated from the University of Toronto and practised briefly in Ottawa, went to British Columbia, where he became in his lifetime that province's most renowned criminal lawyer. Yet he had no office, he met clients on the street corner or in someone else's cubby-hole, and his filing system was in his hip-pocket. Gordon Sr was not quite so disorganized though his filing system was rudimentary. Practising before juries and police magistrates, he did not require elaborate office arrangements, he did not need a typist, he had no telephone, and fees – if there were any – were put straight into his pocket or into the bank. He was more prosperous than his older brother Stuart and young Gordon grew up in fairly affluent surroundings, living for the first twenty-five years of his life – he was born in 1912 – in a genteel, comfortable establishment, the Roxborough Apartments on the north side of Cartier Square, well known and fondly remembered by many in Ottawa today. It was an apartment hotel. Each day the rooms were tidied and the beds made up. Residents could have meals brought to them or they could gather in the dining-room, or they could prepare their own meals. Mackenzie King lived there for a time before he went to Laurier House; Louis St Laurent was a resident and the CPR maintained a permanent apartment on the top floor. It was, one might say, a good address, yet Gordon Henderson Sr, as befitted a Scot, lived frugally though comfortably. He and his wife, English-born, had but the one child, who from the earliest days of his schooling was clearly an above-average student. He attended the Ottawa Model School (now the Teachers' College), where part of the instruction was given by student-teachers, and, later, Lisgar Collegiate Institute, both located on Cartier Square. He was fond of recalling that his whole life had revolved around the square, for his office was on its west side and the courthouse was in it. After graduation from Lisgar he enrolled at University College in Toronto, which his father (and uncle Stuart) had also attended. He joined the Delta Kappa Epsilon (DEKE) fraternity and lived in the fraternity house, and, for the first time, began to think of law as a career. His father spoke to a colleague, George Henderson (no relation), whom he knew well and said that his son was thinking of the law and a stint in a law office as an office boy might cure him or encourage him. George Henderson agreed and each summer between terms Gordon Jr worked at the Henderson Herridge law office in Ottawa licking stamps, cleaning up, and serving drafts and notices of protest regarding 'bounced' cheques upon all persons whose names appeared on them, in conformity with the then law relating to bills of exchange.

Office drudgery did not deter him from a career in the law for on graduation with a BA in 1934 he enrolled in Osgoode Hall. At that time, articling and legal instruction were combined: the student attended lectures for a prescribed period each day, spending the remainder of the day in the law office to which he was articled, in Henderson's case McCarthy & McCarthy in Toronto. Henderson's studies coincided with the great debate about the future direction of legal education in Ontario, with the proponents of academic pursuits (led by Dean Cecil Wright) ranged against the advocates of occupational training – or, as Henderson says, 'Pericles against the plumbers.' The 'plumbers' triumphed but in the short run only. Henderson, who at the time sided with the 'plumbers,' later freely admitted that he was wrong and that the legal education of today is far superior to that which he received. McCarthy's would have kept Henderson on as a junior lawyer after his call to the Ontario bar in 1937 but he never wavered from his intention to practise in Ottawa. He joined the Henderson Herridge firm, where formerly he had licked stamps and posted the mail.

Though his father had not actively discouraged him from law, he had told him that he should stay away from criminal law. Gordon mainly followed his advice but, like many young lawyers, he did appear in the criminal courts. In his first case for an accused person the crown attorney expressed surprise at Henderson's presence, noting that the accused, who had a lengthy record, had made many more court appearances than Henderson. In his later years Henderson was to confine his practice in the criminal law to white-collar crime and to combines offences. One of his particular interests was patents, copyrights, and trademarks, subjects now compendiously lumped into the phrase 'intellectual property.' Henderson had first been exposed to intellectual property cases at the McCarthy firm, which did a lot of such work, and he saw with considerable foresight that the subject held great potential for a young lawyer. The phrase 'intellectual property' is an apt one to describe the three areas of patents, copyrights, and trademarks, since all involve the element of creativity, invention, or art – call it what you will – leading to valuable rights which the courts by statute, or sometimes common law, protect. Broadly speaking, patents are concerned with and result from industrial development. Trademarks are more a matter of marketing and commerce, the primary purpose of which is to identify the source of the product, with the incidental benefit that consumers look to a trademark as an assurance that the product will be of a certain and consistent standard. Copyright heretofore has been the domain of the literary, musical, and visual arts but the lines between it and patents are now becoming blurred: computer software programs are being protected by copyright rather than by patent and, surprisingly, there has been much discussion about extending copyright to functional objects. In the United Kingdom the courts have decided that a tail-pipe for an automobile merits copyright protection, and in Canada a decision of the Federal Court, trial division, suggested that three-dimensional objects of artistic merit might warrant copyright protection. Later legislation, however, seems to have resolved any difficulties posed by the Federal Court's ruling.[1]

Soon after his call to the bar, Henderson immersed himself in the subject of intellectual property and within five years he became, at the request of the publisher, the first editor of a new series, the *Canadian Patent Reporter*, a journal in which the significant decisions in the field were published. He remained editor of the *Reporter* for fifty-one years, surely a record for any professional journal: when Henderson committed himself, he committed himself for the long haul. As editor, he received virtually every written decision of a judge hearing an intellectual property case, and then he decided which were of sufficient importance or interest to warrant publication; published cases were accompanied by digests of the facts involved – known to lawyers as 'headnotes' – and editorial comments, and Henderson prepared both. As a lawyer practising in the field, he would have done his best to keep up with the decided cases in any event and so he looked on his editorship as an extension of his practice, except, of course, that he had to find time to write the headnotes and to compose his comments. In the latter stages of his editorship, he spent five or six hours each weekend working on the journal. An avid football fan (he was at one time a part-owner of the Ottawa Roughriders), he would frequently ensconce himself before the television set in his comfortable study in his Rockcliffe home on Saturday afternoons, where, during breaks in the game, he would edit the case reports. If there was no football game on the screen he would watch baseball. But his active involvement in the field as a practitioner inevitably led to embarrassment for in an editorial comment he might express a proposition which later, on behalf of a client, he contradicted. As a consequence, Henderson gave up writing editorial comments and confined himself to compiling case digests. This episode is but one of a number in which Henderson became involved in conflicts of interest or, at least, in awkward situations.

In 1937 the intellectual property field was occupied by a relative handful of practitioners, notable among them Harold Fox and Russell Smart. This was not surprising, since the Depression had stifled inventive activity – be it mechanical or cultural. Then, as the country edged, or slid, into war, Canadian industrial activity burgeoned, giving rise to increased interest in patents and trademarks; copyright was of lesser significance at the time. Henderson found himself in a firm which had always done a certain amount of work in intellectual property, chiefly by Gordon Gowling, but with the outbreak of war several members of the firm enlisted (Henderson's poor eyesight precluded active service) and Henderson found himself as one of the firm's two counsel after only five years of practice. He was endlessly running, so he recalled, from one court to another. In the days when intellectual property cases were tried in Exchequer Court, and appeals went to the Supreme Court of Canada, he was often in the latter court, unlike today, when appeals from the Federal Court (the successor to the Exchequer Court) go to the Federal Court of Appeal. But during the war years he was doing not only intellectual property work but the whole gamut of litigation.

Henderson, like the subjects of the other portraits, achieved eminence through sheer hard work, coupled of course with native intelligence. Laymen, and even clients, often do not realize how hard a lawyer works in getting up a case. Partly this is because a lawyer must become an instant expert in whatever problem is presented to him; once a particular case is over another replaces it and memory of the earlier one fades quickly. But even that statement is simplistic because at any one moment a busy courtroom lawyer will be juggling a number of cases, and the only way to retain sanity is to be well organized and to have a capable support staff. As for Henderson, he differed from many other lawyers in that his excellent memory allowed him to dredge up legal propositions long after the particular case that prompted them had ended. In other respects, his *modus operandi* was not unusual but he adhered to it all his life. At the end of a day in court he would relax for awhile and then prepare for the following day even though it might take him until ten or eleven o'clock at night. When he was sure he had everything under control, he went to bed, slept well, did not scurry around the next morning tidying up last-minute details, and showed up in court unhurried, and prepared. As he became more senior he relied increasingly on juniors but even at his peak he personally conducted about half the research for a particular case. Henderson's ability to organize his work, to schedule events, to cope with the myriad demands on his time and, withal, to remain genial, was much admired. A fellow lawyer, Hyman Soloway, said that Henderson was 'probably the only person I know who can stretch a twenty-four hour day to meet all his requirements.'

Henderson had other strengths as a counsel. He himself thought that his greatest talent was an ability to absorb knowledge quickly, like a sponge – grasp the facts of a case and master the legal issues and present them to a court with lucidity and persuasion. This talent was not unique to Henderson but that he exercised it in so many fields of law, in the courts and before administrative tribunals, never failed to impress his contemporaries and legal opponents. John Turner, for example, states that he was 'one of the most versatile lawyers that I've ever encountered.' He was flexible in his presentation to the court, never being 'married to written scripts.' Thus, if a judge interrupted him with a question during the course of his argument (though W.Z. Estey says that Henderson spoke in 'non-stop fashion' and was 'a difficult man to interrupt'), Henderson answered it right away, not putting it off by noting that he would deal with it later. Henderson was enthusiastically forthright in putting his client's case; as one correspondent observed to the author, 'It was never difficult for the court to determine what was on Gordon's mind.'

Stamina was another hallmark – the ability to stay the course in a long and complicated lawsuit, particularly where a patent was involved, to carry on his many other activities without diminution while the case was under way, and, at the end of it all, to be so vigorous as to give the impression that the trial had lasted a mere week. Physical powers, of course, would have availed him nothing without great skill. Let anyone try to imagine the concentration and intellectual dexterity required of a patent lawyer – and Henderson was, by common consent, the top patent lawyer of his time – in digesting the intricacies of extraordinarily complicated technical devices and processes and then drawing the line between inventiveness and clever imitation. Yet Henderson, who had studied not engineering but political science, and who by his own admission could hardly draw a straight line, let alone a schematic for an electrical circuit, could with easy confidence discuss arcane matters of circuitry with technocrats. Still another of his characteristics was his inability to say 'no' to someone who turned to him for help in righting a wrong. Some of his contemporaries saw this trait as a fault because it interfered with more serious business. The criticism – if that is what it is – is made kindly, but the fact is that Henderson's response to such requests does him great credit: that is what lawyers are supposed to do – right wrongs – and, in Henderson's case, he often did so without remuneration in those days long before the advent of a structured system of legal aid.

But Henderson, as an advocate, was not without his warts. With so many clients in the intellectual property field, he often found it difficult to steer an ethical course between their competing interests and sometimes he was the target of criticism for endeavouring to do so. Perhaps his largest wart, however – and it was one he acknowledged – was a combativeness in the courtroom that contrasted markedly with his behaviour outside it. As he observed to the author, 'I'm a different person outside of court than in court. I will argue pretty strenuously in court.' This is a common issue of style. One lawyer, such as Lafleur, is dispassionate, calmly viewing every problem as an intellectual exercise. Another, such as Henderson, charges into the fray with high velocity, equally well prepared but with adrenalin flowing at a higher rate. Which of the two is the better lawyer? One cannot answer the question definitely: both are good, yet they are different. Today, many see Lafleur's style as outmoded and Henderson's as too aggressive. But is such combativeness really a fault? Henderson enthusiastically took up every case he was presented with, giving it its best shot. He mastered the applicable law, he never fudged; if he was confronted by a judge or an opposing lawyer who seemed to demolish his argument, he took it in good grace while trying to protect the interests of his client. He was never hang-dog, never subservient. He would unhesitatingly confront a hostile judge, convinced, like the other lawyers portrayed in this work, that the views of counsel are as much deserving of respect as those of judges. On one occasion, Henderson took his fifteen-year-old son with him on an appearance before the Ontario Court of Appeal, with the object of giving the boy an insight into how courtroom lawyers and judges operate. That day he had a very difficult time of it because the judges initially were hostile to his submissions and, by hard questioning, made their hostility even more evident. After an adjournment, Henderson, unperturbed by the onslaught, remarked to his son, 'That is what I do for a living, now wouldn't you like to be a lawyer?' His son cleverly replied, 'No, I want to be the judge.' But the son underrated the father – as often happens, dogged persistence pays off, and the court ultimately ruled in favour of Henderson's client. In his earlier days, Henderson revelled in the cut and thrust of trials, the 'hurly-burly of the trial courts' as he put it. But in his later years he lost his taste for trial work (though he continued to do trials) and preferred appearances before appellate courts where one could concentrate on the legal issues; he told the author that he was most comfortable arguing an intellectual property case in the Federal Court of Appeal, which, in effect though not in law, has become the final arbiter of intellectual property cases. Also, as he grew older, he began to do more work as a solicitor – office, not courtroom work – and at his death he spent roughly a third of his time at it.

Henderson estimated that, of his practice as a whole, about two-thirds was on intellectual property cases. His first appearance in the Supreme Court of Canada, a successful one, was in a patent case, in 1939. At that time, the handful of law firms doing those cases was concentrated in Ottawa because the registration offices, and the bureaucrats, were there. In the fifty years since, there has been a shift away from Ottawa. The causes of the shift are many: the bureaucracy has been decentralized, the federal court now sits in centres across the country, and industrial activity, which spawns patents, has become concentrated in southwestern Ontario, the Toronto area in particular, though the proliferation of high-tech industries in the Ottawa region still results in much work for Ottawa firms. The number of lawyers in the field has grown dramatically, as have the agents who obtain registration of trademarks or patents. At one time lawyers did that work as well, but now they become involved only when there are competing claims in court. The agents, professionals in every sense, are members of a professional organization, the Patent and Trademark Institute.

The whole area of intellectual property rights is changing at dazzling speeds, what with computer technology and software, satellite transmissions and retransmission rights, the information highway, internet – in a word, 'cyberspace.' To keep up with all this, lawyers in the field are becoming increasingly specialized, not just as between patents, trademarks, and copyright, but by subgrouping within each discipline. And big companies holding valuable rights station their representatives in key centres around the world such as Bangkok, Singapore, Hong Kong, and Tokyo to detect, and combat, infringement. All these swift developments in technology make a layman wonder if patents are really worth the effort; by the time an infringement suit reaches court, other alleged infringements will have taken place. Is inventiveness likely to be overwhelmed by the speed of new technology – and global marketing? Henderson recognized the problem and believed that there would have to be a new order of things: existing statutes were no longer 'adequate in Canada or elsewhere to deal with the many demands of rapidly evolving technology and changing business and trade relationships.' A classic case of confrontation between the holder of a patent and the supposed public interest occurred in this country recently when pharmaceutical patent holders (represented by Henderson) were expected by parliament to give up their rights in the interests of cheaper health care by permitting generic manufacturers to infringe patents; no matter how one sugarcoated the pill, it would have resulted in legislated larceny perpetrated in the name of public health. The *modus vivendi* arrived at to settle that issue is of dubious value and, Henderson believed, compromised the whole rationale of protection of intellectual property.

Before we examine a few of the hundreds of intellectual property cases Henderson handled from 1939 onwards, there are some other aspects of his career in the field worth mentioning. He was very much involved in the development of the system to govern performing rights to broadcast music. It is a form of compulsory licensing: the composer and publisher assign their rights to a collective, for example 'PROCAN,' the Performing Rights Organization of Canada, of which he was president. A broadcaster can play the music on payment of a fee set by the Copyright Appeal Board which is paid to the collective; that body in turn pays out the accumulated fees to the composer and publisher, both of whom are thereby relieved of the burden of monitoring large numbers of broadcasters across the country for unauthorized performances. In an allied field, he was a pioneer in complex litigation involving the use by Canadian cable systems of broadcast signals from television stations just over the United States border. Through his efforts, an agreement was reached between the two countries establishing a workable mechanism by which a Canadian tribunal could impose charges for the retransmission by Canadian cable companies of signals received from American stations.

Given Henderson's interest in such matters, it is not surprising that he went into the cable company business in Ottawa as an entrepreneur at a time when cable transmission was just starting. He was very successful, made a lot of money, and eventually sold out to Maclean Hunter. This early experience whetted his interest in communications, but his legal representation of users of wired music – cable companies, broadcasters, and so on – before the Copyright Appeal Board gave rise to allegations of conflicts of interest for at the same hearings he often represented owners of copyright (the licensors or their agents). The obvious difficulties of steering between Scylla and Charybdis must be faced by any lawyer who tries to combine a business career with a legal practice, and opinions differ whether the attempt should be made at all. Henderson's case was different from and trickier than that of Covert, who ran businesses owned by others; Henderson gained much experience in profitably running his own business in a field where, coincidentally, his main interest as a lawyer lay.

And finally, in this general discussion of Henderson's stature among members of the intellectual property community, a few words are in order concerning a report that he wrote in 1991. Commissioned by the federal Department of Consumer and Corporate Affairs and entitled 'Intellectual Property: Litigation Legislation and Education,' the report is an eminently readable exposition of a complex but fascinating subject. Its subject was the problem of how creative works can be protected from imitation or unabashed infringement without imposing a burden of expensive litigation on the producers of such works. Large corporations can usually afford lawyers' fees at lengthy trials, but the small business person holding a patent or trademark more often gives up the ghost rather than risk bankruptcy by paying enormous fees for litigation. As the result of one of Henderson's many recommendations, the Canadian Intellectual Property Institute has been established as a research body to address that problem. Henderson became its first president. Similarly, in an effort to give less affluent litigants quicker and cheaper access to enforcement bodies, he recommended creation of a new tribunal which would combine the function of determining whether a pending application for a trademark affected an existing one with the function of the Copyright Appeal Board in setting fees for performing rights. The amendments necessary to implement this sensible recommendation were contained in an omnibus bill dealing with various aspects of intellectual property which passed the House of Commons but was defeated in the Senate.

Photocopying of printed material has been a lively issue in recent years, pitting libraries, schools, and universities against authors and publishers. A cooperative representing the copyright holders has been established, much like the performing rights societies, but progress in negotiating photocopying rights has been, at best, modest. John Honsberger of Toronto recalls an amusing incident when he proposed to Henderson that they photocopy the report of a decision contained in a legal publication. Standing in the presence of the leading intellectual property lawyer in Canada, Honsberger felt some diffidence in doing so. Henderson said, 'Just flip the paragraphs around and don't worry too much.' Honsberger did, and Henderson went on, 'Anyway, what's the measure of damages?' It is an excellent story which well illustrates the difficulty of maintaining entrenched rights and the moral dilemma that arises when principle is confronted by practicality. In fairness to Henderson, there is a very real question about who holds the copyright in a decision written by a judge – a servant of the crown – that later appears in a legal publication.[2]

There was a bewildering variety in the many intellectual property cases handled by Henderson. Were Coca-Cola and Pepsi-Cola similar products or, more accurately, was the trademark 'Pepsi-Cola,' registered in 1906, an infringement of the trademark 'Coca-Cola,' which had been registered a year earlier? The Supreme Court of Canada ruled that neither one nor the other brand had exclusive rights to the word 'Cola' and that, as far as the names were concerned, one brand could not be confused with the other. Moreover, 'Pepsi-Cola' did in fact contain 'pepsin' and so the use of the word was perfectly legitimate. Though Henderson had little personal contact with the case, his firm acted, unsuccessfully, for Coca-Cola. He thought that the battle between the titans of the soft-drink industry was one of the most important commercial cases in Canada.

Henderson figured directly in a battle between two giants of the tobacco industry, Philip Morris and Imperial Tobacco. The latter had registered in Canada in 1932 the trademark 'Marlboro' for cigarettes; Philip Morris held a United States trademark for cigarettes sold under the same brand name. At the time the litigation started, Philip Morris had huge sales world-wide but only modest ones in Canada – and even these were in duty-free stores. None the less, it sought to expunge the Imperial Tobacco trademark. Henderson, acting for it, raised various grounds on which, he said, the mark was invalid, principally because most smokers identified 'Marlboro' as belonging not to Imperial Tobacco but to Philip Morris. The Federal Court of Appeal ruled against him, however, largely because Imperial Tobacco had held the trademark for nearly fifty years without challenge and a long-standing rule (also applied in the Pepsi-Cola case) gave the benefit of any doubt in such circumstances to the holder of the mark. In another case, the issue was whether the trademark 'Off!' for an insect repellant was infringed by a similar product with the name 'Bugg Off.' Henderson acted for the manufacturer of the latter.

Again, the Supreme Court of Canada decreed that the holder of a trade-mark could not appropriate exclusive use of a word; in this instance, 'Off' was merely descriptive of the result of its use and hence 'Bugg Off' was not an infringement.

Henderson acted in several interesting cases stemming from wartime inventions. In one he represented the government of Canada which, as a wartime measure, had manufactured parachutes of a design patented by an inventor. Understandably chagrined at the failure of the government to pay compensation, the inventor launched a court action. The commissioner of patents had recommended a form of royalty payment, but the courts decided that the inventor should do better than that and ordered compensation based on fair market value. That inventor fared much better than the man, for whom Henderson also acted, who had devised a safe bomb for use by the RCAF in practice bombing runs. Previously, the air force had used a bomb which chemically ignited; the difficulty was that, when stored, the chemicals might leech and so result in an accidental explosion. A civilian inventor suggested a powder mix to be detonated by a device inserted just before the bomb drop, and his method was adopted. Subsequently he joined the armed forces and, in an ill-advised moment, assigned to the crown all his rights of invention. The courts, though sympathetic to his claim for compensation, could do nothing, and the man eventually accepted a modest *en gratia* payment. He presented Henderson with a bomb – presumably harmless – as a memento.

Henderson realized that certain cases were of great commercial significance and he was glad to be involved in them; for example, there was a case involving Bell Telephone and Northern Telecom in which the Federal Court of Appeal, siding with Henderson's client against those companies, broke their monopoly by allowing cable companies to string wires on Bell Telephone poles. Still, he got far greater pleasure out of the offbeat cases, the 'fun cases,' as he called them. In one of these, he persuaded the Exchequer Court that the General Motors Company trademark for a refrigerator, 'Frigidaire,' was invalid because it was merely descriptive of an icebox with cold air and hence Henderson's client could with impunity market a product under the name 'Frozenaire.' In another, an inventor devised a method by which, when an oil tank was being filled, a tube inserted in the fluid containing a whistle would sound so long as air was being expelled by the inflowing liquid; when the tank was full, the whistle stopped. Henderson's client achieved the same result by a flotation device and successfully resisted an infringement claim by the earlier inventor on the basis that the prior patent was restricted to a tubular device.

Two cases that appealed most to his sense of mischief involved the toy manufacturer Reliable Toy, for whom he acted. In the first, which was tried in 1949, Reliable brought out a line of miniature articles of furniture made of plastic for use in children's dollhouses, only to be met with a claim by another manufacturer that it had been marketing similar products for years and had acquired an industrial design which Reliable Toy was infringing. The Supreme Court of Canada, which seldom had to rule on children's issues, said that to produce miniatures of standard items of furniture such as stoves, toilets, and washbasins conferred no exclusive rights. The other case, in 1950, was one of industrial espionage. The chief chemist of Reliable Toy left to go on his own as a consultant. Reliable, on learning that he was probably selling their trade secrets, hired a private detective who, posing as an American buyer, called on the chemist in his room at the King Edward Hotel in Toronto and tape-recorded a conversation in which the two discussed a possible sale of various manufacturing processes. Over the vociferous objections of Arthur Maloney, who acted for the chemist, the court admitted the tape into the evidence, an early example of such evidence; that was the end of the case for the chemist. Similarly, Henderson, about the same time, in a case involving a matrimonial dispute in which it was alleged that the husband had always been quarrelsome, persuaded the court to accept as evidence home movies taken over many years that showed a happy couple; nevertheless, he lost the case.[3]

In litigation outside the intellectual property arena, Henderson often appeared before arbitration tribunals, a method of alternative dispute resolution – to use the rather heavy-handed phrase currently in vogue – that is much less structured than the court system. Citizens, perhaps even lawyers skilled in a certain field, are pressed into service to resolve disputes, not being bound by the strict rules of evidence prevailing in the courtroom, to produce a far faster decision. Henderson, always a practical man who wished to speed the wheels of justice, saw arbitration as a sensible method of avoiding interminable delays in the judicial system. So convinced was he on this score that he predicted the demise of the current system of judicial resolution and its replacement by a less formal and quicker method. He frequently appeared before commissions – royal or otherwise. One of his earlier appearances was before the Norris commission (1961–3) on the controversies surrounding Hal Banks and the Seafarers' International Union; later, two of his most significant appearances involved commissions of inquiry into the affairs of Air Canada and the Bank of Canada, each chaired by W.Z. Estey; Henderson acted for the airline in the first instance and the bank in the second. He never acted as commission counsel, however, always appearing as an advocate for an interested party. Henderson did not think much of royal commissions as a method of resolving difficult issues, partly because the disregard for the ordinary rules of evidence tended to turn the proceedings into a free-for-all, if not a bear pit.

In the courtroom he successfully defended Uranium Canada, the government-owned cartel, on combines charges; his argument was that, as the law then stood, crown corporations were immune from prosecution. He also represented the pharmaceutical firm Hoffman LaRoche on combines charges. The company had donated one million Valium pills to hospitals and it was alleged that it had done so as a form of predatory pricing – its goal was to drive out the competition. The company was found guilty but Henderson's efforts resulted in a small fine – hardly more than a tap on the wrist. As well, he was a pioneer in the field of aboriginal rights and acted for various Iroquois bands in the prosecution of their claims, a good example of his willingness to take on unpopular causes.

But Henderson preferred to look back on a case in which the human element was at the fore. In one such case, two sisters squabbled over who owned the trademark to the product they both sold, a liquid known as 'Fix-So,' which was used as a mending and patching liquid for tears in leather goods. Henderson acted for the sister who claimed that she was sole owner of the trademark and her sister was a mere employee; the other sister asserted that she was a partner and the trademark was a partnership asset and so she could sell the product as widely and as often and wherever she pleased. Thus the issue was purely one of credibility. On the day his client was to testify, Henderson told her, 'You are going to get a dark dress, you are going to have one little jewel, you are going to have a white hat and you are going to get your hair done and you will be made up very quietly and you are going to be very demure when you get in the witness stand.' She followed his instructions to the letter. Her sister, Henderson said, 'wore earrings that you could chin yourself on.' The judge unhesitatingly believed Henderson's client.

The case that Henderson seemed to recall most fondly involved a stand of timber around Victoria Lake, in what is now Algonquin Park. In 1905 J.R. Booth, the millionaire Ottawa lumberman, gave to a good friend, the governor of Vermont, Victoria Lake with a defined area of land surrounding it but reserved the rights to cut the merchantable timber on it. Booth's successor company hired a logging contractor in 1947 to cut the merchantable timber. When the governor's descendants learned that the area had been logged they sued; they were represented by Arthur Maloney, and Henderson acted for the logging contractor. One of the troublesome issues was whether the phase 'merchantable timber' meant the condition of the timber in 1905 or at the time of the logging forty years later. One of the expert witnesses called in an attempt to compare the degree of 'merchantability' between the two periods was a grizzled old logger who, on finding himself in a courtroom packed with spectators (the trial was in Pembroke and attracted enormous interest) and presided over by the chief justice, became flustered and tongue-tied. After a long silence, the chief justice said, 'Give the man a drink' (a glass of water is a standard remedy for any witness in distress). The witness's eyes lit up – relief was at hand, he was given a glass of water which he obviously thought was gin, took a big swig, and, coughing violently, spat it out, drenching the court reporter. After a sudden adjournment the case resumed. Henderson was successful.

Henderson's contribution to the affairs of the legal profession was distinguished; no other word suits. But it was a contribution of one acutely aware of the public interest in the doings of lawyers. On the one hand, he was concerned with the purely regulatory functions of governing legal bodies – the rules of and qualifications for admission to the profession, the circumstances when a lawyer could be disqualified, and the restrictions upon non-lawyers delivering legal services; on the other hand, he was equally concerned about how to maintain or possibly increase the confidence of the ordinary citizen in the working of the legal system and in the integrity of lawyers and judges. For sixteen years he was an elected bencher of the Law Society of Upper Canada, the body responsible for governing Ontario lawyers, and thereafter he continued as an unelected member until his death. He was extremely active in the Society, particularly in the formulation of plans for the provision of legal aid. With others, notably W.Z. Estey and Bryan Williams of Vancouver, he was instrumental in encouraging presentations to the Supreme Court of Canada by satellite communication from a distant location. He was a forward-thinking man, mindful of his own parched – though that would perhaps not be the word he would have chosen – legal education. Until his death, he was actively concerned with making library materials more available to the profession and the public through the use of computers, a reflection of his view that a good lawyer must have a well-rounded education, as witnessed by his membership on the legal education committee of the Law Society and his association with Carleton University and the University of Ottawa. The Law Society, as a recognition of Henderson's work on its behalf, conferred on him an honorary LLD in 1982. Though he was grateful, he was sufficiently amused to question the legal jurisdiction of the Society to grant such a degree – it was not, after all, a university.

Henderson never became treasurer of the Law Society – leader of the profession in Ontario – but he did become in 1979 president of the Canadian Bar Association and thus head of the legal profession in Canada. He was, in a sense, parachuted into the position. Nowadays, presidents work their way up through the ranks – first a member of a provincial branch, then an executive of the branch, then president of the branch, and, afterwards, election to the National Council followed by election as treasurer and vice-president and, finally, president. In contrast, Henderson was asked, through the old-boy network, if he would become treasurer and hence position himself for a rapid ascent to the presidency; he agreed. Even though his ascendancy was accelerated, the result was the same: he had virtually to give up practice for one year. That he, and other presidents before and since, was able to do so was as a result of his being a member of a large law firm which could, without undue strain, afford to lose his earning powers for a year. The author has not done a statistical survey but his impression is that no president of the Canadian Bar Association has come from a small firm; certainly no single practitioner has taken on the task. That very fact caused Henderson concern during his tenure: if the profession is to be run by members of large firms only, how can they be truly responsive to the needs of the entire profession, including those lawyers practising in small centres whose efforts are no less worthy than those of colleagues in larger ones? There is no ready answer to this question. Some think that the president should be sufficiently well paid that a practitioner from a small community, say from Dawson Creek, British Columbia, would not be impoverished by a term on the job. Henderson favoured some form of compensation for such people, if not an outright salary then at least extra-generous travel allowances. During his presidential year, Henderson travelled the length and breadth of the country to meet with lawyers in their communities as well as government representatives, provincial and federal, and generally to act as the voice of the legal profession. But his active interest in the association did not end with his presidency. Long after he stepped down, not only was he frequently asked for advice, but he retained a particular interest in the well-being of the association's scholarly journal – the *Canadian Bar Review*. This was hardly surprising in view of his long editorship of the *Canadian Patent Reporter*.

It is difficult enough for a lawyer, let alone a layman, to grasp the difference between the function of a provincial bar association or law society – they are variously named – and the Canadian Bar Association. To put it crudely, the bar associations are regulatory; the Canadian Bar Association is a lobby and public-relations group which, on behalf of all Canadian lawyers, intercedes with government and private agencies on matters of public policy that somehow involve the judicial system. This is a legitimate function, though one often viewed by members of the general public as self-serving. Henderson, whose own career and character were exemplary and who spent many years trying to improve the image of the profession, sadly confessed that such efforts were likely to fail: 'As far as you want to go back lawyers were not popular and are not going to be popular. Somebody is going to lose generally in a law suit. And when that person loses, his lawyer is to blame ... What is the story, that the hearse horse snickered as he took the lawyer to the grave?' Henderson saw little difference between the public's view of lawyers as voiced by Jack Cade in Shakespeare's *Henry VI* – 'The first thing we do, let's kill all the lawyers' – and present-day attitudes. But this is overstating the aversion to lawyers: the fact is that the percentage of lawyers in the general population has increased markedly in recent years, undoubtedly because society has become much more legalistic and litigious than formerly.

Henderson was interested in the welfare not only of lawyers but also of judges. In 1987 he and two others, Mary Eberts and W.C. Hamilton, were commissioned by the Ontario attorney general to conduct an inquiry into the 'remuneration, allowances and benefits of Provincial Court Judges in Ontario.' They conducted hearings, received written submissions, and heard counsel for various interested bodies, including counsel for the judges themselves, and brought out their report in September 1988; it is fair to say that they came down on the side of the judges; as they pointed out in the introduction to their report, the Ontario Provincial Court decides approximately 93 per cent of all criminal cases heard in the province (these run the gamut from illegal parking to various serious crimes, but do not include homicides) and three-quarters of all family disputes. The court obviously was the one that the ordinary citizen in trouble was most likely to encounter, and therefore, Henderson and his colleagues concluded, its judges should be suitably remunerated, partly out of a sense of fairness and partly to ensure judicial independence.

As noted in the introduction, it was not until the advent of John Turner as minister of justice in the Trudeau government that the treatment of judicial appointments as simply a form of patronage came to an end. From this point on, Henderson, along with other like-minded and highly respected lawyers – for example, the late Leonard Dumoulin in Vancouver – became the unofficial arbiters of judicial appointments in Canada. Although the practice of provincial representatives offering advice to the minister of justice on judicial appointments ceased in 1987, the element of non-partisanship has persisted: hardly any judicial appointments are now questioned on partisan grounds. What has markedly changed, however, is the role of the judges in the era of the Charter of Rights. Since judges now rule on social as well as legal issues, should prospective appointees be interrogated before their appointment about their views on such matters as abortion, euthanasia, capital punishment, sexual harassment, and so on, as is done in the United States? Henderson at first thought not. He firmly believed that an intelligent person of good judgment could render a fair decision on facts presented which might be at variance with the judge's personal beliefs. On the other side of the coin, since prospective judicial appointees in this country are not subjected to scrutiny, he thought that after appointment they should remain silent on public issues. Yet Henderson gradually came to the view that, since judges increasingly are stepping out of the courtroom to make extra-judicial pronouncements on social and political issues, then perhaps after all they should be interrogated before their appointment. It is a rational argument.[4]

Henderson was twice offered a judgeship. On the first occasion, relatively early in his career, he was asked to accept promotion to the trial division of the Ontario High Court; he refused, not because of any ingrained opposition to being a judge, but because he did not feel that at his age he would be effective on the bench. The second offer, more attractive, came in 1972 from Minister of Justice John Turner, who asked Henderson to take an appointment to the Ontario Court of Appeal which, given the age of the sitting members, would likely eventually result in Henderson becoming chief justice. Henderson initially accepted, but then, talking about it with his wife, phoned Turner the next morning to tell him that the judicial life was not for him and, besides, he would have to live in Toronto, a prospect he could not abide. Henderson told the author that he never regretted his decision; what he regretted was his initial acceptance.

Henderson had in reality a second career, one outside the law, through his substantial involvement in a host of community activities in the Ottawa region. Just as was the case with Covert, these activities had nothing to do with his professional career but everything to do with his commitment to the community which had nurtured and sustained him. This

motivation may seem naive to cynics, but with Henderson it was paramount. In the last several years of his life he spent roughly a third of his
time in community or university affairs – and never grudged it – and of
this the largest segment was devoted to the two Ottawa universities. In
1945 he was invited to lecture at the newly established Carleton University. It had no law school – nor does it now – but until 1964 he lectured in
public administration. In 1962 he started to lecture at the University of
Ottawa on intellectual property and continued to do so for almost thirty
years. That university's law school has two components, the civil law
side, teaching the Quebec civil code, and the common law side, teaching
the system which in Canada prevails outside the province of Quebec. By
all accounts from those at Carleton and at the University of Ottawa,
Henderson was a born teacher, enthusiastic, informative, and stimulating,
who did not patronize students and indeed enjoyed rubbing shoulders
with them. On the presentation of his honorary LLD from the University
of Ottawa, he was described as 'the articulate expert' (five years later he
received a similar degree from Carleton). He became increasingly
involved with the administration of the University of Ottawa, first as a
member of the board of governors, then as chairman of the board, and,
finally, in 1991, as chancellor, a post he held until his death. He was an
extremely conscientious board member with a particular interest in the
financial affairs of the institution, including operating costs, the investment of endowed funds, and the liquidity of the pension fund. He
donated to the university a substantial sum which, when matched by the
university itself, endowed a full-time chair of human rights within the
faculty of law.

While chairman he took up the cause of what ultimately became the
university's Heart Institute, located at the Ottawa Civic Hospital. In 1984
he became the founding chairman of the advisory board of the Heart
Institute, a position he occupied until his death. In paying funereal tribute
to Henderson in 1993, Dr Wilbert Keon, under whose medical leadership
the Heart Institute has gained an international reputation, spoke of Henderson's commitment to the institute's work; when Keon visited Henderson a few days before his death, Henderson wanted to be brought up-to-
date on the institute's affairs.[5]

Of the community activities to which Henderson donated his time and
sometimes money – the list seems endless – those closest to his heart were
the affairs of the university, the Heart Institute, and the Community
Foundation of Ottawa-Carleton. The latter was founded in 1987 to raise a
capital endowment fund from which money would be paid to a wide

range of charitable causes – the arts, culture, education, heritage, and a variety of social services – that were beyond the scope of the United Way (which, incidentally, Henderson had headed one year, then staying on as chairman of its bequest and endowment fund). Henderson and his wife initiated the capital fund, donating $100,000 to the foundation, and he became the foundation's first president and chairman.

By 1992 Henderson had practised law for fifty-five years and had been at the pinnacle of the profession for many of them. He could look back at a long and happy marriage of fifty years. His wife had come to work in his law firm in 1941 while pondering a career as a professional skater. Henderson evidently talked her out of it and they were married in 1942. She herself has had a notable record of service in community organizations in the Ottawa area as well as being on the board of governors of the Stratford Festival. As for Henderson himself, like all courtroom lawyers reflecting on their careers, there were the high points – the cases won – and the low points – the cases lost. It seems typical of the breed that the lost cases stir deeper emotions than the victories. The case that seemed to rankle more than any other with him, for he regarded it as the most important of his lengthy career, was his unsuccessful attempt on behalf of Kenneth Dye, the federal auditor general, to secure documents from Petro-Canada and the cabinet relating to the acquisition by Petro-Canada of the shares and property of Canadian PetroFina, the big Belgian oil company. Dye suspected, not without reason, that Petro-Canada had paid too much for the acquisition and, what really amounted to the same thing, did not receive fair value for the taxpayers' money spent. Met with refusal on every hand to disclose documents – stonewalling, Henderson thought – Dye on Henderson's advice went to court in an effort to force disclosure. But the Supreme Court of Canada held that Dye had no standing to sue and that all he could do was to make a formal report to parliament outlining the circumstances.

Oddly, two cases in 1984 seem to an observer more important than the Dye litigation, but evidently they did not make that impression on Henderson. Both involved the seabeds on opposite coasts and legislative jurisdiction over them. The first was the important reference to the Supreme Court of Canada on whether the government of Canada or that of Newfoundland had the legal right to license all exploration in the Hibernia field on the continental shelf off Newfoundland. Seven provinces, including Nova Scotia for whom Henderson acted, supported Newfoundland's claim. The Supreme Court of Canada ruled that any rights by international law acquired by Newfoundland prior to its joining Canada in 1949 had either reverted to the crown in the right of the United Kingdom or passed to Canada by the terms of union. But, more important, the court held that neither Canada nor Newfoundland had any right to explore the continental shelf until the Geneva Convention of 1958, and since by that time Newfoundland was part of Canada only the federal government had jurisdiction, which it could exercise pursuant to the peace, order, and good government clause of the constitution.

The second was also a reference, this time to determine whether Canada, or British Columbia, had proprietorship of the underwater and seabed resources covered by the waters of the Canadian portions of the Strait of Juan de Fuca, the Strait of Georgia, Johnstone Strait, and Queen Charlotte Strait. Henderson once again appeared for Nova Scotia, which, along with Alberta, New Brunswick, and Newfoundland, had intervened to support British Columbia. The Supreme Court of Canada decided that, since at the time the colony of British Columbia entered confederation in 1871 its western boundary was the Pacific Ocean off the west coast of Vancouver Island and its south boundary was the international border through the Strait of Juan de Fuca, all land and waters lying between Vancouver Island and the mainland belonged to the colony, and now the province, of British Columbia. The rulings in both those seabed cases must rank as the most significant constitutional cases in Henderson's long career.

Two very different cases had given him the greatest satisfaction. In the earlier, he acted for Leo Landreville in the latter stages of his struggle to clear his name from a charge that, while mayor of Sudbury, he had corruptly accepted benefits from a pipeline company which was to supply natural gas to the city. The allegation came to the fore after his appointment as a judge of the High Court of Ontario. He was indicted, stood aside from the bench while the charge was being aired, and was cleared of criminal wrongdoing at a preliminary hearing. No further criminal prosecution was initiated. After resuming his judicial post, he became the target of renewed attacks on his conduct; the benchers of the Law Society of Upper Canada issued a report condemning him and urging his removal though they did not give him the chance to defend himself. Henderson was a life bencher and took no part in this process but was angered by it. Mr Justice Ivan Rand, after conducting an inquiry, castigated Landreville and thought he should resign (but made no allegations of criminality), and a joint parliamentary committee also recommended his removal from office. Eventually, his health badly affected by the stress of the long-drawn-out affair, he agreed to step down from the bench if the government would agree to pay the pension due judges who resigned for reasons of health. Unfortunately, he had no more than a verbal assurance of a pension and after his resignation the government would not pay him. At that point he turned to Henderson (at earlier stages of the affair John Robinette and David – now Mr Justice – Humphrey had represented him). Henderson, convinced that Landreville was being unfairly hounded and pilloried, took up the cudgels in an attempt to get Landreville his pension, an excellent illustration of his belief that lawyers should right wrongs. As a preliminary step he succeeded in persuading the Federal Court to quash, on judicial review, the Rand report since Landreville had been denied the opportunity to make full response to some of the allegations against him. He then launched court action for the pension. The Federal Court decided that only the governor-in-council could rule on the issue and directed it to do so. Landreville eventually received a substantial settlement and, as a highly competent criminal lawyer, returned to private practice.

In the later case Henderson was consulted by St Peter's Evangelical Lutheran Church of Ottawa. Having purchased a property in Ottawa on which stood a building designated by the city as a heritage structure, St Peter's applied to the city council for permission to demolish the structure so it could erect a larger church building. Under the Ontario Heritage Act, if a city council refused such consent, it was obliged to give formal notice of its refusal; if it failed to provide that notice, demolition could proceed by default, so to speak. At a meeting attended by the representatives of the church, council refused consent but failed to give official notice as required by the statute, thinking that by their presence the church representatives were well aware of the decision and need not be otherwise notified. At the end of the ninety-day period, not having received the notice, the church tore down the existing structure and started the construction of a new building, whereupon the city launched legal action; the church then consulted Henderson, who realized full well that if the city won the litigation the church would probably be bankrupted through having to pay costs and damages. Which is more reprehensible? Destruction of a heritage building? Or bankruptcy of a church? The Supreme Court of Canada came down on the side of the church: the applicable statute set out a specific procedure or code, the city did not follow it, and therefore the church was free of any liability.[6]

Henderson enjoyed tilting at windmills, as evidenced by this case, but his final tilt did not produce the same happy result; he became involved in the Donald Marshall affair, and the experience left him embittered.

Donald Marshall had been convicted of a murder which, it was demonstrated some eleven years later, he had not committed. In overturning his conviction, three judges of the Nova Scotia Court of Appeal, though acknowledging his innocence, said that Marshall by his conduct had been the author of his own misfortune. A royal commission, headed by Chief Justice T.A. Hickman of Newfoundland, was set up to inquire into the circumstances of Marshall's conviction and the role of the courts and of the police; specifically, its task was to determine whether Marshall, as a Micmac Indian, had been the victim of a judicial and police system rigged against him. During the course of its hearings, the commission decided that it should hear evidence from the three judges; they refused to testify and, in an attempt to force them to do so, the commission applied for a court order. Henderson's law firm (but not him personally) acted as Ottawa agents for the commissioners in preparing and filing the documents necessary to bring the matter before the Supreme Court of Canada, and one of the partners argued the case. The Supreme Court of Canada ruled that it would not make such an order, and the commission concluded its proceedings without hearing from the judges. In its report the commission criticized them for their remarks, which had provoked a public outcry.

Marshall's partisans persuaded the Canadian Judicial Council – a sort of watchdog of the judiciary – to hold a hearing into the propriety of the remarks made by the Nova Scotia judges; a five-member panel, headed by Chief Justice A.D. McEachern of British Columbia, convened in Halifax in July 1990. The three judges retained Henderson, who must have known of his firm's earlier involvement in the matter, or at least, by virtue of a ruling of the Supreme Court of Canada on legal conflicts of interest, would have been presumed to have such knowledge. The lawyers representing Marshall were also aware of Henderson's firm's prior association with the case, but they made no issue of it until Henderson concluded his summary before the tribunal on behalf of the judges. In it, he forcefully attacked the Hickman commission's finding that the judges' remarks were inappropriate; he also strongly reiterated the judges' view that Marshall must bear some of the blame for what happened. At that point, Marshall's lawyers, angered by what they considered as inflammatory remarks, argued that Henderson was in conflict of interest and ought to step down. The inquiry held a closed-door session to consider the allegation, but Henderson obviated any formal ruling by voluntarily withdrawing so that the hearing would not be delayed; however, unrepentant, he insisted that he was not in any conflict. It was a curious situation, made more so by the fact that the objection was put forward by lawyers for Marshall, for whom neither Henderson nor his firm had done any work. The connection of Henderson's law firm with the Marshall inquiry might lead one to ask that, if there was a perceived conflict, who was affected by it? Not the three judges certainly, for they hired Henderson. If there was a conflict, surely only they could raise the issue? Still, it was an awkward situation for Henderson, and it pained him. By an extraordinary circumstance, Henderson's successor as counsel for the judges, Ian Binnie of Toronto, was likewise forced to withdraw since J.J. Robinette, a partner in Binnie's law firm, had also given advice to the commission. In the end, four members of the panel criticized the three judges for 'grossly inappropriate' language; McEachern, the chairman, dissented, holding that the judges' remarks were no more than 'unfortunate.' All agreed, however, that the episode did not warrant their removal from the bench.

Henderson, in reflecting on this episode, attributed it to the tendency of some current members of the profession to be more aggressive in acquiring clients from other law firms and, as part of that acquisitiveness, to look for conflicts of interest where they really do not exist. In former days, he said, when there was a far greater degree of collegiality among lawyers, conflicts were a concern only when there was an unauthorized disclosure of confidential information. But, as law firms grew larger and became more competitive, there was increased emphasis on perceived, but not actual, conflict. In expressing these views, he was far from being a dinosaur; in fact, he was a thoughtful and broad-minded man. He favoured abolition of the appointments of Queen's Counsel, believing them anachronistic and of no value; in this he was rather like his uncle, Stuart Henderson in British Columbia, who spearheaded the movement to abolish wigs. On the issue of 'libel chill,' very much in the forefront these days, he agreed that it exists, that the laws as framed are wrongly weighted in favour of the person allegedly libelled and so the defendant has an uphill struggle. His views on the subject were undoubtedly shaped by his experience in 1988 as counsel for the Ottawa *Citizen* in a libel case involving a federal cabinet minister. Robert Coates, on official business in Germany as minister of national defence, had visited a nightclub featuring pornographic films, nude dancers, and prostitutes. The newspaper suggested that this conduct may have posed a security risk. Coates was forced to resign, and later he sued for defamation. As part of the welter of proceedings both in Ontario and Nova Scotia (where Coates lived), Henderson applied unsuccessfully to the Nova Scotia courts for a declaration that the provincial Defamation Act violated the guarantee of free expression in the Charter of Rights. The law in Nova Scotia was the same as that in other provinces and is still the subject of much controversy. Briefly stated, the usual rule in civil litigation places the burden of proof throughout on the plaintiff; however, in a libel case, once a plaintiff such as Coates establishes that a newspaper article, or book, or letter is in fact defamatory, the burden of proof shifts to the defendant, who, to avoid liability, must establish that the offending words were true, or that they were written without malice, or that the plaintiff suffered no damage. Henderson's contention, one supported by literary and journalistic organizations, is that the plaintiff should prove everything – defamation, falsity, malicious intent, and damages – and to do otherwise is to place a 'libel chill' on writers or journalists.[7]

He was also very much in favour of law firms advertising, particularly the smaller, so-called 'boutique' firms that had no other way to draw attention to themselves and that catered to a particular niche – the drawing of wills, the transfer of property, family disputes, and so on. Although in general he approved of the unilateral patriation of the constitution in 1982 and the accompanying Charter of Rights, he was concerned about the 'silly issues,' as he termed them, raised by lawyers in Charter cases. He deplored the fact that the Charter had spawned a new breed of lawyer committed not to a client but to a cause. Since, under present rules, a lawyer can bring only a client and not a cause into court, there has been a tendency for the client to become incidental to the cause. Henderson was unable to offer any suggestions on how to combat what is, in reality, a form of government by a myriad of dissident groups; all he could suggest was that, with time, the Supreme Court of Canada might set matters right.

In 1992 Henderson became ill with cancer and, because of his deteriorating health and the inevitable onset of age, his general appearance changed from that of robustness to haggardness. The author had lengthy interviews with him that year in anticipation of this portrait; he was an ideal subject: patient, informative and interested.[8] We had a final interview on 18 June 1993. Though clearly unwell, Henderson had driven to his office for the interview and then, with the author, returned to his home, where he, his wife, and I went over his memorabilia. On the 17th of August he died, lamented by all who knew him.

Epilogue

The careers of these seven men spanned more than a century; Lafleur started to practise in 1881 and Henderson's practice ended with his death in 1993. For most of that period, the way lawyers did business and the methods of law-office management and administration remained essentially the same, but there were some significant changes. Telephones and typewriters, which came into common use around the turn of the century, were the first innovations with revolutionary effects on the methods of law practice; the equipment was, of course, refined and improved, but basically the technology remained unaltered until recently. Adding machines then came along, and, when speed was urgent, messages were sent by telegram and frequently delivered by young boys on bicycles. With the advent of computers, word processors, and answering and fax machines, a true revolution has occurred which only Covert and Henderson lived to experience, all in the name of efficiency and service to the client. These are undoubtedly admirable objectives, but they have been accompanied by high office overheads, a certain facelessness, and cold-bloodedness in setting fees, which are now often governed by a programmed machine. One harks back to Geoffrion's method of setting fees, a method that by comparison is positively antediluvian. Farris let others set fees for him but he had a gut feeling about what was appropriate and would have been appalled to be told that the computer should dictate his billings. Covert and Henderson practised in both the pre- and post-revolutionary era. By 1987, when Covert died, the use of computers was widespread; now it is virtually universal. Henderson seemed resigned to the new technology, perhaps reflecting that at his age he would not have to endure it for long.

Other major changes in the period affected litigation generally. First, appeals to the Privy Council were swept away effective 1 January 1950, leaving the Supreme Court of Canada as the court of last resort for the country in all types of litigation. Farris, Covert, and Henderson were known to have favoured abolition and it is almost certain that the other four subjects would also have been in favour. That fundamental change has altered the role of the Supreme Court of Canada. Previously, litigants had virtually automatic rights of appeal to the court if a case met certain defined monetary limits; if no sum of money was involved, then the court would have to consent to hearing an appeal. With the abolition of appeals to the Privy Council, appeals from provincial courts of appeal, which formerly went directly to London – the *per saltum* appeals – wound up in Ottawa. And this circumstance, combined with expansion of litigation generally, has placed the Supreme Court under considerable pressure to the extent that now virtually all appeals must be by consent of the court (some criminal appeals are heard as of right), which will be given only in cases thought to be of general significance. One effect of this development has been to restrict the number of commercial cases heard by the court. As Gordon Henderson pointed out, the Federal Court of Appeal is now the *de facto* court of last resort in intellectual-property litigation. Henderson, in fact, was so concerned about appeals in commercial cases not going to the Supreme Court of Canada that he favoured the establishment of a commercial court which would have at least the status of the Federal Court of Appeal and which would be the final court for commercial litigation, leaving the federal courts to deal exclusively with intellectual property. Alternatively, he supported a division of the existing courts much as in the United Kingdom, where members of the commercial bar appear before judges designated to hear that type of litigation.

Also, these men practised when the British North America Act, and particularly sections 91 and 92 on the distribution of powers between the federal and provincial governments, held sway. Those sections, which assigned specific subjects to the two levels of government, were the touchstone of constitutionality. Whatever effect the founding fathers of Canada intended the peace, order, and good government clause to have, the Privy Council refused to allow it to override or diminish specific powers given to the provinces, though there had been some weakening of that position by the time appeals to it ended in 1950. All the major questions of the day when these men flourished were tested against the BNA Act, and fundamental values such as freedom of speech and freedom of religion were protected by the principles of custom and precedent as enshrined in the British common law and the British parliamentary tradition, a point enunciated by the Supreme Court of Canada in the Alberta newspapers case of 1938. Today the BNA Act, in its amended form as the Constitution Act of 1982, is occasionally involved in litigation, but, increasingly, constitutional issues revolve around the Canadian Charter of Rights and Freedoms. Only Covert and Henderson lived to see the patriation of the Canadian constitution and the advent of the Charter of Rights in 1982. The others would have been deeply suspicious of the Charter for its effect has been to Americanize our judicial system by removing ultimate authority from an elected parliament in the British tradition and handing it over to non-elected judges in the American tradition. Covert and Henderson approved of the unilateral patriation of the constitution by Ottawa, that is, patriation without the consent of the provinces, but, while the other five subjects of these portraits would certainly have favoured patriation in principle, they would not have approved of Ottawa riding roughshod over the wishes of the provinces.

Other changes in the manner in which lawyers function are less dramatic and more subtle but still highly significant. Lawyers increasingly spend time in taking self-protective measures against potential lawsuits brought by disgruntled clients alleging negligence. Until recently, the courts, following the British rule, granted immunity from claims for negligence to barristers in their courtroom role. But that has changed and barristers are now as vulnerable to lawsuits as any other legal practitioner. Formerly clients, dissatisfied with the quality of legal services rendered, took their lumps and changed lawyers, but more and more they tend to engage a new lawyer and sue the earlier one and, to make life more difficult still for lawyers, the courts are tending to side with the clients to the point where errors of judgment, honest mistakes so to speak, are treated as negligence. This trend was unknown from Lafleur's time down to that of Farris, but it was only too well known by Covert and Henderson. One result, as noted in the text, has been the arrival of the specialist and the corresponding disappearance of the generalist. Ironically, the general public, which in effect has dictated these changes, will pay for them since specialization and the cost of insurance taken out by lawyers have resulted in higher fees to clients.

Currently, lawyers are far more conscious of unethical behaviour and potential conflicts of interest which may also result in claims against them. Formerly, lawyers were concerned only about actual conflicts: acting for one client in circumstances opposed to the interests of another; acting for a client one day and against the same person soon after; using information gained from a client when acting against that client sometime in the future; disclosing confidential information and representing two parties in circumstances in which the interests of one must inevitably suffer. Virtually every lawyer encounters such situations, and the subjects of these portraits were not immune. Yet, with the exception of Henderson, they did not seem to be troubled by them. Lafleur, it will be recalled, in the space of one year, 1918, acted against the British Columbia government, then for it, and then against it; four years later, he again represented the province. He rendered an opinion to Emily Murphy in what became the 'Person's' case and seven years later in the actual litigation acted against her, though it must be observed that his argument for the government of Canada accorded with his earlier opinion to her. There are many similar examples. Tilley, as a junior lawyer, acted against the CPR in the Privy Council while representing the company in another, unrelated, case. Geoffrion was asked by the Bennett government to give an opinion on the constitutionality of one of the pieces of Bennett's New Deal legislation, and unhesitatingly declared it was invalid. Six months later he successfully represented Quebec in striking down the legislation; like Lafleur with Emily Murphy, he was at least consistent. Pitblado, however, found himself in a more awkward spot in 1910. He appeared before the Board of Railway Commissioners on behalf of the Winnipeg Grain Exchange and the Winnipeg Board of Trade to seek a reduction in telegraph rates, and soon after he was appointed as counsel to the board, a post that was supposed to be neutral. Later, in 1919, he prosecuted the leaders of the Winnipeg General Strike notwithstanding his active participation in the civic committee formed to combat its effects. Farris, knowing that he was to become general counsel to the British Columbia Electric Railway Company, acted against it before his formal appointment. Covert, in commercial transactions, frequently represented all parties and, in particular, often represented a corporate client and the underwriters when a stock or bond offering was to be made to the public. And Henderson often found himself in difficulties when representing apparently competing interests in the communications industry. These men were honourable, but all the instances mentioned would today be viewed with raised eyebrows and some would likely provoke complaints to the various law societies. Yet, with one exception, the striker, John Queen, no one complained at the time, least of all the clients supposedly affected. The ethical standards of the time were less demanding than they are now.

Perceived conflicts of interest are a new and troubling development for lawyers which can entail unfortunate repercussions. A junior member at a large law firm has no idea what all the other lawyers are doing or who all the clients are; yet, if that junior leaves the firm to join another big law firm which has a client engaged in current litigation or negotiations with a client of the former firm, the second firm may have to withdraw on the grounds that there is always the possibility that the departing lawyer has some snippet of valuable information to impart – or at least had been in a position to acquire it. Even a senior lawyer such as Henderson, in the Donald Marshall affair, fell victim to the new standards governing real or perceived conflicts of interest.

And, finally, the first five subjects and perhaps even a sixth, Covert, would be startled if not appalled by the delays that now characterize litigation. Civil cases have become more complex as government regulation of business and society generally – environmental controls, for example – has proliferated and as advances in science and technology have become difficult to grasp. Thus, medical-malpractice suits, large-scale commercial litigation, litigation in new fields of law, such as aboriginal law and native land claims – all these can result in lengthy trials following lengthy preparation. The ability of word processors to churn out reams of documents has converted much litigation into paper wars and, added to all these factors, is the undoubted increase in litigiousness: if something goes wrong, you sue somebody.

So far as criminal cases are concerned, the delays are more serious. Again, they are partly due to complexity. A big commercial fraud case, for example – a relatively recent development – can be extremely time-consuming, but delays in getting a case to trial currently occur because of preliminary constitutional challenges under the Charter of Rights. Also, the advent of legal aid, worthy though such a scheme may be, frequently results in one lawyer handling a number of cases simultaneously with consequent difficulties in scheduling and, worse, in lawyers stretching out a case to gain more fees. Whatever the causes, and however understandable they are, the fact is that the delays we are accustomed to are of a magnitude unknown to all the subjects but Henderson, who lived long enough to deplore them.

In retrospect, then, these men practised in simpler times. Of course, they faced difficulties, but they were as nothing compared to the complexities and vexations faced by present-day counsel. Lawsuits now are far more complicated than those of fifty years ago, and our subjects spent much less time in arguing a case than their modern counterparts do. Not only that, they could rely on the word of their opponents; a man breaking his word would be ostracized. Today, everything has to be in writing.

The important question is: are the clients better served by the changes in the legal profession? The answer is yet to come.

Notes

AC   *Appeal Cases*
BCR   *British Columbia Reports*
DLR   *Dominion Law Reports*
MLR   *Manitoba Law Reports*
NSR   *Nova Scotia Reports*
OR   *Ontario Reports*
SCR   *Supreme Court of Canada Reports*

PREFACE

1 I confess that this sort of thing is a bit of a hobby horse with me. I have for long, with others, urged the Law Society of British Columbia to set up a mechanism for archival retrieval of lawyers' papers with due regard for client confidentiality, which can be preserved by appropriate restrictions on access. There is a cliché well known to lawyers that their deeds are written in sand. The adage has some truth to it, and one obvious reason that lawyers' exploits are soon forgotten is that zealous housekeepers negligently or deliberately destroy, posthumously, documentary evidence of their existence.

INTRODUCTION

1 F.E. Smith and rude judges: The Earl of Birkenhead, *F.E.*; 'The Task of an Advocate': *Canadian Bar Review*, 1934, vol. 12, 417; Lafleur in the Supreme Court of

Canada: John Honsberger in conversation with G.V.V. Nicholls; the British Columbia land claim case: *Delgamuukw et al. v. The Queen* (1991) 79 *DLR* (4th) 185.

2 'Most of our seven lawyers': Farris Papers (FP), box 10 file 6; Farris-Mackenzie, 15 May 1943; judicial appointments: author's interviews with Gordon Henderson, 2 June 1992, and John Turner, 24 September 1992.

3 There is a surprising paucity of literature on the subject. Those interested may consult the author's biography of Gerald Grattan McGeer, *Mayor Gerry*. As the doughty champion of British Columbia in freight-rate matters from 1922 until 1929, McGeer frequently contended with Pitblado, Tilley, and Lafleur.

4 'Special camaraderie': author's interview with John Farris, November 1981; the case is *Attorney General for B.C. v. CPR* 1927 *AC* 934.

CHAPTER ONE

1 The Shakespeare Dinner: Montreal *Gazette*, 26 December 1964; Lafleur's habits and income: author's interview with R.E. Parsons, and day book, R.E. Parsons Coll.; 'Young Eugene': school reports, High School of Montreal, R.E. Parsons Coll.; 'validity of a will': *Baptist v. Baptist*, (1894) *SCR* 37; the bookkeeper's recollections: W.J. Henderson reminiscences, McCarthy Tétrault Coll; 'involving conflicts': *Logan v. Lee* (1907) 39 *SCR* 311 and *Berthiaume v. Dastous* (1930) *AC* 79.

2 'Whatever the cause': Jerry Mueller, *Restless River*, 69; 'Lafleur's award': ibid., 99; the bill for $50,000: R.E. Parsons in conversation with the author.

3 'Lafleur's courtesy': Hugessen reminiscences, McCarthy Tétrault Coll.; the case is *Outremont v. Joyce* 43 SCR 611, (1912) 46 *SCR* 7; 'a black heart': Hugessen reminiscences; Laurier's offer: Aylesworth-Lafleur, 15 February 1907, McCarthy Tétrault Coll.; 'Family tradition': Borden diaries NAC, MG 26H, 21–3 October 1918.

4 'Legal opinions': McCarthy Tétrault Coll., vols. 1–18, hereinafter cited as 'LP'; 'American professor': LP, Lafleur-Libby, 12 April 1922; Alliance case: LP, Lafleur-Rochester, 10 December 1923; the case is found in (1925) *AC* 384; 'the burial': LP, vol. 4; the *Ne Temere* case: LP, Lafleur-Marler, 23 September 1907, Lafleur-Ames and McMaster, 13 January 1912 and 17 January 1912 respectively; the case itself is (1912) 46 *SCR* 132, (1912) *AC* 880; 'Jewish people': LP, Lafleur-Protestant Committee of Public Instruction for Quebec, 11 November 1924; the case is *Hirsch v. Protestant Board of School Commissioners of Montreal*, (1926) *SCR* 246; (1928) *AC* 200.

5 The Crow rate case: 29 *Canadian Railway Cases*, 238, and (1925) *SCR* 155; 'momentous ruling': 30 *Canadian Railway Cases*, 393; inquiry: 33 *Canadian Railway Cases*, 127.

6 Water case: British Columbia Archives andRecords Service (BCRAS), Bowser-
  Maclean, 16 April 1909, GR 429, box 16, file 3, item 1837/09; the decision is
  Burrard Power and the Attorney General of B.C. v. The King (1910) 43 *SCR* 27,
  (1911) *AC* 87; 'aboriginal title': BCRAS, GR 441, vol. 207, file 53, GR 1323, items
  1398/08, 1412/09, 4563/09, 244/10, 2270/10, 2599/10, 4263/10, 4264/10,
  4413/10, GR 1130, item 37/08; *Delgamuukw*: (1991) 79 DLR (4th) 185; 'aspects
  of fisheries': BCARS, GR 1323, items 4263/10, 4264/10; the case is (1913) 47
  SCR 493, (1914) *AC* 153; 'disallowance': LP, Lafleur-Minister of Justice, 8 April
  1918, vol. 5, order-in-council, 30 May 1918 PC 1334; 'Even Homer': *Statutes of
  British Columbia (SBC)* (1917) cap. 53, *SBC* (1919) cap. 22, *SBC* (1920) cap. 92; LP,
  Lafleur-Dolly Varden Mines, vol. 7, item 77; the liquor case: *Attorney General of
  B.C. v. Attorney General of Canada* (1922) 64 *SCR* 377.

7 'Emergency test': (1920) *SCR* 456, (1922) 1 *AC* 191; 'sterilization': LP, Lafleur-
  Lymburn, 25 January 1928, *Statutes of Alberta (SA)*, 1928, cap. 37, *SA*, 1972, cap.
  87; 'Rupert's Land': LP, Lafleur-Attorney General Saskatchewan, 26 December
  1924; the case is (1931) *SCR* 263, (1932) *AC* 28; water power case: (1929) *SCR*
  200; 'last opinion': LP Lafleur-Lanctot, 19 April 1930; 'Lafleur and Geoffrion':
  the school case is *Attorney General of Quebec v. Attorney General of Ontario* (1910)
  AC 627, and the companies case is (1913) 48 *SCR* 331; the insurance companies
  case: *Attorney General of Canada v. Attorney General Alberta* (1913) 48 *SCR* 260,
  (1916) *AC* 598; the railway case is *Attorney General Alberta v. Attorney General
  Canada* (1915) *AC* 363; '1917 election': LP, Lafleur-Minister of Justice, 11 March
  1918, vol. 6; War Measures Act: LP, Lafleur-Minister of Justice, vol. 6, item 195,
  Co-operative Committee on Japanese Canadians v. Attorney General of Canada (1947)
  AC 87.

8 Morang case: (1911) 45 *SCR* 95; see also Williams, *Duff* 73–4; 'Lafleur going to
  the bench': the *Free Press* issue was 22 December 1920; on King's reasons for
  not appointing Duff, see Williams, *Duff*, 115 *et seq.*; King's diary entries are
  NAC, MG 26J13, 5 May 1924 and 11 May 1924; King's first letter to Lafleur is in
  NAC, King Papers, MG 26JI, vol. 102, 8 September 1924, and his second, 9 Sep-
  tember 1924; Lafleur's letter to King is also in King Papers, 9 September 1924;
  King's opinion of Anglin: King Diaries, 12 September 1924; 'smell of powder':
  Hugessen reminiscences, McCarthy Tétrault Coll.

9 'Lafleur's decision': the hours of labour case is (1925) *SCR* 505, the Alberta
  school case is (1927) *SCR* 364, the Japanese fishermen case is (1928) *SCR* 457,
  the Proprietary Articles case is (1929) *SCR* 409; the 'Person's' case: the letter to
  Emily Murphy's lawyer is LP, vol. 8, item 44, 9 December 1921, the judgment
  of the Supreme Court of Canada is (1928) *SCR* 276, and that of the Privy Council is *Edwards v. Attorney General of Canada*, (1930) *AC* 124.

10 The Macmillan holiday: Macmillan-Lafleur, 30 March 1930, R.E. Parsons Coll.;

Macmillan's appraisal of Lafleur: Lord Macmillan, *A Man of Law's Tale*; tributes
to Lafleur in parliament quoted in Montreal *Star*, 30 April 1930, and the *Times*
obituary appeared the same day; Viscount Dunedin's tribute: proceedings, 1
May 1930 – the first division of the Judicial Committee of the Privy Council,
and his later tribute was quoted by Macmillan; Simon's tribute appeared in the
Times, 1 May 1930; the account of the funeral is in the Montreal *Daily Star*, 2
May 1930, and Lady Macmillan's letter is 2 May 1930, R.E. Parsons Coll.;
Duff's remarks and those of others are found in 'L'Homme et L'avocat,' 1934,
R.E. Parsons Coll.

CHAPTER TWO

1 Tilley lecturing the judges: Gordon Henderson interview with author, 2 June
  1992.
2 'Aloof and cold': David Walker, *Fun Along the Way*; Walker as a student of
  Tilley: Brendan O'Brien to author, 16 June 1994; Walker's case is *Lockhart v.
  Stinson and C.P.R.* (1941) 2 *SCR* 609 and the Privy Council appeal is (1942) 3
  DLR 529; 'silly argument': quoted in (1968) 2, Law Society of Upper Canada
  Gazette, 41; the funeral eulogy: Toronto *Star*, 4 June 1942; 'legal education': C.
  Ian Kyer and Jerome Bickenbach, *The Fiercest Debate*, 134; O'Brien's appraisal:
  O'Brien-author, 7 May 1994; John Robinette's appraisal: interview with author,
  29 May 1991; Mulock episode: O'Brien-author, 16 June 1994; the Currie trial:
  for a full account of this well-known trial, see Robert Sharpe, *The Last Day, The
  Last Hour*. Tilley's education: Hodgins, vol. 23, 83.
3 'Tilley had articled': Ian Kyer interview with author; Tilley's first appearances
  in Privy Council: (1908) *AC* 54; (1908) *AC* 60; fishery arbitration: Proceedings,
  Government Printing Office, Washington 1912, tabled in the *Senate Documents*
  for the 61st Congress – 3rd sess., 5 December 1910 – 4 March 1911, in twelve
  volumes; the remarks by Lammasch: proceedings, vol. 1, 37–8 and 63; Corbett's comment is found in his work *Settlement of Canadian-American Disputes*;
  Tilley and the telegraph inquiry: see 20 *Canadian Railway cases*, 1, and Provincial Archives of Manitoba (PAM), Pitblado Papers, MG 14C64, box 7; the western freight rates case is in 17 *Canadian Railway cases*, 123.
4 The *Empress* case is (1920) *AC* 397, and the *Princess Sophia* case is (1920) *AC* 184;
  the 'train' case is *Ouellette v. C.P.R.* (1924) *SCR* 426, (1925) *AC* 569; the description of the Crow rate hearings before the Board of Railway commissioners is in
  the Montreal *Daily Star*, 25 September 1924, and the Winnipeg *Free Press*, 26
  September 1924; tribute in the Senate: *Senate Debates*, 9 April 1927.
5 Dafoe's testimony: Winnipeg *Telegram*, 9 July 1915; Phippen's testimony: ibid.,
  7 July 1915; for the transcript of Tilley's evidence, and a mass of material relat-

ing to both royal commissions, see PAM, Pitblado Papers, box 4, as well as Marilyn Baker, *Symbol In Stone: The Art and Politics of a Public Building*, and W.L. Morton, *Manitoba: A History*; Tilley and the United Church Commission: see the United Church Archives (Toronto), Church Union Coll., vol. 2, box 10; the separate schools cases of 1916 are found in 1917 *AC* 62 and 76; 'interesting aftermath': see *Trustees v. Quebec Bank and Attorney General of Ontario* (1920) *AC* 230; the 'Tiny' case is (1927) *SCR* 637, (1928) *AC* 363; the overruling case is (1987) 1 *SCR* 1148; the 'British coal case' is (1935) *AC* 500; for a fuller discussion of the bank case, see the chapter on Geoffrion.

6 The aeronautics case: the decision of the Supreme Court of Canada is (1930) *SCR* 663 and the Privy Council appeal is (1932) *AC* 54; the radio case in the Supreme Court of Canada is (1931) *SCR* 541 and the Privy Council appeal is (1932) *AC* 304; Tilley and Geoffrion for Alberta: *Lymburn v. Mayland* (1932) *AC* 318; the 'eccentric will': (1938) *SCR* 1; Tilley's last case in the Supreme Court is (1942) *SCR* 291, W.K. Campbell in conversation with the author, July 1979.

7 Tilley's conversation with Ferguson: David Walker, *Fun Along the Way*; the Smith-Jarvis affair: for a full and entertaining account of this extraordinary episode in Ontario political history, see Peter Oliver, *Public and Private Persons*; Borden's diary entries are 26 August 1917 to 6 September 1917; Tilley and Meighen: see Roger Graham, *Meighen*, vol. 2, 51–3, the law suit is found in ibid., vol. 3, 53–9, and is reported in the Toronto *Evening Telegram*, 4 December 1936; the tribute to Tilley in the Privy Council is recorded in the minutes of the Judicial Committee of the Privy Council, vol. 38, Proceedings, 16 June 1942; abolition of appeals: King Papers, Larkin-King, 29 August 1924.

CHAPTER THREE

1 The city of Toronto case is (1946) *AC* 32 and the temperance case is (1946) *AC* 193; the unsuccessful attempt on behalf of Quebec is found in (1945) *SCR* 600, and the two petitions for leave were recorded in the Privy Council minutes for 4 and 12 December 1945 respectively; the conscription case: *re Gray* (1918) *SCR* 150.

2 See, for example, the author's *Sir Lyman Duff: A Life in the Law*.

3 'Dissatisfaction among Liberals': NAC, Fitzpatrick Papers, MG 27II C1, Elliott-Fitzpatrick, 6 March 1903, and Sifton Papers (SP), MG 27II D15, vol. 141, Fitzpatrick-Sifton, 23 February 1903, vol. 273, Sifton-Blake, 7 March 1903, and vol. 274, Sifton-Duff, 29 July 1903; 'usual civilities': The *Times*, 9 October 1903; Duff's recollection of the tribunal is in *Canadian Bar Review*, vol. 16 (1938), 526, and Geoffrion's remarks are quoted in ibid., vol. 22 (1944), 4.

4 The Japanese fishermen case is (1929) *AC* 111; the association of Lafleur and

Geoffrion: the Bonanza Creek case is (1916) 1 *AC* 566, and the Proprietary Articles (Combines) case is (1929) *SCR* 409; 'sale of debentures': LP, Lafleur and Geoffrion to minister of justice, 2 January 1918; the Gray case is (1918) 57 *SCR* 150; 'The final professional association': Montreal *Daily Star*, 1 May 1930 and 15 October 1946.

5 The *I'm Alone* case: Randell's account, *I'm Alone*, was published in 1930; the *Croft v. Dunphy* case is (1933) *AC* 156, and the attempts to tinker with it are discussed by A.V. Lowe and R.J. Young in 'An Executive Attempt,' *Law Quarterly Review*, vol. 94 (1978), 255; a full discussion of the affair can be found in Williams, *Duff*.

6 In *Mr Sam: The Life and Times of Samuel Bronfman*, Michael R. Marrus is lavish in Geoffrion's praise but makes no mention of the preferred indictment.

7 The Mignault episode: Isaac Pitblado reminiscences are in the Winnipeg *Free Press*, 8 March 1950, and Estey's recollection is in a letter to the author, 12 August 1992; the Bennett election case is (1922) 64 *SCR* 235; the Bronfman preliminary hearing: see the Montreal *Daily Star*, 9 January 1935 *et seq*, and Michael Marrus's biography of Sam Bronfman, *Mr. Sam*; 'forcible closing of a dwelling': *Bedard v. Dawson* (1923) *SCR* 681; the Jehovah's Witnesses cases are *Saumur v. Quebec* (1953) 2 *SCR* 299 and *Switzman v. Ebling* (1957) *SCR* 285; 'lands reserved for Indians': *Attorney General Quebec v. Attorney General Canada* (1921) 1 *AC* 401; 'the militia': in *Re Cape Breton* (1930) *SCR* 554. In 1913, there was a similar occurrence in British Columbia when the militia was called out to assist the police in the disturbances at the Nanaimo coal mines; Farris defended some of the miners at their ensuing trials.

8 Adelard Godbout: Montreal *Star*, 15 October 1946; The Oka case: Ecclesiastics of the Seminary of St. Sulpice, (1912) *AC* 872; the reaction of the Mohawks: *Globe and Mail*, 20 May 1994; the Price Brothers case: (1926) *SCR* 28; 'use of a river': *St. Francis Hydro v. The King*, Privy Council minutes, vol. 35, 12 March 1937.

9 The Newfoundland-Quebec boundary dispute: for the proceedings and judgment, see *In the matter of the boundary between the Dominion of Canada and the Colony of Newfoundland in the Labrador peninsula*, 12 vols. (London, William Clowes and Sons), 'Proceedings'; Quebec's representation: 'Proceedings,' vol. 2, 660; 'the existing boundary': ibid., 333–4; 'a statute of 1825': ibid., 660; the exchanges between Geoffrion and the judges: ibid., 703, 743; 'Scottish streams': ibid., 636–7; Geoffrion's opinion of the award: Guillaume Geoffrion interview with author, June 1994.

10 For the citations of the aeronautic and radio cases, see the chapter on Tilley; 'The New Deal' legislation: Geoffrion's advice to Bennett, *Globe*, 22 May 1935; the labour conventions case is (1936) *SCR* 461; the unemployment

insurance case is (1936) *SCR* 427; the Aberhart legislation: Elizabeth M. Cox, *The Crown and Social Credit, Alberta History*, summer 1992, 25, and (1938) *SCR* 71; the exchange between Geoffrion and Duff: Vancouver *Sun*, 10 January 1938; 'all three acts were unconstitutional': *Reference re Alberta Statutes* (1938) *SCR* 100; 'Canadian political setup': Ottawa *Evening Journal*, 15 January 1938.

11 Abolition of appeals to Privy Council: the decision of the Supreme Court of Canada is (1940), *SCR* 49 and the Privy Council appeal is (1947) *AC* 127; Jowitt's tribute to Geoffrion: The *Times*, 24 October 1946; Geoffrion's support of confederation: Geoffrion-Mitchell, 21 January 1918, Geoffrion Coll., Montreal.

CHAPTER FOUR

1 Thomas Glendinning Hamilton: University of Manitoba, Department of Archives and Special Collections (UMASC) manuscript 14, 'Hamilton Coll.'; Pitblado's letter to Mrs Hamilton: ibid., 25 November 1950; 'Doyle's visit to Winnipeg': Michael W. Homer, *Manitoba History*, spring 1993, no. 25, 9; Pitblado's memorandum to Hamilton: Hamilton Coll., 12 March 1930; King's reaction to Hamilton: quoted in C.P. Stacey, *A Very Double Life*.

2 For a description of this episode, see the author's account of Louis Riel's trial in *With Malice Aforethought*.

3 It is noteworthy that some of the other subjects of this work also thought of themselves as pedogogues: Lafleur took up the law after being turned down for a teaching position at the University of New Brunswick; Tilley taught school for two years; and Geoffrion became a law professor.

4 Duck's Unlimited: Winnipeg *Tribune*, 21 July 1962; 'Indian Jack Jacobs': Winnipeg *Free Press*, 28 November 1959; 'element of discretion': Railway Act, *Revised Statutes of Canada*, 1906, s. 315.

5 'Minutiae': Winnipeg *Telegram*, 13 June 1916; the Coleman dinner: Winnipeg *Tribune*, 20 September 1916; 'contradictory positions': PAM, Pitblado Papers, Pitblado argument General Rate Inquiry, 1947, box 1; 'Alice-in-Wonderland': the Manitoba decision is 27 *MLR* 1 and the Privy Council appeal is (1919) *AC* 935; 'first important foray': PAM box 7, Re Telegraph Tolls, 20 *Canadian Railway Cases*, 1; western freight rates case: 17 *Canadian Railway Cases*, 123.

6 The evidence at the royal commissions, the printed proceedings, and the newspaper reports can be found in PAM, Pitblado Papers box 4; Roblin's tribute to Norris: Winnipeg *Free Press*, 3 July 1915; Perdue commission report: ibid., 30 July 1915; 'staunch Liberal': ibid., 14 November 1905; 'criticized Laurier': ibid., 22 August 1917; Laurier's letter to Pitblado: UMASC MSS48, Pitblado Papers (PP) box 4, folder 2, 4 June 1918; 'speculation grew': Winnipeg

Tribune, 22 August 1917 *et seq.*, and Borden memoirs, vol. 2, 98; 'Pitblado replied to both': the Meighen letter of October 1 and the letter to Borden of October 4 are in PP, box 4, file 3; 'partisan of Meighen': Winnipeg *Tribune*, 19 November 1921; Pitblado and Dexter: PP, box 4, file 10, Pitblado-Dexter, 8 February 1950.

7 Pitblado at Dalhousie: PP, box 20; fees for lawyers: ibid., box 13, file 3; first case for CNR: Winnipeg *Tribune*, 13 September 1921; western freight rate case: Winnipeg *Free Press*, 9 December 1913; engagement by Canadian Northern: Ottawa *Telegram*, 8 April 1914; 'disinfectants in cattle cars': Winnipeg *Free Press*, 15 July 1914; 'retention of the differential': ibid., 2 December 1921; 'Winnipeg and Pitblado had triumphed': Winnipeg *Tribune*, 9 March 1923; 'express rates': Winnipeg *Free Press*, 23 November 1923; 'an obviously unfair situation': see Williams, *Mayor Gerry*, 67, and Winnipeg *Free Press*, 25 February 1927; 'Panama Canal': *33 Canadian Railway Cases*, 127.

8 Duff's letter is in NAC, Duff Papers, vol. 4, N-T, Duff-Pitblado, 18 January 1927, file P, item 13; gratitude of the church: PP, box 4, folder 4, United Church to Pitblado, 25 April 1927; 'Pitblado's speaking style': Winnipeg *Free Press*, 10 February 1925 and Winnipeg *Tribune*, 27 February 1929.

9 The Machray affair: see the report of the Turgeon commission, 29 March 1933, found in the Manitoba *Sessional Papers*, no. 50; W.L. Morton deals with the episode in *One University*; Pitblado's 'brief': PP, box 22, file 5; 'all guns firing': Winnipeg *Tribune*, 14 and 16 January 1933; 'nagging doubts': PP, box 4, folder 5; McWilliams as lieutenant governor: PP, box 4, folder 7. Pitblado-Brockington, 12 April 1940, and Brockington-Pitblado, 15 April 1940.

10 For a full account of the Winnipeg Grain Exchange, see Allan Levine, *The Exchange*; Pitblado and the Privy Council: *Worthington and Forbes v. the Attorney General of Manitoba* (1937) *AC* 260; 'contribution to the war effort': PP, box 14, folder 5; 'general rate increase': Ottawa *Evening Journal*, 15 February 1947; the birthday tribute: *Senate Debates*, 15 July 1947, 744; '21% general rate increase': for the materials relating to this inquiry, see PP, box 1; the cabinet hearing: Ottawa *Journal*, 2 October 1948; 'an additional sum': PP, box 3, Board of Transport Commissioners ruling, 22 September 1949; 'final appearance': Montreal *Star*, 10 January 1950.

11 'Skilled at freight rates': interview with Alan Sweatman, 16 March 1994; 60th anniversary tributes: PP, box 16; assistance to Deacon: Professor D.T. Anderson to author, 5 August 1992; speech in London: PP, box 13, folder 4, box 3, Proceedings of American Bar Association.

12 One of Pitblado's partners was A.E. Hoskin, who had studied law with Tilley. The Pitblado firm in Isaac's day was a major influence in the commercial life of the city, and it still thrives under the name of Pitblado and Hoskin.

13 'Bonny fighter': Winnipeg *Free Press*, 7 December 1964; Cannon's letter: PP, box 4, folder 5; appraisal by Winnipeg *Free Press*: 23 February 1950.

CHAPTER FIVE

1 Farris in Duncan: the author was a witness of this scene. The case which Farris spoke of was actually a petition for special leave to appeal from a decision of the Supreme Court of Canada, *Trans-Canada Forest Products v. Heaps Waterous and Lipsett* (1954) *SCR* 240; Farris was unsuccessful in gaining leave; the margarine debate: University of British Columbia, Special Collections Library, Farris Papers (FP), box 11, file 2, Wyman-Farris, 24 March 1949, Farris-Wyman, 28 March 1949; 'That damn Wendell': John L. Farris interview with the author (FI), November 1981; 'the grateful patient': FI; the Alaska highway: Seattle *Post-Intelligencer*, 29 October 1938; the Copeland recital: FP, box 51, 18 August 1947; the Nell King letter: FP, Nell King-Farris, box 4, file 7, 13 June 1888. The author, whose maternal grandparents and great-grandparents came from Chatham, New Brunswick, often heard about 'pa' and 'ma.' One of the stock family phrases was, 'Have you seen pa's cows?' It was uttered when a visitor was boastful, bovine superiority denoting genuine excellence.

2 The Jewish lawyer: FI; the $25,000 fee: FI; 'a Pinkerton agent': BCARS, GR 429, box 19; for the strike generally, see Lynne Bowen, *Boss Whistle*; 'the special assize': Nanaimo *Free Press*, seriatim, 21 August 1913 – 27 March 1914; the compensation bill: Riots Claims Settlement Act, *Statutes of British Columbia* (*SBC*) 1919 cap. 72.

3 The English Bay case is *Attorney General Canada v. Ritchie Contracting et al.* (1919) *AC* 999; Farris at the Grosvenor House Hotel: FP, box 4, file 1, and box 9, File 9; the 'Grand Day': FP, box 58, file 4, 13 November 1936; for the Esquimalt and Nanaimo Railway case, the decision of the Supreme Court of Canada is (1948) *SCR* 403 and the Privy Council ruling is (1950) *AC* 87; the hearing before the cabinet is reported in the Vancouver *Daily Province*, 30 December 1950; Farris's reaction to abolition of appeals: the Vancouver *Sun*, 22 August 1947, and *Canadian Bar Review* vol. 25 (1947), 557.

4 The distinction of being the last Canadians to argue an appeal before the Privy Council belongs to a group of Edmonton lawyers who appeared on an Alberta case in 1959. Given that the case must have been launched before 1950 to qualify for a hearing, one can only shake one's head at the delays of litigation which sometimes occur. Garson's remarks are in *Hansard*, 20 September 1949; 'Lord Simon ... responded': Judicial Committee of the Privy Council, minutes, vol. 39, 2 May 1951; the *Times* editorial: 4 May 1951; the Canadian govern-

ment's insensitivity: FP, box 7, file 3, Linklaters and Paines to Farris, 25 June 1954, the case was *Trans Canada Forest Products* (see note 1).

5 The CPR fire: *Saturday Night*, 11 April 1953; the McCrae libel: the *Advocate*, vols. 27 and 28; the girl in the whorehouse: A.D. Pool's recollections.

6 The streetcar ticket: author's interviews with A.M. Harper and Mr Justice J.D. Taggart, 7 April 1992 and 8 September 1993 respectively; 'Tilley's a great lawyer': FI; the case is *Georgia Pacific and Bank of Toronto v. P.G.E. Railway Co.* (1929) 4 DLR 607; the Alberta debt adjustment case is (1942) *SCR* 31; arranging a 'bomber': FP, box 10, file 4, Farris-Mackenzie, 18 September 1941; Farris's remark to Davis: F.I.; 'we've abolished appeals': W.Z. Estey to author, 12 August 1992; Farris's last case in the Supreme Court of Canada: *USA v. Harden* (1963) *SCR* 366.

7 The Japanese treaty case: *Attorney General of British Columbia v. Attorney General Canada* (1922) 63 *SCR* 293, (1924) *AC* 203; Japanese franchise: FP, box 10, file 8, Farris-Gordon, 17 April 1945.

8 Sunday sports: the *Lord's Day Alliance of Canada v. Attorney General B.C. et al.* (1959) *SCR* 497; 'milk marketing boards': *Crawford v. Attorney General B.C. et al.* (1960) *SCR* 346; the Ungaro case is (1950) *SCR* 430; 'self-incrimination': *Klein v. Bell* (1955) *SCR* 309; 'the essential ingredients': author's interviews with A.M. Harper and Frank Murphy, 7 April 1992 and 5 November 1992, respectively; 'Farris in action': Gordon Henderson interviews, 1992; 'citation of legal precedent': FP, box 11, file 7, Farris-Lett, 23 June 1953; 'single-mindedness of fair play': FP, box 9, file 6, Farris-Crombie, 28 January 1932.

9 'Erection to resurrection': FP, box 3, file 5, Farris-Farris, 9 September 1943; 'Maitland was a fine man': FP, box 8, file 7, Maitland-Farris, 2 July 1944; Farris and Norris: FP, box 1, file 5, Braidwood-Farris, 20 July 1955, Farris-Braidwood, 3 August 1955; provincial general election of 1907: Vancouver *World*, 9–10 January 1907; resignation of Macdonald: FP, box 50, file 2; 'five measures of greater importance': *Deserted Wives and Children s Maintenance Act, SBC* (1919) cap. 19, *Mothers Pensions Act, SBC* (1920) cap. 61, *Testators Family Maintenance Act, SBC* (1920) cap. 94, *Adoption Act, SBC* (1920) cap. 2, *Juvenile Court Act, SBC* (1917) cap. 20; Helen Gregory Macgill: see Elsie Gregory Macgill, *My Mother the Judge*; Macgill's influence: FP, Farris-MacLean, 14 December 1927; Macgill's tribute to Farris: FP, box 5, file 3, Macgill-Farris, 3 February 1922; 'black-balled': author's interview with Frank Murphy.

10 'Direct Legislation Act': *SBC* (1919) cap. 21; current 'direct democracy' legislation: *Recall and Initiative Act, SBC* (1994) cap. 56, FP, box 11, file 10, Adams-Farris, 6 April 1956, Farris-Adams, 11, 12 April 1956; 'Liquor Control Board': *SBC* (1921) cap. 30; 'liquor and politics': Robert Campbell, *Demon Rum or Easy Money*; 'contemplated moving': FP, box 9, file 1, Farris-MacLean, 6 February 1922.

11 Turgeon correspondence: FP, box 5, file 1, Turgeon-Farris, 19 June 1925; five royal commissions: see Campbell, *Demon Rum*.

12 For the 1924 election, see FP, box 9, file 2, Farris-Oliver, 21 June 1924; the *Province* newspaper reference is 21 June 1924; the 1930 election: interview with Frank Murphy; Farris vs. Green: author's interview with J.D. Taggart; Farris's view of Pattullo: FP, box 10, file 4, Farris-Mackenzie, 17 November 1941; for a general discussion of the fall of the Pattullo government, see Margaret Ormsby, British Columbia, *A History*.

13 Establishment of a law school at UBC: FP, box 7, file 8, correspondence *inter alia*, 14 September 1937, 20 October 1938, 19 February 1940, and FP, box 9, file 10, correspondence of 7 September 1937; for the correspondence with Cecil Wright, see FP, box 20, file 1, Wright-Farris, 15 September 1938, Farris-Wright, 24 September 1938; FP, box 10, file 8, Farris-Norman MacKenzie, 19 May 1945; the Sedgwick correspondence: FP, box 7, file 3, Sedgwick-Farris, 24 April 1936, Farris-Sedgwick, 6 May 1936.

14 The patronage system: see the author's *Mayor Gerry*; Woodward's support of freight rates: Vancouver *Sun*, 21 June 1924; the Carson correspondence: FP, box 2, file 2, Carson-Farris, 21 September 1923; 'this is a law office': FI; 'keep my hands off': FP, box 9, file 7, Farris-Macdonald, 26 April 1934; 'postmaster general': FP, box 9, file 10, Farris-postmaster general, 28 September 1937.

15 'He never appointed himself': FP, box 9, file 3, Farris-King, 21 September 1926; the letter to H.I. Bird: FP, box 10, file 5, Farris-Bird, 6 November 1942; 'a well-known Victoria lawyer': FP, box 11, file 9, Farris-McKenna, 1 August 1955; Martin and Macdonald: D.M. Gordon in an interview with the author, quoted in 'Judges at War,' Law Society of Upper Canada *Gazette*, vol. 16, 331; Macdonald's 'liberality': FP, box 5, file 3, McAlpine-Farris, 22 April 1940; 'The late Oscar Orr': interview with the author, 18 March 1992; Farris's correspondence with Arthur Laing: FP, box 5, file 1, Farris-Laing, 29 May 1963; the J.R. Nicholson correspondence: FP, box 12, file 7, Farris-Nicholson, 5 August 1964; Morrison's opinion of Martin: FP, box 1, file 4, Morrison-Farris, 25 March 1929.

16 'Like to fill a Senate vacancy': FP, box 6, file 4, Pickering-Farris, 29 October 1936, and FP, box 10, file 4, Farris-Hart, 17 June 1941; King's telegram: FP, box 50, file 4, King-Farris, 9 January 1937; 'attack on John Bracken': *Senate Debates*, 8 March 1944; amendments to divorce rules: *Senate Debates*, 2 March 1937, *Court of Appeal Amendment Act 1938*, SBC (1938) cap. 11; 'Canada Evidence Act': *Senate Debates*, 10 May 1948; 'young offenders': *Senate Debates*, 22 April 1948; Senate reform: Victoria *Colonist*, 28 February 1970; 'Charter of Rights': Vancouver *News Herald*, 22 May 1943, author's interview with J.D. Taggart; the Hong Kong debate: King's remark is quoted, and the affair dealt with generally, in

Williams, *Duff*; Farris and WAC Bennett: *Senate Debates*, 9 June 1964; 'in his anecdotage': A.D. Pool's recollections.

CHAPTER SIX

1 Crew selection: letter, Wib Pierce-author, 13 August 1994; 'Covert tersely recorded in his diary': Covert for over sixty years kept a detailed daily diary, and late in life he prepared an abridgement of his lifetime diaries and had it printed. It runs to about 800 pages and an original copy of it may be found in the library of his old firm, now Stewart McKelvey Stirling Scales, in Halifax. The abridgement, for want of a better word, obviously represented to him the most important items drawn from his original diary entries; unless otherwise noted, therefore, the references in this chapter to his 'diary' or 'diaries' will be to the abridgement; the Stewart letter: Stewart-Covert, 14 April 1944, in possession of Covert family; correspondence with Miss Chase: Covert-Chase and vice versa, April 1980–December 1984, seriatim, in possesion of Covert family; Covert as a 'giver': author's interview with Ron Macdonald, 8 June 1992; 'competing against himself': author's interview with Michael Covert, 17 November 1993; 'the child living in him': author's interviews with Susan Covert, November 1993.

2 Covert's social conscience: J.W.E. Mingo, in conversation with the author on 15 November 1993, described Covert as a 'bleeding heart liberal'; 'Leonard Kitz': in conversation with the author, 25 November 1993; 'flying economy class': Beulah Mosher in conversation with the author, 25 November 1993; Covert's diary entry is 1 February 1977; marriage: Michael Covert interview.

3 Ordering last diary: Mosher interview; doing own filing: ibid; Bowater-Mersey at Liverpool: author's interview with Robert Weary, 19 November 1993; management of Ben's Ltd: author's interview with Douglas Sawyer, 19 November 1993.

4 'Covert was years ahead': in the discussion of Covert's activities in the field of labour law, the author has been greatly assisted by his interviews with Innis Christie, former dean of law at Dalhousie and, more recently, deputy minister of labour for Nova Scotia, as well as with Leo McKay; both interviews took place in November 1993; 'man of his word': McKay interview with author; 'Covert always remained collected': interview with John Jodrey, 24 November 1993; 'never lost his temper': Sawyer interview; 'Dalhousie joint labour management committee': see Brian Langille, 'The Michelin Amendments in Context,' *Dalhousie Law Journal*, vol. 6 (1980), 523.

5 'Royal Commission on Transportation': *Report of the Royal Commission on Transportation, 1951* (Ottawa: King's Printer); 'some of the recommendations': *Rail-*

way Act Amendment Act, Statutes of Canada, 1951, 2nd Sess. Cap. 22; for the parliamentary debates, see *Hansard,* 1951, Vols. 1 and 2 and 1951, 2nd Sess., vol. 2, seriatim.

6 'Judicial life too confining': author's interview with Hazel Paul, 19 November 1993, and Mingo interview; 'Liberal of great influence': author's interview with Ron Macdonald, 8 June 1992, and with John Turner, 24 September 1992; Spevak episode: Covert diary.

7 'The church should stick to matters of faith': author's interview with Mollie Covert, 26 November 1993; the Sisters of Charity: author's interviews with Sister Margaret Molloy, Sister Rita MacDonald, and Mary Uhl, formerly Sister Mary Moore, 16 November 1993; 'to hell with it anyway': Mosher interview; Covert's death: Mingo interview, Susan Covert interview and Mosher interview; burial of dog: Susan Covert interview.

CHAPTER SEVEN

1 Henderson's appraisal of Covert: author's interview with Gordon Henderson, 2 June 1992; as well as the interview that day, the author also interviewed him on 18 June 1993; unless otherwise indicated, these sessions will simply be referred to as 'Henderson interviews'; 'Pericles against the plumbers': Henderson interviews; 'functional objects': the British case is *British Leyland v. Armstrong Patents* (1986) 1 All ER 850 and the Canadian case is *Bayliner Marine Corp. v. Doral Boats Ltd.* (1985) 5 CPR (3rd) 289; the legislation is *Statutes of Canada* (1988) Cap. 15.

2 'Stretch a twenty-four hour day': Soloway to author, 22 July 1992; Turner's appraisal: in conversation with the author, 24 September 1992; 'flexible': C.D. McKinnon to author, 22 September 1992; 'non-stop fashion': W.Z. Estey to author, 12 August 1992; 'enthusiastically forthright': Mr Justice James Chadwick to author, 22 September 1992; 'I will argue pretty strenuously in court': Henderson interviews; 'I want to be the judge': in 1986 and 1987 Christina Kates conducted interviews with Gordon Henderson on behalf of the Osgoode Society, the transcripts of which are with the Society; they will be referred to as the 'Kates interview'; 'a new order of things': Gordon Henderson, *Intellectual Property: Litigation, Legislation and Education* (Consumer and Corporate Affairs Canada 1991), retransmission rights: W.Z. Estey to author, 12 August 1992; 'a new tribunal': Bill C–93, 10 June 1993; photocopying: John Honsberger in conversation with the author, 11 May 1994.

3 The Coca-Cola case is *Pepsi-Cola v. Coca-Cola* (1940) *SCR* 17; the Philip Morris case is *Philip Morris v. Imperial Tobacco* (1987) 17 CPR (3d) 289; 'Bugg-Off': (1980) 1 *SCR* 98; the parachute case is *H.M. The King v. Irving Air Chute* (1949)

SCR 613; practice bombs: *Wilson v. The King* (1952) 17 *CPR* 71; the Bell Telephone case is (1978) 86 *DLR* (3rd) 35; the Frigidaire case: *General Motors Corp. v. Bellows* (1948) 7 CPR 1; the oil tank case is *Scully v. York* 23 *CPR* 6; 'children's dollhouses': *Renwal v. Reliable Toy* (1949) 9 *CPR* 67; 'industrial espionage': *Reliable Toy v. Collins* (1950) 13 *CPR* 53; 'home movies': *B. v. B.* (1950) *OR* 721.

4 The Uranium Canada case is (1983) 2 *SCR* 551; the valium case: (1982), 58 *CPR* (2nd) 1; 'very demure': *Booth v. Sokulsky* (1953) 18 *CPR* 86, Kates interview, 113; 'give the man a drink': *Smith v. Daly* (1949) *OR* 601; provincial court judges: Henderson, Gordon, Eberts, Mary and Hamilton, W.C., *The Report of the Ontario Provincial Court Committee* (Ontario Attorney General, 1988); interrogation of prospective judicial appointees: instructive in this regard – and it is only one instance among the many that could be cited to support Henderson's view – is an address given by Mr Justice Charles D. Gonthier of the Supreme Court of Canada to the faculty of law at the University of New Brunswisk on 7 February 1991. In this address Gonthier extols the virtues, as he sees them, of the Charter of Rights – a document that, as a judge, he is called upon to construe. See *University of New Brunswick Law Journal*, vol. 40 (1990), 193.

5 Also in the hospital field, Henderson in 1982 chaired a committee to stage a gala fund-raising event for the Ottawa Civic Hospital Foundation at the Civic Centre. Canadian-born Rich Little agreed to donate his talents and persuaded his friend Frank Sinatra to do likewise; they were joined by the Canadian musician Peter Appleyard. The hugely successful event netted over $750,000 for the foundation.

6 'Judicial life was not for him': Henderson interviews; the Dye case is *Canada v. Canada-Auditor General* (1989) 61 *DLR* (4th) 604; the Hibernia case: reference *Re Seabed etc.* (1984) 1 *SCR* 86; the Strait of Georgia case is *Attorney-General of Canada v. Attorney-General B.C.* (1984) 88 *DLR* (4th) 161; the Landreville case is (1980) 111 *DLR* (3rd) 36; the Lutheran Church case is *Trustees of St. Peter's Evangelical Lutheran Church and City of Ottawa* (1983) 140 *DLR* (3rd) 577.

7 The Canadian Judicial Council hearing: report of a panel of the Canadian Judicial Council, reprinted *University of New Brunswick Law Journal* vol. 40 (1990), 210; Coates and 'libel chill': *Coates v. The Citizen* (1988) 85 NSR (2nd) 146.

8 It was not the first time I had interviewed him. In writing a biography of the outlaw Simon Peter Gun-a-noot many years earlier, I questioned Henderson about his knowledge of the case – his uncle Stuart had successfully defended Gun-a-noot. I vividly recall the moment when I was ushered into his office. Henderson was delighted to meet someone interested in the formidable exploits of his uncle in British Columbia.

Bibliography

LEGAL REPORTS AND PUBLICATIONS

Appeal Cases (AC), 1875 *et seq.*
British Columbia Reports (BCR), 1897 *et seq.*
British Columbia Supreme Court Reports, 1991 *et seq.*
Canadian Bar Review, seriatim
Canadian Patent Reporter (CPR), 1942 *et seq.*
Canadian Railway Cases, 1914 *et seq.*
Law Society of Upper Canada Gazette seriatim
Supreme Court of Canada Reports (SCR), 1894 *et seq.*
The Advocate, seriatim
University of British Columbia Legal Notes

PUBLIC DOCUMENTS AND RECORDS

Attorney General's Papers, British Columbia Archives and Record Service, seriatim
British Columbia Police Papers, British Columbia Archives and Record Service, seriatim
Claim of the British Ship I'm Alone – Brief Submitted On Behalf of His Majesty's Government in Canada in Respect of the British Ship I'm Alone Under Provisions of Article IV of the Convention Concluded the 23rd of January, 1924 Between His Majesty and the United States of America (Ottawa: King's Printer, 1933)

Claim of the British Ship I'm Alone – Statement With Regard to the Claims for Compensation Submitted by the Canadian Agent Pursuant to Directions Given by the Commissioners dated 30th of June, 1933 (Ottawa: King's Printer, 1933)

Hansard, House of Commons, seriatim

Debates, Senate, seriatim

In the Matter of the Boundary Between the Dominion of Canada and the Colony of Newfoundland in the Labrador Peninsula (William Clowes and Sons), vols. 1–12.

Report of the Royal Commission on Transportation, 1951 (Ottawa: King's Printer)

Statutes of Alberta, seriatim

Statutes of British Columbia seriatim

Statutes of Canada, seriatim

UNPUBLISHED SOURCES

1. *Reports and Proceedings*

Privy Council Judgment Registers and Minutes (Privy Council Office, Downing Street, London)

Proceedings, Church Union Commission, Church Union Collection, vol. 2, Notes, Papers and Transcripts, United Church of Canada Archives, Toronto

Proceedings, North Atlantic Fisheries Arbitration, Government Printing Office (Washington 1912), tabled in the Senate Documents for the 61st Congress, 3rd session, 5 December 1910 – 4 March 1911, 12 vols.

Proceedings of the Royal Commission appointed to investigate the charges made by C.P. Fullerton, K.C., 1915 (Perdue report) – Pitblado Papers, Public Archives of Manitoba, MG14, C64

Proceedings of the Royal Commission to inquire into the Legislative Buildings (Mathers report) Pitblado Papers, PAM

Report of the Turgeon commission, dated 29 March 1933, to inquire into the shortage of funds at the University of Manitoba, Manitoba *Sess. Papers*, no. 50

Report to the Canadian Judicial Council of the Inquiry Committee Established pursuant to Subsection 63(1) of the *Judges Act* at the request of the Attorney-General of Nova Scotia, August 1990, rep. (1990) *UNB Law Journal*, vol. 40, 210

Rolls of the Law Society of Upper Canada (Osgoode Hall, Toronto)

2. *Papers, Diaries, Correspondence*

Borden, Robert, Diaries, 1916–19 MG26 H, National Archives of Canada (NAC)

Covert, Frank, Diaries, in possession of family. Printed summary in possession of Stewart McKelvey Stirling Scales, Halifax

Covert, Frank M., Autobiography and Correspondence in possession of family

Duff, Lyman P., Papers MG30, E 141 (NAC)

Farris, J.W. de B., Papers, University of British Columbia, Special Collections Library Vancouver

Fitzpatrick, Charles, Papers, MGII 7, C1 (NAC)

Geoffrion, Aimé, Collection, papers in possession of Guillaume Geoffrion, Montreal

Hamilton, Thomas Glendinning Collection, University of Manitoba, Department of Archives and Special Collections, manuscript 14

Henderson, Gordon, Notes of Interview by Christina Kates for the Osgoode Society, in possession of the Society

King, William Lyon Mackenzie, Diaries and Papers, MG26 "J" series (NAC)

McCarthy Tetrault Coll., Montreal

Parsons, R.E., Collection in McCarthy Tetrault, Montreal

Pitblado, Isaac Collection, University of Manitoba, Department of Archives and Special Collections, manuscript 48

Pitblado, Isaac, Collection, Public Archives of Manitoba MG14, C64

Sifton, Clifford, Papers, MG27, II, D15 (NAC)

Tillenius, Anna, *Learned Friends – Reminiscences Pitblado and Hoskin 1882–1974*, in possession of the firm

Turner, Keith, *A Celebration of the 100th Anniversary of Pitblado and Hoskin*, in possession of the firm

NEWSPAPERS AND PERIODICALS

Montreal *Star*
Nanaimo *Free Press*
Ottawa *Evening Journal*
Saturday Night
Seattle *Post Intelligencer*
The Times, London
Toronto *Evening Telegram*
Toronto *Globe and Mail*
Toronto *Star*
Vancouver *News Herald*
Vancouver *Province*
Vancouver *Sun*
Vancouver *World*
Victoria *Colonist*
Winnipeg *Free Press*
Winnipeg *Telegram*
Winnipeg *Tribune*

PUBLISHED WORKS AND ARTICLES

Angus, William H., *Judicial Selection in Canada: The Historical Perspective* (Canadian Legal Studies 1964–8), with an introduction by John Wilks

Arnup, John D., *Middleton: The Beloved Judge* (Toronto: Osgoode Society 1988)

Baker, Marilyn, *Symbol in Stone: The Art and Politics of a Public Building* (Winnipeg: Hyperion Press 1986)

Beck, J. Murray, *The Government of Nova Scotia* (Toronto: University of Toronto Press 1957)

Birkenhead, Frederick, Second Earl, *F.E.: The Life of F.E. Smith, First Earl of Birkenhead* (London: Eyre and Spottiswoode 1960)

Borden, Robert Laird, *His Memoirs* (Toronto: McClelland and Stewart 1969)

Bowen, Lynne, *Boss Whistle: The Coal Miners of Vancouver Island Remember* (Lantzville, B.C.: Oolichan Books 1982)

Bruce, Harry, *R.A. – The Story of R.A. Jodrey, Entrepreneur* (Toronto: McClelland and Stewart, 1979)

Bumstead, J.M., '1919: The Winnipeg General Strike Reconsidered,' *The Beaver*, June/July 1994, 215

Campbell, Robert A., *Demon Rum or Easy Money* (Ottawa: Carleton University Press, 1991)

The Canadian Encyclopedia, 2nd ed. (Edmonton: Hurtig 1988)

Careless, J.M.S., *Toronto to 1918 – An Illustrated History* (Toronto: James Lorimer 1984)

Corbett, P.A., *The Settlement of Canadian–American Disputes* (New York: Russell and Russell 1937)

Cox, Elizabeth M., 'The Crown and Social Credit,' *Alberta History*, summer 1992

Forsey, Eugene, *A Life on the Fringe: The Memoirs of Eugene Forsey* (Toronto: Oxford University Press 1990)

Fraser, Joan N., 'Judges of British Columbia to 1957: A Sourcebook,' Occasional Paper no. 1, University of Victoria Law Library, 1984

Glazebrook, G.P. deT., *The Story of Toronto* (Toronto: University of Toronto Press 1971)

Graham, Roger, *Arthur Meighen* (Toronto: Clarke Irwin and Company Limited 1960)

Hacking, Norman R. and Lamb, W. Kaye, *The Princess Story: A Century and a Half of West Coast Shipping* (Vancouver: Mitchell Press Limited 1974)

Harvey, Cameron, *The Law Society of Manitoba* (Winnipeg: Peguis Publishers 1977)

Henderson, Gordon, *Intellectual Property: Litigation, Legislation and Education* (Ottawa: Consumer and Corporate Affairs Canada 1991)

Henderson, Gordon, Eberts, Mary, and Hamilton, W.C., *The Report of the Ontario Provincial Courts Committee* (Ontario Attorney General 1988)

Hodgins, J. George, *Documentary History of Education in Upper Canada from the Passing of the Constitutional Act of 1791 to the Close of Rev. Dr. Ryerson's Administration of the Education Department* (Toronto: Warwick Bros. and Rutter 1894–1910), 28 vols.

Hogg, Peter W., *Constitutional Law of Canada*, 3rd ed. (Toronto: Carswell 1992)

Homer, Michael W., 'Arthur Conan Doyle's Adventures in Winnipeg,' *Manitoba History*, spring 1992

Johnson, W.C.V., ed., *The First Century: The County of Carleton Law Association* (Ottawa: Carleton County Law Association 1988)

Johnston, Douglas M., *The International Law of Fisheries* (New Haven, Conn.: New Haven Press 1985)

Johnston, George A., 'Osgoode Hall Lore, An Address Given to the Lawyers' Club, April 14, 1955' (Toronto: Law Society of Upper Canada, 1955)

Kyer, C. Ian, and Bickenbach, Jerome, *The Fiercest Debate: Cecil A. Wright, The Benchers, and Legal Education in Ontario, 1923–1957* (Toronto: Osgoode Society 1987)

Lafleur, Eugene, *The Conflict of Laws in the Province of Quebec* (Montreal: C. Theoret 1898)

Langille, Brian, 'The Michelin Amendment in Context,' *Dalhousie Law Review*, vol. 6 (1980), 523

Levine, Allan, *The Exchange: 100 Hundred Years of Trading Grain in Winnipeg* (Winnipeg: Peguis Publishers 1987)

Lowe, A.V. and Young, R.J., 'An Executive Attempt to Rewrite a Judgment,' *Law Quarterly Review*, vol. 94, 255

MacGill, Elsie Gregory, *My Mother the Judge* (Toronto: Ryerson Press 1955)

Macmillan, Lord, *A Man of Law's Tale: The Reminiscences of the Rt. Hon. Lord Macmillan* (London: Macmillan 1952)

Marrus, Michael R., *Mr. Sam: The Life and Times of Samuel Bronfman* (Toronto: Viking 1991)

Morton, W.L., *Manitoba: A History* (Toronto: University of Toronto Press 1957)

– *One University: A History of the University of Manitoba* (Toronto: McClelland and Stewart 1957)

Mueller, Jerry E., *Restless River, International Law and the Behaviour of the Rio Grande* (El Paso, Texax: Texas Western Press 1975)

Oliver, Peter, *Public and Private Persons* (Toronto: Clarke, Irwin 1975)

Ormsby, Margaret, *British Columbia: A History* (Toronto: Macmillan 1958)

Randell, Jack, *I'm Alone* (Indianapolis: Bobbs Merrill 1930)

Rowe, Frederick W., *A History of Newfoundland and Labrador* (Toronto: McGraw-Hill Ryerson 1980)

Sharpe, Robert, *The Last Day, The Last Hour* (Toronto: Osgoode Society 1988)

Stacey, C.P., *A Very Double Life: The Private World of Mackenzie King* (Toronto: Macmillan 1976)

Stubbs, Roy St George, *Lawyers and Laymen of Western Canada* (Toronto: Ryerson Press 1939)

– *Prairie Portraits* (Toronto: McClelland and Stewart 1954)

Verchere, David, *A Progression of Judges* (Vancouver: University of British Columbia Press 1988)

Walker, David, *Fun Along the Way: Memoirs of Dave Walker* (Toronto: Robertson Press 1989)

Williams, David Ricardo, 'Judges at War,' *Law Society of Upper Canada Gazette*, vol. 16, 1982

– *Duff: A Life in the Law* (Toronto and Vancouver: Osgoode Society and the University of British Columbia Press 1984)

– *Mayor Gerry: The Remarkable Gerald Grattan McGeer* (Vancouver: Douglas and McIntyre 1986)

– *With Malice Aforethought: Six Spectacular Canadian Trials* (Victoria: Sono Nis Press 1993)

CORRESPONDENTS

Professor D.T. Anderson, Ian Binnie, Professor J.E.C. Brierley, Hon. James Chadwick, Antoine D'Iorio, Hon. W.Z. Estey, Father Roger Guindon, Dean D.M. McRae, C.D. McKinnon, E. Peter Newcombe, Brendan O'Brien, A.D. Pool, Hyman Soloway

AUTHOR'S INTERVIEWS

Susan Binnie, Kenneth Campbell, Innis Christie, David Covert, Michael Covert, Mollie Covert, Susan Covert, Hon. G.S. Cumming, Hon. A.S. Dewar, R.A. Dewar, Dorothy Farris, John L. Farris, Guillaume Geoffrion, Marion Tilley Greey, Arthur M. Harper, Gordon Henderson, John Honsberger, John Humphrey, E. Hutton, John Jodrey, Leonard Kitz, Ian Kyer, Sister Rita MacDonald, Professor Ron Macdonald, Webster MacDonald, Leo McKay, J.W.E. Mingo, Sister Margaret Molloy, Beulah Mosher, Cindi Murphy, Frank Murphy, R.E. Parsons, Hazel Paul, Wilbur Pierce, James Pitblado, J.J. Robinette, Douglas Sawyer, Alan Sweatman, Hon. J.D. Taggart, D.A. Thompson, Rt Hon. John N. Turner, Mary Uhl (formerly Sister Mary Moore), Robert Weary

Index

PUBLICATIONS OF THE OSGOODE SOCIETY FOR CANADIAN LEGAL HISTORY

1981 David H. Flaherty, ed., vol. I, *Essays in the History of Canadian Law*

1982 Marion MacRae and Anthony Adamson, *Cornerstones of Order: Courthouses and Town Halls of Ontario, 1784–1914*

1983 David H. Flaherty, ed., vol. II, *Essays in the History of Canadian Law*

1984 Patrick Brode, *Sir John Beverley Robinson: Bone and Sinew of the Compact*
David Ricardo Williams, *Duff: A Life in the Law*

1985 James Snell and Frederick Vaughan, *The Supreme Court of Canada: History of the Institution*

1986 Paul Romney, *Mr Attorney: The Attorney General for Ontario in Court, Cabinet, and Legislature, 1791–1899*
Martin Friedland, *The Case of Valentine Shortis: A True Story of Crime and Politics in Canada*

1987 C. Ian Kyer and Jerome Bickenbach, *The Fiercest Debate: Cecil A. Wright, the Benchers, and Legal Education in Ontario, 1923–1957*

1988 Robert Sharpe, *The Last Day, the Last Hour: The Currie Libel Trial*
John D. Arnup, *Middleton: The Beloved Judge*

1989 Desmond Brown, *The Genesis of the Canadian Criminal Code of 1892*
Patrick Brode, *The Odyssey of John Anderson*

1990 Philip Girard and Jim Phillips, eds., *Essays in the History of Canadian Law*, vol. III, *Nova Scotia*
Carol Wilton, ed., *Essays in the History of Canadian Law*, vol. IV, *Beyond the Law, Lawyers and Business in Canada 1830–1930*

1991 Constance Backhouse, *Petticoats and Prejudice: Women and Law in Nineteenth-Century Canada*

1992 Brendan O'Brien, *Speedy Justice: The Tragic Last Voyage of His Majesty's Vessel Speedy*
Robert Fraser, ed., *Provincial Justice, Upper Canadian Legal Portraits from the Dictionary of Canadian Biography*

1993 Greg Marquis, *Policing Canada's Century: A History of the Canadian Association of Chiefs of Police*
Murray Greenwood, *Legacies of Fear: Law and Politics in Quebec in the Era of the French Revolution*

1994 Patrick Boyer, *A Passion for Justice: The Legacy of James Chalmers McRuer*
Charles Pullen, *The Life and Times of Arthur Maloney: The Last of the Tribunes*
Jim Phillips, Tina Loo, Susan Lewthwaite, eds., *Essays in the History of Canadian Law*, vol. V, *Crime and Criminal Justice*

Brian Young, *The Politics of Codification: The Lower Canadian Civil Code of 1866*

1995   David Ricardo Williams, *Just Lawyers: Seven Portraits*

Hamar Foster and John McLaren, eds., *Essays in the History of Canadian Law, vol. VI, British Columbia and the Yukon*

W.H. Morrow, ed., *Northern Justice: The Memoirs of Justice William G. Morrow*

Beverley Boissery, *A Deep Sense of Wrong: The Treason, Trials, and Transportation of Lower Canadian Rebels to New South Wales after the 1838 Rebellion*